The Campanile
of Florence Cathedral

"Giotto's Tower"

The Campanile
of Florence Cathedral

"Giotto's Tower"

Marvin Trachtenberg

New York University Press
New York   1971

This publication has been assisted by
a grant from the Billy Rose Foundation.

To
Richard Krautheimer

Contents

Preface and Acknowledgments

This study may be regarded as the first in a series of publications surveying Tuscan Gothic architecture, which I have undertaken together with Heinrich Klotz. The project was formed in Florence during the summer of 1965, when it became clear that our previously independent research on partial aspects of the field would be abortive without a deeper understanding of the entire Tuscan Trecento. The first stage of our effort was a photographic campaign, involving some three thousand shots, finished by the summer of 1966. At that time Professor Richard Krautheimer, who first introduced me to the field of Late Gothic architecture, suggested that, for a doctoral dissertation, I write a monograph on the Campanile of Florence Cathedral. The present book is built on the skeleton of that academic effort; it is hoped that the added substance does not overburden or needlessly obscure the old lines of argument.

Perhaps to a greater degree than with most architectural monographs, it has been difficult to demarcate the discussion of the Campanile. The building is central in almost every respect. It is one of the earliest Florentine fabrics for which extensive documentation exists and of which the names of the architects — Giotto, Andrea Pisano, and Francesco Talenti — have meaning. Stylistically it is crucial to the development of the mid and late Tuscan Trecento. Its sculptural decoration is counted among the glories of Italian culture. The Campanile was intended by the Florentines to be an imposing monument, and that it remains, one of the landmarks of the city. From the time of its founding it has been one of the Florentine buildings most frequently discussed. Yet despite — or perhaps due to — its centrality, the tower is, though widely appreciated, poorly understood. The architectural accomplishment of its first two *capomaestri* — whose painting and sculpture have a literature of their own — has largely been the subject of vague and casual passing mention on the one hand, and, on the other, needlessly extravagant notions. Our knowledge of the achievements of Francesco Talenti, one of the major forces in Trecento architecture whose name — unlike many of his lesser contemporaries — was completely lost until modern times, has been little more than an entry in the Thieme-Becker *Künstlerlexikon*. If the results of my study are somewhat overwrought, my intentions have been the best: to do the Campanile, its creators and patrons, full justice.

Several acknowledgments are in order. The ample format of this book is due to a most generous grant by the Billy Rose Foundation. Without aid from the Fulbright Commission and New York University, which has provided continuing support of this project, the three year residence in Florence would have been impossible. I am particularly grateful to Professor Ulrich Middeldorf for full use of the library and photographic facilities of the Kunsthistorisches Institut in Florence and for his continuing encouragement and scholarly advice. To the Opera del Duomo of Florence and its president, Ingeniere Galliano Boldrini, go my thanks for opening normally inaccessible parts of the Cathedral group and for generous cooperation in an archeological probe in the spring of 1969, so kindly executed for me by Professor Isabelle Hyman and Architetto Piero Micheli. Professor Richard Pommer, while in Florence in 1969, checked out, with characteristic acuity, a number of my afterthoughts. Professors James Ackerman, Isabelle Hyman, H. W. Janson, Donald Posner, Willibald Sauerländer, Staale Sinding-Larsen, and Craig Smyth have generously offered invaluable criticism of the manuscript at various stages of its preparation. Dr. Jürgen Paul graciously allowed me a preview of his monograph on the Palazzo Vecchio. Mr. Lonnie Bier and, especially, Miss Patricia Waddy are thanked for their inspired draftsmanship, Professor L. D. Ettlinger, Mrs. Herbert Bier, and Miss Edith Janicke for their help in obtaining photographic materials, Professor Bruce Cole for archival hints, and Professor Mariantonia Ferrucci (among others) for assistance in translation. The exacting cooperation of the staff of Scala in photographing several of the color plates under my direction is much appreciated. I am most grateful for the interest and energy invested in this publication by the New York University Press, in particular, by its director, Mr. Chris Kentera; and the task of the reader has been greatly facilitated by the tireless copy-editing of Miss Harriet Schoenholz. Needless to add, my association with Heinrich Klotz has been of consequence to this study. I want to thank him for the many suggestions and services too numerous here to recount. If one person stands behind my work it is my mentor, Professor Richard Krautheimer: to him my debt is greatest, for his patience and advice, for the scholarly standard and ideal that he sets, and for his friendship. To my wife Heidi, who, while I was happily engaged with my polychrome fabrics, endured the not untrying task of caring for two small boys and a semi-rustic Florentine household and, later in New York, a husband married to a manuscript, I owe more than I can acknowledge.

New York, June 1970   Marvin Trachtenberg

Chapter I

The Campanile in the Eye of History

F. L. del Migliore writes that the task Florence set for Giotto in 1334 was to build for the Cathedral a new campanile "so magnificent, that by height and workmanship it would surpass all those of that genre erected by the Greeks or by the Romans . . . to the honor . . . of a powerfully unified, greatly spirited, and freely sovereign people."[1] Even if reflecting a document lost to the modern historian, the seventeenth-century writer cast the sentiment in his own terms; yet the inner meaning rings true of the early Trecento, particularly of the 1330s, when medieval Florence was proudly conscious of having reached its peak.[2] The vaunting conceit of the builders would have found precedent in the magisterial utterance of the previous generation that Arnolfo di Cambio's Cathedral project was to surpass all the ecclesiastical architecture of Tuscany.[3] To adopt the classical *topos* of civic pride was characteristic; much of the self-image of the Tuscan commune was expressed in terms of antiquity.[4] The age of Giotto was characterized by antique imagery.[5] One easily imagines

[1] Doc. XIV. On Italian historiography in general see J. von Schlosser, *Die Kunstliteratur* (Vienna, 1924).

[2] G. Brucker, *Florentine Politics and Society, 1343-1378* (Princeton, 1962), vii, 3 ff; M. Becker, *Florence in Transition* (Baltimore, 1967 f), *passim*.

[3] C. Guasti, *Santa Maria del Fiore* (Florence, 1887), doc. 24 (April 1, 1300) quoted in Ch. II n. 44). [Hereafter cited as Guasti.]

[4] W. Braunfels, *Mittelalterliche Stadtbaukunst in der Toskana* (Berlin, 1953), 18 ff; H. Baron, *The Crisis of the Early Italian Renaissance* (Princeton, 1955), I 50 ff; N. Rubenstein, "The Beginnings of Political Thought in Florence," *Journal of the Warburg and Courtauld Institutes*, V (1942), 198 ff; E. R. Curtius, *European Literature and the Latin Middle Ages*, tr. W. R. Trask (New York, 1953), 157, 162 ff.

[5] E. Panofsky, *Renaissance and Renascences in Western Art* (Stockholm, 1960), Ch. III; more recently, A. M. Telpaz, "Some Antique Motifs in Trecento Art," *Art Bulletin*, XLVI (1964), 372 ff.

that between April 12, 13, 1334, when the "world's most famous painter" was appointed city architect,[6] and July 18, the celebrative placing of the Campanile cornerstone,[7] the commune, rebounding with mysterious force from the great flood of 1333,[8] conceived its latest undertaking with such antique romance.

Florence had cause to celebrate the founding of the Campanile, for it had before its eyes Giotto's spectacular design (Fig. IX). But if the Florentines were pleased with the structure as it was built — a composite shaft left incomplete around 1364, embodying the transformations of Andrea Pisano and Francesco Talenti (Frontispiece) — they were slow to acclaim it in the Trecento.[9] Giovanni Villani, the first to record the tower, who saw two thirds of it rise before his death in 1348, notes the founding in a surprisingly unsolicitous manner.[10] Yet the very fact that the Campanile breaks into his essentially political and economic chronicle is itself homage: except for the proud description of Florence in the year 1338 — an accountant's soliloquy rather than a survey of monuments — few buildings are mentioned. Only such politically charged foundings as those by the young republic in the 1280s and 1290s — the Third Wall, the Duomo, the Palazzo dei Priori — or the rebuilding of the bridges after the flood find a place in his narrative. In addition, Villani accords the Campanile the aura of its builder, Giotto, "the sovereign master . . . of his age."

Antonio Pucci, born the son of a bell founder around 1309, in that trade himself in his youth, and later a public official,[11] watched the great bell tower rise with avid eyes. In his *Centiloquio* (1373), a versification of Giovanni Villani's chronicle, he devotes eighteen lines to the tower's building history.[12] He relates that the Campanile project was begun to Giotto, modified by Andrea Pisano, then carried to final, though incomplete form by Francesco Talenti. Perhaps Pucci, like Villani, expressed implicit praise with such an explicit account; on the other hand, the final appearance of the Campanile may not have pleased him entirely. It was begun in "good style" by the "subtle painter" Giotto. But Andrea Pisano, attempting to outshine Giotto, whose act was surely hard to follow, succeeded only in raising, with difficulties, a section with "useless" novelties. It is conceivable that Talenti's fenestrated stories above, and especially the Trifora section, may have been too rich for the taste of Pucci's generation, which had been formed by Giotto.[13] The polymorphism, moreover, would have been disconcerting. If so, Pucci remained an arch-Florentine and left the critique unspoken.

---

[6] Doc. 1 f.; see Ch. II n. 44.
[7] G. Villani, *Cronica* (Florence, 1844), XI, 12 (Doc. I). [Hereafter cited as Villani.]
[8] See Ch. VII, 176 below.
[9] On the lack of medieval awareness of architectural achievements, see E. Gall, *Die gotische Baukunst in Frankreich und Deutschland* (Leipzig,
[10] Doc. I.   [1925), I, 9 ff.

[11] D. Manni, "Notizie istoriche intorno ad Antonio Pucci," *Delizie degli Eruditi Toscani*, III (1772), iii ff. Pucci appears in the Cathedral documents as town crier *(banditore)* in connection with the pier competition (Guasti, 120).
[12] Doc. IV.
[13] M. Meiss, *Painting in Florence and Siena after the Black Death* (Princeton, 1951), *passim*.

An anonymous member of the next generation, who came of age during the mid Trecento and wrote a commentary on the *Divina Commedia* around 1395,[14] turned the tables. Not as scrupulous about the tower's building history as Pucci (no one was to be again until 1885), he noted that Giotto had designed the Campanile and that it was "notable . . . and of great cost." Evidently the anonymous writer was pleased with the terminal form. But he records a rumor (founded on truth) that it was Giotto's design that erred. The disgrace was supposedly such that the aged Giotto is said to have died from the shame. How much of his error was included in the "notable" final shape the writer does not inform us. But one suspects he knew the outlines of the building history, if only from Pucci, and that most of the Campanile was not by Giotto. When this same writer notes that Giotto "composed and ordered the Campanile," he is referring to Giotto's "flawed" design, which, we gather, was successfully "reformed" by the later architects. The anti-Giottesque mood was not unknown during the span of the writer's generation.[15]

If, to certain members of the first Trecento generation, the post-Giotto part of the Campanile was somewhat distasteful, and, if to the next, the project of Giotto himself seemed less than perfect, such distinctions and equivocations were lost to later Florentines. The bells of the Campanile pealed the hour of their birth, and they grew to manhood in its shadow. It was, along with its stylistic twin, the Duomo, a determinant of the taste of their generation and those following; their admiration was unbounded.

Goro Dati (1362-1435) as a climax to his *Istoria di Firenze* (1423) gives a proud and, for his time, lengthy description of the city.[16] Included are its walls and bridges, the buildings clustered along the topographic axis that runs from the Piazza della Signoria to the Piazza del Duomo, the Bargello, and the two great mendicant churches. Other structures are mentioned only generically. The Palazzo dei Priori is "of wondrous strength and beauty"; the Loggia della Signoria, "magnificent"; the Palazzo del Podesta "very lordly"; Or San Michele "of marvelous beauty"; San Giovanni, "wondrous," the Cathedral nave, the largest and most beautiful in creation; and finally the Campanile: "who has not seen it cannot imagine its beauty (chi non lo vede non si potrebbe imaginare sua bellezza)." This memorable phrase, the high point of his description of Florence, surely would have been reserved for the Cupola (1420-36) had Dati written at a later date. But in the late Trecento and early Quattrocento, the Campanile, rising brightly, almost with incandescence, above the gray masses of the city, was distinctly the focus of Florentine pride. Small wonder that far from its shadow, but in full view of the campanile of San

---

[14] Doc. V.

[15] Meiss, 1951, 4 ff reveals not only a rejection of Giottesque aesthetics in the mid Trecento, but indications of criticism of Giotto himself.

[16] G. Dati, *Istoria di Firenze dal 1380 al 1405*, ed. Luigi Pratesi (Norcia, 1904), 114 ff, on which see C. Gilbert, "The Earliest Guide to Florentine Architecture, 1423," *Mitteilungen des kunsthistorischen Instituts in Florenz*, XIV (1969), 33 ff, with dating by internal evidence. For its praise of Trecento works, Dati's description is interesting in connection with the contemporary taste for the International Gothic style (cf. *ibid.*, 42 f).

Marco in Venice, a Florentine sculptor (possibly Piero Lamberti) depicted his native land-mark on the Justice capital of the Palazzo Ducale in the guise of an exemplary edifice recommended by an architect to Numa Pompilius, a Roman king renowned as "builder of temples and churches" (Fig. 338).[17]

To Leonardo Bruni (1370-1444), who wrote the *Historiarum florentini populi* at about the same time (completed 1416), the Campanile carried an additional meaning.[18] Dati surely was aware of Giotto's role in the Campanile, but he did not connect great names with monuments; their forms were their glory. Bruni, though aesthetically appre-ciative of the few monuments he mentions, chooses them essentially for their historical and communal significance. As Dante and Giovanni Villani had believed, Bruni stated that the Baptistery was originally a temple of Mars, symbol of the Roman origin of Florence;[19] the fortified outposts in the *contado*, the walls, the Palazzo Vecchio, and the prisons gave monumental shape to the republic and were among its first acts;[20] the Loggia della Signoria completed the civic center.[21] Bruni's discussion of the Campanile[22] carries traces of Giovanni Villani's chronicle, yet is decidedly different. Villani recounted only its founding and with balanced emphasis, church, state, and Giotto each playing a role. Bruni omits all participants but Giotto and ascribes to him the final, "magnificent" form of the tower. The Campanile is now identified with a single Florentine who was considered the greatest artist since antiquity. In this first important Renaissance history, the main tenets of the age fuse with an intense *campanilismo*.

Bruni's formulation was so gratifying to the early Renaissance that three decades later it was repeated by Antonio Divi.[23] However, around the mid Quattrocento it was still possible for Matteo Palmieri in his world chronicle to extol the Campanile without mentioning Giotto's name[24] and, at the same time, for Ghiberti simply to attribute the Campanile to Giotto without praising it.[25] These variations in the incipient canon of

[17] L. Planiscig, "Die Bildhauer Venedigs in der ersten Hälfte des Quattrocento," *Jahrbuch der kunsthistorischen Sammlungen in Wien*, n. s. IV (1930), 71 ff. The contemporary G. Sercambi paired the Campanile with the Baptistery as the supreme Florentine structure (*Croniche*, in Istitu-to Storico italiano per il Medio Evo, *Fonti per la storia d'Italia*, XX [Roma, 1892], P. I, Ch. DLIII, 104).

[18] L. Bruni, *Historiarum florentini populi* (Flo-rence, 1857).

[19] *Ibid.*, Bk. I, 60; a confusion lasting through the 19th century (W. Horn, "Das florentiner Baptisterium," *Mitteilungen des kunsthistorischen Instituts in Florenz*, V [1938], 100 ff).

[20] Bruni, 1857, IV, 460 ff.

[21] *Ibid.*, VII, 510.

[22] Doc. VI.

[23] A. Divi, *Historiarum pars tertia*, Ms. in Bib-lioteca Nazionale, Florence [Magl. XXXIX. 70], II, I. 376; relevant passage cited by R. Sal-vini, *Giotto bibliografia* (Rome, 1938), 12.

[24] "1334. Marmorea Turris, singulari prestantia splendidissimi operis ad Reparate Templum Flo-rentie fundari cepta est," M. Palmieri, *Matthei Palmerii Liber de temporibus*, in L. A. Muratori, ed., *Rerum italicarum scriptores* (n.s. ed. G. Car-ducci and V. Fiorini [Città di Castello, 1906]), XXVI, 113; relevant passage cited by G. Richa, *Notizie istoriche delle chiese fiorentine* (Florence, 1754 ff), VI, 64.

[25] L. Ghiberti, *Lorenzo Ghibertis Denkwürdig-keiten (I Commentari)*, ed. J. von Schlosser (Berlin, 1912), I, 37, 43 (Doc. VII).

homage are readily understood: Palmieri's account was a medieval history of apocalyptic scope, outside the local chronicle tradition that had been decisive for Bruni; Ghiberti, writing of past artists admired, systematically excluded architecture (which he intended to treat in a later volume). In both works, as in Villani, the mere mention of the Campanile was its advocacy.

If Bruni and Dati had spoken for the heroic age of the Renaissance, two lines of the epitaph composed by Poliziano and carved on Giotto's tomb in the Cathedral in 1490 bespoke the Medici court circle of the late Quattrocento:

> Miraris turrem egregiam sacro aere sonantem:
> Haec quoque de modulo crevit ad astra meo.[26]

The dense, beautiful imagery and idealism proclaim the Neoplatonic ambient. From what other context could the boundless individualism of the sentiment arise? In the epitaph given Andrea Pisano at about the same time, the Campanile is not even mentioned.[27] And Francesco Talenti was by then entirely forgotten.

During the period of doubt following the High Renaissance, the bright vision of the Campanile as the pure, noble embodiment of Giotto's genius is darkened. In Poliziano's conceit, Giotto made the model, which bore the all-important idea; it did not matter who, in particular, was responsible for the fabric. But Antonio Billi, writing around 1530,[28] perceived in the model not the essence of the Campanile but a problem: if Giotto died too soon to have completed the building, who did? The oral tradition of its history evidently was now lost and Pucci's poem forgotten. Who then, but "Taddeo Gaddi his disciple."

Billi's note, repeated by the Anonimo Gaddiano in 1540,[29] was but groundwork for that most complex figure, Giorgio Vasari. In the first edition of the *Vite* (1550),[30] he merely elaborated Billi's version of the building history — that Taddeo Gaddi had faithfully executed Giotto's model. We know that the model, mentioned repeatedly, was not Giotto's, but rather Francesco Talenti's 1353 model of wood, which represented the earlier fabric of Giotto and Andrea Pisano along with his own work, and envisioned a never-

---

[26] "You will admire the famous tower sounding in the sacred air: It also grew from my model to the stars."

[27] "Ingenti Andreas iacet hic Pisanus in urna / Marmore qui potuit spirantes ducere vultus / Et simulacra Deûm mediis imponere templis / Ex aere, ex auro candenti, et pulcro elephanto." G. Vasari, *Le Vite de' più eccellenti architetti, pittori et scultori italiani*, second edition (Florence, 1568); ed. G. Milanesi (Florence, 1878 ff), I, 495. [Hereafter cited as Vasari.] For the problem of Andrea Pisano's tomb and epitaph, see

L. Becherucci, "La bottega pisana di Andrea da Pontedera," *Mitteilungen des kunsthistorischen Instituts in Florenz*, XI (1965), 244 ff and n. 12; also Ch. VI n. 4 below.

[28] Doc. IX.

[29] Doc. X. For other early 16th-century estimates of the Campanile, see Docs. VIII, XI, and F. Biondo, *Historiarum ab inclinationem Romanorum imperii decades* (Basel, 1531), cited in Richa, 1757, VI, 64 f.

[30] Doc. XII.

built spire.[31] Since Leonardo Bruni's time, when the true building history was lost, this model was considered Giotto's and eluded critical scrutiny until Vasari, in the second edition of the *Vite* (1568), noted not only that Giotto himself had executed little of the Campanile, but that it was never completed at all: "According to Giotto's [sic] model, this campanile should have had as a terminus over what is seen a spire or square pyramid fifty braccia high."[32]

Even more detrimental to the Campanile's image than its loss of Giotto's autograph (it was now a shop piece), and its incomplete state, was Vasari's characterization of its style: "It was of that *maniera tedesca* of those times," the strongest denunciation possible, if one recalls the philippic on the Gothic style in the "Proemio" to Part I of the *Vite*.[33] Yet had "Giotto's" design been fulfilled, the matter might have been even worse: because, according to Vasari, the spire is "something German and old-fashioned, modern architects have advised that it never be built, things being better as they are." For the modern observer, the Campanile seems strangely deficient when he imagines the outlines of a spire above the soaring prism of dense polychrome. But what could carry more of the *maniera tedesca* than a spire? Incompleteness clearly was preferable to having the entire Gothic elevation: for Vasari, less was more.

The Campanile had other redeeming features. Its foundation was massive and admirable. Giotto's incrustation had been designed "with great diligence" and executed "solicitously" by Taddeo Gaddi. In fact, "the campanile was built in such a manner that it would be impossible to assemble stones with greater diligence." Besides, it was very broad (twenty-five braccia) and high (one hundred forty-four braccia). Vasari, the builder, was always impressed by sound structure, excellent workmanship, and sheer size.[34] Yet, one questions if these qualities were enough to warrant his concluding judgment that the Campanile was "the world's most beautiful tower in its ornament and costliness," adding, in the second edition, that it seemed the most worthy also "for its design."

One cannot justify this surprising laudatory conclusion by postulating the intervention of Vasari's implicit, but obvious chauvinism or by his historical relativism,[35] for the praise is absolute — "la più bella torre . . . del mondo." The apology lies in the genre. Towers were essentially a medieval form and thus inherently inferior. The Campanile was rather less Gothic than most, especially without the spire. All things considered, Vasari was able to fit his verdict into the prescriptive Florentine mold.[36]

[31] See Ch. V.

[32] Doc. XIII.

[33] Panofsky, 1960, 33 f. Also, *idem*, "The First Page of Giorgio Vasari's 'Libro,'" in *Meaning in the Visual Arts* (New York, 1955), 176 ff.

[34] Cf. his discussion of the Leaning Tower of Pisa and the campanile at S. Marco in Venice (Vasari, I, 272 ff).

[35] Panofsky, 1955, 207 ff.

[36] Compare Vasari's plight with the pathetic mid-17th-century attempt by Gherardo Silvani to incorporate the buttress form of the Campanile in his project for the Cathedral facade (A. Venturi, *Storia dell'arte italiana* [Milan, 1901

Down to the nineteenth century local historians had to cope with Vasari's antinomy.[37] Francesco Bocchi, who wrote the first guide to Florence in 1591, *Bellezze della Città di Firenze*, suffered from the problem, but, unlike Vasari, avoided confronting it.[38] He wrote, "When this fabric was built the *maniera tedesca* was in full flower; nevertheless, so much was it improved by Giotto's efforts that he is still commended for his great wisdom." Praise is slyly shifted from the Campanile to Giotto's rare achievement: his melioration of the Gothic. To distract our attention further, Bocchi quotes a famous anecdote: "if the Campanile had a covering (as Charles V already put it . . .) when it would be revealed people would run in great numbers to see such a wonder." Finally, he defers to the common knowledge of the Campanile's excellence — "how beautiful it is, how graceful" — extoling its bells, the design and execution of its decoration, and the perfect structure that has not yielded a single crack or displacement.

For Vasari — and, one senses, also for Bocchi — the *maniera tedesca* was a particularly toxic evil. Even a trace caused him to over-react, as his near contemporary Martin Luther had (likewise with ink) toward an equally malign spirit. The Gothic manner was a less vital issue to the Florentine antiquarians of the late seventeenth and eighteenth centuries, although it was still officially in disrepute.[39] The dynamic, nervous structure of Vasari's *Vite* gave way to a blander approach, in which each monument or artist was discussed more on his or its own terms. Even Filippo Baldinucci, who in his *Vocabulario* vilifies the "ordine Gottico" in Vasari's language,[40] overlooks it in the Campanile,[41] for which he has only praise; he limits the malignancy strictly to the unexecuted

ff], XI, Pt. II, 626, fig. 583; brought to my attention by Mr. Ralph Lieberman).

[37] Foreigners (particularly the French) had no such problems; their praises were pure, if simple. Examples: the perhaps more than apocryphal praise of Charles V (see text below); "nous y vismes . . . le clochier tout revestu de mabre blanc et noir; c'est l'une des beles choses du monde e plus sumptueses," M. Montaigne, *Journal du voyage en Italie, 1580-81*, ed. M. Rat (Paris, 1955), 85; "The steeple standing beside the church is likewise [cf. the Duomo] of fine marble, a very fair and square tower, equal in height to the circuit of the base, with divers stories and things graven in it, so artificial and costly that it deserveth singular praise," W. Thomas, *The History of Italy (1549)*, ed. G. Parks (Ithaca, 1963), 94; "a côté est le campanile ou clocher isolé, riche, élégant et excellent au possible, tout incrusté, comme l'église, de marbre blanc, noir, et rouge. Le dessin est du Giotto," C. de Brosses, *Lettres familières écrites d'Italie*,

1739-1740, ed. R. Colomb (Paris, 1869), I, 249; finally, the Marquis de Seignelai (the son of Colbert) visited Florence in 1671 and declared the Campanile ". . . un très bel ouvrage, du dessin de Giotto: c'est une tour carrée, fort haute, qui ne tient rien à l'église; elle est bâtie de marbre blanc, noir et rouge; toutes les fenetres sont si bien placées et les ouvertures hautes de ce clocher, à l'endroit où sont les cloches, si proprement travaillées, qu'elles le font estimer une des raretés de l'Italie." (In E. Müntz, *Florence et la Toscane*, [Paris, 1897], 225 n. 2).
[38] F. Bocchi, *Le bellezze della Città di Firenze*, ed. G. Cinelli (Pistoia, 1677), 44 f.
[39] P. Frankl, *The Gothic* (Princeton, 1960), 384.
[40] F. Baldinucci, *Vocabulario Toscano dell'arte del disegno* (Florence, 1681), 113 ("Ordine Gottico").
[41] F. Baldinucci, *Notizie de'professori del disegno da Cimabue in qua*, ed. G. Piacenza (Turin, 1768), I, 93 f.

spire in which, at that, it is found to only a limited degree: "it had something of the old-fashioned manner." Del Migliore, after eulogizing the Campanile for several pages, admits as a qualification that "its greatest imperfection is belonging to the *architettura alla tedesca,* though by no means to an exceeding degree . . . [it] being that when it was built those *buone regole* were just being revived."[42] Giuseppe Richa writes much the same: "if one weighs well the design, which was done by Giotto, it is not too much, in Vasari's judgment, to deem it the greatest wonder in architecture, even though it is of the *maniera tedesca* (but not to an exceeding degree)."[43] In Vasari's epic, Giotto had heroically redeemed the Campanile from a contemptible style; for Richa, it begins with absolute excellence and ends only slightly fallen, as somewhat Gothic.

The antiquarians manifest a less hostile attitude toward the Gothic in the Campanile. At the same time they put forth a richer conception of the Campanile's origin, form, and significance. Baldinucci published the *Provvisione* of April 12, 1334, in which Giotto is appointed city architect, and draws the conclusion "that he was the first in those times in all the world to hold that position."[44] Del Migliore (as was seen at the beginning of this chapter) seems to paraphrase a lost document in which Giotto is commissioned to build the Campanile. It seemed to him — in a moral judgment prefiguring Ruskin — that the Campanile was greater indeed than the "obelisks and pyramids" of antiquity, for it celebrated not a mere individual but, rather, a free and great nation. Chauvinistically, he takes care to stress its superiority to the campanili of the other city-states: "the Bolognese and Sienese, in other respects noble communities... constructed towers of imposing heights, yes, but so ordinary and deprived of every adornment that it perhaps would have been better had they restrained themselves from [building them] in order not to have perpetuated the memory of their having failed to earn that praise gathered by magnificence in construction." He chose to overlook the exquisite, if conservative, tower of Siena Cathedral, the soaring, elegant "Mangia," the rich marble harmonies of Pisa, the "Torazzo" of Cremona, San Marco in Venice, and Antonio da Vicenzo's magnificent composition towering over San Francesco in Bologna. As if to reassure the reflective reader, del Migliore returns to the subject several pages later: the Campanile has no equal, not even in confrontation with the "towers of Cremona or those of Venice or even that famous [tower] of Strasbourg in Germany."[45]

One should not demand total consistency of del Migliore. Fine distinctions are lost in the Baroque tumult of his style, characterized by endless, complex sentences and shifting tacks of argument, a dense, intricate (and beautiful) form in which history, description, and associations are fused with impressionistic passion, rather than following in logical order. For the latter, one turns to Richa, a Jesuit writing during the age of reason. His

[42] F. L. del Migliore, *Firenze, città nobilissima* (Florence, 1684), 57.

[43] Richa, 1754 ff, VI, 63.

[44] Baldinucci, 1768, I 26 f.

[45] Del Migliore, 1684, 55 ff.

clear distinction of topics, and the rational progression of his discussion are admirable.[46] Even Vasari had imagined the executed shaft of the Campanile to be an undifferentiated unity; Richa's rationalism leads to the first dissection of the fabric. Having cited the previous literature — the 1334 documents, Villani, Vasari, and various laudatory attitudes — he proceeds to his own description. Comprising the edifice, he says, are a closed lower section, decorated with sculpture, and a highly fenestrated sequence of upper stories. By publishing the document of January 5, 1351, in which Neri di Fioravanti and company are contracted to do the revetment for the Trifora story, Richa implies a third building period after those of Giotto and Taddeo Gaddi. He discovers that the shaft has an interesting interior: "of the hundred other refinements I shall not prolong myself in telling . . . nor of the stairs, nor the lighting arrangements, nor of the squared, cleanly cut ashlar, things that form a new and unexpected wonder." As if to lend this interior historical substance, he cites the story of Bernardo Bandini, one of the principals in the Pazzi conspiracy against the Medici, who sought refuge in the Campanile, and tried to escape his pursuers by lowering himself from one of the lower Bifora windows by the bell ropes, with which the populace thereafter wanted to hang him. Richa then leads us to the seven bells and an even richer discussion of their history than del Migliore's, and dutifully to the imperial standard on the roof. In dramatic conclusion, Richa returns us to the piazza, where we are to attend, on the buttresses, the arms of the commune and the *popolo* that built the landmark.

Richa's image of the Campanile, rich in historical and associative overtones, was the last of its kind. Vasari had broken the crystalline image of the Quattrocento; the writers following Richa ignore, for the most part, the meanings and concentrate increasingly on the fabric. Already in Richa's time, the great folio volume of measured engravings by Bernardo Sansone Sgrilli (1733) reduced the text concerning the Campanile to a few paragraphs, which largely explained the illustrations.[47] The history is reduced to a phrase: "it was built by Giotto." Taddeo Gaddi is omitted. Ritualistically, the presence of Gothic style is denied; the Campanile is described in terms worthy of classical architecture, including "grace, strength, intelligence," and "admirable reason." The sculptural decoration, a major interest of earlier writers, occupies a sentence mentioning Donatello and other "famous sculptors." The real interest is in the fabric, including building materials ("it is entirely [sic] constructed of *pietraforte* ashlar") and means of circulation ("straight stairs hollowed in the thickness of the wall"). The disposition of the building is given a rational explanation. The commodious stair up to the first Bifora section "receives light from some small openings; for to render the fabric more secure the architect chose not to open large windows there, as he did [above] in the other stories, this part having to serve as a base and sustainment for the upper parts, in which it was ventured to build large openings;

[46] Richa, 1754 ff, VI, 62 ff.
[47] B. S. Sgrilli, *Descrizione e studi dell'insigne* *fabbrica di S. Maria del Fiore* (Florence, 1733), 34 f, fig. XVI.

and in the top story four great windows were placed, the less to impede the sound of the great bells gathered there."

In the engravings, the scientific aspirations of the author achieve magnificent actuality. Alongside elevation and section are plans taken at no less than four different levels, even including — in an age of great stairways — precise indication of the stairs buried in the massive walls (Fig. 6). Characteristic of the elaborate architectural publications of its day — bringing to mind the seventeenth- and eighteenth-century encyclopedia, Carlo Fontana, Piranesi — Sgrilli's work revealed structural intricacies rivaled in Florence only by the Cupola and the Baptistery. Yet there was to be no further comment on the internal fabric of the Campanile until two centuries later, when Walter Paatz was obliged to review it in his handbook. The observations of Richa and Sgrilli were ignored; one went on contemplating only the exterior.

But the judgement of the incrustation was reconsidered. Although Vasari's principal demon, the *maniera tedesca,* had paled by the eighteenth century, it still had to be ritualistically exorcized from Trecento monuments. In Giuseppe Molini's shabby 1820 republication of Sgrilli, the ritual is no longer necessary.[48] The Campanile appears "one of the most prodigious works of Tuscany and, in its genre, of the Universe." Vasari would have been disturbed by Molini's judgment of the spire, for he writes sadly, "This enormous structure . . . was never terminated and ends truncated horizontally by a *ballatoio.*" By now even Italy had felt the great wave of Gothic revival that had already swept the North by the late eighteenth century. But though Molini no longer had to make apology for the *maniera tedesca,* he could not quite yet praise the building as "Gothic." In the introduction to the book, he characterizes Florentine Gothic architecture ("Arnolfo's" style): it is "defined today as *Greco-Italico,* because [it was] radically created either by Greeks coming to Italy or by Italians passing through Greece on the occassion of the crusades; it succeeded another style called the *Romano-Barbaro;* [we know furthermore] how it was refined by Giotto and redirected, through the work of Brunelleschi, to Attic purity and elegance."[49] Here is manifest the influence of Winckelmann and the Attic revival, the dream of "gentle, pure" Greek forms. And if the *Laocoön* could be all "noble tranquility and quiet grandeur," why not the hot, coloristic Florentine Campanile as *Greco-Italico?* Even Molini's illustrations manifest the temper, reducing Sgrilli's rich engravings to the open, linear style so characteristic of the Neo-Attic school.

Molini's vision of the Campanile thus was a queer fusion of Tuscan *campanilismo,* Winckelmann, and Gothic revival, a compound surely unsurpassed in its instability. It did not last long. From Vasari to Sgrilli the *maniera tedesca* had been at least theoretically reprehensible; insofar as the Campanile was Gothic, it was unseemly. With the rise of the new *Kunstwissenschaft* in the nineteenth century, this judgment was overturned. Still

[48] G. Molini, *La metropolitana fiorentina* (Florence, 1820), 40 ff.

[49] *Ibid.,* 2.

following the periodization of Vasari, a postclassical work was either medieval or modern, Gothic or Renaissance; but now these epochs were considered to be of separate but more or less equal value. In this dualistic machine, the Campanile and its peers were mangled. By definition not Renaissance, the buildings had to be classified as Gothic, which meant inevitable and detrimental comparison with the thirteenth century French standard. The Campanile was not Gothic enough.

Thus Jacob Burckhardt seems to impersonate a latter-day Vasari: "There was no possibility of a perfect harmony in the case of a secondary, composite style like this Italian Gothic; but within its given limitations something particularly great was accomplished."[50] Burckhardt's attitude is but Vasari's recast; while in an absolute sense lacking, in terms of its restricted domain a building like the Campanile could have merit. For Burckhardt, Franz Kugler, and Carl Schnaase the Campanile appeared a stolid quadratic mass, opened "only as much as absolutely necessary,"[51] "enlivened but by a few windows,"[52] and lacking the kinetic principles and "the energy of northern towers."[53] Architectonically uninteresting, it was appreciated (much as the age of steam was happily struck by savage costume) for its colorful decoration, even for its naïveté. Covered with "richly decorative appointments . . . the entirety is undoubtedly by far the most genuine achievement of the tendency towards decorative taste and . . . in the unassuming innocence of its overall design all the more precious."[54] Burckhardt phrases the sentiment in a loftier manner: "But the fine variations of the incrustation as well as the carved details accord this beautiful building a continually renewed study."[55] Schnaase even was able to perceive in the decoration a certain historical significance: in its "colorative presence" the Campanile was the most highly developed example of the traditional Tuscan incrustation.[56]

The revetment, normally deemed a secondary feature, was emphasized also because it embodied a classical undercurrent in the Italian Gothic, the continuation in Gothic guise of Tuscan Romanesque classicism. Burckhardt felt that "for Italian art the invasion of German or Gothic architectural forms from the North was a misfortune . . . if, for example, in the Florentine Baptistery one perceives the XIII century [sic] well on its way toward a harmonious and classicizing beauty, the observer will quickly realize that beneath the extraneous Gothic ornament of the following times, the fundamental sense of classical form remained intact and indeed that it developed . . . toward the grandest achievement."[57] Once discovered, this classical substream was found issuing into the

[50] J. Burckhardt, *Der Cicerone* (Basel, 1855), 140.

[51] *Ibid.*, 143.

[52] C. Schnaase, *Geschichte der bildenden Künste im Mittelalter* (Düsseldorf, 1876), VII, 152.

[53] F. Kugler, *Geschichte der Baukunst* (Stuttgart, 1859), III, 551.

[54] *Ibid.*, 550 f; F. Schevill still praises it for its "racy, native style," *History of Florence* (New York, 1936), 253.

[55] Burckhardt, 1855, 144.

[56] Schnaase, 1876, VII, 152 ff.

[57] Burckhardt, 1855, 124.

Renaissance. A transitional style, "for Italy... the Gothic epoch was only a corridor to the Renaissance," as Georg Dehio put it somewhat later.[58] The rules are still Vasari's: the date of the Baptistery, essence of the classical in Florence, merely is shifted from antiquity to the Dugento; the architecture of Vasari's transitional *prima età* is termed "Italian Gothic" instead of *maniera tedesca* and is valued primarily for whatever classical it carries.

The approach of the Germans was essentially in terms of epoch and style, occasionally relieved by some remarks on composition.[59] Italians writing general histories tended to parrot the northerners. Pietro Selvatico regarded the Campanile as a major example of the "stile archi-acuto toscano" and felt obliged to rationalize its "antique reminiscences."[60] It was left to a triad of Florentine historians — Camillo Boito, Aristide Nardini, and Cesare Guasti, descendants of the antiquarians of Richa's time — to fashion a basically new approach. The major Gothic revival event in Florence was the international competition for the façade of the Cathedral (1822-1875). In the academic historicism of the time this meant a close scrutiny of the Trecento Cathedral fabric, from which it was believed the originally intended shape of the façade could be reconstructed. We may wince at the elephantine product, but the side effect — on the writing of local architectural history — was quite another matter.

One cannot discount the factor of nineteenth-century positivism in the new approach, in particular the writings of Carl Friedrich von Rumohr, who as early as 1827 hesitated to accept the Campanile as entirely by Giotto: "Now whether the invention [of the tower], which surely is praiseworthy and rather purely Gothic for an Italian building, belongs entirely to him or [instead] was discussed, revised, and recast in one of the deliberations whose protocols are found in the archives of Italian cathedrals, I should like all the less to decide, since I have been able to examine neither the disorderly parchment rolls of the Florentine Cathedral archives nor the archives of the Riformagioni in the same city, where the older sources for the history of the building are preserved."[61]

While the method of von Rumohr and, slightly later, Giovanni Gaye[62] had little effect on the following generation of Germans (who did not go to Florence to get lost in the archives), in the researches of Boito, Nardini, and Guasti it combined with the impetus of the Gothic revival to produce the definitive corpus of documents and the basic critical and historical observations concerning the Florentine Cathedral group. As early as 1857, Guasti published the documents for the Cupola;[63] by 1865 Boito had written a fundamental study of the Cathedral nave that included the isolation of Arnolfo di Cambio's

[58] G. Dehio and G. von Bezold, *Die kirchliche Baukunst des Abendlandes* (Stuttgart, 1884 ff), II, 491.

[59] L. Runge, *Der Glockenturm des Dom zu Florenz* (Berlin, 1853), which includes the only accurately measured elevation of the Campanile, in color; Schnaase, 1876, VII, 160.

[60] P. Selvatico, *Storia estetico-critica delle arti del disegno* (Venice, 1852-56), 162, 242 f.

[61] C. F. von Rumohr, *Italienische Forschungen* (Berlin, 1827), II, 70 ff.

[62] G. Gaye, *Carteggio inedito* (Florence, 1839).

[63] C. Guasti, *La Cupola di Santa Maria del Fiore* (Florence, 1857).

fabric and an appealing, if tenuous reconstruction of his full project, all by way of pivotal documentation and the archaeological and stylistic analysis of succeeding phases of construction.[64] Through the seventies and into the eighties the two final works of the antiquarian trio were in preparation: Nardini's basic monograph on the Campanile (1885),[65] underpinned by documents known to all three historians but published completely only by Guasti two years later in his monumental documentary corpus of the Cathedral (up to the Cupola) and Campanile.[66]

Nardini's *Il Campanile* typifies the new approach. Boito had defined Arnolfo's limited contribution to the Cathedral fabric and reconstructed his full plan; Nardini now startlingly delimited Giotto's portion of the Campanile, largely by identifying the thereafter famous design for a campanile in the Siena Cathedral Museum as Giotto's original project (Fig. IX). Using documents and sources as well, Nardini was able to discover the meaning of stylistic changes in the Campanile fabric, recovering what had been common knowledge in the Trecento — that the Campanile is a composite of the projects of Giotto, Andrea Pisano, and Francesco Talenti.

Although the work of several architects, the Campanile was to the Trecento of such compelling iconic force that it appeared a unity. In the Quattrocento this image fused into perfect crystalline form, only to assume tainted incompleteness with Vasari. For the later antiquarians the Campanile became a gathering of associations, which Sgrilli then unceremoniously stripped away, reducing the proud landmark to a fabric. A charming primitive to the mid-nineteenth-century school of German historians, the Campanile had but small import in the serious categories of their history. Thus Poliziano's magic tower was inherited by Nardini as a disturbingly fascinating, but essentially valueless, historical byproduct. He broke it into a multiple positivistic image. There were now no less than three campanili — Giotto's, or the Sienese dawing; Andrea Pisano's, including a verbal reconstruction of his upper project; and Francesco Talenti's, adapted to the lower parts and missing its spire.

Accompanying the recovery of the Campanile's history was a re-evaluation of the three projects and their authors. To Nardini — and to most writers since — Giotto's project, while alluring, seemed architecturally weak. Although he believed that the Trecento censure of Andrea Pisano's design was unwarranted, Nardini was not overly fond of it, and did not long ponder its style. It was Francesco Talenti, already resurrected by Boito in connection with the Duomo,[67] who was lifted from obscurity to fame; his part of the Campanile seemed the best and historically the most important; from it derived his

[64] C. Boito, "Il Duomo di Firenze e Francesco Talenti" (1865), in *Architettura del medio evo in Italia* (Milan, 1880), 185 ff.

[65] A. Nardini, *Il Campanile di Santa Maria del Fiore*, (Florence, 1885). [Hereafter cited as Nardini.] Many of the observations below were first made by Nardini, as the reader who wishes to determine the extent of my debt can easily discover.

[66] Guasti.

[67] Boito, 1880, 185 ff.

incrustation of the Cathedral. Understandably, it was neither Giotto's magic nor Andrea's lean and articulate precision that attracted the men who built the façade: its pompous style was largely developed from the systematically heavy richness of Talenti and his followers. By the turn of the century the enthusiasm for him was so great that in 1903 an inscription plate was inserted in the pavement of the Cathedral:

> Francesco Talenti, diligent craftsman
> And second to none among the architects of this building
> Placed the admirable summit on the tower begun by Giotto[68]

One had finally awoke from Poliziano's dream to do historical justice.

Behind the efforts of Nardini and his colleagues lay an emotional motive that was as strong as the scientific. Nardini defends the Campanile, and, indeed, the entire Italian "architettura ogivale" on the grounds of nationalistic relativism. One cannot judge Italian architecture, he writes, in terms of a northern language of form as had Viollet-le-Duc; one must consider Italian Gothic on its own distinctly national terms: "In the field of the Arts as in that of Letters every nation has its genius and its particular taste." Then relativism fades: if northern architecture is sometimes more successful on the exterior, he argues, "ours" is certainly better within; besides, he protests, the North has no great "ogival" communal buildings [sic].[69] In the 1880s, the Campanile thus becomes an instrument of national pride and aspirations.

Having deserted positivism for nationalism, Nardini moves into even deeper waters. One Campanile is not enough; placed asymmetrically to the side, it disturbs the composition of the Cathedral group, resplendent with the new façade. Nardini proposed, in all seriousness, that a copy of the Campanile be built in the corresponding position north of the Cathedral.[70] Dr. Jekyl has become Mr. Hyde.

---

[68] "FRANCISCVS TALENTI SEDVLVS OPIFEX ET EX HVIVS AEDIS ARCHITECTIS NEMINI SECVNDVS TVRRI AB JOTTO INCHOATAE FASTIGIVM MIRABILE IMPOSVIT / RERVM S MARIAE A FLORE CVRATORES MCMII." The reasons given for placing the inscription are worth noting. Not only had the researches of von Ruhmor, Nardini, and colleagues proven Talenti responsible for what had been unjustly thought the work of Arnolfo and Giotto, but Talenti's fabric is "la parte più interessante del Campanile cominciato da Giotto" (G. Carocci, "Notizie," *Arte e Storia*, XXI [1902], 6), and, moreover, "questo artefice [Talenti] fosse superiore ad ogni altro nostro della sua età" (P. Franceschini, "Per Francesco Talenti," *Arte e Storia*, XXII [1903],

131 f). Even J. von Schlosser found Talenti's contribution to the Campanile of "the greatest architectural beauty" ("Giusto's Fresken in Padua und die Vorläufer der Stanza della Segnatura," *Jahrbuch der kunsthistorischen Sammlungen des allerhöchsten Kaiserhauses*, XVII [1896], 55).

[69] Nardini, 70 ff.

[70] *Ibid.*, 66 ff. He actually goes so far as to calculate the "braccia quadre" of incrustation that would be required. One might recall that earlier in the century K. F. Schinkel and G. Moller, perhaps more reasonably, but in a similar spirit, envisaged the façade of Strasbourg Münster "complete" (G. F. Koch, "Karl Friedrich Schinkel und die Architektur des Mittelalters," *Zeitschrift für Kunstgeschichte*, XXIX [1966], 208

One fails to comprehend why Nardini did not suggest as well that the obvious deficiency of the Campanile — its spire — be constructed. Perhaps he was aware that several decades earlier one of the most prominent of the English speaking patrons — one should say, *innamorati*[71] — of his city had claimed for himself the idea of building the spire. In *Old Pictures in Florence,* a poem published in 1855, Robert Browning centers an intricate conceit concerning the fate of the artistic patrimony of Florence on Giotto and the bell tower still believed to be entirely his.[72] Eulogizing the city spread before him, Browning exclaims:

> And of all I saw and of all I praised,
> The most to praise and the best to see,
> Was the startling bell-tower Giotto raised . . .
> But the tower had been left incomplete:
> . . . Giotto!
> Thy one work, not to decrease or diminish,
> Done at a stroke, was just (was it not?) "O!"[73]
> Thy great Campanile is still to finish.

Further on Browning records the legend ("as the town-tongues babble it") of the survival of Giotto's design; uncannily anticipating Nardini's "discovery" of the Siena drawing, Browning foresees that "when the hour is ripe" the design will appear and the spire be raised:

> Then one shall propose . . .
> Turning the Bell-tower's altaltissimo.
> And fine as the beak of a young beccaccia.
> The Campanile, the Duomo's fit ally,
> Soars up in gold its full fifty braccia,
> Completing Florence, as Florence, Italy.

ff). Schinkel, in a sketch of the Campanile rising above the Florentine roofs, mistook the Bifora windows for Trifora and gave the tower two stories of the latter (*ibid.*, fig. 8).

[71] See M. McCarthy, *The Stones of Florence* (New York, 1957), *passim*, as an antidote to the Romantic vision of Florence (which continues into our day among schoolgirls, spinsters, tourists, expatriates, and art historians).

[72] R. Browning, *Men and Women* (Boston, 1863), 204 ff. Compare the naive plaint of Henry Wadsworth Longfellow in *Giotto's Tower* (*Flower-de-Luce* [London, 1867], 40 f): "In the old Tuscan town stands Giotto's tower, / The lily of Florence blossoming in stone, — / A vision, a delight, and a desire, — / The builder's perfect and centennial flower, / That in the night of ages bloomed alone, / But wanting still the glory of the spire."

[73] The famous legend that, to demonstrate his craftsmanship for Benedict XI, Giotto drew freehanded, at a single stroke, a perfect circle (Vasari, I, 382 ff).

In a manner characteristic of the English-speaking world since Victorian times, Browning projects his own highly Romantic ego further into the matter, concluding:

> Shall I be alive that morning the scaffold
> Is broken away, and the long-pent fire
> Like the golden hope of the world unbaffled
> Springs from its sleep, and up goes the spire —
> As, "God and the People" plain for its motto,
> Thence the new tricolor flaps at the sky?
> Foreseeing the day that vindicates Giotto
> And Florence together, the first am I!

Writing at about the same time as Browning and Nardini, John Ruskin envisioned the Campanile in a rather different, but equally emotional manner. As a counterpart to Burckhardt's amoral, yes, immoral Renaissance, the Gothic Age became the locus of Christian values, a mainspring of the Gothic revival. In *Mornings in Florence, Being Simple Studies of Christian Art for English Travelers,* Ruskin writes about "The Shepherd's Tower": "Perhaps she may, in kindness, forbid my ever seeing it more, the wreck of it being now too ghastly and heart-breaking to any human soul who remembers the day of old. Forty years ago, there was assuredly no spot of ground, out of Palestine, in all the round world, on which, if you knew, even but a little, the true course of that world's history, you saw with so much joyful reverence the dawn of morning, as at the foot of the Tower of Giotto. For there the traditions of faith and hope, of both the Gentile and Jewish race, met for their beautiful labour: The Baptistery of Florence is the last building raised on the earth by the descendants of the workmen taught by Daedalus; and the Tower of Giotto is the loveliest of those raised on earth under the inspiration of the men who lifted up the tabernacle in the wilderness. Of living Greek work there is none after the Florentine Baptistery; of living Christian work, none so perfect as the Tower of Giotto."[74]

For Ruskin the entire edifice is infused with his interpretation of the sculptural cycle. If, in his better moments, Nardini beheld the Campanile in clear sunlight, Ruskin perceived it through a religious mist. For the first time since Vasari, the moral implications of the Campanile dominate the image. But Vasari called attention as well to the fabric. To Ruskin, the Campanile is but a mirror of his piety.

Thus the fragmented consciousness of the nineteenth century split the image of the Campanile, as through a prism, into a spectrum of pure, though overlapping colorings: Revivalism, Positivism, Historicism, Nationalism, and Romanticism. The fragmentary approach to the building has continued into our time. Julius von Schlosser analyzed the

[74] J. Ruskin, *Mornings in Florence* (New York, 1903 [orig. ed. 1876]), 104f.

iconography[75] and others the style and attribution of its rich sculptural decoration.[76] Wolfgang Braunfels considered the Campanile as *Stadtbaukunst* and imagined its origin in the determination of Giotto to provide his city and himself a great monument, and to vindicate in a relief program the values of urban culture.[77] Andreas Grote studied the building's connection with the history of the Opera del Duomo.[78] All neglected the Campanile as an architectural fabric.

Walter Paatz, finding himself in agreement with an obscure paper of Heinrich von Geymüller,[79] as well as with Nardini and his colleagues, claimed that Tuscan Gothic architecture formed an independent style of great importance and coined a name for it: *Trecento-Architektur*.[80] In his *Werden und Wesen der Trecento-Architektur in Toskana* (1937) he devoted a short chapter to the Campanile.[81] But it was exclusively Giotto's design that he discussed and, at that, only in connection with the system of incrustation, which he termed *Malerarchitektur*. Paatz's attitude toward the Campanile thus was but that of his mid-nineteenth-century predecessors in disguise, even though later in his handbook[82] the additions of Andrea Pisano and Talenti as well as the structure and interior — the latter completely ignored even by Nardini — are nominally described.

Decio Gioseffi's more recent study, *Giotto architetto*,[83] reworks the earlier contributions, avoiding the internal structure of the building except to reconstruct Giotto's interior from the Sienese elevation drawing, with as tenuous a result as his other reconstructions (Andrea's upper zone, Talenti's spire) are awkward. Nevertheless, Gioseffi's book does contribute some intelligent observations. The latest serious publication concerning the Campanile is Heinrich Klotz's derivation of Giotto's spire design from Freiburg Münster.[84]

From these writings a composite "modern" image of the Campanile can be sketched. An assemblage by three divergent architects, it forms a simple quadratic shaft with octagonal corner buttresses constructed about an impressive, but indistinct series of vaulted chambers. More significant appears the polychrome marble incrustation, which was essentially the idea of Giotto and truly a painter's architecture. Andrea Pisano's radical modification of Giotto's design added a second band of relief and niches for full

[75] Von Schlosser, 1896, 13 ff.

[76] See Ch. IV.

[77] W. Braunfels, "Giotto's Campanile," *Das Münster*, I (1948), 193 ff; *idem*, 1953, 170 ff, 179 ff.

[78] A. Grote, *Studien zur Geschichte der Opera di Santa Reparata zu Florenz im vierzehnten Jahrhundert* (Munich, 1961), *passim*.

[79] H. von Geymüller, *Friedrich II von Hohenstaufen und die Anfänge der Architektur der Renaissance in Italien* (Munich, 1908).

[80] W. Paatz, *Werden und Wesen der Trecento-Architektur in Toskana* (Burg, 1937), 1 ff.

[81] *Ibid.*, 129 ff.

[82] W. and E. Paatz, *Die Kirchen von Florenz* (Frankfurt, 1940 ff), III, 359 ff. [Hereafter cited as Paatz.]

[83] D. Gioseffi, *Giotto architetto* (Milan, 1963), 72 ff.

[84] H. Klotz, "Deutsche und italienische Baukunst im Trecento," *Mitteilungen des kunsthistorischen Instituts in Florenz*, XII (1966), 173 ff.

scale statuary. Talenti's richly fenestrated stories above are closely related to the Duomo flanks. Never completed, the Campanile — great civic landmark that it is — was the expression of a communal will, perhaps driven by the force of Giotto. In the scholastic iconography of its sculpture can be discerned a portrayal of the culture of the city.

If the Campanile of Florence Cathedral is indeed all of this, just how much more its stones reveal and its history holds shall be the task of the following chapters to tell.

Chapter II

Giotto's Campanile

On April 12, 13, 1334, the commune appointed Giotto as "master and governor of the fabric and workshop of the church of Santa Reparata."[1] Although according to del Migliore, he was given a visionary commission for the tower design shortly thereafter,[2] it was not until three months later that Giotto's Campanile appears in contemporary sources. Villani writes: "In the same year [1334] on July 18, the new Campanile of Santa Reparata was begun alongside the façade of the church on the piazza of San Giovanni. And to begin the construction the Bishop of Florence was there with the entire clergy to consecrate the first stone, attended by the priors and other high citizens, with a great procession and many people. And the foundation was built in very massive manner down to the water table. And as superintendent and manager of the fabric the commune appointed our fellow citizen Master Giotto: the most sovereign master of painting of his or any age."[3]

Under the direction of the Arte della Lana, invested with control of the Opera del Duomo in 1331,[4] the work advanced at such a pace that the heavy communal subsidies set up in 1331 and 1332 did not suffice.[5] On September 16, 1334, the Opera obtained a

[1] Doc. 1; see n. 38 and 44 below. The original dedication of the cathedral, to S. Reparata, remained popular long after 1296, when it was officially superceded by "S. Maria del Fiore" (cf. Paatz, III, 321).

[2] See Ch. I, 3 f; and Doc. XIV.

[3] Doc. I. If the ceremony was like the founding of the first pier of Talenti's nave on July 5,

1357, it would have been "con torchietti di ciera in mano accesi, con grande triunfo di chanti e di suono di champane d'orghani e trombe" (Guasti, 98).

[4] *Ibid.*, doc. 36.

[5] For the financing of the Opera, see Grote, 1961, 32 ff, 56, 61 ff; Braunfels, 1953, 221 ff.

loan of 150 florins toward completion of the foundations.⁶ The foundations — as Villani tells us — reached the water table, at that time about twelve *braccia* (seven meters) deep in the vicinity of the Campanile. The fact that, in an age of massive construction, they impressed Villani sufficiently to be included in his chronicle suggests that the "massive" aspect of their form — "tutto sodo" — was exceptional. If constructed as four walls on a square plan, those walls would be of enormous thickness. It is even possible that the Campanile foundations form a solid cubic mass, a hidden mountain of masonry as much as thirty-five braccia (twenty meters) per side, a volume of 14,000 cubic braccia (2,800 cubic meters), resembling the Cathedral pier foundations partly uncovered during the nave excavations of 1966-67 (Fig. 244) and costing about 2,000 lira for labor alone. Even the four-wall conformation would have amounted to at least half as much. Small wonder that the financial capacities of the Opera were strained.⁷

⁶ Doc. 2.

⁷ Evidently the procedure Villani witnessed was similar to the construction, two decades later, of the Cathedral pier foundation "fino alla buona ghiaia entro l'aqua" (Guasti, 94), which then seems to have been about 12 *braccia* deep (1 braccio = .584 meters) according to measurements of completed foundations (July 12, 1357, Guasti, 100; Jan. 16, 1358, *ibid.*, 115). Vasari (Doc. XIII) also places the bottom of the Campanile foundations at the water table ("in quella parte donde si era cavata acqua e ghiaia"), but appears to overestimate their depth by 8 *braccia*. Nevertheless the three-part construction he describes probably is largely accurate: at the water level the "primo fondamento," a bottom layer of solid stone masonry ("una piatèa di pietra forte"); then the subfoundation proper, a dense conglomerate mass ("un buon getto") probably laid into, and entirely filling, the lower excavation (a method generally termed *a sacco* in Italian); and above, the rising foundation proper, Vasari's "muro a mano", built in the open below grade, and faced like the Cathedral piers (Fig. 244) with a rough ashlar. The conglomerate core of the foundation would also be similar to the Cathedral piers, for which were ordered "tante pietre di fiume per li fondamenti" on Dec. 7, 1357 and other occasions (Guasti, 113); Piles or solid ashlar were employed only in problematic circumstances, such as those encountered during construction of the Cupola foundations (Guasti, doc. 355; to counteract the problem of ground water, piles or drainage with solid ashlar were suggested as alternatives, and the latter adopted). (See also Ch. V for building methods.) If a solid cubic mass, the Campanile foundations evidently were considered the base for a huge, hollow pier and their breadth probably determined by the same quadrature series as the cathedral piers, where 7-*braccia* foundations carry 4½-*braccia* shafts (H. Saalman, "Santa Maria del Fiore: 1294-1418," *Art Bulletin*, XLVI [1964], 478); this would give the 25-*braccia* Campanile, foundations of about 35-*braccia*. The purpose of such a work would have been to minimize the effects of settling under the huge tower by consolidation through sheer continuity of mass. Precedents of a kind were to be found. Only a few decades earlier the old private shaft incorporated into the Pal. Vecchio as an underprop for its colossal tower was filled to near solidity (Fig. 333; see A. Lensi, *Palazzo Vecchio* [Milan, 1929], 20 f). The foundations of the Pisa campanile — already leaning perceptibly in the Trecento — form an enormously thick ring (ca. 7 m, with the full radius of the campanile base only ca. 9.5 m), a punctured disc rather than a circular wall; because of the soil the campanile leans, but due to the overbuilt underpinnings it at least still stands (as of 1971). (See P. Sanpaolesi, *Il Campanile di Pisa* [Pisa, 1956], figs. 4-12, pp. 15 ff; cf. also the continuous subfoundation, ca. 25 m in diameter, for the original project of S. Aquilino at S. Lorenzo in Milan, 465-511, to counteract

The old Campanile had been built attached to the opposite flank of the church in the common Florentine arrangement, as, for example, at Santa Maria Novella, San Lorenzo, and Ognissanti.[8] But given the intent to relocate the new bell tower — in the most conspicuous site at the corner of the Cathedral toward the heart of the city and on its main axis (Figs. 1, 3, 4)[9] — it would have been difficult to bind the Campanile to the Cathedral, if only because of the breadth of the enormous new foundations.[10] This may have precipitated the decision to treat the Campanile as an independent monument, an arrangement for which there seems to have been deep civic motivation and for which ample precedent would have been found outside Florence in important campanili of major Italian cities, including Pisa, Venice, and Rome.[11]

Construction continued smoothly. Late in 1336 the commune was able to send Giotto "to the service of the Lord of Milan." But, returning, he died in Florence on January 8, 1337. As befitted a great Florentine and *capomaestro,* Giotto was buried in the Cathedral near his most grandiose conception.[12] The documents are characteristically silent as to how much of it he was able to complete. Pucci, the earliest source on the subject (1373), informs us that Giotto "conducted the work so far / That he made the first reliefs in good style."

the sloping, waterlogged terrain, G. Chierici, "La Basilica di S. Lorenzo in Milano," *Palladio,* n.s. IV [1954], 171 ff, figs. 2 f.) Such lessons may not have been lost on the builders of the foundations of Giotto's Campanile, even though the wall that Giotto began above (with thoroughly characteristic Trecento unreliability; see n. 42 below) appears to have been less than well calculated (perhaps *because* of the imperturbable solidity of the foundations).

Cubic measurement of masonry was of highest importance to the *Operai,* for the foundation work was paid by cubic *braccia*—¹/₂ soldi per *braccio* for earth removal; 2 soldi, 5 denari for each cubic *braccio* of masonry (July 12, 1357, Guasti, 99 f; Jan. 16, 1358, *ibid.,* 115 f). 240 denari = 20 soldi = one silver florin or *libra;* the gold florin was broken down into gold soldi and denari in an identical formula, but the exchange rate between silver and gold currency fluctuated.

[8] See Ch. VII.

[9] Braunfels, 1953, 118 f, 170. The main axis runs from the Pza. S. Giovanni down the Via Calzaioli past Or San Michele to the Pal. Vecchio. The history of the names given to the sections of the modern Via Calzaioli is summarized by W. Limburger, *Die Gebäude von Florenz* (Leipzig, 1910), 198. Nearly every block had

a separate name. According to C. Frey (*Loggia dei Lanzi* [Berlin, 1885] 68, Plan I), the 11th-century hospital at the foot of the street, located more or less in front of the present Bigallo, was destroyed in 1298; was this just a step toward the systematization of the piazza and its circulation — or could a new Campanile have already been in mind?

[10] The structural situation would have been similar to that of the campanili set alongside S. Apollinare in Classe and S. Apollinare Nuovo in Ravenna, about which K. J. Conant notes: "Foundation difficulties result when heavy tower masses are joined to other construction; this is sufficient reason for the two belfries being set at a distance from the churches. It seems likely that the precedent established here created the tradition of free-standing belfry towers" (*Carolingian and Romanesque Architecture: 800-1200* [Baltimore, 1959], 301 n. 15). The Florentine placement, to the right of the façade, would also have been in accord — probably coincidentally — with an ecclesiastical tradition recorded by A. Auber, *Histoire et théorie du symbolisme religieux* (Paris-Poitiers, 1871), III, 120 ff.

[11] See Ch. VII.

[12] Doc. I.

It appears, from the context, that this reference to reliefs was, at least in part, intended to indicate the level reached by the fabric. Afterward, Pucci continues, the project was altered by Andrea Pisano.[13] A shadow crosses Giotto's fabric with the cheerless remark of the anonymous Dante commentator: the design was flawed by two errors, "l'uno, che non ebbe ceppo da piè; l'altro, che fu stretto." These faults — a lack of setback near the bottom *(piede),* and overthinness — were so serious that Giotto is said to have died from the shame.[14]

On entering the ground-floor chamber of the Campanile it is soon disclosed how grave, indeed, was Giotto's error (Figs. 25, 26). Behind the double arcade of an inner layer of construction lies the outer wall (its windows cut or altered by the inner shell), which cannot be other than Giotto's masonry (Fig. 32). This visual observation is substantiated by the results of a stripping of intonaco (in April 1969) from two small areas in the corners of the east niche on the south side of the chamber. It could be seen that: the inner shell of piers and the wall flanking the windows do not bond; the window wall is constructed of both stone and brick, the piers exclusively of stone; the piers interrupt the window wall at the joint and continue toward the exterior (Figs. 27-29).[15] Clearly window walls and piers were not part of the same phase of construction; for obvious technical and structural reasons it also appears most unlikely that the piers continue to the exterior with the window wall filled in as a kind of curtain wall (which, at a meter and a half in thickness and bearing the window vault and a good part of the fabric above, it clearly is not). Rather it would seem that the window wall was built as a single and continuous shell of construction, then cut into to an unknown depth to form structural niches into which the reinforcement piers were inserted, effecting a binding of the two layers of construction.[16]

Confirming the laminate nature of this fabric are two further anomalies. In the east niche on the north side of the chamber the window (which, for unknown reasons, is off

---

[13] Doc. IV.

[14] Doc. V. *"Ceppo"* literally means stump or base; in the case of the Campanile it could only be achieved by a setback.

[15] The masonry probe was executed for me under the supervision of Prof. Isabelle Hyman, Ingeniere Galliano Boldrini, president of the Opera di S. Maria del Fiore, and Architetto Piero Micheli of the Comune di Firenze, whose analysis of the findings has been particularly helpful.

[16] Such a binding was not unusual; at least one example is recorded in the Cathedral fabric and documents; the half piers along the side-aisle walls were, at least in certain instances, cut into the pre-existing Arnolfian wall, as, for example,

was decided on Jan. 16, 1359: "Deliberarono di talglare il muro per fare il menbro a la porta de' Chornachini" (Guasti, 124; "men[m]bro" was the term for the half and quarter piers); and in fact, along the north wall of the nave it can be seen that "membri" were sometimes bonded into pre-existing fabric (Fig. 246).

Another interesting example of reinforcement is the Loggia at the Bargello, where the old piers (ca. 1320) were shaved off and a new inner layer added for the vaulting of 1332-46 (W. Paatz, "Zur Baugeschichte des Palazzo del Podestà [Bargello] in Florenz," *Mitteilungen des kunsthistorischen Instituts in Florenz,* III [1931], 308 ff, with an incorrect plan of the pier, fig. 14; cf. fig. 15).

center, canted, and given a lintel rather than a vault) is cut by the inner shell, not only at the top, but at the right jamb, which does not line up with the inner shell, lying instead to the right (east) of it (Fig. 31).[17] Assuming sobriety on the part of the builders, such a configuration can only have resulted from two campaigns. Furthermore, on the exterior of the Campanile in the same area — on the north face between the northeast buttress and the first hexagon frame — can be observed a small lancet window (Figs. II, 8) that originally must have lit some internal compartment (probably a staircase) but which was evidently blinded by the walling up of that cavity with the addition of the inner reinforcement shell now forming a solid mass in that corner.[18]

Giotto's error thus is clear: his Campanile *wall* was too "thin." Only about 1.50 meters thick, and, weakened toward the base by the broadly splayed windows, the wall was intended by the great painter to rise as high as one hundred meters,[19] a structural impetuosity almost rivaling the miscalculation of his Sienese contemporaries that doomed their Duomo Nuovo project.[20] It would have been Andrea Pisano's first act on taking over to thicken the wall inward with a second layer about 1.60 meters thick, doubling its total depth. Giotto's wall rose to a height somewhat below the level of the window in the west wall just beneath the vaulting (Figs. 26, 32). This window, canted laterally away from Giotto's projected elevation but toward Andrea's exterior fabric,[21] reveals a homogeneous structure (Figs. 26, 30), so that from the window up, at least, the entire masonry thickness is Andrea's. Giotto's thin wall obviously allowed for no strong setback; Andrea's thickened wall permitted the setback above the second story (Figs. 7, 46) and also his complex stairway system (Fig. X), to which we shall come in the following chapter.[22]

[17] An observation — among others (see Ch. III) — which I owe to Prof. Richard Pommer.

[18] See Ch. III, 61 f, 65, 70 ff for further observations on this problem.

[19] Including the octagon and spire of the project; Gioseffi (1963, fig. 76 a) calculates 106 *braccia*, or ca. 62 m to the foot of the octagon. According to G. Lami (*Lezioni di antichità toscane* [Florence, 1766], 156) and G. Gozzadini (*Delle torri gentilizie di Bologna* [Bologna 1875], 10 f) not only Florentine but Bolognese towers, as well, of heights occasionally rivaling Giotto's Campanile project, had walls no greater than about 3 *braccia* (1.75 m) in thickness; the closed, stairless private shafts, with a weighty vault only at the bottom, and not subject to the powerful vibrations of bells, evidently required thinner walls than such complex fabrics as the Campanile or the Pal. Vecchio tower, where the massively built upper part (walls of ca. 2 m) rests on the old shaft of the Foraboschi, reinforced on the interior to form walls of more than 3 meters, leaving an open core only 1.25 by 0.65 m (Fig. 333; Lensi, 1929, 20 f). On the Duomo Nuovo project, cf. J. White, *Art and Architecture in Italy, 1250-1400* (Baltimore, 1966), 168 f.

[20] See n. 42 below.

[21] The window is canted so that on the exterior it exits off center but precisely between two of the lozenge frames (Fig. 7): in Giotto's design this opening would not only cut into the paneling but would quite inexplicably confute the centered oculus; thus, the window can only have been planned together with the executed second story of incrustation (without oculus), which, we shall see, was clearly the conception and work of Andrea Pisano.

[22] Should further research reveal the ground story fabric to be of a single campaign, the most con-

Giotto was able to raise structural masonry to a height of twelve to fifteen braccia. How much of the rich decoration that covers the broad exterior planes and corner prisms is his? A fundamental change in revetment design does not occur until above the second story of reliefs. While Giotto's bearing wall at the most rises only a few braccia into the second relief story (Fig. 32), theoretically the incrustation of both relief zones, which seem at first glance so much the same, could be his design. The stylistic variation in the sculpture itself (Figs. 125-132) would not efface this impression: only the hexagonal reliefs in the west face were set simultaneously with the enframing incrustation; the other hexagons were placed after the incrustation itself had been completed; thus, as was common, the execution of the incrustation was not dependent on the completion of the sculpture.[23] But if our naked eye thereby confutes Pucci's testimony, it plays history false: a close analysis of the fabric, aided by detail photographs taken from scaffolding and through telephoto lenses, reveals that Pucci was indeed an accurate chronicler.

The original elevation begins immediately above the bench (Fig. 8), which was added only after the lowering of the piazza in 1339.[24] The first sequence of panels and rounded profiles forming the plinth, socle, and base proper (Figs. II, 8) take as a point of departure the nearly identical elevation of Arnolfo's immediately adjacent Cathedral wall (Fig. 164).[25] Arnolfo's sequence is simpler and clearer than that of Giotto, who has, to begin with, heightened the plinth, dividing it with a pink element that from a mere strip at the buttresses deepens to a bench between them, now largely hidden beneath a bundle of profiles inserted by a later architect.[26] Originally the effect was that of the Campanile poised on a pink cushion that "continued" under the wall and buttresses. Immediately above the plinth, the base and green body of the socle are as nearly identical to Arnolfo's

sequential conclusion I have drawn from my interpretation would still stand: that Giotto was not a professional architect. For what master mason would have designed from scratch the structurally inefficient and visually relatively clumsy conformation?

[23] For the various theories of attribution, see Ch. IV below. Becherucci (1965, 261) notes the evidence for the sequence of the setting of the relief, but interprets it incorrectly.

[24] Doc. 3. The complex profiles of the base of the bench, particularly the overhang, resemble Fra Jacopo Talenti's bases in the Chiostro Verde of S. Maria Novella of ca. 1350-60 (Fig. 173); Paatz, III, 696. The forms of the insert between the piers (above the pink slab) are too clumsy for Giotto, whose foot system they confuse in any case; but when the lower bench was added, the profiles eliminated the redundancy of benches. Dating from the time of Talenti or later,

this detail does not seem to appear in the documents; Gioseffi, who first pointed out that the lower seat is added, connects it with "laborerium de lapidibus marmi" done in 1388 (1963, 77; Doc. 218). Unfortunately this seems to refer strictly to paving.

[25] The two elevations were first well compared by Paatz (1937, 129 ff), who stressed the richer coloration, profiles, and configurations of Giotto. Arnolfo's revetment stops at Talenti's heavy stringcourses in which the consoles supporting the window decoration are set. The extravagant theories of G. Kiesow concerning this wall ("Zur Baugeschichte des Florentiner Doms," *Mitteilungen des kunsthistorischen Instituts in Florenz*, X [1961], 1 ff) are put down by H. Saalman, "Santa Maria del Fiore: 1294-1418," *Art Bulletin*, XLVI (1964), 494 ff.

[26] See n. 24 above.

composition as one could ask. But Giotto has softened the upper profile of the socle by reducing the width of the listel. More importantly, he has entirely altered its relationship to the base above. With Arnolfo, the torus of the base has the same plan as the plinth upon which it rests in forthright, classical manner; Giotto projects the torus beyond, letting it overhang. The listel immediately above Arnolfo's base, which forms the lower border of the first decorative band, is pulled down by Giotto into the base itself; thus the upper torus of his base also becomes the lower frame of the first band.

So by transition — almost as if by progressive mutation — one leaves behind the hard architectonic logic of Arnolfo. From the base of the Campanile to the first cornice one encounters a rich complex of marble incrustation comprising (apart from figured relief and coats of arms) exclusively framing profiles and enframed planes and bands of monochrome and intarsia. The overall scheme, like the sequence at the foot, derives from Arnolfo's Cathedral flanks: alternating dark and light frames about light central rectangles, with the upper- and lowermost strips treated as continuous horizontal bands extended over the buttresses. But if the potent graphic layout of Arnolfo's design was useful to Giotto, its highly abstract planarity ran counter to his intentions. Not surprisingly, he turned for his surface detail to the same source that had inspired Arnolfo's graphic pattern: the Romanesque paneling of the Baptistery attic, framed by bent architraves whose fasciae profiles appear enclosing Giotto's Campanile panels (Fig. 163). Indeed, Giotto's dependence on the Baptistery goes far beyond such detail: obviously his very notion of cladding a fabric in polychrome marbles dominated by rectangular patterns and articulated by classicizing detail derives from the Florentine Romanesque of which the Baptistery — "il bel San Giovanni"[27] — was the pre-eminent example. One would imagine that Giotto's willing acceptance of this tradition was due not only to his own painterly architectural propensities, but to a conscious attempt to harmonize the new Campanile with the Baptistery and Cathedral.

The first story incrustation of the Campanile exhibits brilliant control of relief, characterized by a velvety transition between planes. Three profiles are used: cavetto, tondino, and cyma reversa. The dark bands form the ground plane, from which the fasciae frames of the sculpture step back in two stages, the outer a cyma reversa, the inner a tondino. Fashioned of but the simplest of means, the relief is altogether of an exquisite delicacy and richness (Fig. 9).

An analogous web of polychrome architecture is found in Giotto's illusionistic framework at the Arena Chapel (Figs. 147-153).[28] Whatever its connection to the incrustation tradition of the Cathedral group, the first story revetment of the Campanile is also the frescoed architecture of the chapel turned "inside out" and cast in a dominant rather than

[27] Dante, *Inferno*, XIX, 6.

[28] C. A. Isermeyer, *Rahmengliederung und Bildfolge in der Wandmalerei bei Giotto und den* *Florentiner Malern des 14. Jahrhunderts* (Würzburg, 1937), 4 ff.

subservient role: it is now the figured sculpture that is secondary and decorative. Not only are the Campanile profiles ubiquitous elements in the illusionistic armature of the chapel (as well as in the architectural sets within the scenes), but one observes there precisely the classicizing console cornice that crowns the first Campanile story, consisting of tondino, consoles, and cyma recta (Figs. 11, 12, 152). Indeed, in Padua it extends around the entire chapel. If the originally Roman motif reached Giotto through Dugento central Italian painting, at the Campanile the rather dry version of Padua is enriched. Quite possibly Giotto had in mind the luxuriant classicism of Giovanni Pisano's cornice, which supports the lower row of prophets on the façade of Siena Cathedral (Fig. 162). Here one finds a similar arrangement of consoles, rosettes, and rosette coffering. Characteristically, Giotto intensifies the colorism by setting the rosettes in a ground alternating between pink and green (Fig. III).

As at Padua and Siena, the Campanile consoles support a cyma recta. One senses that a full, powerful cornice is being built up for the first Campanile story to balance the foot. But the outward corbeling stops short, the next profile steps back and with an inclined plane re-enters the wall. Seen from above, the cornice seems incomplete, the re-entrant molding an afterthought added to the monolithic sections of the cornice proper (Fig. 11). In contrast to its delicate classicism, one discovers in the second cornice of the first zone a radically different architectural conformation (Fig. 13). Though constituted of physically monolithic sections, Giotto's cornice seems constructed of clearly separated parts resting additively one upon the other. The cornice above seems carved from a single mass of stone. A modified tondino leads into a cavernous, inverted scotia, followed by an inclined plane decorated with a stud motif, then by a larger inclined re-entrant plane terminating in a tondino. Giotto's classical vocabulary is completely denied. Horizontal and vertical planes dominate the composition of his cornice. Above, except for a single fillet at the point of maximum projection, there are neither horizontals nor verticals, but rather a deeply sculpted forward movement that sweeps suddenly back.

In the second story, the divergence in detail from Giotto continues. Although, as throughout the Campanile revetment, Giotto's intarsia is manifestly rooted in the still active Cosmatesque tradition,[29] it has been suggested that specific Giottesque motives derive from Oriental patterns.[30] The broken, dismembered effect, in any case, is that of looking into a kaleidoscope. The dominant element is the square (Fig. V). Above, the patterns — even if with spiky tips — are both more curvilinear and continuous, and clearly Gothic in origin. The central motif, a variant of the studded quatrelobes on the

---

[29] Compare the dense and dazzling polychrome patterns, the shifting figure-ground relationships, the build up of complex shapes from simple, angular elements in Cosmatesque work (e.g., E. Hutton, *The Cosmati* [London, 1950], figs. 15a,

17, 18, 24, 50 f, 63; *The Encyclopedia of World Art*, III, figs. 481 f for color plates).

[30] Paatz, 1937, 130. The most elaborately "oriental" motifs in Florence are the Giotto school frescoes in the vault of the Bargello Chapel (Fig. 151).

second cornice, floats with concentric clarity rather than activating a flickering figure-ground oscillation (Figs. III, 14). The framing strips differ as well. In the first story, the incrustation bands of intarsia are given subtle emphasis over the flanking monochrome bands by the disposition of the edge moldings, which symmetrically focus on the intarsia by bordering it with their more elaborate profile (the cyma reversa). The monochrome ribbons read as ground, the intarsia as figure. In the second story this distinction is lost: the cyma reversa is replaced by another cavetto so that the framing strip itself becomes neutrally symmetrical and thereby diverts focus from the intarsia.

We have noted the soft, delicate richness of Giotto's inner frames of the hexagonal relief (tondino, cyma reversa); the frames of the lozenges of the second story assume a more vigorously sculpted profile (Fig. 15) — a divergence analogous to that between the two cornices. Although the outer frames of the relief sculpture remain the same in profile, their graphic configuration differs significantly from story to story. Below, the central hexagon and the rectangular ground are quietly balanced. At the inner facets of the buttressing, Giotto simply places a small square (Fig. 7), rather than insert an irregular or a smaller hexagon. How different is the restless angularity generated by the lozenges in the story above, which upset the relaxed equilibrium of the main panels and are squeezed into the corners (Figs. 7, 15). Nor is there affinity between the velvety classicism of the first story (through the console cornice) and the miniature brackets or the metallically delicate trefoil arcade of the second story cornice (Fig. 16). Looking upward, however, it is seen that these latter details match in genre the cornice of the third, or niche story of the Campanile (Figs. 20, 77).

In Chapter III the style of the second and third stories will be examined further. For the moment, it is clear that a sharp change in the shaping of architectural detail occurs above the first cornice of the first story.[31] It seems no coincidence that the incrustation style of this story terminates slightly below the upper limit of Giotto's bearing masonry, a discontinuity entirely in accord with Pucci's testimony.

The hand of Giotto is limited to the first story, then, up to and including the first cornice (though probably not its inclined re-entrant molding). Above, Andrea Pisano departed subtly, but distinctly from Giotto's manner of detail. Did he depart as well from Giotto's overall scheme? Or can Giotto have planned — in imitation of Arnolfo's multi-tiered Cathedral façade (Fig. 239) — a second story similar to the first?

The sole instrument for reconstructing Giotto's project is the famous drawing of a tower elevation in the Museo dell'Opera del Duomo, Siena (Figs. IX, 133, 134).[32] The

[31] Nardini (11 ff), in a less precise and developed discussion along similar lines, excludes — for no apparent reason — the cornice from Giotto's share. Gioseffi (1963, 77) seems to misunderstand the problem completely.

[32] The drawing is on three connected pieces of parchment, with joints at the base of the spire and between the single and double bifore. Although the execution is clearly the work of one hand, the red wash in the triple bifora and spire is more intense than the faded pink below. The change in saturation occurs not between separate

widespread agreement that it closely reflects Giotto's Campanile project might be wishful thinking.[33] This notion is founded upon several observations. The drawing conforms closely, almost precisely, to the exterior of the Campanile to the extent that the executed fabric is Giotto's, that is, up to the first cornice, at which design and fabric diverge (Figs. 7, 8, 135, 136). Above, the drawing is totally different from the executed Campanile. The question has been asked, if not Giotto, what artist would have copied the first Campanile story in such a servile manner, then above have departed from it completely? It could not have been Andrea Pisano or Talenti, whose modifications were of a very different sort. If the draftsman were a Sienese, the argument continues, who might have needed a design for a new campanile around 1339, he would never have copied part of the Florentine project so precisely and then have substituted his own, radically different conception for the rest. If a copy at all, the Siena drawing must be wholly a copy, the argument concludes, and therefore it must reflect closely Giotto's entire project.[34] In addition, it has been stressed that the design evidences a non-architectural, painterly imagination, which again leads to Giotto.[35] Because of his singular eminence as an artist, Florence could have awarded him the commission. But no other painter would have been allowed to transgress the rule that builders, including *the capomaestro,* must belong to the masons' guild. Thus, it is reasoned that the design could not possibly be a variation by Taddeo Gaddi, who never was a stonemason.[36]

On its own terms this argument is inconclusive. Perhaps the most serious oversight is the possibility that the drawing represents an unexecuted project conceived for a competition held after Giotto's death — Andrea Pisano not being mentioned as *capomaestro* until 1340. This would account for both the similarity of the first story fabric to the drawing and the divergence above. Nothing would have prevented Taddeo Gaddi or any other painter, sculptor, goldsmith, or architect from entering such a competition (though

sheets but on the central parchment. Probably the drawing was folded over toward the top, for reasons of its great size, and storage, protecting the color in that part. The image measures 209.6 cm to the foot of the spire angel, the shaft being 131.8 cm, the octagon and spire 77.8 cm. Although tricky to measure (because of warping), the approximate widths of the image are: 29.3 cm at the foot; 28.5 cm across the first-zone hexagons; the shaft above narrows to 28 cm, then to ca. 27.5 at the single bifora, and 27.4 at the triple bifora. The lower angels are ca. 5 cm high, the upper one 7.5 cm. The pinnacles, 40.5 cm high, seem round. Speculation on how the design came to Siena is made by Paatz (1937, 132) and Gioseffi (1963, 78).

[33] For a summary of opinions, see Paatz, III, 436 n. 51, and Gioseffi, 1963, 72 ff. Among serious comment, only Lusini disagrees, holding it for a late Trecento Sienese design connected with restorations of the campanile of Siena Cathedral (V. Lusini, *Il Duomo di Siena* [Siena, 1911], I, 280 ff). The objection is rebutted well by Paatz (1937, 131 ff) who emphasizes the non-Sienese, early (even Dugentesque) character of the design.
[34] Substantially the argument of Nardini (11 ff).
[35] Implicit in earlier writings (see Ch. I above) and suggested by Nardini (12 ff), this point was well illuminated by Paatz (1937, 129 ff), who, in fact, first termed it *Malerarchitektur.*
[36] Nardini, 25 ff n. 2. Amplified by Braunfels, 1953, 221 ff.

he probably would have had to matriculate as a mason to become *capomaestro,* as did Orcagna in the case of the Or San Michele Tabernacle). In the planning activities for the Cathedral in 1366-67, artists of all backgrounds — including Taddeo Gaddi and Andrea da Firenze[37] — took part. Rejected in Florence, the bell tower design could have found its way to a potentially more hospitable Siena.

But even were the logic as such of Giotto's advocates unassailable, it would form little more than, as it were, circumstantial evidence in favor of their claim. After all, to accept the design as Giotto's project for his life's proudest commission demands more than negative chains of deduction and diffuse considerations of painterly qualities. One must determine in concrete manner if the project would be truly characteristic of Giotto as architect.

Unfortunately there is no identifiable trace of his activity as city architect other than the first story of the Campanile. Beyond his connection with the Campanile project, Giotto's position in the Office of Communal Works appears not to have been much more than nominal, and perhaps even honorary.[38] He seems to have played no role in the construction of the Cathedral itself.[39] The commune would not have squandered the precious time of the aged master by assigning him routine construction such as the city

[37] Guasti, doc. 155; cf. Braunfels, 1953, 229 f; Saalman, 1964, 483 ff.

[38] There is a controversy over the nature of Giotto's position as *capomaestro* and city-architect among R. Oertel ("Wende der Giotto-Forschung," *Zeitschrift für Kunstgeschichte,* XI [1943-44], 6), holding that Giotto's fame is rooted in characteristically medieval professional esteem; H. Wiernozowski ("Art and the Commune in the Time of Dante," *Speculum,* XIX [1944], 32), saying that the commission was intended to lure Giotto from his numerous, extra-Florentine callings; W. Paatz ("Die Gestalt Giottos im Spiegel einer zeitgenössischen Urkunde," *Eine Gabe der Freunde für Carl Georg Heise* [Berlin, 1950], 55 ff), giving a profoundly detailed but overextended interpretation; Braunfels (1953, 220 ff), including a list of city projects possibly done under Giotto's term (238 f); Grote (1961, 47 f), summarizing and striking a compromise between Braunfels and Paatz; Gioseffi (1963, 62 ff), arguing with Braunfels about what Giotto did; and Panofsky (1960, 118 f n. 3), stressing the significance of the fact that Giotto was a painter, not an architect. The argumentation has depended largely on varying inter-pretations of the terms of the document of 1334 appointing Giotto *capomaestro* (Doc. 1) — to which I add my own in n. 44 below — rather than on a careful examination of the Campanile fabric, as presented above, and in which a close adherence to the designs of Giotto's own hand is apparent, whether he was on the building site or not, etc. On the other hand, the absence of Giottesque construction other than the Campanile makes the dispute about his position as *Stadtbaumeister* rather fruitless. Gioseffi's attribution of the Arena Chapel itself is highly doubtful, as noted by White (1966, 204). Similar comment is in order concerning the extremely evasive thesis of A. M. Romanini ("Giotto e l'architettura gotica in alta Italia," *Bollettino d'Arte,* III-IV [1965], 160 ff) connecting Giotto as architect not only with Padua but the church and campanile of S. Gottardo in Milan; but the notes of her article do include every conceivable item of bibliography for Giotto, *architetto.*

[39] Paatz, III, 437 n. 52. I now seriously question the theory presented in my Master's thesis (*The Planning of Florence Cathedral from 1296 to 1366/67* [New York University, 1963], 44 ff) on this point.

wall and fortifications, which in any case were nearly complete by 1334.[40] Once the Campanile design had taken full shape, was well understood by all and underway, the commune had fit employment for Giotto, such as dispatching him to the court of Milan late in 1336 on a special artistic mission.[41] Indeed, in view of his structural error at the Campanile — which should have horrified any master mason [42] — he seems to have been a man of little, if any, building experience. If the Ponte alla Carraia was actually reconstructed during his term of office, it may have had his official stamp of approval as city architect, but it hardly would have withstood several floods unless an experienced builder actually had erected it in a thoroughly proven manner.[43] Both Villani and Pucci, even in the context of the Campanile, entitle Giotto purely a painter, as do the terms of his appointment as *capomaestro:* "Magistro Giotto Bondonis de Florentia pittore." [44]

The key to understanding Giotto's architectural imagination lies not in actual construction — nor in such apocryphal attributions of pseudo-architecture as the Tarlatti Tomb in Arezzo Cathedral [45] — but rather in his painting, that is, in the illusionistic framework of fresco cycles, in the imaginary architecture within scenes, and even in the frames of panels. To be sure, all three topics have been studied, but never together

[40] Braunfels, 1953, 64 (however, the wall had suffered flood damage; cf. Villani, XI, 1).

[41] Concerning Giotto's Milanese activity see A. M. Romanini, 1965, 174 f n. 10.

[42] However, one should not be too hard on Giotto. All three of the great Trecento cathedrals were cursed by serious structural flaws: the transept of Orvieto (which had to be rebuilt), the Duomo Nuovo of Siena (abandoned because of gross static miscalculations), and the nave vaults of Florence (bound by tie rods after cracks appeared in 1364). Cf. White, 1966, 165 ff. Of all the gigantic cathedral undertakings, only Brunelleschi's Cupola was structurally flawless.

[43] This is true regardless of Gioseffi's argument (1963, 68). In Villani's record of the rebuilding of the Carraia, which, in Bk. XI, Ch. 12, immediately follows the founding of the Campanile, there is no mention or implicit reference to Giotto.

[44] Contrast the praise of Arnolfo di Cambio as architect: "magister Arnolphus est capudmagister laborerii et operis ecclesie Beate Reparate maioris ecclesie Florentine, et . . . ipse est *famosior magister et magis expertus in hedificationibus ecclesiarum aliquo alio qui in vicinis partibus cognoscatur,* et . . . per ipsius industriam experientiam et ingenium comune et populus Florentie ex magni-

fico et visibili principio dicti operis ecclesie iamdicte inchoacti per ipsium magistrum Arnolphum habere sperat venustius et honorabilius templum aliquo alio sit in partibus Tuscie . . ." (Guasti, doc. 24; italics mine).

The absence of a direct reference to Giotto as architect is particularly telling in the 1334 document of appointment (Doc. 1), so richly extravagant in its praise of Giotto as world famous painter, as master of the "science and doctrine" of art, even as beloved by the Florentines — indeed, as everything *but* builder. It was one thing for the city of guilds to extol the great artist, even to make him *capomaestro* of the Campanile; but to call him an architect in print appears to have been beyond the limit the Florentines would allow the rules to be stretched. In fact, it was probably the acute awareness of the latter difficulty that prompted the extravagant praise as a kind of compensating justification for the office (see n. 1 and 38 above) and the special salary granted, as Villani puts it, "for his virtue and goodness" (Doc. I). See 143 f below for the historic circumstances that brought about this situation.

[45] Gioseffi (1963, 63) tries unconvincingly to attribute the patently Sienese work to Giotto (cf. White, 1966, 287 f).

or in much more than passing connection with the Campanile. Moreover, never has the question of Giotto's basic manner of design entered the discussion.[46]

The architectural drawing of a professional builder is not a final object, but rather a transparent form through which the practiced eye can visualize the projected building.[47] A painter given the same drafting instruments and architectural program, following his professional habit, will quite naturally yield a final image that he means to be a picture of the building.[48] The greatness of Giotto resides partly in the utter finality and absolute density of his images. One can never look *through* an image by Giotto; one looks *at* it. This is true not only of individual forms, but of the overall disposition of a fresco cycle. Giotto sets up a precisely controlled and graduated illusionistic framework, a shallow, classicistic armature of intensively rational complexity and — despite its delicacy of modeling — of lean strength and rigidity (Figs. 147-150, 153). In this grid he seems to suspend a series of planes, the borders of which are disposed and decorated in a manner emphasizing the surface as such. The narrative scenes appear almost tightly stretched tapestries tacked on the surface of the wall.[49]

On the side walls of the Arena Chapel the layout of the enframing armature is completely modular in that, insofar as possible, all the narrative scenes have precisely the same format. One senses an almost compulsive rationalism in the attempt to carry the spacing of the windowless north wall across the vault to the other side, where it can be brought down only to the unfenestrated uppermost zone of narrative (Fig. 148). The subdivision of the frame decoration itself is accomplished with a dauntless geometric spirit, the fields determined by the intersection of equally spaced lines the module of which gives the spacing of the socle panels as well. In the narrative the horizontals and verticals of the frame dominate the composition. Over the scene one feels a geometric, grid-like veil that only the most dramatically critical movement is given to rend (Fig. 147).[50] Giotto set himself the strictest of canons, generating in the spectacular rationalism of frame and composition, the highest tension and suspense. To the flatness and opacity of the wall he opposes the monumental volume and bulk of his figures; against the high static tension

[46] Neither Isermeyer (1937), M. Cämmerer-George (*Die Rahmung der toskanischen Altarbilder im Trecento* [Strasbourg, 1966]), nor J. White, in his profound analysis of Giotto's illusionistic architecture (*The Birth and Rebirth of Pictorial Space* [London, 1957], 105 ff) mentions the Campanile. The best discussion of Giotto's design, that of Paatz (1937, 129 ff) draws certain connections between the Campanile and the decorative forms of Giotto's painting. Gioseffi deals at length with the architectural backgrounds without reference to the Campanile (1963, *passim*).

[47] Such as the design for the façades of Strasbourg and Orvieto cathedrals. See Braunfels's profound discussion of this point (1953, 227 ff).

[48] *Ibid.;* also Paatz, 1937, 133 ff.

[49] Cf. Isermeyer (1937, 6).

[50] The "Koordinatennetze" of T. Hetzer, *Giotto — seine Stellung in der europäischen Kunst* (Frankfurt, 1941), 31 ff. F. Rintelen (*Giotto und die Giotto-Apokryphen* [Munich-Leipzig, 1912], *passim*) also stresses the tight architectural nature of Giotto's art.

of the rectilineal composition he sets their significant action. From scene to scene he can build a progression of movement almost cinematic in power, as in the Betrothal of the Virgin series, and especially in the sequence comprising the *Feast at Cana,* the *Raising of Lazarus,* the *Entry into Jerusalem,* and the *Expulsion of the Money Changers,* where Christ and the Apostles stride ruthlessly forward (Figs. 147, 148).[51]

Asked near the end of his life to design the Campanile, it is reasonable to imagine that Giotto ordered the grand parchment as he had previously articulated walls. Assuming that the Siena drawing represents his design, we see that he first outlined the enframing armature — the octagonal buttresses and the cornices — about the traditional campanile scheme, a stack of cubes. Above the base, each buttress segment is subdivided into seven sections equal in height to the width of the base panels, also seven in number. The latter form, in effect, the frame pulled down around the bottom of the tower, rather than an architectural socle in the traditional sense.[52]

Within this armature a fine grid of squares was constructed by extending lines across the drawing from the buttress panels and upward from the socle panels. In several places, particularly in the monofora story, these construction lines are still to be seen (Figs. 137, 138, 140). To one degree or another, this grid determines the placement of every element on the surface of the Campanile shaft and is so rigid that Giotto — structural problems aside — could allow but the subtlest setbacks in his elevation.[53]

Suspended, as it were, from the armature, and superimposed on the grid, appears a system of panels in which the surface is emphasized by a disposition of borders similar to that of the narrative scenes in Padua. Horizontals and verticals reign. Into the rigid geometric multiplicity breaks the significant action, the windows. Their progressive opening is a traditional Florentine motif; but nowhere does the crescendo have such power as within the geometric web, which amplifies the impact of every change. Crown the shaft with the giant octagon and spire, which, escaping the geometry, loose the tension in upward flight, and the cumulative effect seems not unlike that of the Cana Feast-Money Changers sequence at Padua.

[51] I owe the basis of this interpretation of Giotto to the lectures, never realized in print, of Richard Offner. Cf. Rintelen, 1912, *passim*; Hetzer, 1941, *passim*; White, 1966, 204 ff.

[52] Cf. Paatz, 1937, 133 ff.

[53] Compare the analogous construction grid in the vault decoration of the Arena Chapel, discovered by L. Tintori and M. Meiss ("Additional Observations of Italian Mural Technique," *Art Bulletin,* XLVI [1964], 379 f). The setbacks indicated in the measurements given above (n. 32) are so slight that they have never been noticed. The widths of the square field of each story remain constant; the setbacks are confined to a narrowing of the buttresses themselves. The extreme optical cunning of the recession — a refined version of the normally emphatic setback of Gothic buttresses — is typical of such advanced compositional developments of Giotto (especially in his later years) as "softened oblique perspective" (White, 1966, 211 f). Like the late art itself, the subtlety of the design seems to have been misunderstood by Giotto's contemporaries, who apparently criticized its lack of obvious setback, and grossly misinterpreted by his followers.

Common to the Arena Chapel and the Siena drawing, this manner of design is not to be found elsewhere to any significant degree either in architecture or in painting, except for Giotto's chapels in Santa Croce, where the lack of sequential possibilities precludes its full expression (Fig. 159). In the upper church at Assisi there is only the static equivalence of format from scene to scene. The narrative on the verso of Duccio's *Maestà* runs up and down in no rigorous order, and with scenes occasionally even expanding to double format. Neither in Assisi, in Siena, nor with Giotto's followers is his architectonic code of design followed. At the Baroncelli Chapel in Santa Croce, Taddeo Gaddi develops the vocabulary of Giotto's architectural frames — by adding twisted columns from the Roman school — and retains the tapestry effect of the scenes; but there is not the ghost of geometric control, for example, in the *Presentation of the Virgin,* nor any sequential development between episodes. Indeed, led by certain tendencies in the late Giotto himself, the mid Trecento, first in Siena (Simone Martini, Ambrogio Lorenzetti), then in Florence (Andrea da Firenze), witnesses the breakdown of narrative compartmentalization in favor of continuous narration and unrestrained compositional flux.[54] At the same time, fresco frames become rich, pasty, and flat, of no interest beyond the purely decorative. Composition loses all connection with the Master. The singular affinity in architectural order between Padua and the Siena drawing points emphatically to Giotto as its author — or, if the design be a copy, as the author of the original.

Together with these essential principles of Giotto's architectonic form, the Campanile design reveals, under continued analysis, not only further aspects of his aesthetic method, but the context and specific content of an imagination that can only be his as well. Giotto was a man of years when the project came to him; in it are manifold traces of his long and rich life as observer and artist.

One begins with the skeletal armature — the buttresses and cornices. The foot of the drawing is reflected exactly in Giotto's fabric. But the first cornice of the first story differs (Figs. 7, 11, 135). It commences in both cases with a tondino and a console frieze, the scale of the drawing precluding the representation of the rich classicistic detail exhibited by the fabric. Immediately above, however, the drawing shows not the cyma recta of the Campanile but a tondo, and above the tondo a foliated cavetto, capped in Gothic manner by an inclined plane.

The history of architecture is characterized by such modifications from project to fabric. One need only compare the fate of the contemporary (ca. 1316) elevation projected for the façade of San Giovanni in Siena.[55] Like Giotto's Campanile design, it was followed closely, then, in the third story, all but abandoned; even the lower two zones were interspersed with modifications during the course of construction (Fig. 270). In this

---

[54] Cf. Isermeyer, 1937, *passim*; R. Krautheimer and T. Krautheimer-Hess, *Lorenzo Ghiberti* (Princeton, 1956), 218 f.

[55] White, 1966, fig. 154. For the early date, see the forthcoming study of H. Klotz.

façade — perhaps the most complete synthesis of the Gothic and classical traditions in Trecento architecture[56] — is a clue to the problem at hand. If so much of the Campanile drawing is, in correspondence to the fabric, classicizing, great parts of it are Gothic, particularly the fenestration and the spire. In the context of the Tuscan Trecento, which is not only at the Sienese baptistery but in great part a fusion of antique and Gothic vocabulary and form — and especially in the hands of the great masters: the Pisani, Arnolfo, Maitani, Giotto, Lando di Pietro, Talenti, Orcagna — one naturally expects to encounter a detail such as a cornice mixing the two sources. A more decisive consideration, and one which manifests the identity of the architect, is the manner in which the forms in question are shaped and combined.

The earlier analysis of the first story of the Campanile, particularly of the foot, revealed that Giotto submitted Arnolfian classicism to a dynamic, pictorial, and, indeed, almost playful transformation. The six cornices of the Siena drawing exhibit similar properties. The maximum affinity of drawing and fabric appears in comparing the executed foot sequence with the third projected cornice, capping the monofora section (Fig. 137). Here one finds the same rolling complexity of classical profiles in unclassical — almost "unarchitectural" — combination. One senses here — as in the executed base — a pictoral unity in the synthetic bundle of shapes manipulated for plasticity and tonal values rather than according to standard architectonic logic. One realizes how fundamentally Gothic the conception is by picturing this third cornice, for example, set in the vertical: how closely it would approximate the impression of a bundle pier.[57] The inclined plane, pervasively used in the drawing (and, curiously, anticipated in the most impressive earlier Tuscan campanile, at Pisa Duomo, where every cornice is beveled; Fig. 302), effects a smooth re-entry that preserves the unity of the swelling bundle. The profile fits the silky manipulation of relief, so impressive in the first story fabric. Similar considerations of fluidity dictated, in part, the employment of octagonal buttresses, rather than the traditional, hard rectilinear form.[58] The architect's awareness of the factor of continuity is disclosed by the single exception in the drawing to the use of the inclined re-entrant profile, the fifth cornice, which cantilevers out to a powerful terminal cyma recta in order to support the *ballatoio* separating the lower five stories from the triple bifora section and the spire (Fig. 139). Between the two latter zones the inclined plane is again taken up as cornice terminal, the end being the unity of stories rather than their separation (Fig. 138).

[56] Klotz, 1966, 186.
[57] In contrast to the independent prisms and cylinders that form the compound pier of the classic High Gothic cathedrals (Chartres, Reims, Amiens), the bundle pier, as the term implies, comprises a number of continuous vertical forms gathered about a single structural axis, yielding rich vertical bundles of profiles (from the nave of St. Denis on).
[58] The Giotto who invented the "softened oblique perspective" (see n. 53 above) surely would have thought about the problem of re-entrance.

In cornice design, Giotto achieves what one might call a pictorial Gothic style (if not a personal Late Gothic idiom). Disdaining licentious exploitation, he employs the form in a highly functional manner; in the order there is even rationalism. The first two cornices of the drawing are nearly identical; likewise the third and fourth form a pair. The fifth cornice, as we have seen, differs functionally from all the others. The sixth and last repeats the general outline of the lowermost type, but simplifies the consoles and omits the foliage from the cavetto.[59] The first two cornices are richly decorated — sensitized, according to Gioseffi — and bounded above by intarsia. The second pair, being already rather far from the observer, lacks decoration but, like the immediately following *ballatoio* cornice, forms a fuller, more powerful, plastic composition. The sixth cornice would have appeared rather weak from the piazza far below; its minimal terminal action would have favored the visual unification of the triple bifora section and the octagon, which we shall find Giotto had good reason to desire. The progressive nature of the sequence is clear, an orchestration of succeeding bundles of cornicework playing against each other and the window crescendo in subtle cross rhythms.[60] At the same time, this expressive combination of formal economy and richness not only recalls Giotto's executed Campanile incrustation but is tellingly anticipated in the three illusionistic cornices at Padua, where the lowest — the console cornice at eye level — assumes a tactile density set against the precise, rolling smoothness of the upper two stringcourses, which form an identical pair (Fig. 148).

The divergence witnessed in the first cornice between the drawing and the fabric seems to represent a modification effected between the initial design and construction. Considering the probable speed at which Giotto produced the project, one would expect him to have had second thoughts, at least about certain details. The replacement of the tondo by the cyma recta meant a slight, but noticeable increase in the projection of the cornice, and would at the same time denote, in one detail, a recollection of Padua. Quite possibly Giotto recast the planned details of other cornices, which together with innovations in further elements would have resulted in other versions of the Campanile project. But whatever Giotto's changes might have entailed, it seems most unlikely that the transformation would have ruptured the stylistic envelope defined by the Siena drawing, the first-story fabric, and the Paduan frescoes; the strongly different — even hostile — style of the Campanile above the console cornice is clearly the design of another architect. Nevertheless, it is seen in the next chapter that certain aspects of the second Campanile style — that is, the work of Andrea Pisano — derive from Giotto's design, the most obvious example being the cornice of the second story (Fig. 126), where the upper element is in its scheme almost a copy of the foliated-cavetto and inclined-plane combination of

[59] Nardini (13) reads the foliage, instead, as missing, the drawing supposedly unfinished.

[60] Cf. Giotto's subtle vertical counterpoint between the scenes at Padua (M. Alpatov, "The Parallelism of Giotto's Paduan Frescoes," *Art Bulletin*, XXIX [1947], 149 ff).

Giotto's project. Even the second cornice of the first story (Fig. 13) — Andrea's first contribution — takes up the concave-inclined sequence (though in a quite personal way). It is not surprising that Andrea was affected by Giotto's rich and subtle architecture, especially considering the strong influence of the painting on his sculpture.[61]

In the drawing, the cornices connect and are sustained by the corner buttresses, which function visually as piers forming the main support of the building. The mass of the interlying walls is dissolved by a tapestry-like treatment analogous to the scenes at Padua; thus they appear suspended in an armature like a Gothic window or, indeed, a modern curtain wall. It is even conceivable that Giotto confused the magic of his draftsmanship with the forces of nature and to some degree presumed the octagons to be not merely visually primary but in fact the prime physical support of his tower — a not impossible structural fantasy for the Trecento;[62] if so, he at least expressed this delusion with utter conviction and with absolutely convincing effect.

Paatz and Gioseffi imagined the octagonal shapes of the buttress-piers to be of problematic origin.[63] But as already observed, their octagonal form is part of the supple style of the design. Square buttresses would be harsh, particularly in their direct re-entry. Hexagonal ones would be confusing and embody an acute diagonal thrust. Cylinders — highly un-Florentine — would conflict with the rectangular outlines that dominate the surface and would be, to say the least, difficult to incrust. The octagonal plan was the only real possibility open to Giotto.

Moreover, at this time, in many genres, the octagon was a pervasive, even a basic element. Giotto used it for city-gate backdrops in the Padua frescoes.[64] It appears in small scale sculpture,[65] in the superstructure of important tombs,[66] as architectural piers,[67] buttresses,[68] and defense towers;[69] it forms the body of campanili.[70] The Trecento witnesses the Lombard stacking of octagons at crossing towers and over older quadratic shafts (Figs. 317, 319).[71] And in 1330 the rebuilding of the hexagonal Florentine Badia bell tower had begun.[72] Perhaps most consequential of all are the octagons that frame the

[61] I. Falk and J. Länyi, "The Genesis of Andrea Pisano's Bronze Doors," *Art Bulletin*, XXV (1943), 132 ff; I. Toesca, *Andrea e Nino Pisano* (Florence, 1950), 27 f.

[62] See n. 42 above; and especially J. S. Ackerman, "'Ars Sine Scientia Nihil Est,' Gothic Theory of Architecture at the Cathedral of Milan," *Art Bulletin*, XXXI (1949), 84 ff.

[63] Paatz, 1937, 130; Gioseffi (1963, 82) searches for precedents as far as Sicily.

[64] *The Entry into Jerusalem.*

[65] The *Annunciation* on the Cathedral flank across from the Campanile visible in Fig. 66; the Arnolfian Annunciation relief in London (J. Pope-Hennessy, *Catalogue of Italian Sculpture in the Victoria and Albert Museum* [London, 1964], I, 20 ff, III, fig. 35; also Paatz, 1937, fig. 115).

[66] The tombs by Tino da Camaino and School in Naples; the Tarlatti tomb in Arezzo.

[67] The Bargello, S. Croce — and even the second story of the Baptistery exterior.

[68] Naples Duomo (Gioseffi [1963, 82] suggests this as *the* source).

[69] At the Castel del Monte and other imperial fortifications in southern Italy.

[70] S. Gottardo in Milan (Fig. 318); the older S. Nicola in Pisa (Fig. 303).

[71] See Ch. VII.

[72] *Ibid.* and Figs. 297, 299.

towers of many of the great northern cathedrals.[73] It should not seem unusual that Giotto chose octagonal buttresses for his Campanile; indeed, in the context of his project, where they not only reinforce the style but reflect the Baptistery and prefigure the spire, the astonishment would be had he not.

The decoration of Giotto's buttresses is worth special consideration. Pier striping, as such, was a common Tuscan motif, especially in the schools of Pisa and Siena; but it was not prominent in Florence until the early Trecento, when it suddenly became fashionable. Again, the Baptistery is the key example (Fig. 161).[74] Also of note is the striped tower that appears in the Bigallo fresco, possibly representing the Badia campanile, which may have been given — or intended to receive — such a frescoed revetment (Fig. 285).[75] In his Campanile project, Giotto fused this alien pattern with the indigenous decorative leitmotif, the rectangle.[76] It is the fundamental unit of decoration in the Florentine Romanesque and, for that matter, in Giotto's fresco framework. It dominates the intricate structure of the most developed Dugento Florentine throne image, that in Cimabue's Santa Trinita *Madonna* (Fig. 165). Equally familiar and perhaps more important to Giotto was Arnolfo's Cathedral façade of the following decade, where tiered squares fill the blind bifora panels of the first zone, and mounting rectangles enliven the jambs and outer frame of the main portal (Fig. 239). Arnolfo seems to have appropriated Cimabue's tiny cubes, themselves perhaps derived (via the Byzantine sources for the throne) from even smaller jewelers' forms.[77] In Giotto's Campanile project the motif is daringly magnified to colossal scale (though in the drawing it takes about the same actual measure as in Cimabue). It was characteristic of Trecento architecture to translate forms from non-architectural sources and typical of Giotto as architect to return for inspiration to the great masters of the late Dugento. But most telling was Giotto's transformation of his sources: following Arnolfo's lead, by extreme vertical attenuation of the pattern and its metamorphosis into streamlined pinnacles at the top, Giotto converts the hitherto static motif — vertically compounded rectangles — into the vehicle of Gothic energy and flight.

Within the structural skeleton formed by massive buttress-piers and powerful cornices, Giotto lodged the squares of "curtain wall," in which the disposition of elements

---

[73] Including two of the most influential of all: Laon and Reims.

[74] The striping of the Baptistery piers is ca. 1300 (Paatz II, 174 f).

[75] See Ch. VII.

[76] Nardini is particularly articulate on this distinction (15, 50 ff).

[77] Following P. Metz's definitive discussion ("Die florentiner Domfassade des Arnolfo di Cambio," *Jahrbuch der preußischen Kunstsammlungen*, LIX [1938], 121 ff) the façade represented in the 1587 drawing in the Museo dell'Opera del Duomo (Fig. 239) is substantially Arnolfo's. Metz's argument is accepted by Paatz III, 341 ff. M. Weinberger's counter-thesis ("The First Facade of the Cathedral of Florence" *Journal of the Warburg and Courtauld Institutes*, IV [1940-41], 67 ff) appears untenable. For the thrones, cf. J. H. Stubblebine, "The Development of the Throne in Tuscan Dugento Painting," *Marsyas*, VII (1957), 25 ff.

was determined by a grid of small squares. The expanse is filled by paneling and windows. As with the buttresses, precedent for the configuration lies in the imaginary furniture of late Dugento painting, in this case the arms of the throne in Duccio's Rucellai *Madonna* (Fig. 166).[78] The panels, with their engaged hexagons, derive from decorative motifs encountered commonly in Giotto's frescoes (particularly in the framework, e.g., Fig. 150) and altarpieces.[79] The manner in which these hexagons are disposed, alternating between the inner and outer rows of paneling, is that of the frame decoration of the Ognissanti *Madonna*.[80] This principle of alternating placement of decorative elements in concentric frames is found also at Padua, where the lozenge motives on the inner (green or blue) borders of the narrative scenes are placed between, but never opposite the larger lozenges of the architectural framework. I have not been able to find the pattern in the work of other contemporary artists, though it does appear in the Cosmatesque ancestors of Giotto, the architectural decorator.[81] As in the buttress paneling, a peripheral decorative motif is raised to the role of a principal feature, and then developed in the Giottesque mode.

The question of decorative manner brings up a somewhat digressive consideration. Too often the high seriousness and overwhelming pathos of Giotto's art seem to blind the observer to his amazingly rich and refined decorative imagination and his love of purely aesthetic heights.[82] Giotto knew quite as well as, let us say, a Matthias Grünewald, that in sacred art the depiction of the most solemn, horrifying, and even gruesomely dismal events — such as the Dance of Salome — if rendered in exquisite and colorful manner — as in the Peruzzi Chapel at Santa Croce — achieves an effect of painfully beautiful depth, cutting like a laser beam to the heart of our spiritual awareness. Not surprisingly, the same telling dualism of the dramatic and the decorative inhabits his Campanile project.

We have already observed the decorative impulse in the giant frame-image and in the delicately voluptuous incrustation. But it is in the concentric paneling of the second ("oculus") story that Giotto's decorative fantasy achieves full effect (Fig. 136). Here the total configuration of hexagons assumes a trio of simultaneous visual interpretations: in planarity as concentric or as radial patterns, and in depth as a recession of hexagons toward the oculus. The oscillating effect created by the triple illusion bears deep imaginative affinity with Giotto's kaleidoscopic orientalizing intarsia motifs; and both, with the joyful image of the colossal tower poised at its base on a slender pink cushion.

It is not without calculation that these decorative elements are concentrated toward the bottom of the project, for above they are progressively displaced by the serious content, as it were, of the design. At first the windows gracefully enter the decorative rec-

---

[78] Cf. *ibid.*

[79] Paatz, 1937, 129 ff.

[80] Cämmerer-George (1966, 21 ff) has proven that the frame is original.

[81] Notably at the triumphal arch and portals of the façade at Città Castellana (Hutton, 1950, figs. 15a, 17, 18).

[82] Cf. Hetzer, 1941, 84 ff, 150 ff.

tilinearity; then suddenly, revealing their true, "heroic" nature, the doubled bifore exclude all but the outer frame of paneling; in tripled form, the fenestration banishes even the outer frame; until finally, above, the very paneling of the buttresses is shed, and they rise architectonically pure around the octagon and the spire (Figs. IX, 133, 134). In less hyperbolic manner, this spectacle might be viewed in terms of the characteristically Giottesque contention: gorgeous ornamental fantasy, light, color, and surface on the one hand, and, on the other, severely structured volume and space and ruthlessly pure dramatic characterization and exposition.

But let us return to our analysis of detail. The types of fenestration exhibited in the project appear regularly in Giotto's painting. The round window in the second story, a consequence of the concentric frames (Fig. 136), is found not infrequently in the background architecture especially of the later frescoes, for example, in the church behind the *Raising of Drusiana* in the Peruzzi Chapel or the magnificent structure in the Renunciation scene of the Bardi Chapel. The round-headed monofora (Fig. 137) is a commonplace in Giotto's backdrops; its drop tracery, more filagree than anything yet executed in Tuscany, can be traced to the preoccupation for advanced Gothic openwork manifest in the stage-sets for the *Last Supper* (Fig. 156) and the *Washing of the Feet* in Padua.

In Giotto's architectural settings, fenestration is formed exclusively by the circular window, the round-headed monofora, an occasional neat rectangle, and especially the bifora. Good Florentine that he was, he avoided the trifora (a Sienese commonplace) and more complex types, even when they could have simplified matters. Thus it is that the upper four stories of Giotto's Campanile, in fenestration, were to be composed exclusively of bifore, expanding in number and height[83] and culminating in the towering octagon.

The vocabulary and disposition of the four levels of bifora windows are uniform, except for a slight variation in tracery (Figs. 140-143). Resting on High Gothic bases — in conception not unlike those in the Pentacost scene at Padua (Fig. 157) — a central column and engaged half columns carry rich Gothic capitals and gracefully pointed arches headed by the oculus. The columnar detail closely reflects the most impressive Gothic windows in Florence as of 1334: the Palazzo Vecchio fenestration, where not only the disc-like base profiles of the Siena design, but the flaring and richly foliated capitals, are exhibited (Figs. 174, 231). In outline a classic Gothic scheme (unlike the intersecting tracery of English Decorated origin already known in Siena), the windows are prefigured in Florence in the blind tracery of the bifora panels on Arnolfo's Duomo façade (Fig. 239) — the first of their kind in the city — and appear schematically as the windows of Giotto's illusionistic chapels at Padua (Figs. 154, 155).[84] The diversity among the pro-

---

[83] Cf. the heightening of the upper windows in the Badia and S. Maria Novella towers (Figs. 295-299); Talenti's upper Bifora windows are about 10 per cent higher than the lower. See Ch. VII.

[84] Probably Arnolfo's Duomo flanks, like Talenti's later, projected such a bifora type. On the Sienese tracery, see Jean Bony's Wrightsman Lectures of 1969 (in press).

jected oculi manifests the same logic found in the cornice sequence. The lowest bifora, being solitary, is given the most elaborate tracery: a central hexafoil, circumscribed by six radially aligned quatrefoils (Fig. 141), a late thirteenth-century northern Gothic configuration, but for Giotto's Florence very progressive.[85] Above, the forms become increasingly simplified until, in the octagon, only a single quatrefoil remains (Fig. 143).

With perhaps the partial exception of the octagon (where the decorative relief is difficult to interpret), the projected windows are disposed with extreme planarity, seeming to lack exterior splay or jambs. Appearing to float on the surface, they instead have frames of tondino-edged fasciae similar to the panel borders in the drawing and in the executed first story. The pink frames of the octagon bifore could signify a projection of the frame vocabulary into relief; if so it would be a significant innovation, establishing a prototype for the side-aisle windows of the Duomo Nuovo in Siena, ca. 1339 (Fig. 273), in turn, decisive for Francesco Talenti's fenestration on the upper Campanile (Figs. VII, VIII) and for his Cathedral side-aisle windows (Fig. 248).[86] It will be seen below that Giotto's project had a notable influence on later Florentine architecture.

The frame of the monofora is embellished by a second frame of luxuriant rinceaux, which, in sparer form, decorate many of the framework panels at Padua, notably on the end walls (Fig. 153). The pinnacle forms that flank the single and double bifore have an illogical structural relationship to the wall, before which they seem to hover without physical connection (Figs. 140, 141). Whatever be the cause for this paradox, the forms themselves point to early Trecento Florence. The single pinnacles flanking the double bifore are directly comparable, for example, with the early niche tabernacles at Or San Michele (ca. 1339-40), to the very forms of the crockets (Figs. 202, 203).[87] At the same time, this comparison discloses a familiar Giottesque phenomenon; in that the projected posts represent but the uppermost part of the normal Gothic pinnacle, we witness again Giotto's procedure of abstracting partial elements from their original context and expanding them to prominent, integral features.

The first five stories of the design — that is, through the double bifora zone — are uniformly accorded decorative, planar treatment in all details, including the windows, with the geometric web in control of the outlines. The smooth re-entrants of the first four cornices allow the eye to pass easily from one story to another. The fifth cornice, projecting strongly and capped by a balustrade that screens the beginning of the sixth story, interrupts the continuity and acts as a cumulative cornice for the first five stories, which consequently appear as a unit. In addition the first noticeable setback occurs at this point

[85] The form is encountered in the late 13th century in England (Lincoln Cathedral) and, perhaps more consequentially for Giotto, at Freiburg and Strasbourg. It also appears in choir oculi at Orvieto, entirely in the form of hexafoils, with a date between the reconstruction of the choir in 1335 and the execution of the glass in 1370 (L. Fumi, *Il Duomo di Orvieto* [Rome, 1891], 202).

[86] See Ch. VI.

[87] Probably designed by Andrea Pisano (see Ch. III, 77).

(Fig. 139). This prepares for the two stories above, which, while continuing the inner window vocabulary, depart sharply from the decorative style of the lower zone.

The triple bifore, as already noted, expand laterally right up to the buttresses (Fig. 142). There is no room for enframing panels. Below the windows, the balustrade screens their absence; above, a superstructure rises cutting the cornice. The control grid is all but confounded. The framework and superstructure of these windows have no single precedent. Rather, their design abstractly fuses two of the great Tuscan Gothic façades, those by Giovanni Pisano and Arnolfo di Cambio at the cathedrals of Siena and Florence. The triple arcade compressed between massive, striped piers; the projecting posts and niched pinnacles that cut through the overlying cornice; gables that simply abut the posts; and the rich crockets and triangular panels all point, unmistakably, to Siena (Fig. 269). Even the famous lateral displacement of the upper and lower halves of the Siena façade is reflected in the drawing in the bold vertical discontinuity from the window posts of the triple bifore to the corners of the octagon.[88] If the scheme is Giovanni Pisano's, the detail of these posts is Arnolfian. Comparison with the upper part of the single completed portal of the Florentine façade (Fig. 239, right), reveals a telling correspondence in elevation. In both cases the paneled posts are corbeled forward over heavily foliated consoles (Fig. 139) and subdivided into two segments below the intersection with the gable. To be sure, Giotto brings Arnolfo up to date. The forms are now more slender, the panels are pointed, and the pinnacles are more heavily crocketed; setback via inclined plane replaces the earlier subdivision by soft, dividing profiles; and the heavy rosette and geometric incrustation of Arnolfo's gable yield to finely spun, precise rinceaux (possibly deriving from Maitani's first pier on the façade of Orvieto Cathedral; Fig. 240).[89]

The process unveiled in this analysis is the inverse of Giotto's amplification of normally partial elements, which we have witnessed as a leitmotif in the project. As in the wonderland of Alice, in Giotto's architectural world, scale and significance of forms oscillate violently, as if seen (to borrow a Panofskian simile) through alternate ends of a powerful telescope. Thus, simultaneous with the blow-up of jewel-like cubes to colossal buttress forms, the compelling totalities of Giovanni's and Arnolfo's façades are circumscribed, abridged, and assimilated as but partial components of a new and larger whole.

So it is with the Campanile project's final stage (which simultaneously overlaps and forms part of the "facade" image), for Klotz has made it abundantly clear that the octagon,

[88] The commonly accepted late dating of the façade seems to be a major error, according to Klotz, who (in a forthcoming study) shows it as being substantially complete if not by 1305 then surely by 1315, thus substantiating Paatz's idea that the lateral displacement was Giovanni's intention (1937, 107 ff). Giotto seems to have had the façade in mind for his backdrop to the Paduan *Expulsion of the Money Changers* (Fig. 148).

[89] Compare also the similar tooling of the halo of Bernardo Daddi's *Madonna* in the tabernacle at Or San Michele (R. Offner, *A Critical and Historical Corpus of Florentine Painting* [New York, 1930 ff], Sec. III, Vol. III, 72 f, dating it ca. 1342; pl. XVIII²).

pinnacles, and spire form as close an approximation possible — within the vocabulary of the Campanile drawing — to the most advanced and important Gothic tower then built in all Europe, that of Freiburg Münster (Fig. 167). The Siena drawing appropriates three salient aspects of Freiburg: a completely freestanding octagon with equal windows facing all sides; extremely high pinnacles standing before the diagonal windows, softening the transition from square to octagon; and an octagonal spire rising directly from a crown of gables and richly set with crockets and finials. Even the motif of the surmounting angels seems to be an innovation of Freiburg.[90]

An unresolved problem is how this complex form might have reached Giotto. Nearby, in early Trecento Siena, there was a heavy influx of northern architectural motifs, particularly from Freiburg and Strasbourg, through goldsmiths' work (e.g. Fig. 168; but also Figs. 171, 172). Moreover, displayed in the façades of the baptistery and the Duomo Nuovo at Siena (Figs. 270, 272) and in the Orvieto rose (Fig. 275) are expressions of the northern manner brought (unmodulated by the goldsmiths) directly, either by northern masons or by Italians returning from travels. If a piece of architectural goldsmith work can be imported, a full-scale architectural design can be carried in sketches (like Villard de Honnecourt's) and in the memory. Giotto's own extensive travels had included cosmopolitan Naples and Avignon, where the most advanced Gothic designs would have been a topic among artists. Could he have journeyed as well to the cities of the Upper Rhine, around 1300 among the most vital centers of Gothic architectural development (and where his influence in painting is manifest as early as 1320)?[91]

Although rarely encountered in monumental Florentine architecture, these progressive forms were taken up in Florence in a genre analogous to Sienese metalwork. A recent study has yielded a corpus of Trecento Florentine altarpiece frames,[92] many of which exhibit the very advanced Gothic features found in the work of the Sienese goldsmiths. The development reaches full tide with Orcagna's Strozzi Altarpiece (Fig. 281), comparable to Ugolino di Vieri's reliquary for the SS. Corporale in Orvieto (Fig. 168). Salient

[90] Klotz, 1966, 176.

[91] On the Sienese goldsmith work, *ibid.* See M. Gosebruch, *Giotto und die Entwicklung des neuzeitlichen Kunstbewußtseins* (Cologne, 1962), 215 ff, for a documented *vita* of Giotto; cf. also P. Murray, "Notes on Some Early Giotto Sources," *Journal of the Warburg and Courtauld Institutes*, XVI (1953), 58 ff, esp. 75 ff. In painting, testimony to the existence of lines of transmission between Tuscany and the Rhine is indeed telling in the present context: the earliest manifestation of Giotto's influence in the North is the monumental copy of the St. Peter's *Navicella* in Jung-St. Peter in Strasbourg, ca. 1320 (W. Körte, "Die früheste Wiederholung nach Giottos Navicella," *Oberrheinische Kunst*, X [1942], 97 ff); cf. R. Oertel, *Die Frühzeit der italienischen Malerei* (Stuttgart, 1966), 213 n. 1, with reference to other Giottesque works of the early 14th century in Austria and Switzerland, including the wings of the Klosterneuburg altarpiece, 1324-29. See also Panofsky's comment on this phenomenon (1960, 156 f); his observation that these German painters "ignored the new and significant style of their models and appropriated only the *invenzione*" most aptly describes the converse fate of the Freiburgian tower form in Giotto's hands (see below).

[92] Cämmerer-George, 1966.

are the diagonally placed posts and the pivoting pinnacle series. Although this Florentine development continues to an almost Baroque phase in the frames of Giovanni del Biondo and Lorenzo Monaco,[93] the advanced Gothic ideas are already exhibited in an elaborate work of Giotto's workshop. The Stefaneschi Altarpiece has long since shed its frame, but the original totality is depicted in the Saint Peter panel (Figs. 169, 170) as a "self-portrait" (much in the manner of the model of the Arena Chapel in the Last Judgment scene in Padua). Here Giotto's eclecticism of sources is disclosed in the contrast between the airy, Gothic image of the altarpiece and the heavy Cosmatesque throne of Saint Peter, a close analogy to the contrasting shaft and spire of the Campanile project.[94]

The implications of the connection between Giotto and the North are telling. In Freiburg, the pinnacles, octagon, and spire form the bulk of the tower, rising from a relatively inarticulate quadratic mass, which is bound to the nave of the church (Fig. 167). In manner similar to the manipulation of the Pantheon by Bramante in his project for Saint Peter's, Giotto took the Freiburg tower and placed it on a colossal shaft sixty-five meters high. In doing so, Giotto may have been inspired by the great Lombard octagons and spires set boldly over older quadratic towers in the early Trecento at Modena and especially Cremona (Fig. 319).[95] But if so, the influence of the fussy Lombard brick construction was purely that of example, not style; it was clearly the Freiburgian manner that Giotto had in mind. As he had synthesized the most ambitious creations of Giovanni and Arnolfo, so he was able to accommodate the greatest northern tower form to a traditionally Florentine pattern. He smoothed over its spikiness; he simplified the windows; he closed the airy spire with coloristic paneling; and, with a particularly brilliant stroke of synthetic originality, he assimilated the towering octagon and spire to the traditional theme of progressive fenestration.

The Freiburg tower, completed only in the early decades of the fourteenth century, was an exceptionally up-to-date model for Giotto. So many of the main sources for the Siena drawing — Giovanni's masterwork in Siena, Arnolfo's façade and Baptistery renovation, the thrones of Cimabue's and Duccio's Madonnas — are products of the last two decades of the thirteenth century, the time of the pre-Paduan youth and early manhood of Giotto. One has only to compare his Campanile project — even the spire — with the nearly contemporary Duomo Nuovo at Siena (Figs. 139, 272), or for that matter with the Sienese baptistery façade project of two decades previous (Fig. 270) to realize how old-fashioned Giotto's forms were by 1334. At the same time the endemic notion is discarded that the design is in any manner Sienese. But in more conservative Florence, the project, meant to complement the Baptistery and Arnolfo's Duomo, was still expedient — at least as long as Giotto lived. Indeed, the development of Trecento architecture in

[93] *Ibid.*, pls. 17, 32C, 32D, 33, 34, 35.

[94] Paatz, 1937, 132. On the altarpiece, see M. Gosebruch, "Giotto's Stefaneschi-Altarwerk aus Alt S. Peter in Rom," *Miscellanea Bibliothecae Hertzianae* (Munich, 1961), 104 ff.

[95] See Ch. VII, 159 ff, 172.

Florence, especially in its exterior decoration, was such a continuous, tradition-bound process that had Giotto's design been fully achieved it would probably not seem out of place beside the Cathedral (even with its neo-Trecento façade).

This partly has to do with the manifold influence of the project, directly and otherwise, on the later Florentine Gothic. Considering Giotto's incalculable importance for later painting, should a parallel phenomenon — even if, by comparison, relatively minor — in architecture surprise us? We have already noted the influence of his cornice design on Andrea Pisano. The floating configuration of Talenti's Campanile Bifora stories (Figs. 71, 72) clearly reflects Giotto's design, in particular the single and double bifora sections (Figs. 133, 140, 141); the oculus of Talenti's Bifora (Figs. 74, 75) derives from the single bifora of the drawing (Fig. 141); the inner forms and splaywork of Talenti's Campanile windows (Fig. 70) and the side-aisle windows of the Duomo (Figs. 248, 249) develop the window forms of the octagon. The upper parts of Orcagna's Or San Michele tabernacle (Fig. 282) are a transformation of Giotto's version of Freiburg (Fig. 134).[96] Need it be made explicit that this afterlife of the largely unachieved project — a not uncommon occurrence, as witness the Strasbourg Elevation B, Bramante's Saint Peter's, or Mies van der Rohe's early glass skyscrapers — signals its Florentine origin, leading us within the context of this discussion once more directly to Giotto.

Several aspects of his project remain problematic. Little is revealed of its interior structure. Though the first stories were evidently mural, the wall above was to be increasingly dissolved into pier-like forms. Could they have prefigured the complex pier structure of Talenti (Fig. 88)? In all probability the interior of Giotto's Campanile was to be divided into a series of chambers, vaulted if only for rigidity. The style of the vaulting most likely would have been similar to that in the illusionistic chapels at Padua (Figs. 154, 155) and the illusionistic architecture of the Bardi and Peruzzi chapels at Santa Croce (Figs. 158, 159). This would have meant — unlike the octagonal internal articulation of Andrea and Talenti[97] — the cylindrical forms that Giotto preferred, at least in his painting, even when the real ribs that came with the building were octagonal, as at Santa Croce where he depicts classicizing columns beneath Arnolfo's prismatic vaulting.

Atop the spire and pinnacles of the Siena drawing stand angels. The lower two (Figs. 145, 146) are nameless, but the spire angel, carrying the banner of Christ and an orb, is clearly Saint Michael (Fig. 144).[98] Until the eighteenth century, angels were to be found on the spires of Florentine campanili, for example, at Santa Maria Novella.[99] An angel with a banner is seen above a campanile — possibly the Badia tower — in the Domenico di Michelino panel of *Dante e il suo Poema* in Florence Cathedral (Fig. 289). Angels sur-

[96] Klotz, 1966, 202.
[97] See Chs. III, VI.
[98] Klotz (1966, 176) notes the Freiburg precedent for the placement of the angels on pinnacles. The

St. Michael even connects the two iconographically, for at Freiburg the trumpet-blowing angels sound the Last Judgment.
[99] Paatz, III, 674.

mount the Or San Michele tabernacle. Saint Michael forms part of the iconography of the Duomo decoration: he crowns the Porta dei Canonici.[100] And in 1357 angels were set in place over the Trifora gables of the Campanile, one of which still stands, facing south (Figs. 70, 84).[101]

As they are not iconographically alien to Florentine tradition, so the angels of the Siena drawing do not deny what is stylistically possible around 1330 in Florence, being vaguely Giottesque,[102] but more elongated than one might expect of the master himself. The work of certain followers of Giotto, notably Taddeo Gaddi, is characterized by such attenuation; could an assistant of Giotto have sketched these angels — of distinguished quality — or might, instead, the variation from the canonical Giottesque be due to the possibility that the drawing, after all, is perhaps a copy of Giotto's original?

Crowning the gables of the triple bifore and the octagon are finials of utmost singularity (Figs. 138, 143). Spreading, flame-like leaves form concave vessels filled with pomegranates. The image recalls the bowl of fruit held by the *Caritas* in Padua (Fig. 176). Could the form carry an associated meaning? If so, it might prefigure Donatello's column monument erected a century later, the famous, lost *Abbondanza*, symbol of the city (Fig. 177).[103] To its smallest detail, the Campanile of Giotto would have embodied the pride of Florence at one of its grand moments.

[100] *Ibid.*, 365. However, as in Siena, the feast days of St. Michael (May 7, Sept. 29) are accompanied by no special celebration in the Duomo.

[101] See Ch. V, 117 and n. 58.

[102] Two eminent authorities, Klara Steinweg and Ulrich Middledorf, found the figures difficult to date or place other than as being Tuscan, first half of the Trecento.

[103] As analyzed by R. Freyhan ("The Evolution of the Caritas Figure in the 13th and 14th Centuries," *Journal of the Warburg and Courtauld Institutes*, XI [1948], 68 ff), in the important iconographical innovations of Nicola Pisano and Giotto, the flame and the cornucopia, or fruit basket, were key images, representing the two components of *Caritas*, respectively: *Amor Dei* and *Amor Proximi (Misericordia)*. To synthesize a new symbol of *Caritas* in the Campanile finials — inspired perhaps by the general shapes of the bowl-like lower components of the finial type developed at Freiburg and Strasbourg — would not only have been consonant with Giotto's "iconographical history" and his characteristic condensation of meaning, but would have prefigured the seven virtues didactically added above Giotto's relief program at the first zone of the Campanile; fittingly, *Caritas* is the greatest of the virtues (Cf. Ch. IV n. 46). Following L. M. Bongiorno's uneven and somewhat forced reading of the Padua frescoes ("The Theme of the Old and the New Law in the Arena Chapel," *Art Bulletin*, L [1968], 11 ff), such disguised architectural symbolism would have been an important Giottesque method.

Moreover, the intention would relate to the tradition of the columnar monument (W. Haftmann, *Das italienische Säulenmonument* [Leipzig-Berlin, 1939], *passim*) exemplified by the Croce al Trebbio of 1338 or the nearby Column of S. Zenobius of 1388 to the north of the Baptistery where an elm is said to have blossomed the winter of 429 (Figs. 4, 161). From his treatment of the Campanile base and from the profound civic meaning of the Campanile connected with its pointed isolation, among other things (see Ch. VII), Giotto — whose architectural imagination we have witnessed as having limitless flexibility — might even have consciously regarded the tower as a gigantic, Gothic amplification of the antique columnar genre. The fruit basket had been appropriated — or misappropriated, in Panofsky's sense of the medieval divorce of antique meaning and form — from the arms of an antique market genius (a type of columnar monument known in the Trecento; Haftmann, 1939, 139 ff) or *Abbondanza* figure. Donatello, in his *Dovizia* (or *Abbondanza*), ca. 1428 (H. Kauffmann, *Donatello* [Berlin, 1936], 41 ff), returned the image of plenty to its rightful owner, and both to the original context (Haftmann, 1939, 139 ff), for Donatello's columnar monument stood in the market (now the Pza. della Repubblica, where the site is occupied by a copy of the replacement of the 18th century, when the original figure crashed to the ground; Fig. 175).

Let it merely be mentioned in this context that as early as 1321 the Compagnia Maggiore della Misericordia, a prominent charitable institution, established itself around the corner from the eventual Campanile site (opposite the south portal of the Baptistery), and that its loggia-oratory directly across the way from the tower (Fig. 4) was built contemporaneously with the Trifora (1352-60; cf. H. Saalman, *The Bigallo* [New York, 1969], *passim*).

Chapter III

Andrea Pisano

Giotto's death in January 1337 probably spared the commune the embarrassment of having to relieve of his high post the great painter so ceremoniously invested only two years before. Amidst the pomp of his burial in the Cathedral were surely to be overheard scandalized whispers, as well as speculations about who would be the next *capomaestro*. In Florence since 1330, Andrea Pisano had finished his magnificent Baptistery door (Fig. 178) the preceding summer;[1] upon Giotto's passing he became the dominant artist in the city. Already associated with the Campanile in connection with the hexagonal reliefs on the west face — executed and placed during Giotto's time[2] — the goldsmith and sculptor from Pontedera was the likeliest choice for the task of completing the imposing Florentine monument.

The external evidence that Andrea did take over is minimal but consistent. On April 26, 1340, mention is made of "master Andrea, principal master of the works" as member of a council of the Opera del Duomo.[3] This reference substantiates Pucci's testimony that Andrea Pisano succeeded Giotto as *capomaestro* (to be followed himself by Talenti).[4] Most of the Trecento Campanile sculpture (Figs. 125-132) is connected with Andrea Pisano: even if aspects of their design can be traced to Giotto, the hexagonal reliefs are in execution partly autograph Pisano, partly shop or school, as are indeed most of the lozenges above; the Sibyls and Kings originally on the west face are very near to

[1] White, 1966, 303.
[2] See Ch. II, 26.
[3] Doc. 5. Other than Andrea Pisano, there appear no Andrea's of special mention in Florentine architecture in these years. Andrea Orcagna matriculates as stone mason only in 1352 in connection with the Or San Michele Tabernacle. Cf. I. Falk, *Studien zu Andrea Pisano* (Hamburg, 1940), 11.
[4] Doc. IV.

Andrea's own hand, and the Prophets from the south face are by followers.[5] But we shall see that the architectural fabric itself provides the conclusive evidence for Andrea's role at the Campanile.

It is possible to determine, by way of deduction, the fabric for which Andrea could have been responsible and the period in which it would have been built. The records concerning the history of the Campanile during the decade following Giotto are so few that it is wise first to leap forward to solid ground and then thread our way back. Between 1350-51 and 1359-60 the Trifora section was erected under Francesco Talenti. Although the documents first mention him in 1351 in connection with the Trifora zone, on stylistic grounds it appears that Talenti was responsible as well for the two Bifora stories.[6] In February 1348 an official of the Opera was directed to obtain timbers "for the centering of the Campanile vaults."[7] This could hardly concern the chambers below the Bifora level, for if so there would have remained only two years — even less, with the Black Death — for the construction of the Bifora section (Fig. 6). The document can only indicate that the Bifora chamber was vaulted and the section completed following February 1348, which would dovetail the commencement of the Trifora story in 1350.

Although the Trifora section was not completed until 1360, most of it was standing by 1357, when attention, funds, materials, and workers were diverted to the Cathedral. With work proceeding at full speed, the Trifora story could have been finished in seven to eight years. The Bifora section is roughly equivalent in magnitude and complexity to the Trifora. With the partial interruption of the year of the Black Death,[8] construction seems to have been continuous in the mid and late forties. Projecting back seven or eight years from 1350, we arrive at 1342-43 for the beginning of the Bifora stories. The relief and niche sections below, shown substantially complete in the Bigallo fresco of 1342,[9] and which also form about one third of the total fabric, would have taken a reasonable nine or so years of the total twenty-seven.[10]

Working forward from the death of Giotto in January 1337, we are led to the same *terminus ante quem*, 1342-43, for the fabric of Andrea. On February 1, 3, 1337, the Opera puts its account in order with the commune, behind in its contributions.[11] In December the Opera is assured of additional income.[12] The building revenues in this period

---

[5] See Ch. IV.

[6] See Ch. VI.

[7] Doc. 10.

[8] Grote seems to overestimate the effect of the Black Death on building activity (1961, 60). The fact that very few documents are to be found in the two years following means little in view of the scarce documentation for the entire history of the Opera before 1351. In fact, the three new documents Grote cites, recording the election of *Operai* as early as March 1, 1349 — even if not

on schedule — evidence a recommencement of activities that spring.

[9] Saalman, 1964, 472 n. 6; 1969, 9 f.

[10] This would, of course, include the foundations; however large, their construction was probably, like that of the Cathedral pier foundations, comparatively rapid, involving local building materials and the least skilled architectural labor.

[11] Guasti, doc. 51.

[12] *Ibid.*, doc. 52.

are so high — largely siphoned from the *gabelle,* which peak in the late 1330s[13] — that in June 1339, the combined workshops of the Cathedral and the Baptistery (backed by the Calimala guild) can afford the luxury of systematizing the level of the Piazza del Duomo and repaving it.[14] In December 1339, it is decided that the houses of the canons be destroyed to facilitate the construction of the Cathedral "and its campanile, being constructed anew."[15] A few months later, the Opera, together with the *capomaestro,* Andrea, decides to build a new residence for the canons to the south of the Duomo (on the present Via della Canonica),[16] and in August it is voted to buy them some houses.[17] In January 1341, the Signoria writes the Bishop of Luni concerning special conditions for the quarrying of marble by the Opera,[18] and in April 1342, complains to Siena about defective shipments of pink marble, indicating substantial work of incrustation.[19]

But in the early 1340s the city income wanes. Under the Duke of Athens (1342-43) it dwindles to an amount so meager that the treasury can barely meet the overhead and daily expenses. The period "marked the nadir in communal finance."[20] By January 4, 1343, the Opera was forced to petition the Duke (successfully) to restore the communal subsidy, which had not been received for the preceding two months.[21] But considering the fall of the *gabelle* revenues, even if the Duke kept his promise the Opera would have gained little profit. Following his expulsion, in August and early September of 1343 only scarce *gabelle* revenues entered the state treasury: the "judicial authority of the courts had collapsed so that it was virtually impossible to enforce the law."[22] The months of chaos and weakness witnessed the loss, through successful revolts, of much of Florence's hard gained territory; in what remained all was not pacific. The state of affairs is reflected in a letter from the Signoria admonishing all towns still under its control not to hinder the transport of marble "over the Arno river toward Florence for the construction of the mother church of the city."[23]

Civic disorder and dwindling building income meant a slowdown, if not a break in the construction of the Campanile, which had proceeded so fruitfully from 1334 into the first year or two of the 1340s. But the depressed conditions alone would not have caused Andrea's departure. He would not have voluntarily resigned the lucrative post of *capo-*

[13] M. Becker, "Economic Change and the Emerging Florentine Territorial State," *Studies in the Renaissance,* XIII (1966), 9 ff.

[14] Doc. 3. Grote (1961, 55) notes that as late as 1289 the piazza had been repaved (R. Davidsohn, *Forschungen zur Geschichte von Florenz* [Berlin, 1908], IV, 462). The cost may have been the cause of a loan of 200 florins to the Opera from the Arte della Lana on May 31, 1340 (Grote, 1961, n. 176). But it could well have gone toward the Campanile itself.

[15] Doc. 4.

[16] Doc. 5.

[17] Guasti, doc. 58.

[18] Doc. 6.

[19] Doc. 7.

[20] M. Becker, "Florentine Popular Government (1343-1348)," *Proceedings of the American Philosophical Society,* CVI (1962), 361 ff. Also, Becker, 1966, 10 ff.

[21] Guasti, doc. 61.

[22] Becker, "Popular Government," 1962, 361.

[23] Doc. 8.

maestro, losing the high salary of 100 florins per year and numerous fringe benefits, including the opportunity to carve large amounts of well-rewarded sculpture. Nor would the Opera have released a man of Andrea's abilities, but somehow would have maintained at least his salary.

Yet, were there a strong undercurrent of dissatisfaction, the difficult, trying months of 1343 could have precipitated Andrea's dismissal. According to Vasari, Andrea was the court architect of the Duke of Athens, giving shape to his outrageous building program.[24] Although modern critics have concluded that Andrea was expelled along with his patron for this transgression,[25] Vasari's architectural attributions to Andrea are brought into serious doubt by his failure, among other things,[26] to mention the one building on which we are certain Andrea worked, the Campanile. Nevertheless, as we shall discover below, it seems likely that he was given more responsibility for other communal architecture than Giotto. Assuming that Andrea's high office continued into the reign of the Duke of Athens, he could have been associated with the dictator's "anti-communal" projects. But even if so, in the case of a highly gifted artisan — as with a well entrenched bureaucrat — the ensuing political restoration would not necessarily have led to a purge from office.

The underlying cause for Andrea's departure is suggested by a more reliable source. Pucci records that, in contrast to Giotto, who overcame every obstruction and completed a fragment of the Campanile with [at least] its decoration in "bello stile," Andrea met only with difficulties ("affanni") in his campaign. His vain attempt to better the project was adjudged a failure:

> Because of a useless labor,
> Which was done for improvement,
> The [post of] *capomaestro* was taken from him.[27]

Clearly, in the trying months of 1342-43, discontent with Andrea's work, perhaps going back several years, broke into the open and he was forced to leave.[28]

With what aspect of Andrea's design can the *Operai* have been displeased? His structural modification discussed in Chapter II (and again below) was an eminently sound step, in no manner open to criticism. Nor can the style of the interior chambers, shortly to be examined, have deeply or adversely affected the *Operai*. It was the exterior with which they — and Pucci — were primarily concerned, the Campanile as a monumental landmark.

---

[24] Vasari, I, 483 ff, 490 f.
[25] E.g., Nardini, 30; Guasti, L f; J. Lányi, "L'ultima opera di Andrea Pisano," *L'Arte,* n. s. IV, Vol. XXXVI (1933), 204; Becherucci, 1965, 230.
[26] W. Kallab, *Vasaristudien* (Vienna, 1908), 321 ff, 328 ff.

[27] Doc. IV.
[28] Gioseffi (1963, 88) finds that dissatisfaction with the Campanile (which, however, he misconstrues) rather than Andrea's connection with the Duke of Athens was the primary consideration.

Andrea's first modification of Giotto's elevation was to repeat the initial story (Fig. 7). By the abridgement of Giotto's first cornice and the addition of an equally scaled, if differently formed, one immediately above (Fig. 10), the division between the zones of relief was minimized. At the same time, Andrea transported the foliated cavetto and inclined plane of the first cornice projected in the Siena drawing (Fig. 135) upward to cap the new second story (Fig. 126).[29] The effect, combined with the setback and radical modulation in design above, is that one reads the first two stories as a cubic unity, forming a massive base from which the shaft of the Campanile rises (Fig. I). Giotto's design — as the anonymous Dante commentator appears to have noted — had no base in this grand, abstract sense. Rather, the great shaft was to be poised on a relatively minute set of classical base profiles; the first story was not meant as a base in the traditional architectonic manner, but as the lower section of a colossal, frame-like armature. Giotto's base, while overtly classical, was — like his cornices — in essence a Gothic conception: in every High Gothic elevation is manifest the same phenomenon of miniature bases carrying enormously high piers and colonnettes. Andrea's reform — characteristic of the unpredictable interweaving of classicizing and Gothic architectonics in Trecento Tuscany — despite its trappings, is more truly in the classical tradition.

By repeating Giotto's fabric, Andrea transformed its architectural significance. The bands and panels now form the rhythmic, horizontally oriented decoration of a massive cubic form. The bands — for Giotto static elements of a frame-like configuration — are given new meaning, especially the broad series between the two zones of panels, which now seems a tensely stretched belt. Above, in the niche section, freed from nominal compliance with Giotto's manner of revetment, Andrea eliminates the moldings dividing the bands. The latter are now set directly against each other so that they seem even more a taut membrane stretched around the Campanile (Figs. 19, 22).[30]

For Giotto the incrustation was an ingenuously plastic, naked form. Andrea's polychrome ribbons form a structural skin, covering and binding the hidden body and structural bones beneath. From the tautly draped, cubic base rise set-back, analogously covered shafts: the octagonal buttresses and lesene. Only at the level of the niches does the skin terminate, stripped, as it were, to reveal a vertical armature beneath, and between which appears the heavy curtain wall of windows and niches. Wall and armature are enveloped again by a narrower series of bands, then re-emerge, the deep niches now blind. A broad series of bands follows, symmetrically disposed to the series below the niches, thus

[29] Noted by Nardini, 21 ff.

[30] The patterns of the two intarsia bands of the niche section, in a manner characteristic of the Campanile history, represent a simplification (in particular for the marble workers) of the second story motifs and at the same time a partial revival of the discontinuous patterns of Giotto's intarsia, not so much as executed in detail at the fabric but as schematically represented in the Siena drawing (with a reversal of the figure-ground coloration, however); Figs. 23, 135; cf. Ch. II, 28 f.

unifying the sequence. The cornice above terminates the fabric of Andrea (Figs. 20, 21, 77).

The *Operai* could not but have marveled at the vitality, sophistication, and grandeur of the design, by which the wall assumes nearly the guise of a living organism — to use an Albertian simile[31] — the bones (piers), flesh (curtain wall), and skin (horizontal membrane) clearly defined and articulated. The idea was that of a born sculptor. How wonderful an elevation is the elegant massiveness of the base, the setback of veiled forms that appear undraped, appropriately, at the level of figure sculpture (Fig. 23); with what architectural magic the piers are run again beneath and from repeated zones of bands disappearing and reappearing as does the window itself! Nor could one ignore Andrea's inspired manipulation of the restricted triad of color, not only in the taut rainbow bands but the jewel-like concentrations of crimson richness in the niches (Figs. I, IV).

Can the *Operai* have objected to the visionary nature of Andrea's conception and adjudged it "a useless labor," something too intricate for their conservative Florentine taste? I should think not. Giotto's design was equally complex in a different manner. Later, the very illusionary structural effects of Andrea are taken up and developed by Talenti and eventually Giovanni d'Ambrogio. And they come to characterize the revetment of the Duomo designed and executed from the 1350s into the Quattrocento, transmitting Andrea's ideas to Brunelleschi, for whom they were of substantial importance. Indeed, rational complexity and structural intellectuality form the essence of the seminal building of Florence, the Baptistery, where the wall is also analyzed into pier, horizontal overlay, and curtain wall,[32] although in static rather than the dynamic configurations of Andrea and his followers (Fig. 161). Likewise, Andrea's refined colorism stands midstream in a current that runs from the Baptistery through Giotto, Talenti, and the Quattrocento Cathedral fabric. Nor can the razor-sharp thinness of Andrea's surface have disturbed the *Operai;* a Florentine characteristic, it is found in other important mid-Trecento fabrics, such as Santa Trinita[33] and the facade of Santa Maria Novella (Fig. 236).

What proved fatal to Andrea's design was not the style, but simply its basic scheme. Underlying Giotto's project was the traditional Tuscan stack of cubes with windows opening progressively upward and topped by a pyramidal spire. The elevation is characteristic of all the important Florentine campanili — Ognissanti, Santa Maria Novella, San Pier Maggiore, and even the Badia, allowing for its hexagonal shape (Figs. 293-300).[34] Andrea Pisano's unpardonable crime was his denial of this tradition.

His project aligns with the orthodox only in the cubic base. Above, one would imagine that the two lesene on each side were to continue upward several times their

[31] L. B. Alberti, *De re aedificatoria* (Florence, 1485), Bk. III, Chs. VI, VIII, IX.

[32] W. Horn, "Romanesque Churches in Florence," *Art Bulletin,* XXV (1943), 123 ff.

[33] Against the untenable Dugento dating of Paatz

(1937, 23 ff), see H. Saalman, *The Church of Santa Trinita in Florence* (New York, 1966), 31 ff.

[34] See Ch. VII.

executed length,[35] repudiating both fundamental aspects of the tradition: the stacking of cubic stories and the progressive opening of their windows. Instead, the body of the Campanile would have appeared a continuous shaft overlain by pilaster strips and marked by a severely limited, almost inconsequential fenestration.

The heresy of Andrea was deeply rooted in his past. Growing up near Pisa, pilaster articulation figured strongly in his earliest architectural impressions. He may even have lived in one of the supposed 10,000 examples of the *casa-torre* (house-tower) reported in Pisa in the twelfth century.[36] This basic local house type had a façade formed by a high armature of stone piers appearing as pilasters closing in arches and supporting stone architraves at the floor levels; this frame was filled out by a brick curtain wall punctured by windows (Figs. 224, 225).[37] Andrea would have known the campanile of San Nicola, with its cylindrical and, above, octagonal body articulated by buttress strips (Fig. 303). He would have been well disposed to appreciate the canonical tower form of Venice, where he may have been working when called to Florence in 1329-30.[38] The type, exemplified not only in Venice itself but all over the Veneto and Emilia-Romagna (Figs.

[35] Nardini's hypothesis, that they were arranged to line up with the buttresses of an octagon similar to Giotto's, is repeated by Gioseffi, who renders an awkward reconstruction (1963, 88 ff and fig. 76), and Klotz, 1966, 178 f.

[36] According to the *Chronicle* of Benjamin da Tudela, cited by L. Pera, *Il razionalismo e l'architettura pisana*, (Pisa, 1936), 24 f, with evidence for such great numbers. C. Lupi ("La casa pisana e i suoi annessi nel medio evo," *Archivio Storico Italiano*, s. V, Vol. XXVII [1901], 264 ff) explains that their narrowness gave the effect of towers, though at ca. 10-20 m in height, most of them were not.

[37] Lupi *(ibid.)* gives the soundest historical and structural account of the type, for which he finds related examples at Lucca, Pistoia, and even — from a very early period — at Siena. See also Pera, 1936, 24 f, figs. 5, 10; and A. Bartalini, *L'Architettura civile del medioevo in Pisa* (Pisa, 1937), pls. I, II. Interestingly enough, with regard to Andrea Pisano, the broadest and highest of Pisan towers, the *Torre vittoriosa*, was built in 1336 at the Pontenovo della Spina, according to G. Rohault de Fleury, *Les Monuments du Pise au moyen age* [Paris, 1866], 81; he also notes (82) that, after the second conquest of Pisa by Florence in 1509, all the Pisan towers were razed to the height of 15-16 m (about 25 *braccia*, or half the Florentine limit).

[38] On June 11, 1329 Piero di Jacopo ("orefice di Firenze") is sent to Pisa to make a drawing of the Cathedral bronze doors and thence to Venice, with instructions to find a maker — "un maestro a lavorare la forma" — for the bronze doors of the Baptistery; six months later Andrea Pisano appears as "maestro delle porte"; and when, within two years, the casting stage is approached, it is a Venetian, Leonardo d'Avanzo, who directs the intricate process (G. Vasari, *Le Vite de' più eccellenti pittori, scultori ed architettori*, ed. K. Frey [Munich, 1911], I, 350 ff). [Hereafter cited as Vasari-Frey.] Falk ([and Lányi], 1943, 132 f) insists that Piero di Jacopo's Venetian mission involved seeking only a bronze founder, not the sculptor. But if so, one would imagine the instructions to have read "un maestro a *fondare*," and that such a specialist, rather than Andrea Pisano, would have appeared a few months later. Is it not more reasonable to assume that the Florentines knew quite well their immediate need was for a metal sculptor of great artistry and that he would know what specialists to summon when the time came? O. Mothes (*Geschichte der Baukunst und Bildhauerei Venedigs* [Leipzig, 1859], 181 f) and I. Falk (*Studien zu Andrea Pisano* [Hamburg, 1940], 17 f) discuss Vasari's attribution to Andrea of the Venetian arsenal work of the early Trecento with respectively positive and negative judgments.

310-312), consists of a closed quadratic shaft divided on each side by from one to three lesene terminating in an arched corbel table frieze. Sometimes there are several such sections. Surmounting the trunk is the belfry *(cella),* a short section with large windows. The whole generally is capped by a low pyramid or spire.[39]

Andrea Pisano's Campanile project clearly incorporated both sources: the complex masonry of the Pisan *casa-torre,* whence derived the separation of high pilaster or pier armature and the curtain wall; and the scheme of the Venetian campanile.[40] The Pisan reminiscences went beyond the schematic: the lozenges forming the centerpiece of the second relief story take their geometry from the diamond shaped, inset panels that not only are an omnipresent decorative motif of the Pisan Romanesque but in particular — and with singular richness of detail (compared with its duomo) — ring the base of the Leaning Tower (Fig.302).[41] That Andrea had Venice in mind is indicated by a prominent, but curiously overlooked, detail in his fabric: the vertical fenestration formed by a double row·of circumscribed quatrefoils (Figs. 19, 23, 24). This is precisely the canonical window type of the Venetian palace, examples of which still exist from the early Trecento, for example at the Palazzo Ariani (Fig. 223).[42] As a single row, the motif appears in the arcade of the Doge's Palace. But Andrea seems to have worked also in Siena,[43] and was inspired by the advanced Sienese architecture of the times as well. The dynamic manner in which the buttresses and lesene spring from the massive base of the Campanile bears the impact of the façades of Siena Baptistery and Orvieto Cathedral (Fig. 270, 275).[44]

Andrea's intentions should have been obvious at the outset. But it was only as his fabric slowly rose that it dawned upon the Florentines that Giotto's quintessential Florentine design was being replaced by a Pisan's version of the bell tower of San Marco in Venice, with Sienese overtones to boot.[45] In the unsettled months of 1342-43, when public

[39] See Ch. VII, 158 and n. 35.

[40] Certainly the Venetian *cella*-plus-pyramid terminus is just as plausible a hypothesis as the reconstruction of Nardini, Gioseffi, and Klotz (see n. 35 above), the awkward belfry of which (Gioseffi, 1963, fig. 86) neither the Florentines nor Andrea would ever have envisioned. The spacing of the lesene resulted from a number of factors, including the Venetian source, the continuation of the divisions of Giotto's ground story, and the niches and "Venetian" window (see below).

[41] See p. 81 below for the intermediate link between the Campanile and the Leaning Tower detail.

[42] G. Fontana *(Cento palazzi fra i più celebri di Venezia* [Venice, 1865], 373 ff) dates the Pal. Ariani (later Minotto) in the very early Trecento.

[43] M. Wundram ("Studien zur künstlerischen Herkunft Andrea Pisanos," *Mitteilungen des kunsthistorischen Instituts in Florenz,* VIII [1957-59], 199 ff) connects Andrea with the Trecento stream of Sienese sculpture; he argues, however (211 n. 34), that the "Andrea Ugolini" who appears in the Siena Cathedral documents in 1299 as a witness in a money matter (P. Bacci, *Documenti e commentari per la storia dell'arte* [Florence, 1944], 44) is not Andrea Pisano.

[44] Klotz, 1966, 186.

[45] The contemporary awareness of such formal distinctions can be seen in contemporary painting; for example, at the upper church at Assisi, in the *Dream of Pope Innocent* the Lateran campanile is depicted in characteristic Roman form, whereas in the *Expulsion of the Demons from*

hostility to alien ways reached the flash point, the *Opera* was finally able to throw out Andrea Pisano and his project. Fortunately, he had executed only a cube-like segment of the shaft,[46] so that the emphatic return by Talenti to the traditional scheme above did not critically disrupt the unity of the whole.

In the previous chapter, it was observed that the details of Andrea's fabric are patently non classical. In this also the Florentines could have found fault: from San Giovanni to Brunelleschi the vocabulary of Florentine architecture is, to one degree or another, rooted in antiquity. Andrea's Campanile fabric is the single outstanding exception to this tradition, apart from such inherently non classical forms as spires, crockets, and tracery or an occasional run of Gothic capitals (as in the early parts of Santa Maria Novella). In contrast to Giotto's rich, delicate classicism in detail, Andrea's unfamiliar forms are endowed with an almost metallic sharpness (Figs. 16, 24, 77). Even the leaves in the second-story cornice are reduced to a crisp, but uniform texture (Figs. 16-18).

Andrea must have been trained first as a goldsmith and — even in his other callings — *orefice* he remained.[47] The quality of goldsmith work is evident in the high precision and refinement of his sculpture, particularly in bronze.[48] His architectural forms fall within the same context.[49] Who but a goldsmith would place a tiny arcade on delicate, razor-sharp consoles and decorate it with paper-thin trefoils, ten meters up (Fig. 16)? These trefoils relate to the equally planar, if larger, trefoils inside the niches, themselves rubious foci given sharp edges everywhere and capitals set into their elevation like jewels (Figs. IV, 24). Who but a goldsmith would form the barbed intarsia motifs of the second story (Fig. 14) and the metallic leaves of the second-story cornice (Fig. 16), or devise the set-gem motif of the cornice immediately above Giotto's (Figs. III, 13, 14)? Who else would fancy the lotus-and-trilobate-leaf frieze, a motif derived from the vocabulary of crowns, in the cornice of the niche section (Figs. 20, 77)?[50]

It is not surprising, then, to find many motifs of Andrea's Campanile decoration — a kind of marble *bijouterie* — at his Baptistery door, where decorative forms abound in the sleekly plastic and finely ornate frame, in the exquisitely monumental furniture and architecture of the miniature settings (themselves highly reminiscent of contemporary reliquary architecture), in the platform supports, and in the brilliantly tooled garments and trappings (Figs. 178-188).

The freedom with which Andrea applied small scale decorative forms of bronze sculpture and goldsmith work to monumental architecture is remarkable. Inside the Cam-

---

Arezzo a more Tuscan campanile can be observed (see Ch. VII for these building types).

[46] Despite its appearance, the niche section is nearly cubic (ca. 25 *braccia* high, and 23 broad), according to the measured drawing in Runge, 1853.

[47] Vasari-Frey, I, 352, Regs. 26, 27.

[48] Wundram, 1957-59, 200 ff.

[49] A suggestion of Prof. Richard Krautheimer.

[50] For example, Maitani's Madonna over the central portal of Orvieto (Fig. 276); the Madonna of Andrea and Nino Pisano in the Spina (Beccherucci, 1965, fig. 40); the *Presentation of the Head of St. John* in Andrea's Baptistery door (Fig. 183).

panile, the vault of the second chamber is capped by perhaps the most astonishing keystone in Florence (Fig. 58). Inscribed in a pierced quatrefoil similar to the frames in the Baptistery portal is a disc bearing the Florentine lily. The triangular and semicircular fields at the margin bear leaves in a manner reminiscent of the miniature architecture in the bronze door (Figs. 184, 188); and the six-pointed stars in their starfish form bring to mind the fibulae worn by a number of Andrea's contemporary marble figures, for example, his *King David*. Indeed, the very layout of the keystone probably derives from a type of fibula[51] exemplified by the Sienese piece of about 1330 now in the British Museum (Fig. 220).[52] In both cases the tangential relationship between the circle and the scalloped border is a distinguishing feature. In adapting the form to the Campanile vault, Andrea cast it in massively abstract, yet delicate plasticity. The notion to employ a fibula motif for the keystone is characteristic of a goldsmith's imagination; as a fibula binds the garment, the keystone binds the vault.

The tympanum of the street portal to the Campanile seems to be Andrea's, at least in design (Fig. 65).[53] Like the keystone, its form derives from ecclesiastical metalwork, in this case, the paten.[54] The preserved Trecento example closest to the tympanum seems to be found in the treasury of the cathedral of Sulmona (Aquila) (Fig. 221).[55] In both cases the figured central disc is bordered by a trefoiled scallop. The remnant triangular spaces are decorated with leaves. The differences between the related patterns of the Sienese fibula and such patens are consequential. The fibula is small and spiky, easily adapted to the keystone, where its function could be fancied active. The larger, closed, and circular form of the paten emphasizes surface and was well appropriated for the flatness of the tympanum, which spreads, as in the paten, to the frame beyond. To a Trecento goldsmith, such distinctions, to us perhaps rather fine, would have been obvious.

The unorthodoxy of Andrea Pisano's Campanile elevation and detail is unique, and may have contributed to his downfall during the crisis of 1342-43. But at the same time certain aspects of his exterior are closely linked to indigenous tradition. It has already been emphasized that architectonically conceived, structurally analytic incrustation is a

---

[51] A suggestion of Prof. Richard Krautheimer.
[52] C. G. E. Bunt and S. J. A. Churchill, *The Goldsmiths of Italy* (London, 1926), 50. P. Toesca (*Il Trecento* [Turin, 1951], 901, fig. 791) considers it mid-Trecento Florentine.
[53] The head of the lamb, especially the carving of the eye area, which carries an almost human expression, is comparable to such figures of Andrea as the nearby Hercules, not to mention the bronze lion heads of the Baptistery door (Figs. 132, 180). Likewise, the curls of wool are similar to the beards of Hercules and, even more, the adjacent Navigator. The rich, yet precise and con-

trolled leafwork in the cusps is manifestly akin to that of Andrea's second cornice, and the delicacy of the leaf in the upper corner is prefigured in the Baptistery door. Certainly, all of this, as well as the smooth manner of relief, has little to do with the harsh, mid-Trecento style of Talenti and his followers.
[54] A suggestion of Prof. Richard Krautheimer.
[55] Other comparable examples are found in the Perugia Galleria Nazionale (Alinari 47561) and the early Trecento paten of Benedict XI (Alinari 52246).

central theme of medieval Florentine architecture. The triple form of Andrea's last cornice, even the equality of proportions, is found at the Baptistery (Figs. 77, 234). Certain details derive from Arnolfo's Cathedral façade, where there were not only deep niches for sculpture in the lower tier, but blind niches flanking them, prefiguring Andrea's vertical arrangement (Fig. 239). Moreover, the pink frames of Andrea's niches reflect, perhaps even coloristically, the jambs of Arnolfo's main portal (Fig. IV). And the two rows of fleur-de-lis running along the lower façade prefigure the crown motif exhibited by Andrea's upper cornice (Fig. 77).[56]

In noting that Andrea Pisano's Campanile design reflects the Florentine, and specifically the Arnolfian inheritance, we are led to a well-justified digression: consideration of the intricate question of the origins and comparative historic positions of the Campanile architects, not only within the context of Florence but more broadly speaking. The lifespans of Giotto (ca. 1267-1337), Andrea Pisano (ca. 1290-1348), and Francesco Talenti (ca. 1300-69) not only significantly overlap one another but form entangled, yet definable relationships with the generations of their Tuscan peers. To gain a perspective on their styles we might at this point — midway in our discussion of the Campanile architects — pause to reflect upon their lineage.

The architecture of the fountainhead of Tuscan Gothic, Nicola Pisano (active 1258-78), is characterized by bold, free, and rich configurations molded in dense plasticity (Fig. 232). Classical and Gothic forms mingle freshly, in carefree manner, without inhibitions about their miscegenation. His art was ripe with possibilities and indeed was a cornucopia of unexplored formal directions that spared his great followers the doom of servile imitation or sterile mannerism.

Although it is dangerous to generalize about their rich artistic personalities, it is clear that Nicola's inheritors polarized their legacy. Arnolfo di Cambio (ca. 1245-1302) cast a Florentine chill over Nicolesque flux. His classicizing, as well as Gothic, conceptions are rigorously abstract in outline, severe and frozen in detail (Figs. 237-239). If Arnolfo, more than any Florentine-trained master, manifests himself the arch-Florentine, Giovanni Pisano (ca. 1250-after 1314) — the first recorded titanic personage in Italian art — animates Nicolesque ease with a mercurial excitement more Sienese than the art of any artist Siena-born. The passionate architectonic and dramatic rhythms of his major work, the Siena Duomo façade (Fig. 269), the compelling tactility of its swelling, twisting, blooming, colorific forms looms unforgettably but always again quite unbelievably as one approaches its presence.

It is perhaps because of their utter divergence that in the work of both Arnolfo and Giovanni there is a white-hot intensity of imagination, an extremism born, conceivably, of the compulsion to differ creatively from the relaxed broadness of their master's style.

[56] Compare the similar motif in the architectural setting of Giotto's *Birth of the Baptist* in the Peruzzi Chapel, S. Croce.

Giotto, following by half a generation, arising from a different ambient, working with a brush rather than in marble, was evidently spared — despite Dante's famous quip[57] — the deforming pressure of a follower syndrome. Indeed, like Nicola, his was the art without which a whole epoch is unimaginable. Even so, Giotto was deeply linked with his great historical peers. The volumetric plasticity of his figure style, for example, is unthinkable without Arnolfo and Giovanni. Yet, as figural bulk is lent to personages of a composure and dignity alien to Giovanni's world of explosive emotions and yet possessed of a breath of life denied Arnolfo's frozen effigies, so Giotto's architecture forms the third alternative of the post-Nicola generation; to this his Campanile project belongs, despite its delayed birth in 1334.

To further clarify Giotto's architectural kinship with Nicola's followers, one might again examine such a revealing detail as Giotto's Campanile base, this time confronting it not only with Arnolfo's Cathedral sequence but also with the foot of Giovanni's façade (Figs. 8, 164, 233). It is immediately clear that the inspiration of Giotto's pictorial transfiguration of Arnolfo's frozen stolidity could well have been Giovanni's equally vivid composition. But if pictorial, Giovanni's forms dramatically express, in spreading, cushioned stages, the impact between the load of the mighty façade and the earth beneath. Giotto's base is instead, we have seen, a fanciful bundle of profiles forming part of a painter's frame-like architectural metaphor. Indeed, it is just this fluid sense of play that we have observed to be so especially and profoundly alive in the interpenetrating images, sequences, and transformations of Giotto's Campanile project.

While the romantic, yet cohesive pictorialism of Giotto's architecture forms the third manner of the post-Nicola generation, Andrea Pisano — deeply indebted not only to Nicola's immediate school but also to such advanced younger masters as the designer of the Siena Baptistery façade — is already beyond the pale of their epoch, falling into an ill-defined, but well-represented, architectural period between Giovanni, Arnolfo, and Giotto on the one hand and, as will be evidenced below, Orcagna's and Talenti's new aesthetic of the 1340s and 1350s on the other.[58] The systematic composition and sharp precision of Andrea's Campanile project — alien to the individualizing temperaments and classic stylistic phase of Giotto and his elder peers — typify a number of major works of Andrea's time, running from about 1310 to the 1330s:[59] the façades of the Siena Baptistery, 1316 ff (Fig. 270), and Orvieto Cathedral, 1310 ff (Figs. 275, 276); the Duomo Nuovo in Siena, 1339 ff (Figs. 272-274); in Florence, Santa Trinita, 1340/50, and the bell towers of Santa Maria Novella and the Badia, 1330s (Figs. 295-299). It is no accident that Andrea Pisano's Sienese counterpart during his leadership at the Campanile, Lando di Pietro, was also a goldsmith whose architectural ideas — manifest at

---

[57] "Credette Cimabue nella pintura tener lo campo, e ora ha Giotto il grido, sì che la fama di colui è oscura" (*Purgatorio*, XI, 94-97).

[58] See Ch. VI.
[59] Klotz, 1966, 186.

the Duomo Nuovo (Figs. 272-274) — embody the refined grace, high precision, and occasional fussiness of their craft.

At the same time Andrea's design embodied certain of the main currents of northern Gothic architecture. Not only is jewel-like detail a major characteristic of the French court style,[60] and refined thinness a leading quality of Gothic architecture from the time of the south transept façade of Paris and Saint Urbain at Troyes well into the fourteenth century,[61] but Andrea's organic elevation can be seen as an astoundingly original, polychrome Florentine version of the tensile, interwoven articulation of the most progressive northern wall elevations and vaulting of the time.[62] So modern was Andrea's manner that even the widely traveled, highly sophisticated Talenti, years later, still bent himself to the task of transforming these northern themes into Tuscan language.

It was thus not merely chance, but also because his style of design was the *dernier cri* on all horizons, that Andrea Pisano was chosen Giotto's successor. Yet the circumstances of Andrea's promotion in a manner predestined his eventual fate in the city. The name of Giotto had lent his own, already dated, project authority. But with the passing of the master, Florence — shaken perhaps by the near structural catastrophe — realized suddenly that his dazzling greatness had eclipsed what was transpiring in the world. And Florence, though in its own manner profoundly conservative, was not one to be left behind. Indeed, so violent was the awakening that in the rush to the latest fashion, the Florentines forgot the depth of their own conservatism and were blinded to the alien conformation accompanying Andrea's modernism. At the time they must have deeply appreciated being brought up to date with his project.

As was mentioned earlier, Andrea's handling of the interior structure and decoration was, from any point of view, unexceptionable. In solving the structural deficiency at the base Andrea doubled the thickness of Giotto's walls, but around Giotto's windows left voluminous barrel-vaulted niches (Figs. 25, 26, 32). While they allow light to pass and the narrow space to expand, thus profiting the use of the room as meeting quarters (suggested by the bench), it would not be unreasonable to imagine that the subchambers were more specifically designed as tombs of a type *(avelli)* known best at the façade of Santa Maria Novella (Fig. 236; see also Fig. 297).[63] Their presence in the Campanile

---

[60] R. Branner, *St. Louis and the Court Style in Gothic Architecture* (London, 1965), 58 f.

[61] W. Gross, *Die abendländische Architektur um 1300* (Stuttgart, 1948), *passim*.

[62] See my forthcoming study of this phenomenon.

[63] Though the façade of S. Maria Novella is misdated by G. Kiesow (it is not late Dugento, but mid Trecento, not only according to Paatz's fairer reading of the documents, but stylistically), his discussion of the *avelli* places them in a Tuscan ambient reaching back well into the Dugento

("Die gotische Südfassade von S. Maria Novella in Florenz," *Zeitschrift für Kunstgeschichte*, XXV [1962], 1 ff). U. Schlegel's convincing interpretation of Giotto's illusionistic chapels at Padua (Figs. 154, 155) as imaginary tomb chapels for the Scrovegni, which she connects in type with the S. Maria Novella *avelli* ("Zum Bildprogramm der Arena-Kapelle," *Zeitschrift für Kunstgeschichte*, XX [1957], 130 ff), is extremely thought-provoking in the suggestive parallelism to the Campanile subchambers; there are even rings in the

would have been prompted by the displacement of graves from its site — the ancient cemetery along the south flank of the Duomo[64] — and necessitated by the pressing need for building funds. The rectangular niches in the intermediate piers would have served the memorial service of the dead as well as the assembly of the living; and the need of both purposes for light partly might explain the steepness of the internal splay of the window just below the vault on the west wall (Figs. 26, 30, 32), through which illumination might be channeled down even in the late afternoon, but which would also allow exit to the otherwise trapped fumes of incense, candles, and torches.[65]

In the unavoidably awkward corners — the exigencies of inherited windows and necessary added mass left Andrea little choice[66] — were set octagonal colonnettes that support the octagonal ribs of the vaults, the first such composition in Florence.[67] The ledge profiles of the niche flooring interlock with the colonnettes, physically as well as visually, holding the shafts in place (Fig.44). It may have delighted Andrea to have placed the small stone octagons at these inside corners opposite the massive octagonal buttresses of the exterior.

Campanile vault (Fig. 25) for the lamps that "belong to every Christian grave" and which Giotto hung in his "sepulchres" (*ibid.*). On the dado of the bench at the foot of the Campanile, on the west face, are six coats of arms with sepulchral inscriptions (one dated 1472, according to Richard Pommer); might the fact that there are also six subchambers inside be more than pure coincidence? For Florentine burial customs in general, V. Fineschi, *Memorie sopra il cimitero antico della Chiesa di S. Maria Novella* (Florence, 1787), 3 ff.

[64] Frey, 1885, plan II, no. 17a; V. Follini and M. Rastrelli, *Firenze antica e moderna illustrata* (Florence, 1789 ff), II, 365 f. The systematic removal of tombs from the Cathedral precinct began in the late Dugento around the Baptistery (Frey, 1885, 65 ff).

[65] A suggestion of Mr. Ronald Malmstrom. Such diagonal air/light shafts appear in fortifications, e.g., the tower of the Duke of Athens at Volterra (G. Rohault de Fleury, *Toscane au moyen age: Architecture civile et militaire* [Paris, 1870-73], I, pl. XXXIII).

[66] The responds are barely given seating; seen in elevation, the minimal corner contrasts clumsily with the broad ashlar face of the central pier. This unsightliness resulted from forming the inner shell symmetrically about the pre-existing windows; had the second architect instead lessened the mass of the central piers and increased the plan of the corner reinforcement into an "L," thus achieving a more balanced elevation for the reinforcement shell, the windows would all have been off center vis-a-vis the niches. Of the two alternatives of the dilemma, the one chosen is at least the more efficient structural solution — the reinforcement piers being all about the same in plan, and the vaulting juncture between window and niche aligned. If both shells had been part of a single campaign, a solution would have been formed satisfying both structural and visual considerations (assuming the architect to have been reasonably competent).

[67] As opposed to the Dugento round colonnettes, figured capitals, and rounded ribs of the S. Maria Novella choir and side chapels; in effect, the side chapels of S. Croce, in which Giotto's illusionistic responds are columnar but Arnolfo's actual ribs octagonal, are a transitional step (Figs. 158, 159). The little known chapel to the rear of the apse of S. Croce (Figs. 205, 206), probably ca. 1348 (Paatz, I, 662 n. 376) is nearly a copy of the articulation of the ground floor Campanile chamber. In the late Trecento triconch chapels of the Duomo, broken corner bundles support embellished octagonal ribs.

The octagonal colonnette first seems to appear in Florence a half century earlier, in the responds of the nave piers of Santa Maria Novella. But their three-sided form is in reality a beveled corner. In the Campanile, the octagon takes definition as five sides are loosened from the wall, in manner related to the precisely contemporary occurence in Or San Michele (Figs. 192, 193), hardly a coincidence, as we shall see. The base of the chamber respond, of which only one example is preserved (Figs. 37, 38), is also most progressive: though a canonical sequence, it follows neither the leaden shapes of Florentine Romanesque profiles nor the compass-drawn curves found in Santa Maria Novella, or in the work of Arnolfo and even Giotto. Rather, Andrea gives the base profiles a new swing and spread that reflect his Pisan and Sienese years. Certainly the capitals (Figs. 39-42) are essentially non-Florentine in their foliage, but instead traceable to Siena (Fig. 222) in the high proportioned opposition of a striated inner leaf to one that encloses it, curling over at the tip. The crisply grooved dryness of this foliage is comparable in intent, if not quite in quality, to the leafwork of the second-story cornice (Figs. 16-18). The diagonal, prismatic cutting of the structural components of the capital — astragal, bell, abacus — is characteristic of the jeweler's hand of Andrea. Yet, as on the exterior, local influences (here the execution by local craftsmen) play a role. The classicizing core is common in the colonnette capitals of Florentine communal architecture, found — in more expansive form and with richer leafwork — at the windows of the Bargello and the Palazzo Vecchio (Figs. 174, 231). Not only does one of the chamber capitals (Fig. 41) poorly copy the evident prototype version (Fig. 39) but another (Fig. 42) substitutes a free-form leaf that is found in the Santa Maria Novella workshop (Fig. 227) and in Arnolfo's arcade on the interior Duomo façade (Fig. 229). The ledge profile — although a common terminal form comprising an ovolo, fillet, and cyma recta (Fig. 44) — interestingly enough resembles Giotto's illusionary cornice at the base of the Peruzzi Chapel frescoes (Fig. 159). The Campanile molding could even be a re-used detail from Giotto's time, but its dryness, and the beveling of the upper edge, suggest the workshop, at least, of Andrea. The keystone is also ambiguous in attribution. Unlike the imaginative version in the second chamber, it forms a simple figured disc (Fig. 43). Its iconography, however, is worth noting: the Agnus Dei is the same as the entrance tympanum, a point to which we shall return.

The ground floor chamber, conceived within the restrictions of Giotto's fabric and the exigencies of its reinforcement, was a prototype for the more fully developed, finely executed, and better preserved version above (Figs. 46-49), a disparity already having been observed in the keystone. A fully profiled bench runs around the meeting room.[68] The vaulting system begins about two meters up, where a cornice articulates a setback of about 20 centimeters (Figs. 52, 53). The cornice is but a slight simplification of

---

[68] Now used as storage. The white objects in the photograph are the plaster molds for the copies of the relief sculpture recently removed to the Cathedral Museum.

Andrea's first exterior cornice (Fig. 13): tondino, scotia, listel, inclined plane, and horizontal. The sequence is perfectly adapted to the function: transition from the vertical wall surface to a narrow shelf on which the vaulting system rests. Once again Andrea reveals his past, for the configuration suggests the Pisan archetype of columns resting on a jutting cornice, found, for example, at the Duomo and the Leaning Tower (Fig. 302).

Lifted above eye level, the octagonal corner shafts are placed on bases related to those in the first story, but higher, more plastic and precisely delineated. The lower torus seems to spread more under the weight, the scotia is springier. The shape of colonnette is itself developed: between its five visible sides and the wall is inserted a squarish spur (Fig. 54). The octagon itself is thus further detached and defined, and the angular play with the massive flatness of the wall — and above with the vault web, transversed by ribs continuing the profile — is accentuated.

It is worth noting that this configuration is akin to the shifting diagonal orientation of the prismatic responds and ribs in the exterior niches (Figs. 23, 24). These form Andrea's most highly developed Campanile vaults. The sharp fluting of their prisms may reflect his years in Siena, where similar grooving is a leitmotif, for example, in the baptistery façade (Fig. 222). But Andrea employs the form functionally rather than merely for tactile value, implicitly dividing the prismatic respond in a manner corresponding to the profiles of the ribs and arches above. By the same considered architectural logic, the otherwise similar diagonal prisms forming the frame of the niche are left ungrooved. The niche capitals (Fig. 119) are prefigured in the rudimentary, but similar shapes in the Baptistery door (Fig. 185); like the niche bases, the capitals form tight, dense versions of the comparatively richer forms of the second Campanile chamber (Figs. 54-57).

The details of the chamber capitals are eclectic. The contrast between the closed structural core and the free, almost wind-blown leaves ultimately derives from the High Gothic. The wanton variants of acanthus leaves in the lower row come from Santa Maria Novella and the interior façade of the Duomo (Figs. 228, 229). The upper leaves are of two types: one is identical to the leaves of the ground story capitals (Figs. 39-42, 54); the other (Figs. 55-57), a folded-over, abstract form, ultimately a French type (the crocket capital) traceable in Tuscany to Nicola Pisano (Fig. 226), is found, again, in Arnolfo's blind arcade on the interior façade of the Duomo (Fig. 229) and in Santa Maria Novella Fig. 230). The astragal and abacus present shapes already familiar to us in Andrea: they too ultimately derive from the High Gothic.

The Florentine sources are in need of no explanation, Andrea having spent over a decade in the city and now head of a shop filled with Florentine masons. His sculpture reveals experience in Siena and knowledge of French thirteenth-century forms.[69] Like Giotto, Andrea succeeded in fusing divergent sources into an intensely personal style, in this case exploiting, perhaps even encouraging the rough execution by local workmen of

[69] Falk, 1940, 6; I. Toesca, 1950, 14, 24 ff. Wundram, 1957-59.

the eclectic leafwork to achieve the highly effective textural, almost airily sculptural play of foliage against the finely conceived and uniformly executed structural elements of the capitals (Fig. 51).

The second chamber has other notable features. Light flows in through two of Andrea's "Venetian" windows (those to the north and south are blind) past broad splay-work that emphasizes the massiveness of the walls, lighting up the beautifully textured surfaces (Fig. 50). One's eye is led to the elevated vaulting system and finally to the color-ful (the figure is red), ingenious keystone (Fig. 58), which is set so that the lily is seen upright on looking up from the entrance.

In contrast, the third chamber is altogether plain (Figs. 46, 59). Although Andrea's windows continue on the exterior into this level, the chamber is almost in darkness, the only light filtering in through stairways or glaring down from punctures in the vault. The simple rib vault resting directly on a cornice can barely be made out. The keystone is in-complete. The style of the cornice seems too harsh for Andrea. The vaulting is probably Talenti's, as will be seen in Chapter VI.[70]

Although we have explored the purpose of the ground story, the utility of these vaulted chambers can perhaps be clarified by the analysis of the complex circulation arrangement that Andrea's thickened wall permitted (Fig. X).[71] It comprises two inde-pendent stair systems, each with its own entrance and function. The first is entered at street level through the portal on the east side of the Campanile (Figs. 60, 61). Through the door at the end of the antechamber one accedes directly to the ground floor chamber; through another doorway to the side one passes (to the south) into the staircase, a broad, comfortably paced[72] series of flights winding in long passes around the four sides of the Campanile and in its lowest reaches set largely within the thickness of Andrea's inner masonry shell (Figs. 6, 36).[73] It bypasses the second chamber on the second, third, and

[70] See Ch. VI, 135 f.

[71] The stairs of the Florentine campanili (e.g., S. Maria Novella, Ognissanti, the Badia) are mini-mal arrangements hung on the interior face of the walls. But as a Pisan it would have been na-tural for Andrea Pisano to imagine commodious stairways in bell towers; cf. the great spirals in the campanili of Pisa Cathedral and S. Nicola (cf., however, also the stair in the Pal. Vecchio shaft [Fig. 333]). It might even be argued that Andrea's stair system was a cause for his extreme thickening of the wall structure, which the stairs penetrate (see below). While, due to our ignorance of the Trecento mathematics of the structural cal-culations involved, this must remain a moot point, I would prefer to think that the thickening was dictated essentially by Giotto's structural inade-quacy, and that this was cleverly exploited to achieve the added benefit of the commodious, in-tegral stairways. A major basis for this opinion is the fact that, as we shall see (70 ff), the com-plex stairways discussed below only evolved gradually in a series of building phases, and that the primary stair was not even present in the thickened wall of Andrea's original project, at least at ground level.

[72] Approximate gradient, 1.42 (Patricia Waddy).

[73] In the first flight, except for a bonding with Giotto's masonry, the staircase appears to be set entirely within the inner shell, as Sgrilli correctly indicates. However, Sgrilli errs above, for al-ready in the second flight the staircase is moved toward the center of the wall, as one can see in the reinforcement arch in the east niche on the

fourth turns. But on the fifth flight, that is, back on the east side, a small doorway in the staircase wall gives to the third chamber. The stairway itself continues up past this door, then across the south face in a sixth flight that issues onto the floor of the Bifora section.

The second set of stairs begins at an elevated portal (Figs. 66, 67) entered originally via a bridge from the Cathedral, where a corresponding, now walled-up portal is found (Fig. 68), and which was reached presumably by a winding stairwell in the nave wall, still identifiable by small windows running alongside the second buttress from the façade (Fig. 164). Through the elevated Campanile portal one entered a landing. There is no trace of stairs leading down. One can only go upward, to the east; partway up the second flight — that is, roughly in line with the doorways to the first and third chambers in the first stair — one finds the entrance to the second chamber (Fig. 48). Continuing past this door and on around the south side, one reaches a landing halfway up the west flight (Fig. 46). The stairway continues no further; a door at the landing leads to the third chamber; across the room, that is, to the east, one finds the doorway already mentioned communicating with the first stair system.[74]

Today the second set of stairs serves only one indispensable function: access to the second chamber. But nothing prevented the simple puncture of a doorway in the wall of the first stairs at the floor level of the second chamber. Why was this simple solution rejected in favor of the expensive dual stair system? The builders probably had in mind something more than the simple problem of access.

In effect, the first stairway is the main, public communication, entered from the street and leading uninterruptedly to the great, airy spaces in the Bifora zone above. It also passes directly to the ground floor chamber, which could have functioned as a meeting room for the Opera. Both the keystone of this chamber and the portal tympanum carry the emblem of the Arte della Lana, of which the Opera del Duomo was a subsidiary. In 1362 it is recorded that the Opera did indeed meet in the Campanile ("congregati in campanile").[75]

Although one could reach the second set of stairs via the first through the third chamber, it entails unnecessary climbing and passage through at least two locked doors. The proper movement was through the Duomo, up the spiral stairs in its wall, across the bridge and through the richly decorated, elevated Campanile portal, and up the two half-flights of stairs to the entrance of the monumental, and very much isolated, second chamber. The orientation of the path of entrance, as well as the presence of the Madonna in the elevated portal, suggest an ecclesiastical function for the room. Moreover, whereas

south side of the ground chamber (Fig. 27); a central position is obtained in the subsequent flights (Fig. 32).

[74] R. Salvini notes the stair accurately, but summarily ("Arnolfo e la Cupola di S. Maria del Fiore," in *Atti del 1° Congresso Nazionale di* *Storia dell'Architettura* [Florence, 1936], 31). Paatz, based on the report of Siebenhüner, gives a somewhat garbled description of the stair (III, 362, 483 n. 201a, 551 n. 441, 553 n. 447).

[75] Doc. 211.

no sculptural program was originally intended on the north face of the Campanile in the lower relief zone,[76] in the upper series, the common scholastic iconography of the Planets, Virtues, and Liberal Arts was pointedly completed on the north side by the highly unusual representation of the Seven Sacraments,[77] poorly visible from ground level (Fig. 7)[78] but prominent indeed from the bridge (Figs. 66, 67). And surely it is not fortuitous that the Consecration of the Priest, the sacrament involving exclusively the clergy, was set over the portal. Could the second chamber then have been a meeting place for the canons, whose quarters were torn down after 1339 (and who would have particularly appreciated the keystone)?[79]

The second set of stairs may have served a purpose beyond that of private access to the second chamber. The old Campanile was attached to the Cathedral in the traditional Florentine arrangement, as at Santa Maria Novella, San Lorenzo, or Ognissanti. Though unable to adjoin the new bell tower with the nave,[80] the Duomo officials seem finally to

[76] The two Trecento reliefs were displaced to the north face by the superstructure of the street portal (see 72 ff below); the five panels of Luca della Robbia clearly are extraneous to the Trecento program and, with respect to the Liberal Arts in the second story on the east side, largely redundant. See Ch. IV.

[77] According to Mrs. Susan Koslow (engaged in study of the problem) the only significant sacraments cycle in Italy prior to the Quattrocento other than at the Campanile is in the Incoronata frescoes in Naples; even in northern manuscript illumination the subject is exceedingly rare, the earliest example being mid 13th century; Pucelle, however, did execute an example in the Belleville Breviary (F. G. Godwin, "An Illustration to the 'De sacrementis' of St. Thomas Aquinas," *Speculum*, XXVI [1951], 609 ff, with explicit reference to the campanile cycle). On this subject, see also H. von der Gabelentz, *Die kirchliche Kunst im italienischen Mittelalter — ihre Beziehungen zur Kultur- und Glaubenslehre* (Strasbourg, 1907), 241 ff, with added examples. Dating of the Campanile series ranges from the 1330s (L. Becherucci, "I rilievi dei Sacramenti nel campanile del Duomo di Firenze," *L'Arte*, XXX [1927], 220) to the 1350s (Paatz, III, 389); in the latter case their complete absence from the rich documentation of that decade is a difficulty, while any dating prior to 1343 would have to take into account the stylistic break with the Andrea Pisano shop that executed the other three

faces. I would suggest the period 1343-48, Talenti's early years at the fabric; primarily an architect, he would have been satisfied to commission the remaining relief sculpture to Arnoldi to whom the work seems securely attributed (Becherucci, 1927, 214 ff) and who appears later as a major contractor for the decorative detail of the tower (Ch. V). Talenti would have been busy with the fabric and, if with sculpture, then perhaps the life-size prophets in the south niches (Paatz, III, 558 f n. 462 f; see also below, Ch. V n. 58). While the hard geometricity of the Sacraments is moving away from the time of Giotto and Andrea, their unaffected naturalism and ingenuous narrative certainly do not belong to the post-Black Death period. Whether pre- or postdating 1348, the iconography certainly might be connected with th findings of Meiss concerning "The Exaltation of God, the Church, and the Priest" (1951, 27 ff). Cf. Ch. IV, 95 ff.

[78] Von Schlosser was puzzled by the contrast between the high quality of the reliefs and their obscure location (1896, 63).

[79] It also might have been where the powerful confraternity of the Laudesi of the Cathedral met for business; their cemetery lay between the Campanile and the Cathedral below the bridge (communication of U. Krause, engaged in a study of Florentine burial customs and their relationship to architecture). Cf. Follini and Rastrelli, 1789 ff, II, 164, 365 ff, on the function of the bridge.

[80] See Chs. II, 21 ff, VII, 174 ff for the reasons.

have succeeded in obtaining at least direct passage from their church. The bridge solution was by no means an innovation, for many of the private houses and defense towers were linked above the street level by such structures, usually of wood and ready for removal in bad times.[81] By closing the street entrance, the Campanile itself could have become, to a degree, an ecclesiastical defense tower.[82] But even were it merely privacy that was behind the arrangement, the double communication of the third chamber could be explained: through it one might reach that part of the Campanile not in direct communication with the second stairway. It would have functioned as a kind of buffer, insulating the two sets of stairs and thus isolating the second chamber, but at the same time allowing intercommunication when necessary.[83]

The placement and decoration of the stair portals involve intricate considerations. The elevated portal on the Campanile (Fig. 67) sits precisely in the center of the north side. Andrea sunk the doorway into Giotto's fabric, cutting down through his predecessor's cornice to the lower frame of the intarsia strip below; above, he carefully limited the archivolts to allow space for half a figured lozenge. The decisive management of the matter is characteristic of Andrea.

The configuration of the portal seems to have been dictated partially by the exigencies of the bridge from the Cathedral. The doorposts sit on massive corbel blocks and could support a substantial weight on their large and solid capitals (Fig. 66). In the portal on the Cathedral, the support surface is instead at the bottom (Fig. 68). The only possible explanation seems to be a drawbridge pivoting over the capitals on the Campanile portal. It could be lowered to the foot of the opposite portal or swung up flush to the face of the "defense tower" by means of a rope from above.[84] This arrangement

[81] R. Davidsohn, *Storia di Firenze* (Florence, 1956), I, 821; M. Borgatti, *Le mura e le torri di Firenze* (Rome, 1900), 24, noting that the bridges rested on large consoles, some of which are still to be seen; A. Schiaparelli, *La casa fiorentina e i suoi arredi nei secoli XIV e XV* (Florence, 1908), 53 (the bridges — or *cavalcavie* — were taxed and regulated to have a minimum height from the street of 5 braccia).

[82] The Bishop himself had a defense tower nearby, at the corner of the Borgo S. Lorenzo and the Via de' Cerretani (Borgatti, 1900, pl. I), the base of which, with its magnificent rusticated portals, still exists (Fig. 329). Similarities between the Campanile and private defense towers have been drawn by Lami (1766, I, 161), comparing the isolated position, and J. Wood-Brown (*The Builders of Florence* [London, 1907], 114). As late as 1371 the tower at the Badia a Settimo was aggrandized together with the fortification of the

monastery (Fig. 301; see Ch. VI n. 83). Ecclesiastical defense towers were particularly common in the violent Midi (R. de Lasteyrie, *L'Architecture religieuse en France à l'époque gothique*, ed. M. Aubert [Paris, 1926 f], II, 143 f). On fortified churches, see also, S. Toy, *A History of Fortification* (London, 1955), 186 f. For what it is worth, the Duke of Athens had a private stair built (supposedly by Andrea) on the Pal. Vecchio on the side toward the Via della Ninna going all the way to the *ballatoio* (N. Rodolico and G. Marchini, *I palazzi del popolo nei comuni toscani del medio evo* [Milan, 1962], 157).

[83] Although rarely as programatically complex as the Campanile, multiple stair systems were not uncommon; the Baptistery has two, the Cupola four.

[84] If Andrea was indeed the architect of fortifications for the Duke of Athens he would have been well qualified to design this little draw-

would explain the flush archivolts of the Campanile portal, which otherwise contrast senselessly with the powerful posts.[85]

The hand of Andrea is strongly felt in the portal detail. The archivolts are shaped with metallic precision. The capitals — a familiar outline — exhibit a goldsmith's taste and carry a double row of acanthus closely akin in cut to those of Andrea's second cornice. The leaves of the door frame brackets are folded like those in the capitals of the second story chamber. The Madonna is possibly autograph Andrea,[86] and the rolling, finely controlled plasticity of the frame in which she is placed is reminiscent of the Baptistery bronze door, as are the base profiles. The latter are differently conceived from those in the Campanile chambers in order to harmonize with the Giottesque incrustation. The same is true of the frames of the doorpost panels, the door frame, and the tympanum, which take up the profiles of Giotto's outer relief frames.

Andrea placed the elevated portal on the axis of the Campanile even though it entailed misalignment with the corresponding portal on the Duomo, the location of which was determined by the pre-existing window opening and buttress. Symmetry favors monumentality, and it is quite clear from the richness and quality of the Campanile portal and the relief program that the clergy wanted to be impressively greeted crossing the bridge. Though Andrea probably cut the opening necessary for the Duomo portal (together with the presumed winding stair) in the fabric of Arnolfo's nave, which still lacked incrustation on the level of the upper two thirds of the doorway, the style of the portal decoration is that of the mid-Trecento Talenti circle.[87]

bridge. Neither the offset landings nor the tricky geometry would have been an insuperable problem. See M. Viollet-le-Duc, *Dictionnaire raisonné de l'architecture française du XIᵉ au XVIᵉ siècle* (Paris, 1864), VII, 314 ff ("Portes fortifiées"), for the extremely varied and complicated geometry of drawbridges.

[85] Noting that the bridge seems to be visible in the Bigallo fresco, Saalman suggests that the overpass was the "lavorio che mosse vano" that was Andrea's undoing (1964, 472 n. 6). But we have seen that a) there were stronger reasons, in the eyes of the Florentines, to dismiss him; b) the double system of communication, and especially the direct access from the Duomo, was evidently not Andrea's personal idea, but the wish of his patrons (even were it his, it would have been no grounds for dismissal, but merely for modifications, quite different from the profound dissatisfactions with his exterior elevation); c) the *Operai* had the bridge completed only later, together with the Talentian portal of the Cathedral ter-

minus; d) the bridge existed until at least 1397 (as pointed out by Saalman himself); e) its destruction probably occurred in the early Quattrocento and resulted from two related events: the systematization of the Pza. del Duomo going on since the late 14th century (the cause for the destruction of Brunelleschi's nearby Cupola model in 1431; see Ch. V, 124 f) and the completion of the sculptural decoration of the Campanile, which involved the placing of Lucca della Robbia's five reliefs and eventually the transfer of the Pisanesque prophets to the north side of the Campanile (Cf. G. Vasari, *Die Lebensbeschreibungen*, ed. A. Gottschewski [Strasbourg, 1906], III, 28 n. 5). Visual considerations now overruled a function that probably no longer obtained, the quasi-military associations of the Campanile be-[ing extinct.

[86] Becherucci, 1965, 239 ff.

[87] Compare the tympanum with the side portal near the Campanile, the columnar detail with the Bigallo, and the intarsia motifs of the jambs with the Trifora.

The eccentric placement and problematic form of the street level portal of the Campanile and the disposition of the chamber and staircase to which it leads is an even more complex matter. To unravel the knot we must return to the ground story chamber. The east side of the reinforcement shell, which the entrance penetrates and through which the first flight of the staircase now in question runs, does not form the double arcade of the three other sides (Figs. 32, 33, 35). To the south it includes a walled-up arch (Fig. 35) identical in elevation to the vaulted niches of the other sides. The remainder of the east side (to the north) is solid, except for the entrance portal.[88] The placement of this portal is determined by two considerations: the "pier" in the center of the wall, and the apparent attempt to keep the cavity away from the northeast corner, which may have been weakened by the original presence of Giotto's spiral stair.[89]

We have already observed two stages of construction at the Campanile bottom: Giotto's wall, and Andrea Pisano's reinforcement shell. Now there is evidence that the staircase, which runs south from the entrance antechamber through the central "pier" and behind the walled-up arch (Fig. 33), was not present in Andrea's original reinforcement shell, but rather that the stair was an afterthought cut through the partially completed fabric. The ceiling of the staircase does not run above the arch, but cuts diagonally across it. In other words, the ceiling at that point rests in the wall filling the arch (Fig. 33). Thus, the staircase cannot have existed or been planned without the filling wall. This wall, in turn, does not seem to have been present in the original state of Andrea's inner shell: it would have made little sense, particularly structurally, to have built an arch while planning to wall it up. In any event, lines in the intonaco of the staircase (Fig. 34, extreme right) correspond to the outline of the arch,[90] indicating that originally the arch was open — as a seventh niche. That the stair was added would explain several further peculiarities. While perfectly executed ashlar lines the interior of the flights above, the first flight of the stair is lined for the most part with intonaco (Figs. 34, 36). This makes sense if we assume the flight was cut into finished fabric, for to cut away more to add a layer of unbonded ashlar facing would further weaken the structure, while to add the ashlar inward would narrow the staircase considerably. A thin layer of intonaco was the obvious solution. Finally, the position of the entrance antechamber (Fig. 6) — part of the original state of Andrea's design and for manifest structural reasons best left alone — appears to have prevented the architect from beginning the stair far enough to the north to rise comfortably up over either the seventh niche or even the first chamber niche on turning the southeast corner. At that turn, in place of the broad landing forming

[88] There are also three small openings, ca. 15-30 cm deep, in the east wall; the two over the doorway conceivably might have been the seating for a wall tomb; the one alongside the door, about a meter long, has a mysterious passage going up behind the wall.

[89] See below, concerning this stair. For the awareness of the builders of the structural disadvantages of staircases, cf. Guasti, docs. 170, 352 ff.

[90] My thanks to Prof. Richard Pommer for this observation, as well as the details in n. 88 above.

every corner above (Fig. 36), the stairs continue around a bunched curve (Figs. X, 34). But even this device does not bring the stair high enough; for its support the architect finally had to resort to the bridging arch dropped into the east niche on the south side of the chamber (Figs. 25, 27, 32, 35).

Thus, the bottom of the Campanile appears to have involved three campaigns: Giotto's wall, Andrea's reinforcement layer — including a seventh niche — and finally his staircase cut up through the substantially completed ground story fabric. It would mean that originally Andrea Pisano — and his advisors — planned only the second, or upper stair. With the street portal giving only to the ground story chamber there would have been no direct means of circulation between street level and the upper parts of the tower, accessible only from the church via the bridge. This arrangement was far from singular; in fact it was characteristic, if not of church campanili, then of the private defense towers, to have a chamber at the bottom open to the street and commercially exploitable, but sealed by a vault from the levels above, which were entered only from the adjoining residence of the landlord.[91] A perfect example is the Bargello tower, its lower part originally a private, family keep (Fig. 247).[92]

The interior disposition of the Campanile, then, appears to have been a matter not immediately settled, but involving a conflict between private and public interests. At the time of Giotto's project, which seems to have included merely a spiral corner stair-case entered from within the Campanile, itself accessible from the street,[93] the issue had not yet emerged. It materialized with Andrea's elevated portal and its stair, which would have transformed all but the ground-floor chamber into the private reserve of the church. It must have been the reaction of the public — or a powerful public institution, such as the Arte della Lana — to that exclusive arrangement, which forced the difficult and structurally disadvantageous addition of the other stair. Thus, the conflict was solved by a compromise. The church was alloted one, possibly two isolated chambers and allowed private access; the remainder was given over to the public (Fig. X).[94]

Perhaps Andrea's final project even included, in its upper reaches, a zone of the vertical vastness — though not the expansive fenestration — of Talenti's spectacular ambient, the chamber that rises thirty meters through the Bifora zones (Figs. 88-90). In a later chapter we deal extensively with the style of that remarkable interior.[95] But its immediately apparent, visionary quality allows us, in the present discussion, to place it

[91] E. Rocchi, *Le fonti storiche dell architettura militare* (Rome, 1908), 175, noting that many had no street opening at all.

[92] Not all such vaults were sealed; an alternative was to leave an opening in the vault for communication (by wood or rope ladder), an easily defensible arrangement (Wood-Brown, 1907, 75, 184; Schiaparelli, 1908, 65 ff).

[93] See below.

[94] Concerning contemporary tensions between church and state see M. Becker, "Some Economic Implications of the Conflict Between Church and State in 'Trecento' Florence," *Medieval Studies*, XXIV (1959), 1 ff; idem, "Church and State in Florence on the Eve of the Renaissance (1343-1382)," *Speculum*, XXXVII (1962), 509 ff.

[95] See Ch. VI, 136 ff.

in the context of the Florentine development of public spaces that earlier saw the carving out of the Piazza Santa Maria Novella and the Piazza della Signoria, and later was to witness the immense swath cut around the new Cathedral. At the time of the Campanile, this process not only yielded the small, yet ornate Bigallo loggia across the way (1352-60) and the majestic ground floor of Or San Michele up the street (1336 ff), but witnessed the birth of the prodigious Loggia della Signoria, which, although not executed until 1374, was officially projected in 1356 (Figs. 1, 3, 258).[96] In fact, it was in all likelihood because of the priority of first the Campanile and then the Cathedral nave that the great Loggia was not put up until the latter was complete; but all three served, in different ways, the powerful Florentine thirst in the Trecento for vast communal interiors.

Returning to the foot of the Campanile, the final complexity that we must examine is the matter of the street portal. Giotto's original entrance to the Campanile was probably a nominal, inconspicuous opening at street level, interfering minimally with the incrustation system and similar to those seen in the upper stories of the Siena drawing (Figs. 139, 143), but missing from the rendering at the foot because intended for one of the secondary faces of the tower, that is, either the north or east.[97] It need not have led directly to Giotto's spiral stairs in the northeast pier, but, as already noted, could have given to the main space with an internal door opening to the stairwell, as in the Cathedral façade.[98] Considering Giotto's simple wall structure, it is most unlikely that he would have chosen for his portal the present eccentric location dictated to Andrea by structural complications. Giotto's portal must have been subsequently walled up and the revetment extended over it, leaving no visible trace. Andrea cut a new opening in Giotto's fabric for his entrance, facing the freshly exposed raw masonry and the contiguous reveal of the inner, reinforcement shell with a layer of ashlar. Attention to the walls of the small antechamber at the entrance discloses, indeed, a homogeneous revetment: the *pietraforte* courses manifest no breaks or irregularities and run smoothly along the walls from the exterior portal into the central chamber.

The location of the street portal is Andrea's; but is its decoration his as well? The answer is problematic. We can date neither the execution nor the emplacement of the hexagonal reliefs with accuracy. We know only that the reliefs of the west face were set in place together with the enframing incrustation and that the others were placed afterward.[99] This would mean that the west hexagons were executed and imbedded in Giotto's

[96] For the history of the Loggia, Frey, 1885, 15 ff; on communal places, Braunfels, 1953, *passim*. On the Bigallo, Saalman, 1969; concerning its place in this development, cf. my brief remarks in a forthcoming review of Saalman's book in the *Art Bulletin*. For Or San Michele, see below, 76 ff.

[97] Suggested by Gioseffi, 1963, 77.

[98] As noted above (p. 25) the presence of the spiral stair is indicated by a tiny lancet window alongside the buttress on the north face (Figs. II, 8). Andrea's stair, entered almost from the portal itself, is prefigured in the stairs in the Siena Cathedral façade, entered at the portal wall.

[99] Becherucci, 1965, 261.

time, but the others (excepting, of course, Luca della Robbia's five early Quattrocento reliefs on the north side) in all probability under Andrea, from whose hand or workshop they all derive.[100] If Andrea himself was the author of those to the east — and perhaps even had first conceived the notion to extend Giotto's program beyond the west face — would he also have designed and been permitted to construct a portal superstructure that cut brutally into the zone of the hexagons (Figs. II, 60, 61), displacing two of his own reliefs (to the shadowy north side, originally devoid of sculpture in the lower relief zone)? Would Andrea not rather have planned a smaller, more genial door similar to Giotto's, leaving the rude, extant superstructure to a later, less respectful architect? On the other hand, Andrea held office for as long as six to seven years; in that time the portal, originally merely an access to a dim chamber, became an entrance by which the public could move from the newly (1339) systematized and repaved piazza to impressive, even grand, ambients planned (and eventually realized) above. There is no reason why Andrea could not have executed and placed the hexagons early, then later, with the new stair, have decided to give the portal a greater monumentality, even if it entailed the displacement of two of the hexagonal reliefs.

The fabric of the street portal itself seems to indicate a complicated history. We have already observed that the paten-like tympanum reflects the presence of Andrea (Fig. 65). The frame of the tympanum and the inner frame of the doorway (Figs. 61, 62) can also easily be linked to Andrea; one need only compare the similar forms of the elevated portal (Fig. 67).[101] On the other hand, the ponderous superstructure of double-storied posts, the three-sided octagonal colonnettes and archivolts, the gable and the foliate detail point rather to Talenti's workshop. The top-heavy elevation reflects his Duomo portal adjacent to the Campanile (Fig. 249). The rich, blossomy capitals[102] bring to mind the Talentian portal (dei Cornacchini) on the north side aisle (Figs. 248, 251). Octagonal jamb elements typify Talenti's windows (Figs. 82, 250). The cornice of the gable (Fig. 63) is to be found at random in his work, especially in the flanks of the Duomo, commencing with the first set of profiles above Arnolfo's socle (Fig. 68). Even the prickly crockets, with their deep grooving and saw-toothed lower leaf edge, fall within Talenti's idiom (although his crockets are usually more frontal).[103]

While the Talentian adaptation of the superstructure to Andrea's pre-existing fabric was quite smooth, it is betrayed at several points. The most obvious discontinuity is the

---

[100] Paatz, III, 387 ff.

[101] But as the elevated portal itself is in many respects adapted to the essentially Giottesque character of the surrounding incrustation, its similarity to the street portal's inner detail is somewhat inconclusive. Conceivably parts of it, in particular the cornice and frame, could be re-used from Giotto's lost portal.

[102] Only the capital to the left is original (Figs. 61, 62, 124): the right one (Fig. 64) is a very good reconstruction; cf. the 19th-century state of the left original in Fig. 124.

[103] The idea of paneled posts derives from the same source as Andrea's elevated portal: Arnolfo's facade (Fig. 239).

manner in which the capitals, especially the one to the right, cut Andrea's door frame (Figs. 62, 64). The awkward joint above, where the section of cornice belonging to the superstructure meets that of the inner portal, is also revealing. The shape of the cornice seems to be Andrea's; the section at the lintel itself would be his. Talenti would have extended the cornice around his superstructure in a manner characteristic of his Cathedral articulation, for example, at the tracery level of the side-aisle windows. In the homogeneous decoration of the Cathedral flanks such corners and angles achieve great smoothness (Fig. 250),[104] in contrast with the somewhat imperfect adaptation to pre-existing fabric at the Campanile portal. It is not only the joint that suggests the complex history, but also the manner in which the delicate, harmonious profiles of the straight cornice become dissonant and aggressive in their relationships when folded around the superstructure.

A hypothetical history for the portal can now be posed. To maintain the integrity of Giotto's incrustation, Andrea first constructed a small, modest doorway at the point dictated by structural exigencies. With the new stair it was decided to enrich the portal. This second version may have been set somewhat lower than at present, the Talentian shop later raising it above new steps and bases. If so, originally it need not have displaced the overlying hexagons but, in a configuration akin to the elevated portal, instead might have pushed up between them (though somewhat off center), cutting away only the lower parts of the framing panels. Later the portal was adjudged insufficiently monumental, especially as it was located opposite Talenti's huge new Cathedral side entrance, ca. 1360 (Fig. 5). Thus the posts and superstructure were added in a third campaign, and the two reliefs, were they still in place, transferred to the north side.[105]

Other hypotheses are of course possible. The knowledge of Andrea's architectural range of possibilities is not secure; many of Talenti's ideas derive from the goldsmith. Conceivably, the entire portal could be Andrea's. Theoretically, although even less likely, it could also be entirely by Talenti, who might have appropriated Andrea's goldsmith forms for the tympanum, adapted ideas from the elevated portal, etc. Nevertheless, the more complex version of the story presented above seems, at least at this time, the best.[106]

* * *

[104] Kiesow's observations to the contrary (1961, 14) are untenable.

[105] The five missing hexagons on the north face were not sculpted until the 15th century (1437-39; Paatz, III, 389), in all likelihood because of the dark, cluttered (Doc. 220) location; only after the completion of the Cupola and the rest of the Campanile sculpture did the systematic process reach this least prominent tract of the tower.

[106] The history of the portal seems to have been fraught with complexities. In 1431 it was decided to supply a capital still missing ("capitellum de novo ubi non est") and to place three figures from the Opera on top of the portal (Doc. 224). On the basis of the missing capital, Paatz (III, 552 f n. 446) suggests the erection of the portal superstructure at this late date together with the removal of the two reliefs, following the argument of J. Länyi ("Andrea Pisano," in Thieme-Becker, *Künstlerlexikon*, XXVII [1933], 97),

Despite the opinion of the Opera, Andrea Pisano as *capomaestro* of the Campanile manifest himself as a consummate architect. The problems of structure, circulation, lighting, functional space, and above all, decoration were treated with great intelligence, imagination, and skill. Yet, other than the Campanile, no building — Vasari's imaginings aside — has been connected with him. Like the phenomenon of Brunelleschi, who also was first goldsmith and bronze sculptor, Andrea appears as architect with little warning. Both men had about the same number of years to quietly develop grandiose ideas, which they carried out with a goldsmith's precision and a sculptor's plasticity. In two decades, Brunelleschi changed the face of architecture for all time. Might not Andrea's activity as architect extend beyond the magnificent section of the Campanile?[107]

If his position as *capomaestro* was at all similar to Giotto's, and his building skills more professional, one would expect to find Andrea's traces in the communal architecture of the years 1337-43. These were years of continuing activity at the Bargello. At that ambitious building quite possibly the civic arms over the north portal to the court owes its design to Andrea; in its deeply sculptural brilliance and precision and its affinity with the "fibula" keystone in the Campanile it seems literally — and uniquely — stamped with his style (Figs. 58, 189).[108] But however fascinating one finds this superb ornamental

who gives a late date to the entire portal, including the opening; Paatz objects (III, 483 n. 201a) that the opening, at least, being at the foot of Giotto's [sic] stair, must be original. We have seen, contrary to both, that the stair, opening, and probably the inner parts of the portal, are Andrea's, the superstructure Talentian. On Mar. 22, 1491, we are informed of a dissatisfaction with the "stipidi" of the portal; presumably it was intended to replace Gothic panels with classicist pilasters. Fortunately the matter was dropped. Nardini, who published a summary rather than the text of the document (Doc. 225) seems to have misinterpreted it, reading a completion of the portal; but the 1431 document makes it clear that the portal was then completed, only needing the one capital (the twin form makes it impossible to determine which) in order to carry the three figures. G. Brunetti (denying Vasari [Doc. XIII]) assigns the lateral figures to the early Nanni di Bartolo ("I Profeti sulla porta del campanile di Santa Maria del Fiore," *Festschrift Ulrich Middeldorf* [Berlin, 1968], 106 ff).

[107] Falk (1940, 17 f) refutes Vasari's attributions (including the Castello in Scarperia, the Arsenal in Venice, the Florentine wall from the Porta San Gallo to the Porta al Prato, the Pal. Vecchio fortifications of the Duke of Athens [which she allows to remain a possibility], and the Pistoia Baptistery).

[108] This is particularly evident in a comparison with the arms over the opposite entrance to the court, those in the court, and those at the Pal. Vecchio (Fig. 204); the main portal to the north on the Pal. Vecchio received its decoration in 1351 (Frey, 1885, doc. 106). The Bargello carving would not have been a unique instance of Andrea's sideline pursuits; his continuing activity as metal worker is recorded in a payment for an iron stamp for marking imported cloth made for the Arte dei Baldrigai (cutters of cloth), a subsidiary, like his own Orefici, of the Arte della Seta (Por Santa Maria; Vasari-Frey, I, 379 Reg. 2; Falk, 1940, 11). To Andrea's shop can also be attributed the monument of Giovanni Cacciano (d. 1338) in the cloister of S. Spirito (Fig. 190); cf. M. H. Longhurst, *Notes on Italian Monuments of the 12th to 16th Centuries*, ed. I. Lowe (London, 1962), Reg. G. 14, but ill. G. 15; W. R. Valentiner, "Giovanni Balducci a Firenze e una scultura de Maso," *L'Arte*, XXXVIII [1935], attributes it to a follower of Giovanni Balduccio. The upper cornice band of the Baptistery attic (Fig. 163), added in 1339 (Paatz, II, 175, 225

carving it is at the great communal work initiated during Andrea's Florentine years — Or San Michele — that our major interest lies.

The old grain hall being a disgrace to the community, the commune decided in 1336 to rebuild it in monumental form; a special building committee was appointed. By July 29, 1337, things were well enough in order to celebrate the laying of the cornerstone for a building to consist of three vaulted stories.[109] No mention of an architect is made until March 27, 1338, when the Arte della Seta, now given control of the fabric, decided to appoint a treasurer, two *Operai*, and a *capomaestro*.[110] It is not known whether it was to be a new *capomaestro* or merely the formal acceptance by the guild of a man originally appointed by the commune. In 1339, with the piers already partly standing, it was decided that each guild was to place a monumental figure of its patron saint in a pier niche. In 1342 the fabric was provided with additional income. But in the late 1340s progress seems to have slowed — most certainly with the plague — for in 1350 it was noted that the piers of the ground-floor hall had been standing frescoed and ready for vaulting for some time; even the scaffolding was up, awaiting building funds. By 1357, the ground story (Figs. 191, 192) was substantially complete.[111]

The earliest stages of planning fall in the period when Giotto was still alive. But according to Villani he would have been in Milan during much of late 1336 and hardly can have been deeply involved in the initial arrangements. If he submitted a design, it seems to have had little consequence. Andrea, on the other hand, could have taken high office immediately after Giotto's death, a full half year before the laying of the cornerstone. He could have guided construction until 1343, giving the great hall at street level its definition, even if not its completion.[112]

At Or San Michele the piers of the ground floor form a double system: a broad, massive outer arcade (originally open), to which are attached highly articulate half and quarter piers corresponding to the full, freestanding shafts in the center of the room (Figs. 191, 192). The six bays of vaulting seem to rest entirely on the inner system, to which, in effect, the outer arcade forms a buttressing shell, while, at the same time, supporting the huge wall above. Though the two systems are kept neatly distinct, they are bound by a common base, shaft ring, and abacus. Furthermore, the full niches on the exterior are reflected inside by shallow, frescoed versions.[113]

This high tectonic complexity would have been well within Andrea's power, to judge from the Campanile. Though he had no chance there to form such elaborate piers,

n. 24), was at least influenced by Andrea Pisano (the Baptistery had its own *capomaestro*; Doc. 158).

[109] Paatz, IV, 482 f.

[110] U. Dorini, *Statuti dell'Arte di Por Santa Maria* (Florence, 1934), 141 f n. 3.

[111] Paatz, IV, 483.

[112] Paatz, seemingly unaware of Andrea's architectural abilities and style, and overlooking his important position in Florence during the critical years for Or San Michele, places him last and least on a list of possible candidates (IV, 511 f n. 24).

[113] Cf. White's description (1966, 173).

the double arcade of the ground-story chamber (Figs. 25, 26), serving both structural and spatial purposes, is not so unlike the Or San Michele system. Even the exotic marbles of Andrea's Campanile exterior are profoundly and intricately architectonic in conception (Fig. 19). Moreover, certain details of the two buildings are highly analogous. The octagonal colonnettes in the piers of Or San Michele and the Campanile interior were simultaneously the first of their kind in Florence: free, five-sided shafts. The base profiles of Or San Michele have a swelling plasticity and spring uniquely like those in the second-story chamber of the Campanile (Figs. 52, 53, 193, 195). Likewise, the capitals in that chamber — related in shape to details in the architectural settings of the bronze door — seem but schematic, less delicately executed versions of the magnificent capitals in Or San Michele (Figs. 54-57, 197), the leaves of which recall Andrea's second cornice on the Campanile exterior (Figs. 16-18). Andrea's ground floor Campanile capitals are related to those more expressive forms on the portal to the stair in Or San Michele (Figs. 39-42, 201). The beveling and rounding of edges is typical of both fabrics. If one need find a single detail in Or San Michele that suggests the presence of Andrea it is the base of the colonnette at each exterior corner, decorated with the stalks of the grain that the structure was designed to store and protect — if not to sanctify (Fig. 200).

Not surprisingly, the *capomaestro* was involved with the sculptural embellishment of the grain hall. It is not known whether Andrea executed the original statues of patron saints for the Arte della Seta (not only sponsor of Or San Michele but Andrea's own gold-smith's guild) and the Arte della Lana (with which he would have had excellent connections as *capomaestro* at the Campanile).[114] However, the niche frames for these sculptures (Figs. 202, 203)[115] exhibit, in their polished elegance and precision of design and detail, not only stylistic continuity with the building itself, but unequivocal affinity with the Andrea we have come to know. The goldsmith is unmistakably present in the finely dentilated outer frame;[116] in the exquisitely refined intarsia patterns of the interior, and their framework; and, above all, in the crockets and finials of the pinnacles and gable, which in their metallic shapes form marble cognates of the analogous details in the stage sets at the Baptistery door (Figs. 182, 188). Even the vaulting seems to develop the style seen at the Campanile, especially in the niches.

Thus, the bell tower of Andrea and the grain hall manifest a similar structural intricacy and display closely related forms and details. If the ground-floor system of Or San Michele has affinities with the interiors of Francesco Talenti, to whom it often

---

[114] Both Trecento figures were replaced in the Renaissance; the original St. Stephen of the Lana appears lost, but the St. John the Evangelist of the Seta seems to have ended up in the Museum of the Ospedale degli Innocenti (Paatz, IV, 504, 552 f n. 177 f; R. Krautheimer and T. Krautheimer-Hess, *Lorenzo Ghiberti* [Princeton, 1956],

94 f n. 13; see Ch. IV below on Andrea Pisano's part in the conception of the two works).

[115] Documented 1339/40 (Paatz, IV, 493 f, 522 f n. 88, 528 f n. 97).

[116] Compare the hexagonal niches on the interior (Figs. 192, 197).

has been ascribed,[117] it is, I think, because he may have learned much from the building. Indeed, after Andrea's departure, he even may have run the Or San Michele workshop, giving, perhaps, certain of the forms slight modifications.[118] But the design and spirit of the ground story certainly have little to do with the severely intellectual, hyperplastic, and often ambiguously slick style of Talenti. The contrast could not be greater than between the piers of Or San Michele, which would be Andrea's fullest such conception, and Talenti's Cathedral piers, derived from the former but drained of their plastic vitality and crystalline architectonic form.

In Andrea's pier the socle is cleanly separated from the base, and the base from the shaft, in which the cross-shaped main mass is kept distinct from the octagonal responds (Figs. 192, 193).[119] These distinctions — which recall the structural clarity of Andrea's Campanile elevation — are blurred in Talenti's pier, lost in a sequence of ambiguous relationships between succeeding shapes (Figs. 194, 244, 252). Here one cannot determine which set of profiles forms the base, nor if the grooved octagonal corners are meant as independent colonnettes or as cartilaginous extensions of the core. One reads the Cathedral pier as a congealed, homogeneous mass bound by heavy, cast-iron-like shaft rings and effusive foliate bands (the capitals) — as bundle piers rather than the compound piers of Or San Michele.[120] The profound antithesis extends to the very tactile qualities of the stones. As with all works of Andrea — who, in this sense, continues his Pisan predecessors' and Giotto's classic manner of, as it were, living masonry — one wants to touch the piers of Or San Michele and sense directly the fine, healthy plasticity of their shapes (Figs. 195, 196). One shrinks instead from the idea of touching Talenti's "cast-iron" fabric — the works of a new aesthetic.[121].

Talenti's curious, but, as we shall see, quite momentous, style goes back to his earliest known work, the Bifora section of the Campanile, begun as early as 1343, too closely following the Or San Michele design — to say nothing of the continuing execution —

---

[117] *Ibid.*

[118] On the exterior, a shift in style away from the massive, beautifully textured arches and the smooth plasticity of the capital-level stringcourse is to be noted in the harshness of the cornice of the ground floor (Fig. 199) and in the planar, artful window detail above, comparable to Talenti's style in the upper Campanile; the window-arch decoration rather resembles the interior face of the Trifora arch (Figs. 112, 198). See Ch. VI. On the interior, the second-story piers are a radical simplification of the ground-floor models (Fig. 243); the bundled springing of the ribs over a blocky capital is notably close to the great hall of the Bargello, vaulted 1340-46 by Neri di Fioravanti, whose name comes up often, by no ac-

cident, in connection with Or San Michele in the 1350s and afterward (Paatz, IV, 511 n. 24), and who, as on the Campanile Trifora, could have subcontracted construction from Talenti — or whoever was the architect — though here with a freer hand in the detail (cf. Ch. V, 111 ff).

[119] The elevation of the arms of the cross-shaped core unmistakably derives from Arnolfo's buttresses on the side aisle of the Cathedral, including the high socle, ponderous base, shaft ring, and blind niche (Figs. 164, 192, 193).

[120] These forms are defined in Ch. II n. 57.

[121] There is even something very much resembling the shapes of bones in Talenti's cathedral profiles. One is, of course, tempted to mention the Black Death in this connection (See Ch. VI, 139 f, 149 f).

for the grain hall to represent an earlier stage of his personal development. The lack of other promising candidates and, more importantly, the profound coherence between the known work of Andrea Pisano and Or San Michele make the early building very likely his.

Andrea's architectural style displayed at the Campanile and Or San Michele is so mature and attractive that a search outside Florence — where, after all, he spent less than a decade and a half — might yield at least traces of his activity as architect. Before he appeared in Florence, he worked, we have observed, in the Pisan-Sienese ambient; in his last years he was, for a brief time, *capomaestro* of Orvieto Duomo. If anywhere, these should be the *loci* of his building efforts.

One building stands apart from the rather uninspired architecture of Pisa following the passing of Giovanni Pisano: the oratory of Santa Maria della Spina. In spite of the merciless restoration, particularly on the exterior, of the late Ottocento when the dilapidated fabric (Fig. 207) was lifted up from the Arno bank to modern street level, there can still be perceived the lines of the original structural and stylistic discontinuities resulting from a number of building campaigns.[122] The awkward fill of the arcade (Figs. 207, 209), for example, indicates that the building was, in an earlier state, largely an open loggia,[123] but probably closed when the elaborate door to the choir was walled up and the columnar, blind arcade of its rear wall eliminated (Figs. 208, 209, 213, 215).[124] Similarly, the decorative superstructures are patent superimpositions. Even the row of figures by followers of Giovanni Pisano was clearly meant for a deeper ledge (Fig. 209). It was probably the direct exposure of the building to the wrath of the Arno that largely occasioned the restoration and reforming of the fabric. The oratory, rebuilt following 1323 (then, for reasons of scale and probably style), seems to have been the victim of the great flood of 1333, for the exterior clearly exhibits the mid-Trecento Tuscan manner of Talenti's generation in the compounded, hot richness of its interpenetrating formal ambiguities and its pictorially conceived detail.[125]

---

[122] Rohault de Fleury (1866, 100 f) appears to have been the first, and very nearly the only critic to have noted that the building has suffered almost too many changes and additions to reconstruct the original form, which he felt was maintained (as of 1866) on the side facing the river. L. Tanfani's monograph (*Della chiesa di S. Maria del Pontenovo, detta della Spina* [Pisa, 1871], 83 ff) notes the numerous restorations of the building, including even a 15th-century reconstruction of foundations, but ventures nothing about changes in form. The sacristy off the choir toward the river that still existed in Tanfani's day (*ibid.*, 70, engraving on 67) appears to have been eliminated in the restoration that followed.

[123] White, 1966, 174.

[124] The choir wall exterior preserves the bases for the columnar mullions of the tracery (presumably blind) of the original project.

[125] Following the documents published by Tanfani (1871), in 1323 a council of eight Pisan citizens, including the *capomaestro* of the duomo and Nocco del Abaco, a prominent mathematician-engineer, receive permission from the commune to begin an enlargement of the oratory by extending the foundations out over the bank and into the Arno to a specified dimension (*ibid.*, doc. I); but construction cannot have begun before 1325, when the Archbishop grants permission to enlarge the oratory itself — evidently

But the oratory of the 1320s appears not to have been entirely lost. Notable components of the original Trecento building, essentially at the choir, seem to be preserved. In contrast to the exterior, they exhibit a cool spatial grace and a refined, yet strongly plastic, delicacy of detail that not only gives the early date but suggests a connection with the early Andrea Pisano — already known in the history of the Spina through its famous interior sculpture of his later years.[126]

The three bays of the choir appear to have retained their original vaulting and support system (Figs. 213, 214). The piers of the arcade separating choir from nave and the matching pilasters on the rear choir wall exhibit bases and capitals (Figs. 216, 217) conceived and cut with a highly expressive, yet refined plasticity, and point, singularly, to what would be Andrea's later work in Florence: details such as the Or San Michele base, his first exterior cornice of the Campanile (Fig. 13), and the ledge in the second chamber (Figs. 52, 53). The Gothicizing bases of the Spina would form a link between the much richer Sienese prototypes of Giovanni Pisano (Fig. 233) and Andrea's Florentine bases, which adapt to the Florentine classicizing tradition but retain much of the Sienese spring. The unique vaulting at the Spina (Fig. 214), in which the broad flatness of the dividing arches contrasts with the slender, rounded delicacy of the ribs, which run in semicircular curves across the billowing vaults and come to rest on the most refined conical imposts, suggests that fusion of the imaginative processes of goldsmith and architect that we have come to recognize in the work of Andrea.

Andrea's traces at the Spina appear to extend beyond the choir articulation — and with it the arcade on the river side of the nave with its similar capitals (Figs. 213, 216)[127] —

legally distinct from building the foundation platform alongside the primitive building (*ibid.*, doc. II); in 1331 the project of 1323/25 was not yet complete, for when the *Operai* receive permission to sell an inconveniently located property (vineyards at the farthest reaches of Pisan territory), the proceeds are to go into charity and the fabric (*ibid.*, doc. V).

The slow pace of construction may have been due to the sharing of Pisan financial capacities in the 1320s and early 1330s, with the rebuilding of the dilapidated drainage channels — storm sewers — around 1327 (*ibid.*, 81 f) and the construction of similar oratories (now destroyed) at the feet of two of the other bridges — S. Maria del Pontevecchio, 1322 ff (*ibid.*, 21), S. Maria del Ponte-novo della Degazia del Mare, 1332 ff (*ibid.*, 23). The year 1333 must have been a turning point for the Spina: it brought not only the great flood, and doubtlessly severe damage to whatever had been completed, but the gift of a fragment of the Crown of Thorns, from which the oratory has taken its popular name (*ibid.*, 79 f); now it became imperative to transform the fabric resplendently and at the same time financially possible to do so because of the offerings that any institution sheltering such a relic receives (cf. *ibid.*, 71 ff, for evidence of such offerings). Thus the final state of the building — White calls it a "jewelled casket" (1966, 174) — reflects not only the mid-Trecento Tuscan manner, but a tradition of reliquary architecture reaching in the Gothic period back to the Ste. Chapelle, and ultimately far beyond (Branner, 1965, 57).

[126] Becherucci (1965, 227 ff) argues strongly for a post-Campanile, pre-Orvieto period (1343-47) in Pisa for Andrea, when he would have carved at least the powerful Madonna del Latte for the Spina (a work emphatically his).

[127] The capitals of the nave arcade on the land side exhibit, despite an intended classical refinement, rather crude proportions and slippery,

to the walled-up choir portal (Fig. 210). Its base profiles, which continue around from the choir wall (Figs. 208, 209), are nearly identical in their depressed form to the choir piers. Moreover, they end abruptly at the left edge of the portal, where heavier and entirely upright bases begin in the columns articulating the nave-wall arcade and continue around the façade (Figs. 209, 211) — clearly part of the post-flood fabric. But it is the jambs of the choir portal that capture our attention; in contrast to the clumsy richness of the side portal to the nave (Fig. 212) and the impotent carving at the façade portals, here (even after the Ottocento restoration) is evident the goldsmith's touch in the taut shapes and proportions, in the jewel-like presentation of sharply conceived, highly tactile motifs, and even in the fiery delicacy of the frame and polychrome ground. Striking parallels to these jambs exist in Andrea's later work: the intarsia in the two niches at Or San Michele represent the same imagination in a completely planar mode; and conversely, related forms assume an even bolder plasticity in the great travertine cornice at Orvieto (see below). Moreover, the lozenge patterns of the Campanile reliefs and the Or San Michele intarsia would find at the Spina portal an intermediate link with their Pisan Romanesque prototypes.[128]

Andrea's early activity in Pisa is unrecorded but strongly suggested in this small, but highly personal work.[129] His architectural opportunities as the documented *capomaestro*

impotent movements characteristic of the non-Andrean detail at the Spina. It should be noted that, in contrast to the bold, in part Gothicizing profiles of Andrea, the other moldings and cornices at the Spina, particularly on the exterior (Figs. 207-209) issue directly from the Pisan Romanesque; in their dense compounding of leaf and dentil friezes the Spina details would fit perfectly into, for example, the cornice of the nave arcade at the duomo, the side-aisle cornice on the exterior (Fig. 302), or, for that matter, into Giovanni Pisano's pulpit. If the *capomaestro* of the duomo was ever connected with the Spina, as Falk suggests (see below), it would have been with these later phases.

[128] The lintel is equally worthy of note. Its magnificent rinceaux descend from a long and distinguished Pisan line of foliated lintels; the energy of its carving, and such details as the emerging horse put it in the tradition of the Pisani; cf. the similar horse on one of the two great foliated columns of the Siena facade. Obviously, this would bear significantly on the question of Andrea's beginnings were the Spina lintel to prove his.

[129] According to Ghiberti, Andrea was responsible for "moltissime cose" at the Spina ("Santa Maria a ponte"; ed. von Schlosser, 1912, I, 43). Vasari (I, 483) writes that it was by the sculpture of his youth at the Spina that Andrea Pisano achieved much of the fame that gave him the great commissions at the Cathedral group in Florence ("Perchè, conosciuto l'ingegno e la buona pratica e destrazza sua, fu nella patria [Pisa] aiutato da molti; e datogli a fare, essendo ancora giovane, a Santa Maria a Ponte alcune figurine di marmo, che gli recarono così buon nome, che fu ricerco con instanza grandissima di venire a lavorare a Firenze per l'Opera di Santa Maria del Fiore"). Falk (1940, 20 f) objects to any architectural connection of the building with Andrea on three grounds: first, that Andrea does not appear in the 1323 document (see n. 125 above) which she completely misinterprets as concerning "some models" ("einige Modelle") [of the building] "with express mention of the artist who made them" — when, in fact, the upshot of the document is the determination of dimensions of the new foundation-platform; secondly, she notes that Andrea was already working on the Baptistery door in 1331, when, according to her account of Tanfani (1871, doc. II), the building was only in its beginnings — although, in fact, the docu-

of the epochal — but nearly complete — cathedral fabric at Orvieto from May 24, 1347 into 1348 and possibly 1349 (when, perhaps already deceased, he was succeeded by his son Nino)[130] appear to have been anticlimatic after the major Florentine projects of his prime.

On June 10, 1347, several weeks after he is first mentioned in connection with the fabric, several lengths of a new cornice are commissioned, "a flore de tiburtino."[131] On July 1, 1347 more lengths of the travertine floral motif are contracted, now supplemented by two further components, one "a foglia," a leafwork frieze, and the other "ad becchytellum,"[132] a console frieze later called more precisely "ad beccatellum et rosas."[133] These three forms — commissioned in great quantities in succeeding months[134] — clearly are the components of the travertine cornice that (as noted by Fumi)[135] tops the aisle walls of the Orvieto nave and runs on around the transepts (Fig. 218). A glance at its extreme plasticity, its sharply cut, rhythmically spaced forms, and particularly the singular central frieze ("a flores") of metallically carved rosettes set like jewels in deep quatrefoil frames, indicates Andrea Pisano — the eminent architect for whom, sadly, there was little left at Orvieto to design — as its certain author.[136]

Andrea's other minor contribution to the cathedral at Orvieto seems to have been connected with his continuing activity as marble sculptor. A Madonna flanked by two angels, in the Orvieto Cathedral Museum, probably meant for a portal tympanum, has been rather convincingly attributed to him.[137] All of the Orvieto portals carry sculptural groups except two: the Porta del Vescovado on the south flank and the first portal from the façade on the north, the Porta di Canonica (Fig. 219). Although it has been suggested that the former was the site for Andrea Pisano's *Maestà*, the Porta di Canonica, before

ment only indicates that the 1323/25 project was not complete; finally, Falk objects that the exterior sculpture is largely Giovanni Pisano school — a fact which, considering the succession of three versions of the Spina in the years during which the sculpture could have been executed (the primitive oratory, the 1323/25 project, and the post-1333 fabric), need not have prevented Andrea's presence at some point. There is no reason why the young, but manifestly gifted artist could not have been given the responsibility for the architecturally unambitious project in 1325; beginning at the choir, even with limited funds, the fabric I have connected with him could easily have been executed within an extremely short period, a year or two, leaving plenty of time for him to get to Florence and even Venice in the interim. Certainly there is no reason to suppose that Lupo, *capomaestro* of the cathedral, who was included in the council of 1323, built the

Spina — although he might, as an active sculptor (Tanfani, 1871, 68), have participated at some point in its decoration.

[130] Fumi, 1891, 60 ff, doc. CLI ff. Andrea is last mentioned in Orvieto (or anywhere) Apr. 26, 1348 (cf. Falk, 1940, 12; but see also Becherucci's speculations about his supposed burial in Florence Cathedral [1965, 244 ff], and below, Ch. VI n. 4).

[131] Fumi, 1891, 60, doc. CLII.

[132] *Ibid.*, 60, doc. CLIV.

[133] *Ibid.*, 61, docs. CLXI, CLXII.

[134] *Ibid.*

[135] *Ibid.*, 30.

[136] See Fumi, 1891, pl. I following p. 250, for an elevation and section of the cornice.

[137] Länyi, "L'ultima opera," 1933, 204 ff; P. Cellini, "Appunti orvietani per Andrea e Niccolo Pisano," *Rivista d'Arte*, XV (1933), 1 ff; Becherucci, 1965, 277 ff.

1412 when its walled-up tympanum was given a painted *Maestà*, could equally have served,[138] a possibility that stylistic considerations would seem to favor.

The Porta di Canonica clearly was broken into the already incrusted late thirteenth-century wall and therefore theoretically could be contemporary with Andrea's sculpted group. Its form falls out of the local tradition, differing from the primitive, roughly textured, pre-Sienese Porta del Vescovado; from the flat-framed, richly jambed Sienese sophistication of the façade portals (Fig. 276); and from the Porta del Corporale (or "di Postierla"), which mixes Sienese and strictly native tradition. The Porta di Canonica

[138] There is an unresolved controversy over the name and Trecento decoration of this portal and the second one on the north flank, the Porta del Corporale (being adjacent the Cappella del Corporale). Documents of 1338 and 1360 (Fumi, 1891, 447) refer to a *Maestà* in the "porte Pusterle"; according to a 17th-century source the Porta "Pustierlese" was the one next to the Capella Corporale, the name arising — as often was the case — for the quarter to which the portal gave; thus the Porta del Corporale would be in modern Italian the "Porta di Postierla", and originally would have held a sculpted *Maestà*, lost in the 16th century, and replaced in the 1890s by the Trecento seated Christ and flanking angels exhumed from the storehouse and placed over the completely new lintel, cornice, and bases (*Ibid.* 439 ff). In the portal on the south flank — which Fumi informally calls, for want of a proper title, the "Porta del Vescovado," as it faces the Papal Palace — the tympanum held an annunciation relief up to the 17th century; afterward the sculpture was removed and at some point before 1890 the tympanum was given "modern" painted decoration; in 1890 the pair of twisted columns that had been sitting awkwardly in the tympanum all along, and which may have come from the de Braye monument in S. Domenico, were removed to the Opera del Duomo and the tympanum was opened and given a translucent alabaster wall like the façade portals (*ibid.*, 443). Against this account of Fumi — which appears reasonable to me — Cellini (1933) insists on a different story: he assumes, without any documentation, that the Porta di Postierla is identical not to the Porta del Corporale, where he imagines the group of Christ and Angels now there belonged originally, but to the "Porta del Vescovado," which he argues would be the original site of Andrea Pisano's *Maestà*, that is, the *Maestà* mentioned in the "porte Pusterle." It is obvious that Cellini's theory fails to take into account at least three facts: first, that the *Maestà* documented in the "porte Pusterle" was already there in 1338, a decade before Andrea carved his group; secondly, the 17th-century identification of the Porta "Pustierlese" with the Porta del Corporale — which Fumi, a native antiquarian who knew the local traditions, the history of the building, and the archives thoroughly, accepted (Fumi's nomenclature is accepted by R. Bonelli, *Il Duomo di Orvieto e l'architettura italiana del duecento trecento* [Città di Castello, 1952], 83 f; I fail to comprehend why the guide of the Touring Club Italiano [*Umbria* (Milan, 1950), 325] accepts Cellini's nomenclature); thirdly, the Annunciation relief that was in the "Porta del Vescovado" tympanum in the 17th-century. It would seem that Fumi's version is by far the more tenable, which would mean that in Andrea Pisano's time the Porta del Corporale — or di Postierla — held a lost *Maestà*, and that the "Porta del Vescovado" may have already included the lost Annunciation relief; even were it empty, there is no necessity that the latter was designated for Andrea Pisano's group. Similarly, Cellini's insistence (1933, 10) that even prior to the frescoing of 1412 (Fumi, 1891, 443) the tympanum of the Porta di Canonica never contained sculptural decoration, is equally unfounded; without the filling layer of masonry there would have been ample space for Andrea's small figures (the Madonna is 85 cm high, and the headless angels originally probably ca. 60 cm [Länyi, "L'ultima opera," 1933, 204]).

instead suggests the presence of Andrea Pisano.[139] The door frame, tympanum, outer jamb, and inner archivolts all are formed of a tondino-cavetto-tondino profile highly reminiscent of Andrea's frames, for example, at the Baptistery door (Figs. 178-180). The shape is not found elsewhere in Orvieto in this context. The base profiles of the Orvietan portal are reminiscent of the Campanile portals, as are the folded bracket leaves, a rarely encountered motif. Even in the capitals and cornice, clearly deriving ultimately from the portals of Siena Baptistery (Fig. 222), the hand of Andrea is evidenced, in the adaptation of the spiky Sienese roughness to his smoother, more delicate and rounded style. The cornice — comparable, to a degree, with the manner of his first Campanile cornice (Fig. 13) — thus achieves compatibility with the rolling profiles of the portal frames and the archivolts.

The presence of Andrea becomes even clearer when we allow for exigencies of execution and demands of local tradition. The cutting of unfamiliar forms by indigenous craftsmen resulted in the leaves, for example, becoming drier and the moldings and rosettes somewhat brittle. Conversely, as Andrea exploited the textural richness of native travertine in the side-aisle cornice, here he acknowledged the Orvietan portal formula not only by including the twisted jamb column (similar to those of the Porta del Corporale) but also in the disposition of the outer archivolts and the tympanum, in their original state possibly framing a window as in the other entrances.

No major work, the Porta di Canonica seems to have been Andrea's frame for his last known sculpture. Thus, from the beginning to the end and however profoundly architectonic the project, Andrea Pisano, the goldsmith who became an architect, was always concerned about Andrea the sculptor.

---

[139] Bonelli dates the portal generically in the 1340s (1952, 83 f).

Chapter IV

The Sculptural Program

Comment on some aspect of the sculptural program that decorates the Campanile fabric of Giotto and Andrea Pisano (Fig. 126) has been prominent among the leitmotifs of art-historical literature since the days of Pucci and Ghiberti. Involving the greatest Trecento painter and the most important Italian school of medieval sculpture, depicting central themes of the encyclopedic art of the Gothic Age, and forming the ornament of a pre-eminent landmark at the center of Florence, the Campanile statuary has generated an endless bibliography. Indeed, one of the themes that the wise historian might best avoid is the attribution of the numerous Campanile reliefs and standing figures to a varying group of sculptors.[1] The controversial question of the iconography, however, is another matter. Unlike the treacherous problem of attribution it is a quicksand that may have a bottom; at least a tangible and relevant structure of meaning is worth seeking. Although within the scope of this monograph a full-scale discussion of the sculptural program is not feasible, a review of the standing readings of the iconography and an outline of new directions of interpretation are not only in order but integral with our central subject.[2]

[1] Cf. the masterful review of the older literature by Paatz, III, 388 ff, 549 ff n. 440 ff; Falk, 1940; A. Valentiner, "Andrea Pisano as a Marble Sculptor," *Art Quarterly,* X (1947), 163 ff; I. Toesca, 1950, 28 ff; P. Toesca, 1951, 313 ff, 333 ff; J. Pope-Hennessy, *Italian Gothic Sculpture* (London, 1955), 194; L. Becherucci, 1965; White, 1966, 309.

[2] The discussion omits, for understandable reasons, the five reliefs of Luca della Robbia (cf. Paatz, III, 389, 551 f n. 442); the standing figures at the street portal (cf. Ch. III n. 106); and the multiple problems connected with the Quattrocento niche sculpture of Donatello and his associates (see Paatz, III, 390, 555 ff n. 457 ff, and H. W. Janson, *The Sculpture of Donatello* [Princeton, 1957], II, 33 ff.).

That the hexagonal panels in the Siena drawing are devoid of relief (Figs. 133, 135) is open to at least four interpretations. The drawing is a Sienese copy and therefore naturally excludes the Florentine iconography; the drawing is Florentine but simply omits the projected relief as too small to represent and irrelevant to the purpose for which the rendition was made; relief was intended but its program still undecided; finally, no relief was planned at all in the primitive project, with the hexagonal *specchi* meant as a purely decorative motif in the bottom story as well as above. Whichever the case, we know that when the time came for Giotto to emplace the hexagons on the west face[3] they had been carved with the Biblical and scholastic images that initiated two belts of such relief and a third zone of monumental freestanding figures.

Quite possibly Giotto himself conceived the entire Trecento program of the first zone (Figs. 60, 125, 126).[4] Certainly the iconography of the west face — the Creation of Adam and Eve, their First Labor, Jabal (first herdsman), Jubal (inventor of musical instruments), Tubalcain (first smith), and Noah (first cultivator of the vine) — is continued on the south and east sides with Gionitus (first astronomer), *Armatura* (the Art of Construction),* Medicine,* Hunting (or Horsemanship),* Weaving,* Phoroneus (inventor of law and order), the flight of Daedalus (master of all arts and patron of artists), and then Navigation,* Hercules and Cacus (purifying the earth for civilization), Agriculture,* Driving (or *Theatrica*),* Sculpture* and Painting* (displaced to the north side by the portal), and finally (in distinction to *Armatura*) the Architect.*[5]

The nature of Andrea Pisano's role in this first zone of relief is, to say the least, uncertain. Whether or not he played a part in its conception, and just which hexagons he — or Giotto — designed or executed will remain an interminable controversy.[6] What is clear is that Andrea's project added a second band of relief comprising, from the west around to the north, the Planets, the Liberal Arts, the Virtues, and, clearly executed by a different shop, the Sacraments.[7] He was also responsible for the sixteen niches above, now regrettably empty,[8] but which by the 1430s were filled with a most impressive series of prophets and other typological pre-Christian personages initiated on the west face by Andrea himself with Kings David and Solomon, and the Erythraean and Tiburtine Sibyls.[9]

---

[3] Cf. Ch. II, 26 and n. 23.

[4] Braunfels (1948, 193 ff, and esp. 205) gives the most evolved (if not always the most convincing) argument for this possibility.

[5] Essentially the reading of von Schlosser, 1896, 53 ff. Those marked by an asterisk (*) represent the canonical seven *Artes Mechanicae* of Hugo of St. Victor, Vincent of Beauvais, and other scholastics, with Architecture, Sculpture, and Painting as subcategories of *Armatura* (on the latter point [as against Braunfels's erroneous assertion,

1948, 204], see H. von Einem, "Bemerkungen zur Bildhauerdarstellung des Nanni di Banco," *Festschrift für Hans Sedlmayr* [Munich, 1962], 68 ff, with the sources).

[6] Cf. n. 1 above.

[7] Probably Arnoldi (cf. Ch. III n. 77).

[8] See Ch. V n. 133.

[9] The initial group of the Kings David and Solomon and the Tiburtine and Erythraean Sibyls (agreed by nearly all to be at least of Andrea's shop) originally were on the west face, but were

We shall see that Andrea's sculptural project, particularly the niche statuary, derives ultimately from the schemes of the great High Gothic façades. Conceived, however, in direct response to Giovanni's powerful Sienese program (Fig. 269) and Arnolfo's adjacent Cathedral façade (Fig. 239), it manifests that ruthless inventiveness and will to outshine his famous predecessors which we have seen in Andrea's architectural elevation. Bearing in mind the "vaulting ambition" of the virtuoso goldsmith we meet with scarce surprise when we turn briefly from his sixteen Campanile niches to the fourteen at Or San Michele (Fig. 191). They were as unprecedented in the grain-hall context as the former on the face of Italian bell towers. It is no coincidence that both programs appeared during the initial years of Andrea's high Florentine office — between 1337 and 1339. As his Pisan predecessors, in their pulpits and façades, had given magnificent form to the unshaped desires of their patron cities to glorify God and the commune with art,[10] so now did Andrea in Florence, following the lead of Arnolfo and Giotto before him, and having established his own creative authority at the bronze door. By 1343 Andrea Pisano and his workshop had executed at least four of the Campanile figures;[11] in the same years he is said to have completed several statues, now lost, for Or San Michele,[12] where the two most important Trecento niche frames bear his stylistic traces (Figs. 202, 203). Had he retained his post beyond 1343, one can be certain that many more of the thirty niches would have contained the melodious prophets, apostles, and saints of Andrea Pisano and his shop. A sculptor's dream at the heart of Florence, they were eventually filled by the most impressive works of the heroic age of the Florentine Renaissance.[13]

Disregarding the political and social background for the genesis of the program,[14] and the levels of meaning that were attached to the Early Renaissance figures,[15] the statuary at Or San Michele (aside from the incidental relief) was quite simply a presentation of the patron saints of the guilds that ruled the city.[16] The Campanile program, as it finally evolved during the offices of Giotto and Andrea Pisano (and here the relief counts most prominently) was anything but simple.

---

displaced to the poorly visible north side in 1460 by Habakuk (the "Zuccone"), Jeremiah, John the Baptist, and Abdias of Donatello and Nanni di Bartolo ("Il Rosso") which originally had been set there (Fig. 23). The southern group of four anonymous prophets is agreed to be mid Trecento, but attributions range from the late Andrea himself (Becherucci, 1965) to Francesco Talenti (which I tend to favor; see Ch. V n. 58), his son Simone, Arnoldi, the Orcagna circle, and, in the case of one figure, even Maso di Banco. The two prophets on the east (bearded and beardless), the Abraham-Isaac group, and the Moses (?) are by Donatello and Nanni di Bartolo. See n. 2 above for the literature.

[10] See Wiernozowski, 1944, 14 ff.

[11] See n. 9 above.

[12] See Ch. III n. 114.

[13] Cf. F. Haart, "Art and Freedom in Quattrocento Florence," Essays in Memory of Karl Lehmann (New York, 1964), 114 ff.

[14] Cf. Braunfels, 1953, 211 ff; F. Antal, Florentine Painting and Its Social Background (London, 1947), 16 ff (but see the review by M. Meiss, in Art Bulletin, XXXI [1949], 143 ff).

[15] See among others, Krautheimer, 1956, 71 ff; Janson, 1957, II, 16 ff, 23 ff, 45 ff; and Haart, 1964, 119 ff.

[16] Cf. Villani's account of its founding (Bk. XI, 66).

The first major effort to understand it was von Schlosser's famous study of 1896. In high authoritative manner, he set forth a solidly structured interpretation. The sculpture is the end product of the great Gothic programs of the North and the Italian visions of the Pisani; not without accident is it formed in the creatively scholastic Florence of the academy of Santo Spirito, of Brunetto Latini, Dante, and the Dominicans of Santa Maria Novella (and their eventual Thomistic ambient at the Spanish Chapel); the Campanile sculpture portrays man's creation and fall into the yoke of necessity, his efforts to raise his existence through the manual crafts and plastic arts (including the canonical *Artes Mechanicae);* through the Virtues and Liberal Arts man's activity, always under the powerful influence of the Planets, becomes truly human and worthy of God; but it is only through the Sacraments that fallen man attains a state of grace, awaiting the Second Coming of Christ just as the prophets depicted above awaited the Incarnation.[17]

One questions if von Schlosser's interpretation goes far enough. That the program is creatively, yet solidly scholastic is made abundantly clear. But one would expect nothing less of a major Florentine monument involving Giotto and Andrea Pisano; and its scholasticism, as such, was the very mental language of the age.[18] Von Schlosser's reading, while anchoring the program in Florence of the schoolmen and analytic of its message according to the universal criteria of the age, does not touch (beyond theological matters) on its specific historical genesis and, at least equally important, its topographic situation. Rather, it presents the sculpture as if it had been conceived as a single entity, instead of in several phases; and the interpretation to which this supposed iconographic monolith is subjected is that of dead-center Christian dogma, ignoring the many important cultural byways established particularly in the later Middle Ages, as well as the twists so characteristically given to the focal beliefs themselves by preeminent artists and patrons.

If von Schlosser avoids the descent to historical particulars, Braunfels's attempt (in a study that includes a number of acute observations) to center the entire matter on Giotto presents a tangle of highly speculative presumptions. He tells us that Giotto was at odds with an iconoclastic faction led by the Franciscans, who were fighting architectural and decorative luxury; that their abusive opposition to fresco decoration in particular was an insult to Giotto; and that, to make matters worse, the reform orders forbade towers, an architectural genre which Giotto is pictured as having long wanted to pursue, as prideful symbols. In revenge (Braunfels continues), Giotto pushed Florence — which already had the Bargello and Palazzo Vecchio shafts as landmarks together with a functioning Cathedral bell tower, and which was in dire need of completing the amplified space of the new Cathedral to hold its teeming populace — into erecting another costly tower. At that most prominent corner in Florence the eminent painter (and not the guilds which, as Braunfels would have it, were soon to be involved with their sculptural image exclusively at Or San Michele) devised an unprecedented cycle of magnificent relief glorifying the crafts and particularly the visual arts far beyond their minimal lot in scholastic theology. This would be, Braunfels concludes, a second attempt on Giotto's part to raise the status of his art, for Filippo Villani informs us that already next to Dante's portrait in the Bargello Giotto had painted his own.[19]

Braunfels's transformation of Giotto into a proto-Albertian hero, carrying the most vital and factional of cities into an oblique campaign against personal enemies makes most fascinating reading. But, to take the matter seriously, the Franciscans, particularly the Florentine chapter at Santa Croce, hardly mistreated Giotto and his fellow artists; and, indeed, his whole art is inconceivable without the religious force of Saint Francis. The plot Braunfels imagines would have had slight welcome in Florence; besides, we would have to imagine Giotto to have been not only highly paranoiac but very naïve as well to conceive revenge in such terms. And, among the burgeoning objections to Braunfels's thesis (to be distinguished from his many fundamental observations as such), one wonders why Giotto's depiction of the plastic arts was shunted to the least conspicuous of the Campanile's three original faces of relief.[20]

The historical expansion of von Schlossers's study is clearly not to be directed toward such unrecoverable iconographic idiosyncracies of the *capomaestro*. In fact, we might now do well to return to von Schlosser's view as a point of departure. In the first band of relief (following strictly a tradition that includes, among others, both Vincent of Beauvais and Bonaventura) von Schlosser perceived man's Fall and his partial redemption through the canonical *Artes Mechanicae* and numerous other crafts: by manual labor man is delivered from the necessities to which his body has been subject since the Fall. But does this narrowly dogmatic, rather less than positive, reading fully explain the singularity of the twenty-one reliefs? Perhaps it is just that singularity which needs further scrutiny.

In medieval art the subject of man's labor appears rather unevenly in a number of diverse contexts. Although, as a category, the *Artes Mechanicae* found a place in the hierarchy of medieval theology, their direct translation into monumental art was rare.[21]

[19] Braunfels, 1948.

[20] Braunfels's history of the fabric is clouded as well: not only does he categorically state that the second relief zone — including the Sacraments [of Arnoldi] — "all belongs stylistically to Andrea Pisano's shop" (*ibid.*, 205), but — in an error that might be consequential for his argument — that the niche zone is Talenti's (210)! Nor can I let the apodictic statement pass that "Andrea Pisano . . . was incapable of inventing" the reliefs of the Painter, Sculptor, and Architect (208).

[21] P. Brandt, *Schaffende Arbeit und bildende Kunst im Altertum und Mittelalter* (Leipzig,

1927), 307 ff; Braunfels, 1948, 204 ff, 209. For the literary and iconographic history of the *Artes Mechanicae*, see R. van Marle, *Iconographie de l'art profane au moyen-age et à la renaissance* (La Haye, 1932), II, 252 ff; and esp. von Einem, 1962, with emphasis on representations of the visual arts. (Mrs.) V. W. Egbert takes up the latter theme in *The Mediaeval Artist at Work* (Princeton, 1967), which includes an extensive appendix (89 ff) of examples indicating that the crafts may have been somewhat more common in the minor arts, particularly manuscript illumination, than in the monumental media.

Leaving the Campanile aside for the moment, the best known examples of their systematic inclusion in encyclopedic programs are (with one exception) comparatively minor, fragmentary, and even disputed carvings in much larger wholes — as at the controversial socle of the Chartres north transept porch, or the capital in the ground story loggia of the Palazzo Ducale in Venice.[22] Only in the outer archivolts of the central portal of San Marco in Venice, where fourteen crafts are carved, do the *Artes Mechanicae* achieve relative prominence. But inasmuch as in this latter case it is quite distinctly the Venetian crafts that are depicted, the San Marco cycle moves in the direction of the widespread genre of the donor's portrait.[23] Examples range from the inset reliefs on the columns of Piacenza Duomo,[24] sponsored by the guilds, to the keystones of the vaults donated by the guilds of Lodi Vecchio and Erfurt (in the Franciscan church),[25] and to the famous forty-seven windows of Chartres in which guildsmen are depicted at work at the base of each stained-glass lancet.[26] In contrast to these donors' portraits, which fall outside the official iconographic programs of the buildings in which they appear, and the true representations of the *Artes Mechanicae,* which are so rare and fragmentary, there are the extremely common and programatically integrated cycles of the Labors of the Months. They appear prominently on many Gothic portals, for example, at Senlis, Reims, and, most famous of all, Amiens. Italian instances are equally widespread, including Pisa Baptistery, Arezzo Pieve, Lucca Cathedral, and the Fontana Maggiore at Perugia.[27] In distinction to the *Artes Mechanicae,* the yearly cycle is concerned, all but exclusively, with the labor of the land, thus leading us to perhaps the most common, and, indeed, the original context of human labor: the narrative in Genesis of the toil of Adam and Eve, Cain and Abel, and their descendants after the Fall.[28]

---

[22] See p. 91 and notes 30 ff below.

[23] O. Demus, *The Church of San Marco in Venice* (Washington, D. C., 1960), 161 ff; see also his discussion of the reliefs of the Piazetta columns, 117 f, 162. H. Kraus notes analogous French examples of sculpture referring to prominent local industry (*The Living Theatre of Mediaeval Art* [Bloomington, 1967], 85 ff).

[24] G. de Francovich, *Benedetto Antelami* (Milan-Florence, 1952), 17 ff.

[25] Brandt, 1927, 309 ff.

[26] The Chartres series is complemented by 45 windows given by the kings and nobility, and 14 by ecclesiastics. Brandt (*ibid.,* 314 f) points out several cases in which more than the simple representation of the donor (active or passive) was involved: certain Bourges windows include Biblical "typology" of the crafts (e.g., the Offering of Isaac in the butcher's window), related to the Noah window at Chartres, donated by the carpenters; the landworkers' window at Tours depicts the first farmer, Adam, ploughing. On the well known examples at Le Mans and Semur, see Musée des arts décoratifs, *Vitraux de France du XIᵉ au XVIᵉ siècle,* ed. J. Guerin (Paris, 1953), nos. 21, 41. Cf. E. Mâle, *L'Art religieux du XIIIᵉ siècle en France* (Paris, 1931), 63 f; also, the suggestive, if sometimes questionable, discussion of the subject by Kraus, 1967, 72 ff (esp. his discussion of the Chartres St. Lubin window).

[27] On the subject in general, see von der Gabelentz, 1907, 233 ff; Brandt, 1927, 147 ff; Mâle, 1931, 64 ff; and, for the broadest discussion to date, J. C. Webster, *The Labors of the Months in Antique and Mediaeval Art* (Princeton, 1938; but see the review by M. Schapiro in *Speculum,* XVI [1941], 134 ff).

[28] For examples, p. 92 and notes 36, 39 below. Cf. Braunfels's analysis of these categories (1948, 206 f). The subject of human labor appears in

From this brief description it is clear that the Campanile cycle is not confined to any one of these categories. In this it was not unique, for several related instances involve the combining of groups; even when there is no overt mixture, the categories tend to take on particular meaning from the context. The crafts occupy the major ring of archivolts at San Marco; but the others include a calendar cycle and the Virtues, and the tympanum is occupied by a Last Judgment mosaic. Thus, for Otto Demus, every detail of the portal "relates to the realm of ethics," the trades representing the "effect, as it were, of the working of the powers of order which are symbolized by the Months and the Virtues," and the whole is "a belated attempt to give to San Marco some sort of 'cathedral character.'"[29] The eight crafts may fill the leafwork on an entire capital of the arcade of the Palazzo Ducale, but the thrust of meaning is given by the secular emphasis of the forty capitals of the full colonnade.[30] The right portal socle of the Chartres north transept porch includes Adam with his shovel, Cain ploughing, Abel tending flocks, Jubal and his lyre, and Tubalcain at the anvil on the left jamb; on the right, one finds — if not the traditional, but now disproven interpretation of Hippocrates, Archimedes, and Apelles — that there is included at least the city builder, Henoch, holding a square, along with a representative of Philosophy.[31] One is tempted to see here a partial representation of the *Artes Mechanicae,* together with several of the Liberal Arts. But from the context it would appear that the tools and instruments function perhaps more as attributes of the largely inactive figures in their role as pre-Flood ancestors, than as symbols of the crafts as practiced by their Biblical inventors.[32]

We shall come to the question of the final context of the Campanile reliefs further on. But what of the matter of their iconographic composition? What principle or desired significance governed the selection of the subjects of the twenty-one reliefs and the manner of their combination and emphasis? Unlike the juxtaposed categories of, for example, the San Marco archivolts, the Campanile reliefs form a continuum. That continuum is given a narrative impulse by the initial presentation of Genesis, which gathers enough momentum to carry through to the succeeding subjects. After the depletion of the stock of Biblical figures, the sense of chronological progress is maintained by the

other contexts as well, for example the six maidens in the archivolts of the north porch at Chartres who symbolize the active life in their industrious manufacture of textile (A. Katzenellenbogen, *The Sculptural Programs of Chartres Cathedral* [New York, 1959], 74); see also Brandt, 1927, 213 ff, 254 ff, *passim.*

[29] Demus, 1960, 150, 161.

[30] On their iconography, F. Zanotto, *Il Palazzo Ducale di Venezia* (Venice, 1853), not entirely reliable; G. Rossi and G. Salerni, *I capitelli del Palazzo Ducale di Venezia* (Venice, 1952), esp.

73 ff, 79 ff. Cf. the forthcoming study of the Pal. Ducale by S. Sinding-Larsen.

[31] Against the older literature (e.g., Mâle, 1931, 93), see W. Sauerländer, *Von Sens bis Straßburg* (Berlin, 1966), 96 f, figs. 144, 152, 155, 156.

[32] The portal as a whole, and in a general way, is dedicated to the Old Testament ancestors of Christ (but cf. the extremely complex reading of Katzenellenbogen, 1959, 67 ff, 74 ff); for Sauerländer this is true, in particular, of the socle figures of the right porch (1966, 96). Cf. n. 39 below.

inclusion of characters from antique fable. But it is the Genesis series that provides for an unequivocal reading of the program. Not only do the Biblical reliefs set the theme for what follows; it is in the interpretation of early Old Testament history that we have rich, yet precise visual traditions and, moreover, contemporary Italian examples in monumental art — at Orvieto, Perugia, and Florence itself — against which to set the Campanile cycle.

Among the purest and most prominent expressions of this are Maitani's relief at Orvieto (Fig. 240) and the Florentine Baptistery mosaics (Fig. 241). In both instances the initial events in Genesis are depicted *in extenso* with the standard dogmatic emphasis on man's irrevocable fall into toil: following the Creation of Adam and Eve, in each case four to five scenes are taken up with the Warning (in Orvieto only), Sin, Apprehension, Expulsion, and the First Labor (and thence to the tragedy of Cain and Abel).[33] At the opposite extreme to this Biblical directness is the Fontana Maggiore of Perugia, whose iconographic heterogeneity is confused by successive dismantlements and reconstructions, but which appears to form an abbreviated history of the world with Perugia as the teleological product. Included among the statues, for example, is the hero Aulestes, legendary Etrurian king and founder of the city, alongside Ermanno di Sassferrato and Matteo da Corréggio, the current *capitano del popolo* and *podestà*.[34] Yet even so, the message of the early Biblical iconography is clear, for the only primal scenes of Genesis to be included are the twin reliefs depicting the Temptation and the Expulsion:[35] thus the significance of man's beginnings is condensed into the barest dogma of Creation and Fall (Fig. 242).

[33] To be sure, the Orvieto pier includes, at the top, the geometer and Tubulcain the smith: but they appear all but incidental in the context of the dominant tragic drama depicted beneath — particularly in comparison to the Campanile program.

[34] Following the reading of G. Swarzenski (*Nicolo Pisano* [Frankfurt, 1926], 46 ff) the relief program falls into three cycles — Labors of the Months, Liberal Arts, and a condensed Biblical and early Roman history (with Adam and Eve, Samson and Delilah, David and Goliath, Romulus and Remus, the Roman wolf and Rhea Silvia) — separated by symbolic animals and fables and leading to the ring of figures in the upper stage, which appears to represent the historical makers of the religious and political life of the cities Rome and Perugia. Cf. the detailed material of G. Nicco Fasola, *La Fontana di Perugia* (Rome, 1951) and the interpretation of J. Seznek, *The Survival of the Pagan Gods*, tr. B. Sessions (New York, 1961), 128. To support his thesis of Giotto as the arch-protagonist of the new urban culture, Braunfels stresses the contrast between the "rural-agrarian" Monthly Labors at Perugia and their "urban" counterpart in the *Artes Mechanicae* at the Campanile (1948, 208); however, even if valid, the significance of this distinction would apply to the Campanile program regardless of its "author."

[35] With explicit emphasis on the guilt of Eve, not only in the relief composition but in the inscriptions — "EVA DECEPIT ADAM — EVA FEC[IT] ME PECCARE" — a pointed misogynic sentiment even if in good Biblical and churchly tradition, for among all possibilities the following relief depicts Samson and Delilah. The contrast to the lofty humanism of the Campanile relief could not be greater (despite the inclusion of the Liberal Arts elsewhere in the Perugia cycle).

In sharp contrast to both the polarization of uninhibited chauvinism and stringent dogmatic symbolism at Perugia and the apocalyptic starkness of Maitani and the Baptistery, the Campanile in its first zone of relief celebrates, in effect, the theme of creativity.[36] God's creation of Adam and Eve is not followed by the Fall — which, compared with the other cycles, is expressly absent. Rather, the creatures of the Lord immediately take up their own works. The First Labor of Adam and Eve leads not to the continuing misfortunes of Cain and Abel but is succeeded directly by the works of their descendants — husbandry, music, metalurgy, viticulture,[37] and so on, around the three originally decorated sides of the tower. Included are not only the labors of Genesis and the canonical *Artes Mechanicae,* but two representatives of the higher spheres of human striving as well. The Liberal Art Astronomy (Fig. 128; as we shall see, singled out from its sisters by more than chance) was first praticed, according to Latini, by Gionitus, said to have been a "fourth" son of Noah who fittingly lived on the Euphrates. Phoroneus (Fig. 129), in ancient fable, was arbitrator at the dispute between Hera and Poseidon, and in Latini and his scholastic precursors he became the inventor of law and order (or the *Jus civile* of the discipline *Ethica,* which in the scheme of the churchmen falls between *Mechanica* below and *Theorica,* subsuming the Liberal Arts, above).[38] Subtly following and intermingling, and including two further personages of fable (Daedalus and Hercules, discussed below), the twenty-one reliefs of Giotto and Andrea Pisano, which comprise such diverse levels of the encyclopedic frame, are cunningly fused into a singular continuum in which the works of Adam and Eve are openly marked not as the wages of sin, but as the first creative acts of mankind.[39]

[36] The Perugian condensation of early Genesis is far from being an isolated example; cf. Brandt, 1927, 226 ff. Further examples of Italian Genesis iconography are given by S. B. Loessel, *S. Maria in Vescovio* (Master's thesis, New York University, 1942), esp. App. XI (manifesting considerable variety, but no parallel to the Campanile).

[37] Even the "nakedness" of Noah (Fig. 127) is not the tragic embarrassment of Genesis, but almost a drollery not only identifying the protagonist but manifesting the power of his invention. Contrast Bartolo di Fredi's version in the Collegiata at San Gimignano or, for that matter, Ghiberti's (Krautheimer, 1956, fig. 82, pl. 89). Cf. also the examples discussed by Brandt (1927, 254 ff), such as the Porte St. Ursin at Bourges.

[38] Cf. von Schlosser for this interpretation (1896, 67 ff) and for his helpful charts of the relevant aspects of the scholastic system (37 f); Braunfels suggests — I believe unnecessarily — that Gionitus may be the remnant of a Liberal Arts cycle

planned at some point for the first zone (1948, 208).

[39] To bring French examples into our account, it is clear that, in distinction to Mâle's equation of the two programs (1931, 93 n. 2), the Campanile contrasts sharply with the orthodox Genesis cycle in the voussoirs of the north transept rose at Reims (P. Vitry, *La Cathédrale de Reims* [Paris, 1919], II, pl. LII). Similarly with the outer voussoirs of the central porch of the Chartres north transept, which rigorously depict the creation of the world and the Fall of man; it may be worth noting that here the last scene of the tragedy is the condemnation to labor — which, it would seem, possibly carries to the archivolts of the right porch, where the Labors of the Months are found (E. Houvet, *Cathedral de Chartres, portail nord* [Chelles, 1919], II, pls. 21 ff, 77 ff). As a unique — though, naturally, historically disconnected — northern precursor of the Campanile cycle, there might be suggested the porch socle re-

The celebrative character of the reliefs was in full keeping with the protohumanistic epoch; with the undoubted influence of the great iconographic poet Giotto in his old age; and particularly with the celebrative character of the Campanile itself.[40] Moreover, its impact was strengthened by an iconographic aspect that has been ignored by all but Seznek. These reliefs embody the "euhemeristic" tradition — in which the ancient gods and fabulous heroes were but pagan disguises, as it were, for the great mortal benefactors of mankind — "at its purest and noblest."[41] Indeed, we have witnessed that it is not only the crafts themselves as impersonal categories that are celebrated, but their inventors as human heroes — collectively, the Promethian nature of man himself. Thus appear, together with the Biblical protagonists and initial practitioners of the arts, several tellingly related "euhemeristic" heroes. The reader will realize that Phoroneus is just such a personage.[42] And not only does Minerva, associated with the origins of weaving,[43] preside majestically over that relief (Fig. 131), but there is Daedalus, patron of artists, who captured the imagination of man as first conquerer of the air (Fig. 130). Perhaps the spirit of the program is embodied most clearly in the figure of Hercules standing triumphant over the monster Cacus (Fig. 132), deified for his aid to man in having, as von Schlosser puts it, "cleansed the earth as a basis for cultural life." He is the very Hercules who, from the end of the Dugento, appears as protector and symbol of Florence on the seal of the Signoria with the legend: "Herculea clava domat Florentia prava" (with the club of Hercules, Florence subdues the wicked).[44]

liefs of the right portal of the Chartres north transept; crafts and liberal arts as practiced by their Biblical inventors. But the differences clearly outweigh the similarities. Not only is there the enormous contrast in the extent of the programs and in the prominence of presentation, but there is the distance between the comparatively static groups of precursors to Christ, only incidentally the inventors of mechanical and liberal disciplines, and the sweeping narration of the creative accomplishments of man following his creation by the divine. Cf. p. 91 and notes 31 f above, and also White's comment on the Campanile cycle (1966, 309). See H. W. Janson, *Apes and Ape Lore in the Middle Ages and the Renaissance* ("Studies of the Warburg Institute," XX [London, 1952]), 132 ff for a medieval undercurrent stressing the positive nature of Adam. A solitary discordant note at the Campanile would be the bear in the scene of the First Labor. A symbol of fornication (*ibid.*, 66 n. 103), its reaching for fruit might be intended as a compensating reference to those immediately preceding, tragic events of Genesis so conspicuously absent.

[40] See Ch. IV, 104 ff and Ch. VII, 174 ff.
[41] Seznek, 1961, 30 f.
[42] *Ibid.*, 18.
[43] *Ibid.*, 22.
[44] E. Müntz, *Les Précurseurs de la renaissance* (Paris, 1882), 48; Seznek, 1961, 20 n. 27 (on the seal, Hercules is shown brandishing his club in one hand and with the other at the throat of the Hydra). Cf. H. Wentzel, "Italienische Siegelstempel und Siegel all'antico im 13. und 14. Jahrhundert," *Mitteilungen des kunsthistorischen Instituts in Florenz*, VII (1955), 73 ff (with bibl.); Davidsohn, 1956, Vol. II, Part II, 221. A life of Hercules was included in Petrarch's biographical collection, *De viris illustribus*, written in 1337 or shortly thereafter ("Le 'De viris illustribus' de Pétrarque," ed. P. de Nolhac, in *Notices et extraits des manuscrits de la Bibliothèque Nationale*, XXXIV [Paris, 1891], 134 ff for Hercules); for the date of the ms, and its influence in contemporary iconography see T. E. Mommsen, "Petrarch and the Decoration of the 'Sala virorum illustrium' in Padua," *Art Bulletin*, XXXIV (1952), 95 ff.

That this interpretation is not unconscionably overextended in a humanistic direction is indicated by the fate of the Campanile program itself. The naked humanism went too far. The Florentines — like their Sienese contemporaries who, in a violent reaction, destroyed the antique Venus Pudica they had proudly set up at the Fonte Gaia[45] — quickly had misgivings and took steps, if not to eradicate, then to counterbalance the stark celebration of man of Giotto's project.[46] In a move that foreshadowed the turning away from early Trecento humanism in the 1340s and 1350s (so clearly recorded by Millard Meiss),[47] they ordained a second story of relief and on its main face expressly set up the Seven Planets which, according to the most elementary astrology, all but govern man's fate.[48] If the first zone was possible only in Giotto's Florence, paradoxically it was the very epoch during which astrology, endemic in the early Middle Ages, growing

Prof. L. D. Ettlinger has been so kind as to provide me (in time to be inserted in the proof) with the text of a talk on "Hercules in Florence" given in 1970 in London (and soon to be published in the Florentine *Mitteilungen*), in which the Hercules relief and civic seal are paired and put in the context of civic symbolism, with justifiable stress on the fact that "the exploit of Hercules selected shows him with a defeated and dead robber who had terrified the countryside." This latter observation, which had not struck me, ties in neatly with my interpretation. In the seal, Florence is identified with Hercules in overcoming wickedness. In the relief, conversely, wickedness — which is not particularized in the seal (except for the inscrutable Hydra) — takes shape specifically as the evildoings of Cacus, whose infamous contemporary counterparts, as I now realize, were the lawless nobles who originally had terrorized the land but who had finally been beaten down by the Florentines (perhaps there was also an allusion to their urban cousins whose disruption of life was only definitively curtailed by the Florentines in the 1340s [see 176 ff below]). One might say that relief and seal complement each other perfectly: by implication, the relief identifies at least certain of those "wicked" parties of the seal, and, by way of cross-reference, the inscription of the seal seems to provide the missing "text" for reading the self-image of the Florentines into the victorious hero on the relief.

45 See Ghiberti's account (ed. von Schlosser, 1912, I, 63; II, 189 ff) and Panofsky's interpretation (1960, 112, 151, 155). The Venus, probably discovered in the mid 1330s, was dismembered in 1357 for having brought down on Siena their recent defeat by the Florentines (in whose soil the remains of the "carcass" were buried in hopes of transfering the Lord's wrath). Panofsky relates this to the general turn away from the humanistic, classicizing art of the early Trecento at mid century, as described by M. Meiss (1951). Oertel's discussion of post-Giottesque Tuscan painting before Orcagna should be weighed carefully here (1966, *passim*). Cf. Ch. III n. 77. (See Ch. VI on the architectural ramifications of this problem.)

46 A kind of iconographic counterbalance may have been intended at the Campanile from the beginning: if, in the Italian Trecento, Hercules embodies the moral virtues (Panofsky, 1960, 150 n. 4), he would be countered — or better, complemented — by the St. Michael at the tip of Giotto's project (Fig. 144) embodying the theological trio *(ibid.)*, reinforced by the possible symbolism of the flaming finials (Figs. 138, 143) as *Caritas*, greatest of all the Virtues (*I Cor.*, XIII, 13; cf. Ch. II n. 103).

47 Meiss, 1951. Meiss himself (100) notes that "none of the 'mechanical' arts so intensely practiced in Florence and represented a generation earlier on the Campanile is included in the scheme" of the encyclopedic fresco of the left wall of the Spanish Chapel (1366-68).

48 Cf. A. Jahn-Rusconi, "Il campanile di Giotto," *Emporium*, XIX (1941), 241 f, 250. It might be noted that the sequence of Planets at the Campanile is the canonical one, corresponding to the Seven Ages of Man.

during the twelfth and thirteenth centuries through Arab influence, scholastic assimilation, and widespread propagation, attained a powerful hold over the Western consciousness.[49] As Seznek tells us, "In Italy, astrologers directed the life of cities, *condottieri*, and prelates."[50] Not only such visionaries as Dante[51] but, by Villani's own testimony, even that most tough-minded of communes succumbed. Those consulted about the causes of the great flood included astrologers whose reply was that the "diluvio" in large part was due to the "celestial course and strong conjunctions of planets," the unbelievably complex detail of which the chronicler records in full.[52] Together with the upsurge in astrological mentality naturally came the penetration of the Planets into monumental iconography, from which they had been restricted in the encyclopedic French programs of the thirteenth century.[53] If the first Campanile zone of relief includes, as Braunfels emphasizes, and as we have seen,[54] the first complete and most monumental depiction of the *Artes Mechanicae*, the Seven Planets above not only are among the earliest manifestations in monumental art of their genre but undoubtedly, as Seznek suggests, the most exalted.[55]

Again, a few comparisons clarify the express meaning of the Campanile iconography. At the Palazzo Ducale in Venice the Planets are restricted to a single capital where they compete with the glorious foliage in which they are set; and later in Florence at the Spanish Chapel, confined to small *tondi*, they decorate the gables of the thrones grandly occupied by the Liberal Arts.[56] At the Campanile not only are the Planets (following the system of Dante and other scholastics) coordinated for the first time in monumental art with the Liberal Arts and the Virtues,[57] but by their placement on the west face are given a tactical predominance that in an age of hierarchical acuity and endless protocol can only have meant symbolic prepotence.[58]

[49] Seznek, 1961, 42 ff.

[50] *Ibid.*, 52.

[51] E.g., *Purgatorio*, XVI, 73; *Paradiso*, XXII, 112; and, indeed, his underlying scientific outlook.

[52] Villani, XI, 1; following several pages of astrology, Villani recites the major acts of divine justice recorded in the Bible and antiquity, spells out the sins of Florence (including pride, violence, "infinite avarice," usury, vanity and disordinate expenses of the women, gluttony, etc.), concluding, "per li oltraggiosi nostri peccati Iddio mandò questo giudicio [the flood] mediante il corso del cielo." Astrological discussions appear so frequently — at least six times in Bk. XI alone (Chs. 1, 20, 33, 67, 99, 113), in fact, to explain every natural or calamitous event — that it imposes a fatalistic overcast (particularly with such chapter titles as "Della Congiunzione di Saturno e di Giove e di Marte nel segno d'Aquario"

[XII, 41]). And Villani was a rather representative, hard-headed Trecento businessman.

[53] Seznek, 1961, 127.

[54] 1948, 207.

[55] Seznek, 1961, 128. Could the set-gem appearance of the rhomboidal Planet reliefs have anything to do with the tradition by which the effigies most efficacious in magically influencing the heavenly powers were those carved in precious stones? Is it mere coincidence that the common astrological manual, the *Picatrix* (the Arabic *Ghâya*), that prescribes this method is the very source for the puzzling iconographic details — which also must be correct if the image is to have effect — of the Campanile Planets (*ibid.*, 52 ff, 160 ff)? (But cf. Ch. III, 81.)

[56] *Ibid.*, 70 (with further examples).

[57] Von Schlosser, 1896, 40 ff.

[58] Cf. Jahn-Rusconi, 1941, 242.

Thus the historically more central Liberal Arts and Virtues[59] were shunted around to less conspicuous sides of the tower (Figs. 60, 126). There was probably more than a compulsive scholasticism behind their presence, more than mere encyclopedic correspondence for its own sake. In their concern for balance, the Florentines countered the humanism of the first zone with the astrological reliefs. At the same time they were undoubtedly aware of the theological tradition in which the stars, which determine individual character and its flaws, lead (though not force) man into sin.[60] The Liberal Arts and the Virtues, of course, direct him out. In fact together with the *Artes Mechanicae* they carry him to the maximum recovery from the effects of the Fall possible without the Sacraments and the Grace of the Lord.[61]

If it was thus inevitable, given the system of correspondences between these categories and the emphatic will to balance at the Campanile, that the Virtues and Arts would take their place alongside the Planets, perhaps it was the same convergence of general scholastic habits and the particular dynamics of the Campanile that resulted in the nearly unprecedented depiction of the Sacraments on the north face. Clearly their immediate origin was in the bridge to the church from which the ecclesiastical officials would view them (Figs. 66, 67).[62] But even if poorly visible from the piazza (Fig. 7) the presence of the Sacraments would have been known and felt; from the tacit balancing of themes on the three exposed faces of the tower their transcendental significance for the program would have been clear. In fact, how fitting it was to set the mysteries of the church not openly exposed to the life of the street, but huddled in shadows next to the nave of the Duomo where only the clergy who were spiritually intimate with the Sacraments might be visually so.

Whatever the domain of the reliefs of the Sacraments, the prophetic figures proudly displayed in the niches above clearly reach out to the observer on the street (Figs. 23, 126). It is, I believe, inescapable that, in part, and in a decidedly general and indirect manner, they represent a transfer, both formally and iconographically, from the Gallery of the Kings that crosses the upper façade of so many of the great High Gothic cathedrals. Surely the placement of a band of large statuary, of typological import, high on the face of a monument is a shared arrangement.[63] It is also reasonable to imagine, as does von

[59] On the Liberal Arts, Curtius (1953, 36 ff) is particularly illuminating; on the Virtues, besides A. Katzenellenbogen's *Allegories of the Virtues and Vices in Mediaeval Art* (New York, 1964), see Offner, 1930 ff, Sec. IV, Vol. IV, Pt. I, 22 n. 9, for for a survey of the Tuscan iconography.

[60] Seznek, 1961, 48.

[61] Poetically expressed in the *De animae exilio* of Honorius of Autun, on which see von Schlosser, 1896, 50 f; von Einem, 1962, 68 ff.

[62] See Ch. III, 66 ff.

[63] Except for Reims, the Kings in the French galleries are, of course, not — as was long believed — the Kings of France, but the Old Testament Kings and Patriarchs that form — as in the Tree of Jesse — the genealogy of Christ and even more importantly, the Virgin, to whom the cathedrals were dedicated (Mâle, 1931, 167 f). We shall see that the same iconographic bond obtained at the Campanile. In medieval theology David and Solomon not only are Kings, but prophets and major types of Christ as well —

Schlosser, that they raise the Campanile iconography one more rung up the anagogic ladder by implicit reference to Apocalypse, the Second Coming of the Lord whose first earthly appearance they prophecied and prefigured. Thus they would form a still further expansion and internal balancing of the iconographic scheme.

But is this all? To push this direct exegesis onward immediately meets a diminishing of meaningful returns. Yet to abandon the search at this point evokes a sense of incompleteness in our understanding. Even the most fundamental questions are still unanswered: why, for example, the Campanile sculpture was completed while the Cathedral façade was abandoned, or why, for that matter, the Campanile was given the grandiose program at all, when traditionally bell towers were sculpturally naked.[64]

These questions lead us to a nearly unexplored approach — perhaps latent in von Schlosser's interpretation of the prophet cycle and, indeed, in Braunfels's emphasis on the civic implications of the tower and its decoration. Might not a key to the hidden meanings of the Campanile sculpture be simply the Campanile itself, that is, implicit in its nature as a tower and in its specific historic and topographic situation? We have, in fact, already reaped the benefits of this approach in the case of the Sacrament reliefs. In the final chapter an analogous inquiry reveals the circumstances for the Campanile's realization. Here, perhaps, are the means to unlock the still elusive programmatic substance of the sculpture.

In the Campanile we may imagine that two independent formal systems interpenetrate: the horizontally spreading flatness of the Cathedral façade, which the Campanile, considered as a folded plane, extends; and the axially gathered verticality of the Campanile as an independent, free standing tower. In both these formal systems — façade and tower — reside various levels of properly distinct, yet overlapping and interweaving meanings crucial to our understanding of the Campanile sculpture.

As surface, the Campanile is meant as a folded extension of the Cathedral façade, aligning its initial (west) face with the plane of the façade and continuing (as Gioseffi has shown, at least for Giotto's project) the spacing of Arnolfo's tiers (Fig. 239) in its lower stories.[65] This pointed formal continuity was bound up with the decided icono-

---

just as the Abraham-Isaac group of Donatello pressages God's sacrifice of His Son (Cf. *ibid.*, 152 ff; on the multiple roles of David, see H. Steger, *David Rex et Propheta* [Nürnberg, 1961]).

[64] Even the grandiose marble campanile at Pisa Duomo has only a Madonna at the entrance and some minor, incidental decorative relief set in the wall (Sanpaolesi, 1956, fig. 2). In the North, however, where the towers are integral with the façade, the sculptural program tends to spread upward not only as Kings' Galleries but to the

towers themselves — the most famous example being Laon West.

[65] Gioseffi, 1963, 80 ff (with the calculation that the breadth of the Campanile between buttresses corresponds to the width of the Duomo side aisle), fig. 73. But the continuity is already implicit in Villani's account of the founding: the new Campanile is "alongside the façade of the church" (Doc. I). Cf. Ch. II n. 77 for the Metz-Paatz reconstruction of Arnolfo's façade (so far as executed, nearly identical in its architectural features with the 1587 drawing; Fig. 239).

graphic orientation — latent in von Schlosser's discussion, and suggested by Kauffmann and Metz[66] — of the Campanile sculpture toward the façade. This relationship, which centers on the manifest connection between the Campanile prophets and sibyls and the essentially Marian façade, is not as casual, however, as it first appears, but can be historically delineated with some precision.

Arnolfo's façade project is not known in its full extent. Unlike his more fortunate contemporaries, the great Florentine mason died before more than a few components of his most complex conception could be carved: essentially the Nativity, the Madonna Enthroned, and the Death of the Virgin, from left to right in the three portal tympana; for local tradition, figures of San Zenobius and Santa Reparata flanking the Madonna; and to reflect pontifical patronage, the stupendous Boniface VIII in a niche above.[67] Yet one can scarcely imagine that in the decades of maximum iconographic activity of medieval Tuscany — in fact, precisely between the high drama of the Sienese façade and the Arena Chapel — Arnolfo did not have a profound sculptural poetry in mind. A fragment of such a conception is in fact recorded by the façade drawing (Fig. 239). At the left portal, celebrating the Birth of Christ, there appears a "window" opening in the wall of the tympanum for God's creatures, the farm animals, to view the sacred event. The scene is revealed to us from behind drawn curtains, heralded by angels, and flanked on the right by the Annunciation to the Shepherds who gesture towards the Star of Bethlehem in the gable that surmounts the central scene.[68]

A half century — and the construction of the Campanile — passed before Trecento sculptors began to fill out the Arnolfian frame. When they did, it was not only with the loss of Arnolfo's vision, but with a confusion and lack of clear — let alone inspired — iconographic focus and direction, which was to characterize the late Trecento Cathedral workshop in general. By the early Quattrocento the façade included, beyond its Arnolfian inheritance, the four seated Evangelists, and standing in tiers above, groupings of martyred saints, the Church Fathers, adoring and musical angels, together with a few miscellaneous prophets; Arnolfo's sixteen niches in the jambs of the central portal held a series of apostles and other figures. Moreover, not only the façade, but the four portals ranged along the flanks of the Cathedral, became weighted with a progressively less inspiring iconographic (as well as stylistic) load: two Annunciations, three standing Madonnas, and an army of attendant figures. Only the inventor of the Porta della Mandorla jambs

[66] Kauffmann (1936, 71), notes that the Campanile prophets refer to the mother of God whose story takes up the façade; Metz (1938, 142) agrees and offers further that the Campanile sculpture represents the Old Testament, the façade the New — forgetting, it seems, that a good deal of the iconography of the Campanile is hardly Old Testament, in particular, the Sacraments.

[67] Paatz, III, 392 f; cf. Pope-Hennessy's more expansive reconstruction (1955, 185).
[68] For the various detailed reconstructions of this portal see n. 67 above, and H. Keller, "Der Bildhauer Arnolfo di Cambio und seine Werkstatt," *Jahrbuch der preußischen Kunstsammlungen*, LVI (1935), 22 ff. Keller suggests a Joseph in the niche to the left of the tympanum, Pope-Hennessy (1955, 185) an Annunciation above.

and Nanni di Banco, in his great Assumption relief, were able to break the late Trecento spell.[69]

Thus it is that we meet an impasse upon trying to reconstruct the unexecuted bulk of Arnolfo's program, as we must in order to fathom its relationship to the program of the Campanile. It is not possible to assume the façade iconography of the late workshop — with all its heterogeneity (to be sure broadly ecclesiological in nature), even confusion, so painfully apparent in the drawing — to represent Arnolfo's intentions. What, after all, would have been the fate of the Siena façade, the greatest work of the school of the Pisani, had Giovanni not lived to carve that awesome belt of sculpture (Fig. 269). In Florence one can be sure that the executed niches and whatever framework Arnolfo intended above[70] were meant for an assemblage of sculpture far more coherent than the eventual outcome in program, type, scale, not to mention style. Yet just because this conformation of marble would have been so rich and personal it is impossible to imagine with any precision what Arnolfo's grand design might have been.

Nonetheless, from the Marian iconographic tradition, its tendencies in Arnolfo's time and the multiple possibility for grouping within his façade frame, it would seem safe to assume the inclusion of a typological group somewhere in his project.[71] On Siena Duomo (Fig. 269) prophets are ranged both in great horizontal bands and (together with Apostles) about the rose (with the Madonna at top center).[72] Arnolfo's plan may have shared aspects of this configuration. But it is conceivable as well that Arnolfo's sixteen small niches in the main portal jambs (Fig. 239) were originally meant to receive the typological assembly in question or part of it, perhaps even the canonical four major and twelve minor prophets, which would have converged intimately on the tympanum Madonna.

In any event one thing is clear: the Arnolfian typological program would be included along with the Siena façade and the northern Gallery of Kings as the sources for the unprecedented Campanile program of standing statuary.[73]

This very transferal of typology from façade to Campanile would reinforce the concept of iconographic unity — or at least continuity — between the two buildings, particularly in Andrea Pisano's time. Moreover, it leads to a further consideration.

---

[69] For the dating, see Paatz, III, 393 ff, 364 ff.

[70] Cf. the Metz-Paatz reconstruction, Ch. II n. 77.

[71] Cf. R. Jaques, "Die Ikonographie der Madonna in Trono in der Malerei des Dugento," *Mitteilungen des kunsthistorischen Instituts in Florenz*, V (1937), 1 ff. Arnolfo's façade project was really a sculptor's equivalent on the grand scale — and well in advance — of the great Tuscan *Maestà* type definitively achieved by Duccio, Giotto, and Simone Martini.

[72] A. Kosegarten ("Einige sienesische Darstellungen der Muttergottes aus dem frühen Trecento," *Jahrbuch der Berliner Museen*, VIII [1966], 103 ff) has shown that the Madonna dates around 1300, and indicates that the rest of the upper Sienese façade, as well, is also very early Trecento (and not 1377 ff as has been commonly believed; cf. the concurring study of H. Klotz [forthcoming]).

[73] Cf. Ch. III, 59, for a formal architectural connection.

Although it has been shown that many formal aspects of Arnolfo's façade are linked to strictly Italian traditions,[74] Florence, vital intellectual and artistic center that it was in the Trecento, was far from ignorant of cosmopolitan European forms. We have seen this in the work of Giotto and Andrea Pisano, for example, and it hardly needs mentioning that Arnolfo's monumentally conceived Marian tympana are impossible without at least the indirect knowledge of the northern tradition, as is indeed his very notion of the sculpturally profuse wall.

Yet by comparison with the encyclopedic programs of the northern cathedrals, the Florentine façade, even in terms of its maximum possibilities, would have finished programmatically emaciated. Arnolfo's own project may have been an inspired one, but it is obvious that beyond the Marian portals the architectural frame — insofar as we can imagine it[75] — simply did not provide for much more than tiers of a relatively few, large-scale figures mostly standing individually. For Arnolfo's generation this was evidently a more than satisfactory prospect: indeed, it was a splendid one according to the document of 1300 praising the "visible and magnificent beginnings" of the new Duomo — which can only have meant the façade.[76] But Arnolfo's generation was also taken by Brunetto Latini's vulgarization of the great scholastic systems in his informally constructed *Li Livres dou Trésor* of 1284, which he personally transformed into the even more picturesque versified Italian version, the *Tesoretto*.[77] When the Campanile program was conceived the work of a follower of Latini had already been written: Dante's *Divina Commedia*,[78] constructed, it has often been rightly said, like a Gothic cathedral. Could its readers of the 1330s have been happy with Arnolfo's façade project, not only half finished and abandoned for more than a decade, but holding a scholastically threadbare future. Where were to come the compounding cycles representing Saint Vincent's *Speculum Mundi* seen on the definitive French façades, or for that matter, more recent examples like Strasbourg West? Even the very sculptural forms — the rows of socle relief, jamb figures (except for the still empty central portal niches), multiple archivolts — were lacking. Surely it is not unreasonable to suggest that the possibilities of the façade that had seemed so promising to the Florentines of Arnolfo's generation might have appeared rather barren to their descendants during the decades between the *Divina Commedia* and the Spanish Chapel.

In this light it is not hard to imagine that the Campanile sculpture, seen as a whole now, may have been conceived quite literally as a programmatic supplement to the façade, both formally (its bands of relief substituting for those "missing" at the base of the façade) and iconographically (its relief a scholastic enrichment in several dimensions

---

[74] Metz, 1938, 148 ff; Panofsky, 1960, 116 f.
[75] The Metz-Paatz reconstruction, Ch. II n. 77; Kauffmann suggests in addition gable mosaics such as the Coronation of the Virgin (1936, 71).
[76] Guasti, doc. 23.

[77] Cf. von Schlosser, 1896, 40 ff.
[78] Completed 1320; for an impression of its effect not only on *litterati* but more ordinary upper-class citizens, see Villani's two chapters of tribute to Dante (Bk. IX, 133 f).

to the limitations of Arnolfo's sculpture and frame). The typological statuary, while in all probability not an addition to the original façade program, which according to the present hypothesis included the theme, in effect became such to a degree. Certainly in their magnificent perch and full-scale form the Campanile figures — truly in the spirit of the northern Gallery of Kings[79] — carry the message of Christ's Coming more power-fully than would have Arnolfo's typology either in stacked, miniature form at the central portal or (more probably) mixed in the niche tiers above.[80]

But a persistent (if unfair) critic — say from Orvieto — might still have queried: even considering the two programs as an iconographic whole, where, beyond the story of the arts and a few central New Testament scenes on the façade is to be revealed God's universal plan of world history? The expected modern scholarly reply would defer to the traditional Tuscan — even Italian — sculptural reticence and partial programming. But for a Florentine of the second quarter of the Trecento the defense conceivably would have been less evasive: the apocalyptic vision was not lacking to the Cathedral group but was magnificently expressed in the newly completed Baptistery mosaics that depict Genesis from the Creation to the Flood; the Lives of Joseph, Mary, Christ, and the Baptist; and the spectacle of the Last Judgment, together with attendant Church Fathers, Deacons, Bishops, Patriarchs, and Prophets.

In the rationalization might lie a profound historical truth, for it is possible indeed to view the decoration of the Florentine Cathedral group as an iconographically inte-grated, or at least collectively iconographic entity, the product of a grand impulse that ran from the twelfth century through the sixteenth. It can be seen as cumulative and piecemeal (rather than systematic) in conception, fragmentary in realization, each phase grounded in particular and often fleeting historical circumstance, with attendant and increasing overlappings, redundancies, and imbalances (like the liturgy itself), and — as we have seen at the façade — with the labors of some periods manifesting more icono-graphic direction and unity than others. Not the least powerful and synthetic cycle of the process was that of the late thirteenth and early fourteenth centuries, destined to

---

[79] Cf. n. 63 above.

[80] In its outlines, Arnolfo's project seems to re-flect such comparatively uncomplicated compo-sitions as the interior façade, west, at Reims (which H. Keller, "Die Bauplastik des Sieneser Doms," *Kunstgeschichtliches Jahrbuch der Biblio-teca Hertziana*, I [1937], 141 ff, connects with the Sienese façade) and the peculiarly English front at Wells and Salisbury, rather than the more intricate standard High Gothic configurations (e. g. the external façade at Reims) suggested here as an inspiration for the Campanile program. Such gradual assimilation of central French proto-

types would not be unique; it characterizes, in fact, to a great degree, the stylistic evolution of the Pisani from Nicola to Giovanni to Andrea to Nino (see M. Weinberger, "Remarks on the Role of French Models within the Evolution of Gothic Tuscan Sculpture," *Acts of the Twentieth International Congress of the History of Art* [Princeton, 1963], I, 198 ff), or, for that matter, the shift from the still Byzantinizing Duccio to Simone Martini. For Giotto's awareness of the High Gothic programs (including Reims) see H. Jantzen, "Giotto und der gotische Stil," in *Das Werk des Künstlers*, 1939-40, 441 ff.

witness the initiation of the Cathedral façade (1294), the completion of the Baptistery mosaics (begun at an unknown point in the Dugento, finished by 1325), and the casting of Andrea's bronze door (1330-36). The Campanile program — begun in 1334, expanded in 1337 — clearly rode the crest of this great late medieval wave (just as the later Trecento activity wallowed in its wake).[81]

With this in mind it is suggested that the Campanile sculpture may have been intended as a partial iconographic complement — or at least a supplement — not just to the Cathedral façade but to the content of the entire Cathedral group as it had evolved by the early Trecento, and especially as it had so intensively developed in the previous decades. The sense of unity both between and within the buildings may have dissipated in the later Trecento; but near its height in the 1330s it could hardly have been less than a powerful synthetic force. This would place the Campanile program in a specific iconographic topography at a meaningful iconographic moment, opening up an interpretation of the fully evolved Campanile program along the following lines: the prophetic figures of the Campanile announce and await the appearance of Mary (not only as Mother, but as the Church) and the Coming of Christ dramatized on the façade (as well as in the Baptistery); but the Incarnation is to be seen within the whole of Universal history, particularly those events represented on the Baptistery ceiling. Within this apocalyptic scope, however, one must not neglect — as the scholastics themselves allow, and as the times cry out — man's own heroic efforts, depicted in the Campanile relief, to cope with necessity, to improve his earthly existence through manual skills and the arts, through imagination and the intellect, though not without defining the limits of this fallen creature's potential, his subjection to heavenly powers, and his ultimate dependence through the Sacraments and the Church, together with the intercession of the Virgin, on the Grace of God.

In imagining that the decoration of the three buildings forming the Cathedral group generated a common iconographic field affecting the emphases of meaning in each, we must be careful not to imply — any more than a theologian would concerning such speculation about the Trinity — a loss of identity by any of the monuments in question. In fact, the process of juxtaposition as well as suggesting affinities sharpens the distinctions. It is obvious, for example, that the repeated representation of the Life of the Baptist

---

[81] Kauffmann explicitly connects the Donatello Cantoria with the Trecento *Mariencyclus* of the Cathedral exterior, the impulse of which he finds to be still at work in the early Quattrocento, but transferred to the interior (1936, 71; but cf. the review of U. Middeldorf, *Art Bulletin*, XVIII [1936], 570 ff, esp. 576 f). Not unrelated to the Florentine dynamics are the iconographic histories of the multiple porches of the French cathedrals, such as Chartres, where the cumulative interrelationships of diverse campaigns stretching nearly a century are emphasized by Katzenellenbogen, 1959, *passim*. In the context of the present discussion, the erroneous terminology of A. Billi (Doc. IX) and the Anonimo Gaddiano (Doc. X), who entitle the tower the "Campanile di San Giovanni," may not be intirely without significance.

in San Giovanni was utterly appropriate, just as the Marian façade (and later side portals) was the clear choice for the new Cathedral, no longer dedicated to the obscure Santa Reparata (or Santa Liperata, as she was often called) but rather to the Mother of God.[82] What then, can we suppose to have been the significance of the Campanile program in terms of the monument itself?

The 1330s, when the Campanile was conceived, is intimately akin to two other periods in Florentine history: the decades around 1100 and the early Quattrocento. Their common bond is twofold. Each of the periods witnessed an explosion of civic and cultural energy: the earliest thrust Florence onto the center stage of history; the latest saw the incandescent bloom of the aged republic in the heroic decades following the defeat of Milan; and the last days of Giotto knew the quite conscious peak of the medieval city. Each epoch had good reason to be proud; and, lifted by mysterious energies, each chose to express that emotion with the building of an unprecedentedly monumental vertical structure characteristic of the period: the Romanesque Baptistery, the Gothic Campanile, and Brunelleschi's Cupola.[83]

Because the Campanile was above all a profoundly civic monument (and we shall uncover evidence for this in addition to that of Braunfels as we continue, particularly later on)[84] we may imagine that the Florentines, perhaps affirming the donor portrait tradition exemplified at Chartres and Venice, saw in its sculpture not only the Universal Mirror of Saint Vincent of Beauvais, but, as we have already implied above, reflections of their own self-image (happily, the reliefs are called *specchi*). Dante was just another Florentine in his predilection to gather Apocalypse and Florentine politics, even gossip, in the same breath. Like the stage of the *Divina Commedia*, the sculptural cycle of the Campanile embodied a double thrust — toward the scholastic universalism of the Cathedral group and now toward the universal pride of the Florentines.

This complex emotion was closer to exultation than vainglory. It compounded several levels of shared experience. Intimately connected with the very will to build the Campanile was the dramatic pride born of an epochal political struggle that culminated in the early Trecento, and to which we shall come in Chapter VII.[85] But equally telling was the self-esteem expressed by the communal documents concerning Arnolfo and Giotto,[86] or by Giovanni Villani in the very scope and tenor of his chronicle and particularly in his description of the city in the 1330s, a cumulative exultance of the sheer

---

[82] Paatz, III, 321. The apocalyptic cycle of the Baptistery mosaics could, of course, be linked with the web of meaning of Baptism.

[83] Though already projected in the mid-Trecento, the Cupola as *built* — especially the heroic process of construction, and the celebrative cumulation of the lantern — not only intimately belongs to the early Quattrocento, but, indeed, is a prime

measure of it. One is tempted to imagine Michelangelo's *David* as the counterpart expression of the penultimate republic.

[84] Braunfels, 1948; 1953, 170, 180f, *passim*. Cf. Ch. VII, 173 ff.

[85] *Ibid.*

[86] Guasti, doc 23; Doc. 1.

physical magnificence — "al modo di Roma"[87] — of Florence and in the economic, professional, cultural and moral achievements of its citizens. Conditioned by the extended geneology of the world chronicle form,[88] surely they could not but have seen their affinitive ancestors depicted in the first band of relief: the heroic inventors of the skills and institutions that made possible the new urban culture of which they — under the seal of Hercules — were manifestly now among the leading exponents in all of Christendom. Similarly with the guiding moral forces and intellectual disciplines personified above in the Virtues and Liberal Arts: without doubt these aspects of life appeared at least as pervasive and highly refined in Florence as anywhere. How else would a companion of Villani have been of the opinion that "more charity [caritas] is practiced in Florence in a day than in a week at Pisa?"[89] The fact that these as well as the crafts were part of God's plan would, if anything, have given them further cause for swagger. And if the Planets sometimes frowned on Florence, Fortune quite commonly smiled.[90] The chauvinism was so heated that even the very personages of universal history that occupy the Campanile niches could be turned toward Florence. In a manuscript of 1339 that in concentrated form lavishes an even richer praise on the city than Villani's of the previous year — particularly concerning the moral character of the citizens — appears a belief "held by many": that the vision of the Erythraean Sibyl (and the related words of her Tiburtine sister) of "dazzling white lilies [that], under Mars, will be born from the dew of the noble descendants of Romulus" and which, after a long and difficult formation, will rise to great power, foretold exclusively the rise of "Florentia," city of the lily.[91]

In all of this can be felt a groundswell of the grandiose pride in their character and accomplishments, real and imagined, that in the early Quattrocento of Leonardo Bruni would mount, in antique form to heroic pitch.[92] But in the early Trecento such humanism was still at the exploratory stage, expressing itself publicly in veiled, double-edged forms. In the Campanile sculpture — as in the shifting attitudes of such early humanists as

[87] Villani, Bk. XI, 93.

[88] Seznek, 1961, 11 ff.

[89] Villani, Bk. XI, 134.

[90] Such as in the case of the two lion cubs born in Florence in 1331, said to be a "segno di buona fortuna e prospera per lo commune di Firenze" (*ibid.*, Bk. X, 185), or the six cubs of 1337, according to "l'agurio delli antichi pagani . . . segno di grande magnificenze della nostra città di Firenze" (*ibid.*, Bk. XI, 86).

[91] "Videtur hec esse ciuitas, de qua Sybilla loquitur Erithrea, que de tractibus partium Asie transiens ad partes Europe, ponit hec uerba. 'In Europe partibus ex rore nobili descendentium Romuli Romulene flos quidem floridus et candore mirabili liliatus, sub marte nascetur. Sed citra florum morem cum difficultate ac dierum longitudine deducetur in formam. Ante tamen quam arescat, sibi subiciet multarum gentium nationes. Et erit fortitudo eius in rota et rota dabit partes eius quasi pares.' . . . Sunt et alia multa iudicia, quod propheta hoc de Florentia loquatur, que omittuntur, gratia breuitatis. Sed hoc non omittitur, quod post Erithream tempore Octauiani claruit Tabertina sybilla, que tractans de quadam ciuitate, ponit quasi similia, sed per alia uerba, cuius dicta per multos ad ciuitatem Florentiam uerisimiliter reducuntur" (Frey, 1885, 123).

[92] Baron, 1955, *passim*; Haart, 1964, 114 ff.

Petrarch and Boccaccio[93] — man despite his accomplishments remains strictly subject to celestial forces, dependent on the Sacraments, at the mercy of God's will, and, awaiting the Second Coming, inextricably enmeshed in His universal plan of history.[94]

By now it is apparent that the spheres of meaning associated with the Campanile in its different aspects are by no means isolated. This becomes even clearer upon consideration of the symbolism of the tower in medieval times. One interpretation of the architectural genre, stressed by Braunfels, was pride: "Turres superbiam huius mundi significant," proclaims Rabanus Maurus ("Towers symbolize worldly pride").[95] Yet at the same time the tower — as impregnable fortress — was an important symbol of Chastity, Temperance, Fortitude, indeed a symbol of the Church and of the Virgin herself: Peter of Capua writes, for example, "Turris . . . id est Virgo Maria."[96] The thrust of meaning here (if one may allow the presence of such allusion in the case of this symbolically charged edifice) is thus double, toward the celebration of *civitas* (a legitimate pride) and at the same time toward the Church. Now we encounter that subtle iconographic feedback, as it were, so characteristic of the situation: the new Cathedral is dedicated not just to the Virgin in general but, in a sheer pagan spirit, to the Virgin especially inclined toward Florence — Santa Maria del Fiore.[97]

The final aspect of the Campanile that bears on the sculptural meaning is the most obvious: that the building is after all not just a tower but a bell tower, a campanile. The very intricate medieval symbolism of church bells is well worth reviewing. Already in the early Middle Ages they acquired, by their sounding out emergency, death, against the devil, and at great occasions, rich layers of popular meaning that survived, indeed thrived beneath the symbolic interpretations added during the scholastic centuries.[98] The scholastics were characteristically thorough in their treatment of the bells. Their typology is the silver trumpets of the priests of Moses, sounding to assemble the tribes for sacrifice and

[93] Cf. Petrarch's famous ascent of Mont Ventoux, in which antique reminiscences succeed to Augustinian gloom; J. H. Robinson and H. W. Rolfe, *Petrarch* (New York, 1914), 307 ff; on Boccaccio, Meiss, 1951, 157 ff.

[94] And increasingly so toward mid Trecento (cf. p. 95 above).

[95] *De Universo*, Bk. XXII, Ch. III; Braunfels, 1948, 196 ff; 1953, 179 f.

[96] Auber, 1871, III, 116 n. 1 f, with further sources; cf. Panofsky's discussion of the "tower of chastity" (*Early Netherlandish Painting: Its Origins and Character* [Cambridge, Mass., 1953], 132). In the lower church at Assisi the *Allegory of Chastity* depicts Chastity safe up in a tower set within a walled fortress (Alinari 5302); see also the related tower symbolism (Fortitude,

Temperance) in the Codex of the Ambraser collection of the Kunsthistorisches Museum in Vienna (von Schlosser, 1896, 19 ff, pl. II).

[97] In the "City of the Virgin" (Siena), the claim of Mary's patronage was even more explicit, dominating, for example, Duccio's *Maestà* (see N. Rubenstein, "Political Ideas in Sienese Art: The Frescoes by Ambrogio Lorenzetti and Taddeo di Bartolo in the Palazzo Pubblico," *Journal of the Warburg and Courtauld Institutes*, XXI [1958], 179 ff).

[98] J. Sauer, *Symbolik des Kirchengebäudes und seiner Ausstattung in der Auffassung des Mittelalters* (Freiburg, 1924), 140 ff. Follini and Rastrelli attest to the continuation of the popular meanings through the 18th century (1789 ff, II, 375 ff).

to excite adoration; for Joshua at Jericho the trumpets embodied unified power. So now the church bells symbolize the unity, power, and triumph of the new children of God; they sound the message of the preacher through the whole world; their beating is like the preacher's tongue, ringing out on two sides the truths of the two Testaments; the beam from which they hang is the Cross; the bands connecting them represent charity; the bell cord, always in motion, represents the supernatural life and the humility of the worshipper (we ascend toward God, He descends toward us); even the knots at the end of the cord have a significance, the perseverance to announce the truth.[99]

Yet surely the most tactile symbolism of the church bells was not that of the anonymous Christian preacher or the somewhat contrived readings of uninspiring mechanical parts, but rather the impassioned ancestors of Christ: the vividly human and individualistic prophets and sibyls who preached the message of His Coming. "The Bells are Prophets," declares Honorius of Autun.[100] Small wonder then that in the Trecento it was the Campanile, and not the façade, that was chosen for a cycle of monumental prophetic figures. Perhaps it was even the notion of Andrea himself — it would have been characteristic of his fluid imagination — that prophets on the Campanile would give icon to their voice and sound to their image. How else to outshine Giovanni Pisano's mighty but silent drama staged at the Siena façade?[101]

All these considerations evoke a final surmise, whether the inspiration for Donatello's most heroically rhetorical figures, the Habakuk ("Zuccone") and the Jeremiah (Fig. 23), might not have been in part the power of the symbolic matrix at the Campanile: on the one hand the Campanile bells as the emphatic voice of the Church; on the other, the Campanile as civic symbol for the triumphant republic that conceived itself in terms of antiquity. Again we would experience that telltale iconographic feedback of the Campanile sculpture, for Donatello's figures are at once the orators of antiquity in the guise of impassioned prophets, and passionate prophets in the guise of antique orators.[102] Is it too much to suppose that the undying and outspoken love of the Florentines for these figures, in particular for the "Zuccone," was not a function, at least in good part, of this profound

[99] Hugo of St. Victor, *Speculum de mysteriis Ecclesiae*, I (J. P. Migne, ed., *Patrologiae cursus completus series Latina* [Paris, 1844 ff], CLXXVII; passage cited by Auber, 1871, III, 122 f; amplified in the liturgical compendium of W. Durandus, *Rationale divinorum officiorum*, [Naples, 1839], Bk. I, Ch. 4 [cf. Sauer, 1924, 147 ff]).

[100] "De campanis significatio. — Campanae sunt prophetae. Campanae sonabant, quia prophetae Christi adventum praenuntiabant," H. Augustodunensis, *Gemma anamae*, Bk. I, 5, in J. P.

Migne, ed., *Patrologiae cursus completus series Latina* (Paris, 1844 ff, CLXXII, 544 f); similarly in Durandus (see n. 99 above) Bk. IV, Ch. 6, Reg. 15; cf. Sauer, 1924, 147.

[101] Their iconography is more than generically related: not only are the sibyls present in both cases, but David and Solomon are the central figures.

[102] Cf. H. W. Janson, "Donatello and the Antique," *Donatello e il suo tempo, Atti dell'VIII Convegno Internazionale di Studi sul Rinascimento* (Florence, 1968), 94.

integration of the double meaning of the sculpture with the double iconographic thrust of the Campanile itself?

Although sounding on only seven notes at most, the pealing of the Campanile bells seems to have carried an astoundingly rich symphony of allusion and meaning to the darkest back streets of Florence. In full view of the bell tower — yes, a colossal musical instrument, polychromed and symbolically adorned — the resonance of the clamorous ringing, the architectural splendour, and the reverberant iconography surely produced an effect in the Florentine consciousness little short of overpowering.

Chapter V

The Upper Campanile: Building History

The closed section built by Giotto and Andrea Pisano forms only a third of the Campanile. Above rise two huge stories pierced on each side by a pair of richly decorated Bifore, and even higher soars the final section lit by enormous Trifore and capped by a massive *ballatoio* (Frontispiece). It is to the history of the upper Campanile that we now turn.

The Bifora section suffers the same paucity of documentation as the fabric of Giotto and Andrea Pisano. The only archival entry referring directly to its building history is the decision of the Arte della Lana, taken on February 28, 1348, to obtain timbers "for the centering of the Campanile vaults."[1] The arrival of the Black Death in the summer of that year surely interrupted the work, delaying completion of the uppermost structure and decoration of the Bifora section.[2] The length of the delay can be elicited from Trecento building practice. The placing of revetment normally seems to have been phased closely following the progress of completed structural fabric; the marble components were always commissioned well in advance of projected emplacement, usually about a year to a year and a half.[3] Thus, in early 1351, with the lowermost decoration of the

---

[1] Doc. 10. See Ch. III, 50.

[2] See Ch. III n. 8, for the effect of the Black Death on the progress of the Campanile.

[3] This is apparent in the following discussion. The reason was, of course, that the same scaffolding and lift wheel used for the structural fabric be employed for the decoration, and also in order to maximize the productivity of the multipurpose crew, which could work the fabric as the various materials arrived, often in random order

and behind schedule. Saalman's apodictic statement on procedure ("masonry construction and incrustation are *always* [italics his] two separate phases, since the very process of building a masonry wall, with its lifting of stones, bricks and mortar, represents a serious danger to any expensive polychrome marble panels below"; 1964, 496) is untenable; according to these purely speculative rules, the entire bearing wall of the the Campanile would have been completed be-

Trifora section being commissioned,[4] it appears that the Bifora stories were substantially complete and the Trifora bearing wall nearing or already under construction.[5]

From the building rate of the Trifora section (based on extensive documentation discussed below), the magnitude of the fabric, the time available, and other circumstantial grounds, it was found (see Chapter III) that the Bifora section had been begun around 1343. During the difficult times immediately following the expulsion of the Duke of Athens (August 6, 1343), the construction, headed by a new *capomaestro*, may have proceeded at first somewhat slowly. On October 18, 1343, Florence entreats all cities still under its power not to hinder the transport of marble for the Opera.[6] On July 7, 1344, the Signoria asks the Bishop-Count of Luni to grant the Opera special conditions for the extraction of marble from his quarries.[7] This marble would form part of the extensive area of white incrustation at Bifora level. Progress soon must have accelerated, quickened by the reordered civic conditions and the upsurge in *gabelle* revenues under the popular new government,[8] and by early 1348 preparations were already being made for vaulting the Bifora section.

But after five years of rising fortune, the Opera succumbed to the universal catastrophe. Not only did the Black Death sweep away workmen and *Operai*, but in the chaos, the communal subsidy appears to have been lost. Order was restored with astounding swiftness, however. In March 1349 the Opera is returned its income; the commune makes it clear that the Duomo (which, in the context, includes the Campanile) is being built to the honor not only of God but also of the city; any official who disobeys the financial directive concerning the Cathedral subsidy must pay the enormous fine of 3,000 florins within three days of judgment or suffer decapitation — "eidem capud a spatulis amputetur."[9] Characteristic of the ever-surprising Trecento economics, the *gabelle* and other city revenues recovered rapidly, in fact, almost immediately upon the subsidence of the Black Death,[10] enabling the Opera, now solidly funded, to finish the Bifora section by 1350-51 and to begin the Trifora zone.

Through the chance preservation of the books of two succeeding Opera officials (*Provveditori*),[11] the building history of the Trifora story has a richer documentation than any previous and, indeed, most following Florentine structures. Not only can the Trifora fabric be traced almost step by step from start to finish, but, as we shall find, in the process new light is shed on the complex and elusive practices of medieval Florentine construction.

---

fore the incrustation was begun. For the way materials were lifted, see Doc. 148.

[4] See pp. 111 f below.

[5] Nardini gives no basis for his termination of the Bifora section in 1353 (37).

[6] Doc. 8.

[7] Doc. 9.

[8] Becker, "Popular Government," 1962, 363 ff; *idem*, 1966, 14 ff.

[9] Guasti, doc. 67.

[10] Becker, 1966, 14 ff; Brucker, 1962, 11 ff.

[11] For the role of the *Provveditori*, Guasti, LV f.

On January 5, 1351, a company of four subcontractors headed by Neri di Fioravanti and including Alberto Arnoldi is commissioned to execute 4,100 florins worth of sandstone and white, red, and "black" (green) marble piecework, sufficient to decorate major aspects of a ten-braccia section of the Campanile.[12] The masons are to shape the components "to the specifications given them by Francesco Talenti, the principal master of the fabric" and deliver the finished work within fifteen months, the marble near the lifting wheel at the foot of the Campanile and the interior revetment of *pietraforte* to the quarters of the Opera.[13] The masons, required to maintain Florentine residence during the term of contract, are permitted to execute, in excess of the ten, one extra braccia in altitude of revetment, but not more; the Opera is given the option to commission unlimited additional piecework according to the prices and terms of the contract.

It is specified that the completed work is to be placed "in four windows and in [their] jambs, shoulders, frontispieces, [and as] red 'colonnettes' and intarsia" and that it will constitute "everything pertaining to ten braccia in height of the said windows" (qualifying the following clause that the material is to be sufficient "to furnish ten braccia in height, all around, of the Campanile"). The revetment, then, is for ten braccia in and about four windows set in the four sides of the Campanile, which can refer only to the Trifore, where red colonnettes ("colupnellis rubeis"), lacking in the Bifora decoration, are indeed present in the jambs (Figs. VII, VIII). The specifications of the piecework indicate that the section in question is the first ten braccia of the window, that is, beginning with the splay below the balustrade and ending about a third the way up the columns (Fig. 83).[14]

[12] Doc. 12. (The *Verde di Prato*, a rich, deep green marble is termed "black" in the documents.)

[13] The interior revetment is *pietraforte* except for the *ballatoio* in the Bifora section and the ceiling of the stairways for which the veinless and thus structurally sounder *macigno* was employed. F. Rodolico (*Le pietre delle città d'Italia* [Florence, 1953], 238 ff) discusses the nature of these two main Florentine building stones. *Pietraforte,* quarried from the hills to the south of the Arno — including the Boboli area — is a warm-colored, fine-grained and highly weather-resistant calcareous sandstone. In fact, it contains so much lime (24 per cent against 35 per cent silica) that Rodolico calls it a sandy limestone; it forms the bulk of Florentine architecture, including the Pal. Vecchio, S. Croce, Or San Michele, the Pal. Medici, Rucellai, Pitti, etc. *Macigno,* a rather pure sandstone (65 per cent silica, only 4 per cent lime) from the hills of Fiesole is divided by color into two categories: the earthy-tinted *pietra bigia* —

seen in the façades of the Pal. Gondi, Antinori, Capponi, Pandolfini — and the cool gray *pietra serena* of Brunelleschian fame, used also at the Mercato Nuovo and the Uffizi, of great strength and beauty but comparatively vulnerable to the elements (see the present state of the Loggia at the Innocenti).

[14] The list (Doc. 12) includes 20 items. Many are difficult to identify precisely. However, the altitude of the 10 braccia section can be fixed. Item 15 specifies 40 braccia of plain white slabs ⅞ braccia broad to be placed at the bottom splay of the window between red borders, 72 braccia of which are specified for the very purpose in item 13 ("Septuaginta duo bracchia colonnellorum dictorum marmorum rubeorum, que poni debent ad planum fenestrarum ad pedem isguanciatorum"). Of the 18 braccia per side of the red moldings, ca. 10 are for the bottom and ca. 8 braccia for the shorter upper section of frame. Immediately above comes the even shorter bal-

Included in the commission is dressed stone "to be placed on the interior at the stair," probably meant to line the stairwell in the northeast pier of the Trifora section (Figs. X, 88). But the stairwell, and thus the pier, cannot have been begun before April 5, 1353, when the Opera asks the *Provveditore* "to determine if it is more work, or less, to make the stair square [in plan] instead of round," as specified in the contracts.[15] Indecision about the form of the stairwell — finally executed as an octagon (Fig. X) — may have delayed the construction of the northeast pier until the last possible moment. It is in the least conspicuous corner of the Campanile, and the Opera, ever anxious to manifest to the public the dutiful execution of its responsibility (a recurrent theme in the history of the Cathedral), probably would have directed the other three piers to be built first in any

ustrade of item 18, 12 panels ("compassate") including 8 of 2²/₃ braccia length and 4 of 1²/₃ — i.e., per side two of the former and one of the latter, coming to 7 braccia (2²/₃ + 2²/₃ + 1²/₃). Over the balustrade run 7 braccia per side of the 28 braccia of cornice of item 17 ("Viginti octo bracchia dicte cornicis albe pro davanzalibus fenestrarum"), to be carved in the same manner as item 16, i.e., as a tongue molding ("laborata ad linguaczas") to continue as an extention of the balustrade cornice (or vice versa) around the piers ("cinghiant pilastros et facciuolas usque ad columpnellos").

For the section below the level of the lower frame of the lower splay, I could find no item. However, the jamb intarsia is given in item 14 as 75 braccia of intarsia work ⁷/₈ braccia wide ("Septuaginta quinque bracchia inpetrati pro isguancitis fenestrarum, que poni debent in medio colupnellorum rubeorum, largitudinis septem ottavorum bracchii") which, divided by the 8 jambs, breaks down to 9³/₈ braccia per jamb. The corresponding red framing is found in item 11 as 152 braccia of red "colonnellorum . . . que cinghiari debent inpetratum isguanciati fenestrarum," which comes to 19 braccia per jamb, or about 9¹/₂ braccia of height, which, allowing for the unmitered placement of the vertical upon the horizontal members of the frame and the diagonal cut of the jamb at its lower corner, corresponds closely to the 9³/₈ braccia of intarsia.

This ca. 9¹/₂ braccia, together with the breadth of the lower frame strip, ¹/₃ braccia (item 13; the frame is identical all around), comes close enough to the 10 braccia section specified. This tallies with item 10, which specifies 192 braccia

of twisted columns of all three types (the half- and full tracery columns, and the doubly large — and doubly paid — ones of the frontispiece), breaking down into 48 braccia per window or 8 braccia per column (computed probably ideally for accounting, since the 3¹/₂- and 6¹/₂-braccia sections in which the column pieces must come, would result in some columns less and some greater than 8 braccia). Since the columns begin ca. 2 braccia up (the frontispiece columns over the 2 braccia socles of item 1, 16 braccia of "stipidorum," or 4 braccia per window) it is clear that the same 10-braccia section is meant (in item 10, the payment for the columns is reckoned at 16 lire per braccia, the different sizes of columns being given braccia factors according to their relative sizes — ¹/₂, 1, 2 "braccia" — different from their much smaller absolute diameters. Thus, for the half columns are paid 8 lire for each braccia of length, the central — normal — column 16, and the outer 32).

Two further points are worth noting. The remaining items (2-9, 12, 16, 20) provide only partial incrustation of the "piers." Thus, the clause that the material is "omne id quod pertinet ad dictas fenestras, altitudinis decem bracchiorum" is to be interpreted rather strictly. Secondly, the list includes only one intarsia ("inpetrati") item, the ⁷/₈-braccia-wide jamb decoration. But between the jambs and the half columns of the tracery is a narrower intarsia strip. This discrepancy might indicate a slight modification of the design during execution, which may even be reflected in the document of Apr. 5, 1353 (Doc. 15) concerning a discrepancy in the jambs.

[15] Doc. 14.

case. This order of events is substantiated by the fact that on the same day as the stairwell inquiry, April 5, 1353, it is discovered that some of the structural masonry of the window jambs is less beveled than the plan specifies ("meno ismusso che non è il disegniamento") and must be redone.[16] One surmises that by April 1353, substantial parts of the three "prominent" piers of the Trifora story were up and probably even partly incrusted with the marble Neri di Fioravante and company were to have had ready by mid 1352.[17] The jamb error would have been discovered in the process of emplacing the revetment.

On August 14, 1353 the Opera orders the construction of a wooden model of the Campanile.[18] A design for the Trifora already existed, from which the jambs are recorded (on April 5, as noted above) to have deviated. Following its specifications, by the summer of 1353 a great deal of the fabric of the Trifora story had been executed. Not only the piers and revetment, but even the complex, expensive window tracery had already been begun. The course of the Trifora section was already determined.[19] The wooden model cannot have entailed its substantial modification, but must have primarily concerned the independent elements projected above. It could well be that the novel form of the "andito," or *ballatoio*, first mentioned only on March 9, 1356,[20] then took shape, and also the great spire that was begun immediately above the Trifora section and abandoned in its initial stages. The model then would be the one known two centuries later to Vasari as Giotto's: "According to Giotto's model, this campanile should have had as a terminus over what is seen a spire or square pyramid fifty braccia high."[21]

The L-shaped pier stumps under the roof of the Campanile give little basis for a reconstruction of what was to come above (Figs. 88, 114, 116).[22] But the fact that the massive piers contain no stairs indicates that another prismatic window story definitely was not planned.[23] Vasari's quadratic pyramid surmounting the enormous Trifora story would have been but a gigantic example of the pre-Giottesque Florentine archetype seen, for example, at Santa Maria Novella (Fig. 295).[24]

[16] Doc. 15.

[17] On Apr. 5, 1353, Benozo — the Benoczo Niccolay who was one of the four contractors of Jan. 5, 1351 (Doc. 12) — reports to have finished about 1000 florins worth of his share of the contract (Doc. 19).

[18] Doc. 34.

[19] Gioseffi's notion (1963, 92 ff, figs. 77A, B, 82C, D) of a first, radically different Trifora design, based on a slight anomaly in the Spanish Chapel view of the Campanile of 1366 (Fig. 69) is unreasonable (compare the distortions of parts below Trifora level) and belongs in the same category of speculation as Kiesow's reconstruction of the "Arnolfian" Duomo flanks (1961, fig. 8).

[20] Doc. 111. This would be substantiated by the irregularity in the incrustation pattern just below the *ballatoio;* the "missing" two strips could have resulted from a modulation of the *ballatoio,* perhaps an enlargement — or from its invention.

[21] Doc. XIII.

[22] Cf. Gioseffi's reconstruction, 1963, fig. 77b.

[23] In each of the three stories of the upper Campanile the stair begins with a spiral in the northeast pier (in the Bifora section quadratic in plan, in the Trifora, octagonal) climbing to a level from which a straight flight can be run up over the windows, and up the south side where all the exits to the floor levels are located (Figs. X, 6).

[24] A revival not without historical significance (see Ch. VII). Cf. Gioseffi's notion that Talenti planned an octagon and spires like Giotto (1963, 94).

Whatever was in question in August 1353, a model was not necessary to build it. Rather the model served a public function in a state project. The citizenry, all along paying the enormous expenses of the fabric, wanted to see how it would appear. A hint of their anxiety is given by the decision of the Opera in June 1353, to remove, prior to the approaching feast of San Giovanni, "the scaffolding catwalks so that the fabric might be seen."[25] The model of the Campanile served the same purpose as did those for the Cathedral shortly later. It was important that the citizens be pleased; were they not, trouble could be made, funds withheld, subsidies cancelled. Pleased, they were to back the Opera to the limit. The Siena design, a colorful affair over two meters high (Fig. IX), was surely done at least partially toward this end.[26] No layman would understand or appreciate the forms rendered in a working drawing. Like the building committee of today, he needed a realistic rendering or even better, a model, in order to judge. Presumably the Campanile model would have been given polychrome decoration and would have included not only the projected, but the already completed parts so that one could conveniently evaluate the success of the totality.

Naturally the designer himself would have been interested to see the visualization of his ideas. It seems more than likely that the man responsible for the Campanile model was Francesco Talenti, who had been *capomaestro* since at least January 1351, when it was recorded that the incrustation components were to be shaped following his specifications. On May 29, 1355, he was commissioned to solve problems concerning the design of the Cathedral, on which work was again about to be taken up, and to present the solution, which was eventually accepted, in the form of a wooden model.[27] Talenti alone was *capomaestro* until 1357-58, when the Cathedral construction began with great impetus. The added responsibilities seem to have been too much for one man, at least for the aging Talenti. Within a year, Giovanni di Lapo Ghini, a structural specialist who had made his way into the circle of power as subcontractor for the Cathedral pier foundations, was co-*capomaestro* alongside — or perhaps slightly beneath — his senior.[28] Moreover, for a brief period beginning in 1358, Alberto Arnoldi achieves the same rank; a first-rate sculptor, long providing the Opera with incrustation components and now entrusted with completing certain details of Arnolfo's façade, Arnoldi appears as a complementary appointment to Ghini, as a specialist of architectural decoration.[29]

[25] The scaffolding thus was not built up from the ground (as is generally the current practice) but lodged in the putlog holes and, covering only a section at a time, moving up with the building as it grew. Doc. 23.

[26] Cf. Braunfels's (1953, 227 ff) and Grote's (1961, 113 ff) lists of such models and designs.

[27] Guasti, 81 ff.

[28] Having proven his abilities in the preceding months, on Oct. 26, 1357 (Guasti, 110) Ghini is put in charge of the Cathedral pier construction under the direction of Talenti, who is still in control of both fabrics. But Ghini does not receive the title of *capomaestro* until Nov. 22, 1358 (Guasti, 121), when he and Talenti together are called "chapo maestri di questa opera." Saalman's implication (1964, 480) that Ghini is *capomaestro* already on Oct. 26, 1357 is misleading.

[29] Cf. "Alberto Arnoldi," in Thieme-Becker, *Künstlerlexikon.*

But the sharing of responsibility seems to have applied only to the Cathedral, at least initially. On November 28, 1358, a substantial error is detected in the execution of the Campanile incrustation; moreover, the work is behind schedule. The blame is laid directly to Talenti. "It's Talenti's fault," notes the *Provveditore*.[30] Thus, from its beginning in 1351 to late 1358, when it was substantially complete, the Trifora section went up under his design and personal supervision. Only later, and in a secondary capacity,[31] did Ghini enter the final stages of construction of the Campanile.

One should not imagine that the position of Cathedral *capomaestro* was in any manner onerous. His social status seems to have corresponded to that of a high public official.[32] The yearly retainer was one hundred florins, high on the scale of salaried individuals. Special commissions contributed considerable income in addition. Talenti was paid twenty florins for his wooden Cathedral model.[33] The mechanical work of carving stringcourses, paneling, intarsia, etc., was subcontracted, as we have observed, at relatively low rates and on stiff terms. Although Talenti received no commission for delivering the full-scale drawings and templates for this piecework, which was considered a normal part of his job, he got first crack at the more complex and better compensated elements of decoration, particularly those forms difficult to render other than by prototype examples.

On June 26, 1355,[34] Talenti finishes carving the tracery of one of the Trifore — termed a "*lunetta*" (Figs. 82, 87) — which was begun sometime before June 25, 1353, when it is noted that he has received a fifteen florin advance toward completion of the work.[35] We are not informed of the outcome of the appraisal ordered made of the piece at its completion. But the fact that an appraisal was necessary indicates it was the pilot model, after which the other three sets of tracery were copied. On the basis of the valuation of Talenti's example, the others were commissioned at a set price (though always as "low as possible"). They required much less time to carve than it had taken a busy *capomaestro* to shape the prototype. The second set of tracery, presumably commissioned shortly after the completion of Talenti's, seems to have been more or less ready by January 1356, six months later, when there was talk of contracting the third, which Talenti himself even may have received.[36] It was commissioned on March 18, 1356.[37] Two months later, on May 10, it was decided to consign the fourth set after the festival of San Giovanni "for less if possible."[38] Apparently there was still haggling over the price of Talenti's

[30] Doc. 197.

[31] He helps Talenti to estimate remaining work; significantly, it is Ghini who is sent to Siena to procure desperately needed material in 1358, and not Talenti, who thus is still the indispensable director of the fabric. Grote's attempt to belittle the role of Talenti (1961, 70 ff) is inexplicable.

[32] Braunfels, 1953, 216 ff.

[33] The approval of his model on Aug. 31, 1355

(Guasti, 84) does not give the amount; presumably it was the 20 florins promised in the comission of May 29, 1355 (Guasti, 81).

[34] Doc. 78.

[35] Doc. 32.

[36] Doc. 100.

[37] Doc. 113.

[38] Doc. 116.

prototype; only on May 31 was the dispute settled ("La lunetta di Franciescho. — Istral-ciaronla").[39] Perhaps on the basis of that price, it was resolved on the same day that the "ultima lunetta" — the one to be commissioned after the feast of San Giovanni — should be contracted "for 150 lire, or as best you [the *Provveditore?*] can."[40] Presumably Talenti's prototype would have grossed him somewhat more than the copies.

Almost certainly Talenti had a hand in executing the rich capitals of the Trifore (Figs. 82, 87, 120), which would be the "other works" ("altri lavori") mentioned in connection with his work on the "lunetta." Shortly later, on August 31, 1357, he seized the large commission (320 lire) for the prototype of the huge pier capitals of the Cathedral (Fig. 252),[41] the carving of which must have been partly responsible for the negligence of his duties on the Campanile that became a problem at this time.[42] Finally, like Giotto and Andrea, Talenti took part in the figural decoration: following January 11, 1357, he carves a prophet for twenty-five florins.[43]

The timing of the commissioning of details, as has been noted, was connected intimately with the progress and projected future advance of the fabric, and entailed the additional reckoning of the time required for the subcontractors to fulfill their commitments. Nothing was readily available. The most basic materials, even timber and rubble, were obtained piecemeal in the cheapest manner possible. Everything had to be made by hand. Even transport — at best, backbreaking cartage and bargework — sometimes meant a risky passage through unfriendly places. A modern building contractor carried back to the Trecento would throw up his hands in horror. One respects a man like Talenti, who could co-ordinate so many variables and reply to the question of whether or not to order certain marbles on February 5, 1356, with astounding precision: "It seems that we won't contract them," notes the *Provveditore*, "because Franciescho says they will not be placed for two years."[44] Or on August 14, 1353, asked about "ordering marble for working upward from the top," it is recorded, with chronological precision at least, that "Francesco said there's work for a year."[45]

With the synchronism of the various aspects of construction in mind, it is possible to follow the building history of the middle section of the Trifora story from the seemingly random documentary references. On September 26, 1353, there is the first mention of placing a window,[46] followed on November 5 by discussion of "which window to complete."[47] The parts that had been contracted in January 1351 probably were mostly

[39] Doc. 119.

[40] Doc. 122.

[41] Guasti, 108.

[42] Talenti seems to have undertaken too much in 1357-58. He had to obtain an extension of the completion deadline of the nave capital on Feb. 16, 1357 (*ibid.*, 116); even the figure that he was supposed to carve after Jan. 11, 1357 (Doc. 138) was delayed until after Oct. 17, 1358 (Doc. 193),

at which time he is allowed only a 10-florin advance on it. There is no record of a final payment, and the figure may never have been finished.

[43] See n. 42 above.

[44] Doc. 102.

[45] Doc. 35.

[46] Doc. 41.

[47] Doc. 43.

finished; additional, similar components seem to have been ordered in the intervening time at the original rates, accounting for the continuing references to the contract of Neri di Fioravanti and his colleagues.[48] Indeed, so much incrustation was commissioned by late 1354 that on December 15 there was an inquiry about "the intarsia lacking on the Campanile."[49] One gathers that less, rather than more, than half the intarsia work remained to be contracted or completed, at least for the Trifora section.

In February 1355, and again in April,[50] several barges of columns and other marble items arrive from Carrara for the Trifora windows, one of which already is being placed on February 27 ("The window. Go on with it," notes the *Provveditore*).[51] On March 18, the work continues.[52] Talenti's tracery prototype was commissioned a year and a half before (by June 25, 1353) in order to have it ready by early 1355. On June 8, 1355, there was an inquiry about the tracery and other forms being carved in Talenti's workshop: "Estimate when it [will] be completed."[53] Finished by June 26, the tracery was quickly appraised[54] and freed for placement, which must have occurred shortly thereafter.

By January 1356, another window must have stood to the level of the tracery, which was sorely needed ("have a lunette delivered by any means at our expense").[55] Following the staggered raising of the piers, the commissioning of the final two sets of tracery in March and June would have anticipated the basic completion of the framework of the two windows in question in late 1356 and early 1357. This is borne out by comparison of three lists of components remaining to be commissioned. On June 20, 1356, a price schedule of piecework still includes red colonnettes ("colonnelli rossi") and various items of arched intarsia (for example, "empetrato in archo di 7/8" braccia in width and "empetrato in volta del 1/3") indicating that work is still in progress on the window jambs and archivolts (Fig. 82).[56] A year later, on July 5, 1357, in an inventory (made by Talenti) of the items of white marble needed "to raise [the Campanile] eight braccia higher, in one year," nothing seems to belong to the zone of the windows themselves.[57] That the level of activity had reached the incrustation over the windows is also indicated by the instruction in June 1357 to place "the Angels," one of which — totally absent from the literature — still stands above the southern Trifora gable (Figs. 70, 84).[58] The gradual upward progress of the revetment is evident in Talenti's next list, compiled on September 28, 1358, of what was lacking up to the *ballatoio;* nothing conceivably belonging to the window is men-

[48] "Sommo" is the term for contract, see e.g., Docs. 65, 74. For further discussion of contracting see Docs. 13, 35, 84.

[49] Doc. 57.

[50] Doc. 58.

[51] Doc. 59.

[52] Doc. 64.

[53] Doc. 72.

[54] Doc. 78.

[55] Doc. 92.

[56] Doc. 130.

[57] Doc. 162.

[58] Doc. 154 (cf. Docs. 98, 109, 120). The small figure (ca. 1½ braccia) — discovered by my wife — is close in style to the Andrea Pisano-school prophets originally on the south face of the Campanile, now in the Cathedral Museum. Could it — and the prophets as well — be by Talenti?

tioned, but rather numerous components of the *ballatoio* (Fig. 85), in particular the three ranges of consoles ("bechadelli grandi, mezani, e picholi").[59]

Following the setting up of the first tracery in the summer of 1355, the window arches were begun.[60] In a council of February 9, 1356, it is directed that these arches be constructed of large stone voussoirs consolidated by metal ligatures: in vaulting the window "there should be employed large blocks of stone with leaded clamps to bind everything."[61]

The structural core of the Campanile wall — like that of, for example, Or San Michele and the Cathedral — consists largely of *pietraforte* courses narrower and far less presentable than the large, well-finished blocks of the interior revetment (Figs. 27-29, 112).[62] It probably even contains considerable rubble masonry in the huge corner masses, as in the cores of the end piers of Or San Michele,[63] the foundations of the Cathedral, and the city wall (Fig. 245). This would account for the references to "ripieno" (aggregate) in the Campanile documents, such as the request on May 10, 1356, for an unspecified quantity, "either new or old, whichever is better for the fabric."[64] The rubble was commonly obtained from the destruction of older fabrics ("ripieno vecchio"), nothing being discarded.[65] But sometimes the need outstripped this supply, as on December 7, 1357, when quantities of river-bed gravel ("tante pietre di fiume") were requested "for the foundations" of the Cathedral piers.[66] Brick — nearly always covered with an intonaco in Florence — was much employed in construction, sometimes together with stone in rough masonry, as in the ground-story Campanile wall, but particularly for arches and vaults because of its lightness, its availability in thin, uniform units, and its great adherence to mortar.[67] In Or San Michele, the window arches in the upper stories are composed of brick;[68] the ribs, at least in the second story, alternate brick and stone voussoirs; the webs,

---

[59] Doc. 191.

[60] It may seem perverse to first put up the tracery and then the arch, but that is the way the documents would seem to have it. In any case, the span of the arch was not great (7-10 braccia) and the scaffolding would have protected the rather massive tracery — which would have stood without the columns. A particularly close fit between tracery and arch may have been desired.

[61] Doc. 103. In this context "raguagliare" (to level) can only refer to the vaulting of the window.

[62] As can be seen in the innumerable places where the interior revetment is missing, in scaffolding holes, and in the uncovered stumps of the spire (Figs. 112, 114, 116).

[63] According to Prof. Antonio Bigazzi of the Sopr. ai Monumenti, Florence. Such masonry is visible at the break in the city wall at the south

of the Pza. Torquato Tasso (Fig. 245); see also the cross section of the Pisan campanile in Sanpaolesi, 1956, fig. 5, and his analysis on 22 f. The material was not always competently employed, as witness the sudden collapse of S. Pier Maggiore (early Trecento) in the 18th century when it was shockingly discovered that the structure was largely of rubble masonry (Paatz, IV, 629, 643 n. 8).

[64] Doc. 118. The material can be only for the Campanile, as work was not begun on the Cathedral until a year later.

[65] For example, the materials of the old Cathedral campanile, when dismantled in 1357, were used for the new Cathedral foundations (Doc. 166).

[66] Guasti, 113.

[67] According to Prof. Antonio Bigazzi.

[68] In the third story, even the piers, which carry

as in the Campanile, are of bricks oriented cross-axially (Figs. 49, 89, 243). The space above the vaults in a multistoried building was filled to the superior floor level with rubble masonry. But the employment of massive stone blocks was rare;[69] their use in the Trifora arches was an extraordinary measure, the solution, by a special council, of an unusual problem. To withstand the oscillations and the powerful vibrations of the bells hung within it and the stresses of the huge spire that was to surmount it, the Trifora section had to be structurally flawless. In the lateral thrust of the Trifora arches resided a potential weakness, and the *Operai* were not taking any chances. The clamping of the voussoirs (and probably the adjacent fabric as well) would neutralize much of the thrust. To be efficiently linked, the masonry would have to be of exceptionally large blocks.

As further insurance, on May 31, 1357, it was directed that the Campanile "be bound all around with sufficiently heavy iron chains in the wall"[70] — forerunners of Brunelleschi's Cupola. Still further tensile binding of the fabric with metal devices is encountered during construction of the Trifora section. On June 19, 1953, a directive is issued concerning the rationing out of lead and bars ("piombo e ispranghe").[71] Even in the later history of the Trifora story, after January 4, 1358, when the workers are reduced to a skeleton crew, a man is retained to work lead ("a pionbare").[72] He would have performed the same task as his counterpart in the previous register of Campanile workers drawn up on June 14, 1357,[73] a mason "a allacciare," to fasten and connect, referring to the common method of attaching and connecting revetment with leaded dowels and cramps.[74] But it might also mean that a great deal of the structural fabric of the upper Campanile, at least, is interlocked with metal devices.

After the completion of the Trifora windows in 1356 and early 1357, the construction, which had proceeded with such deliberate speed since 1351, loses momentum. The causes are complex. The problem was partly one of materials. The structural fabric and interior revetment were of local stone,[75] but the marble, with the exception of the *Verde di Prato*, was extracted from Pisan and Sienese territory.[76] The procedure for obtaining this marble was multifold. As already noted, agreements were made with in-

only a timber roof, are constructed of brick (covered, of course, with intonaco).

[69] Another example: the jambs and especially the lintels of the rectangular niches of the ground floor chamber (Figs. 25, 26).

[70] Doc. 148.

[71] Doc. 25.

[72] Doc. 182; this does not refer to the process of plumbing the fabric, which any of the *maestri* could do well enough.

[73] Doc. 155.

[74] According to Prof. Antonio Bigazzi.

[75] Florence is built literally in a quarry that in-

cludes not only a variety of strong, beautiful, and finely carvable building stone (see n. 13 above), but, as well, limestone for mortar (the "alberese" from just south of the Ema) and riverbed gravel for aggregate (cf. Rodolico, 1953, geological map, p. 236).

[76] As stated, for example, in the contract of Jan. 5, 1351 (Doc. 12), the white comes from Carrara, the red from "Sancti Iusti ad Montem Rantali" (in the Chianti near Cintoia), and the black (green) from Monte Ferrato (Prato). See Rodolico, 1953, 242.

dependent contractors, such as Neri di Fioravanti and Alberto Arnoldi, to provide set amounts of piecework at fixed prices. These contracts, or *sommi*, seem to have provided the bulk of the incrustation. But there were supplementary resources. Other Florentine workshops, perhaps with masons not fully employed, were granted work. Or San Michele,[77] Santa Croce,[78] and the Misericordia[79] (now the Bigallo) are mentioned in this capacity, as well as the Baptistery, where the *capomaestro* himself is named subcontractor.[80] The Opera del Duomo seems to have sent its own workmen to procure marble from Carrara alongside the private companies.[81] Finally, if the contract with Siena mentioned in 1342[82] reflected a general phenomenon, there were arrangements for other communes to provide piecework, a practice that seems to have been eliminated, however, by the 1350s.

The pragmatic combination worked well until June 15, 1357, when a subcontractor by the name of Sibellino fell behind on his agreement to deliver large amounts of white marble items from the Sienese quarries.[83] On November 29, 1357, the Opera grudgingly grants him an extension until November of 1358.[84] On October 17, 1358, he is awaited in Florence, where he is to give an account of himself.[85] But apparently little, if anything, of his contract is then delivered. On January 10, 1359, the Opera admits "the greatest need" ("grandisimo bisongno") for "consoles of white marble, small, medium, and large," that is, the *ballatoio* consoles (Fig. 85). Benci di Cione is to try — in vain — to secure their delivery.[86] By January 29, the delay has become a public scandal: Talenti, Ghini, and the *Provveditore* beg the Opera to "obtain by any possible way or means the lacking white marble for the flanks of the church, and similarly for the Campanile"; expressly, they ask "to be pardoned for the murmuring [*mormorare*] going around."[87] The next day the Opera dispatches Ghini himself, badly needed to direct the structural work in the Cathedral, to the Sienese quarries to determine what has gone wrong and to get the marble to Florence at all costs (though as cheaply as possible), "especially the consoles, cornicework, little arches [etc.] . . . for the Campanile."[88]

The second problem was financial. The main source of building funds was the communal endowment. In 1331 it was decided that two denari deducted from every lira paid

[77] Doc. 186.

[78] Docs. 60, 63, 86, 102.

[79] Docs. 99, 142.

[80] Doc. 158. To this day all major Florentine fabrics retain a *capomaestro* or the services of an equivalent for the continuing care required of venerable buildings.

[81] A mason is sent from the Opera on Jan. 7, 1354, to Carrara for marble (Doc. 51); in the lists of marble shipments arriving from Pisa in Feb. and Apr. 1355 (Doc. 58) it is distinguished between the work of the subcontractors ("iiii colon-

ne del sommo") and of the Opera *maestri* ("39 pezi di marmo dell'opera").

[82] Doc. 7.

[83] Doc. 156. The original contract of Nov. 7, 8, 1356 specified delivery for Jan., 1358 (Doc. 134).

[84] Doc. 172. The turn to Siena might have had to do with the abandonment of the Duomo Nuovo project in 1356, which would have freed marble workers, at least temporarily.

[85] Doc. 192.

[86] Doc. 201.

[87] Doc. 207.

[88] Doc. 208.

out of the city treasury, a discount of 0.8 per cent, be given to the Opera.[89] In 1332, this was supplemented by two denari that the tax farmers were to pay of every lira of the purchase price of the *gabelle*.[90] But beginning around 1340 at least one of the major *gabelle*, the tax on contracts, could no longer be sold; by 1350, the city had taken over its administration directly.[91] The Opera successfully petitions the city in March 1350 to adjust the 1332 law to the new situation, the Opera to receive two denari per lira collected by the city officials.[92] But by June 1353, funds are again short: the *Provveditore* is directed by the Opera "to reclaim the income from the [city] treasury and the *gabelle*,"[93] which perhaps had been diverted to military purposes during the war with Milan between 1351 and 1353 or to the purchase of grain during the famine of 1352-53. The plea is repeated on September 26, 1353,[94] and perhaps again in 1354.[95] Only on August 14, 1355, is the endowment returned to the Opera.[96]

Despite almost cyclical variations in income from the state, the Opera managed to finance the Campanile project uninterruptedly. Other sources had been periodically available, such as the head tax of two soldi, the indulgences, and the discount of the *estimo* during Arnolfo's period; the Inquisition revenues assigned to the Opera between 1318 and 1328; and the law of 1331 that disputed testaments fall to the Cathedral fabric. There were as well substantial gifts, beginning with the 3,000 florins of Boniface VIII in 1296.[97] Especially after the Black Death private donations poured into religious coffers,[98] and there is no reason to except the Opera del Duomo. Finally, as in the case of Giotto's foundations, money could be borrowed from the Arte della Lana in a tight situation,[99] promises made, and payments postponed.

With only the Campanile going up, the Opera managed to get along. But in 1355, Talenti formed the new design and model for the Cathedral, which by June 1357 was begun at an impressive pace. The discount rate of the state subsidy had been established in the 1330s at the height of Florentine prosperity. Even though the economy rebounded miraculously after the plague, it did not recover its former level.[100] The income provided was barely enough, together with secondary means, to keep the Campanile workshop running at a good tempo; but it was not sufficient to finance both projects simultaneously. The Opera therefore petitions the commune on January 11, 1357, to grant it a discount of six denari per lira instead of the current two. With the additional funds they would

[89] Guasti, doc. 35. On this and the following endowments see Grote, 1961, 43 ff.

[90] Such taxes were not collected directly by the state; rather the privilege of taxation was sold to the so-called tax farmers who realized high profits on the transaction.

[91] *Ibid.*, 61.

[92] Guasti, doc. 67.

[93] *Ibid.*, 75.

[94] *Ibid.*, 78.

[95] *Ibid.*, 79.

[96] *Ibid.*, doc. 74.

[97] Grote, 1961, 32 ff.

[98] Meiss, 1951, 78 ff.

[99] Cf. also Guasti, doc. 133 (as noted by Saalman, 1964, 476 n. 24); and "CC fiorini" from the Arte della Lana on May 28, 1353 (Guasti, 75).

[100] Brucker, 1962, 11 ff.

promise to complete the Campanile in four years for 40,000 florins instead of the 70,000 florins and twenty years they calculated it was going to take with the old income. Hoping to achieve what a modern economist would term economies of scale, the Opera wanted to dispatch the Campanile project, weighing on its shoulders for more than two decades, so that all energies could be channeled to the awaiting Cathedral.[101]

The Opera was obliged to repeat the request four times.[102] Only on April 14, 1358, did it meet with success, the commune granting a tremendous financial boost, retaining the old tax on the sale of *gabelle*, hiking the discount of city disbursements to 1.6 per cent, and adding a new discount of 1.2 per cent of all city income.[103] Florence had to back the Cathedral project founded so ceremoniously in June 1357. But because it had delayed funds so long, the Campanile's future was darkened. Already on the same day as the approval of Talenti's Duomo model, August 31, 1355, it was seen that a choice might have to be made between the Campanile and the Cathedral, for there was talk of fewer workers on the tower.[104] The impending commencement of the Cathedral precipitated the decision on June 14, 1357, to transfer laborers from the Campanile to maximize the raising of the Duomo.[105] The combination of limited funds, the freshness and newly established precedence of the Cathedral project, and the failure of the marble supply in late 1357 brought about the further reduction of the number of Campanile workers on January 4, 1358, leaving only a skeleton crew at the Trifora section: two marble workers, one master "a pionbare," one stonemason, and assisting common laborers.[106] The irresolute future of the Campanile was now fated. The high hopes for a rapid completion manifest a year earlier had been broken and the opposite way taken. Now that the eyes of the citizens were diverted to the dramatically rising Cathedral, it was possible to protract the completion of the Campanile at a minimal rate.

We have already seen that the incrustation for the wall above the Trifora windows was executed through 1357 and possibly into 1358, when a final inventory (made by Talenti and Ghini on December 20) of revetment missing up to the *ballatoio* ("fino a l'andito") includes only marbles for the *ballatoio* itself;[107] the lacking elements are those which Ghini is sent to bring "at all costs" from Siena a month later,[108] indicating that work on the *ballatoio* continued at least into 1359. The revetment for the upper wall of

---

[101] Doc. 140. Saalman (1964, 476 n. 24) assumes this to concern the Cathedral project, which, however, was not even begun until 6 months later, and which, in any case, could never have been executed in 4 years, nor for 40-70,000 florins. Only in the later requests for funds, after the Cathedral is begun, is it included as partial beneficiary together with the Campanile (in making his point Saalman, after discussing an event of 1365, returns to one of 1357 without dating it

other than to note ambiguously that it happened "at this time," i.e., 1365?).

[102] May 12, 1357 (Guasti, 90), June 10, 1357 (*ibid.*, 91), July 7, 1357 (*ibid.*, 98), Apr. 14, 16, 1358 (*ibid.*, doc. 77).

[103] *Ibid*; Grote, 1961, 63 f.

[104] Doc. 90.

[105] Doc. 155.

[106] Doc. 182.

[107] Doc. 200.

[108] Doc. 208.

the Trifora story could have been placed in the second half of 1357, when the uppermost wall structure must have been complete in order to carry the bells transferred from the old campanile — which was destroyed shortly after September 19, 1357[109] — and ordered to be hung in the new belfry on January 30, 1358[110] (following preparations that had been going on since October 26, 1357[111]).

Soon thereafter the vault of the Trifora section must have been sprung; its completion on March 29, 1359 was celebrated by the workers with wine provided by the Opera.[112] While waiting for the remaining *ballatoio* components to arrive from Siena, the Opera evidently decided to employ the otherwise wasted manpower to begin the construction of the spire. Judging from the meager height to which it rose (Figs. 88, 114, 116), the remaining marble items seem to have arrived and been emplaced within the year.

Meanwhile, the committee that had been appointed on March 22, 1359,[113] to audit and review within four months the "account of expenses incurred in the construction of the Campanile" must have delivered its findings.[114] At the same time the *Operai* may have given the Campanile project a hard look. After twenty-five years of their nearly exclusive attention it towered magnificently over the beginnings of the new Cathedral and was almost as high as the tower of the Palazzo Vecchio. With the *ballatoio* it received a degree of formal completeness — and, as we shall see, symbolic fulfillment.[115] As the Cathedral once had been abandoned for the Campanile, now the relatively inefficient skeleton crew on the tower was transferred to the Cathedral nave, where all hands were needed.

Although the building of the Campanile seems to have substantially terminated in late 1359 or, at the latest, 1360, final touches may have continued for several years, a haphazard process in which even important decorative details — namely, the pinnacles of the Trifora frontispieces, the crockets, and, on two sides, the finials of the gables — were postponed into the unkind future along with the spire (Figs. VIII, 70, 84). But the fabric remained officially on the boards until well into 1364, when the city twice gave substantial funds "to the works and fabric of the campanile and church of Santa Reparata";[116] as late as December 12, 1364, the Campanile is still mentioned with the Cathedral in a directive insuring the communal subsidy.[117] But on December 20 Talenti, sole *capomaestro* of the Campanile since at least 1351, is no longer needed by the Opera and

[109] Doc. 166.

[110] Doc. 188. On Feb. 7 the belfry beams are ordered (Doc. 189), and on Feb. 16 the contract is made for the actual hanging of the bells (Doc. 190).

[111] Doc. 169. The medieval bells all seem to have been replaced between the 15th and 18th centuries (Richa, 1754 ff, VI, 68; Follini and Rastrelli, 1789 ff, II, 375 ff).

[112] Doc. 210.

[113] Doc. 209.

[114] The accounting is still going on Aug. 30, 1359 (Grote, 1959, 69).

[115] See Ch. VII, 173 f.

[116] Jan. 31, Feb. 1, 3, 1364 (Guasti, doc. 112); May 29, June 1, 3, 1364 (*ibid.*, doc. 117).

[117] *Ibid*, doc. 123.

is discharged.[118] When the commune obtains money for the Opera the following October, the Cathedral is mentioned, but the Campanile omitted.[119] In 1366-68 its terminal portrait is duly executed (with uneven accuracy) by Andrea da Firenze in the Spanish Chapel at Santa Maria Novella, rising behind a loosely conceived version of the newly planned colossus of a Cathedral (Fig. 69).[120]

Its construction abandoned after late 1364, the Campanile was found to be a convenient place for various types of mischief, so that a custodian had to be appointed on August 19, 1367.[121] On the same day an ancient monk is granted five florins honoring his past services as adviser to the Opera, which go back "a long time and even to the time when the Campanile was being built."[122] These are the years of the great controversies over the form of the new Cathedral. In the din the not so distant decades when the Campanile had been the Opera's major responsibility already seemed long past. Yet the completion of the spire at some future date was still at least overtly intended. It was not until 1387 that it became clear that this time was to be very far away, after the raising of the impossibly huge Cupola, or perhaps even never, and that it was therefore necessary to cover the incomplete fabric with a protective roof.[123]

Although the spire never was completed, the Campanile continued to concern the Opera. The lowering of the piazza following 1339 was only the beginning of the ambitious systematization and reshaping of the surrounding area. On April 6, 1367, the Opera decided to destroy one of its own buildings nearby "for the decorum of the Campanile" and to open the formal space around it.[124] Following the momentous decision of August 26, 1388, to extend the Piazza del Duomo in a great swath around the entire Cathedral (which should now be renamed the Corso-Parcheggio del Duomo),[125] on September 2 it was decided that the tract to the west of the Campanile be paved with marble together with the area around the Baptistery.[126] On May 9, 1391, the Opera ordered the dismantling of the large, unsightly enclosure of the Cathedral model near the Campanile and its replacement by a simple wooden cage.[127] In 1397 it was directed to raze the indecorous "clutter" (probably tombs) between the Duomo and Campanile under the bridge — itself now an arched masonry construction in place of Andrea's originally intended drawbridge — and to pave the spot.[128] In 1407 "marble tombs" — probably including antique sarcophagi — were removed from the adjacent area.[129] The nearby model of the Cupola con-

[118] Doc. 212.
[119] Guasti, doc. 133.
[120] Cf. Paatz, III, 721. Meiss, 1951, 94 ff.
[121] Doc. 214.
[122] Doc. 215.
[123] Doc. 216. Gioseffi (1963, 97) feels that the spireless shape may have influenced the towers of Lincoln Cathedral (as Boccaccio did Chaucer); unfortunately, he does not take into account the fact that at Lincoln there were originally spires.
[124] Doc. 213.
[125] Doc. 217. Cf. Braunfels, 1953, 128 f.
[126] Doc. 218. And in the manner already achieved in front of the Duomo.
[127] Doc. 219.
[128] Doc. 220. (Cf. Ch. III n. 85).
[129] Doc. 221.

structed by Brunelleschi in 1419 was ordered destroyed in 1431 "for the convenience of the Opera and to honor the beauty of the Campanile."[130] At about that time the sculptural decoration was completed by the reliefs of Luca della Robbia (presumably with the attendant dismantling of the bridge),[131] the prophets of Donatello and his workshop, and the three figures from the Opera storeroom that were placed on the street portal in 1431, after the missing capital had been supplied.[132] Only then was the Campanile the building we know today.[133]

[130] Doc. 223.
[131] Cf. Ch. III n. 105; Paatz, III, 551 ff n. 442,
[132] Cf. Ch. III n. 106. [456.
[133] It has, of course, been often restored, as is clear from old photographs (Figs. 5, 124) showing a patchwork of weathered and restored pieces.

The present purity of appearance has resulted from a thoroughgoing restoration of 1950-58. The niche sculpture was removed during World War II to the Cathedral Museum (but, unfortunately, not replaced by casts); the reliefs were removed in 1964-67 and replaced by copies.

Chapter VI

Francesco Talenti

Pucci writes that following the dismissal of Andrea Pisano, the Campanile project was:

> Then directed [by] Francesco di Talento
> Until all was abandoned
> To give completion first to the Duomo.[1]

Andrea's fabric seems to end with the cornice of the niche section; thus, the Bifora section would be Talenti's as well as the final story shown clearly to be his in Chapter V. Although, to the extent that we can document the history of the Campanile, Pucci's version is upheld, the attribution might be more soundly based. Later sources neglected both Talenti and Andrea Pisano; Pucci may have omitted a fourth man. If the Bifora stories indeed be Talenti's they would not only break with the style of Andrea, but manifest convincing affinities with the Trifora story as well. To resolve this question, the entire upper Campanile invites close scrutiny, which it richly deserves quite apart from the question of attribution.

Not only does the Bifora section rudely interrupt Andrea Pisano's sleek fabric; it rejects the organic structuralism of his style. Andrea had stretched taut horizontal bands over articulate vertical piers; in this tectonic grid was rested the dense curtain wall (Figs. I, 19, 22). The stylistic principle of the Bifora section is instead purely decorative and painterly. The paneling of the buttresses alternates between pink and white marble, denying Andrea's clean structural logic (Fig. VII). There is no sense of organism or resilience in the broad cornice friezes, which seem to be pasted onto the wall, breaking into separate panels at the corners, and confuting the illusion of tension found in Andrea's

---

[1] Doc. IV.

horizontals (Figs. 71, 72). No longer is there a functional distinction between buttress and cornice; both now form part of an uninterrupted frame. Indeed, wall, pier, and cornice seem fused into a monolithic mass, over which a continuous crust of framing and enframed elements lies slackly. The latter form a rich, but shallow constellation of plastic shapes floating at the wall surface. The window elevation (Fig. 73) — comprising an inner screen of balustrade and tracery, a frontispiece formed by a crocketed gable resting on twisted columns, richly intarsiate jambs and archivolts, and a single stringcourse running between the capital structures — determines the disposition and shapes of the flanking lancets and rectangular panels and the overlying triangles. The whole is governed not by architectonic order, but by a free distribution and balancing of elements following common methods of planar design.

Andrea had reformed the painterly tendencies of Giotto. The Bifora stories manifest a reactionary attitude; they return unmistakably to the Siena drawing, where much the same superpositioning of cubes faced with an ornamental skin was projected (Figs. 133, 134).[2] Indeed, the Bifora elevation embodies several motifs found in the drawing: the separation of elements by a continuous dark strip, the arrangement of the windows and panels at the monofora and single bifora zones, the doubling of the bifora form itself. Even such a specific detail of the Siena drawing as the tracery of the single bifora is now revived (Fig. 141).

But in the visual sense, Giotto's piers and cornices were to function structurally, forming a rigid skeletal armature supporting a tapestry-like curtain wall. While it lacked the dynamic three-dimensionality and organic analysis of Andrea's fabric, Giotto's design, however strong its decorative qualities, maintained a firm architectonic integrity. The incrustation of the executed Bifora section represents, in effect, a reworking of the purely decorative aspects of Giotto's project, lifted from their architectonic context.

Giotto's determination of all elements by a modular grid was not a painterly device as such, but a method of design rooted in his feeling for the rectilinear and the solid. He employs it in the Siena drawing to consolidate the architectonic framework. In the executed Bifora stories the pattern is exploited instead for its purely painterly possibilities. The disposition of the Bifora incrustation is determined to an extent by the seven vertical divisions of Andrea's section, which in turn continue the spacing of Giotto's socle (Fig. 22). The elevation of the Bifora stories is divided horizontally into three unequal tiers corresponding to the balustrade, lancet, and gable of the fenestration (Figs. VII, 71, 72). The resulting vertically elongated, loose and uneven, gridlike pattern serves no architectonic function, but forms the field for a checkerboard play of alternating pink and white paneling and a sophisticated juxtaposition of open and blind lancet tracery. Likewise, Giotto's muscular cornices are replaced by an ambiguous assemblage. One cannot decide whether the charming rosette frieze above the Bifora windows is meant as an

---

[2] Cf. Gioseffi, 1963, 90 ff.

enframement of the square below, or as part of the surmounting classicistic cornice. Even strengthened by the rosette frieze, the cornice is too brittle to sustain an illusion of resilience. It can only be read as surface, as part of a non-structural and ambiguously bounded frame. Giotto's sophisticated control of illusion had enabled him, by very subtle means and within very shallow relief, to differentiate the structural armature from the thin curtain wall seemingly suspended within it. In the Bifora section there is no such illusion: all is brought like froth to the surface. Even the windows, though deeper than Giotto's, seem to float. Like most reactionary events, the Bifora section is the parody of a great original.[3]

Giotto's death in 1337 spared him the discomfort Andrea would have suffered upon seeing the pastry-like Bifora stories riding his crystalline fabric when he may have returned to Florence toward the end of his life.[4] Andrea's architectural vocabulary, however singular, had inner logic and utter consonance. The Bifora incrustation not only mangles Giotto's idea, but assumes certain of Andrea's decorative particulars and adds still different sources in a rough manner, with a resultant indigested richness. One need only compare the perfect smoothness, precision, and clarity of Andrea's final cornice with the decoration immediately above it to realize the change (Fig. 77). The loose geometric motifs and inarticulate flatness of the intarsiate panels at the foot of the Bifora section clash with the precision and plasticity of the molding above, which demonstrably derives from Andrea. The frontispiece of the window rests on richly foliated consoles, between which, however, the elements sit on an arched intarsia frieze riding rather clumsy trilobes that mimic the trefoiled arcade in Andrea's terminal cornice. The cavetto-tondino molding immediately above the intarsia frieze is again reminiscent of Andrea, but clashes in its soft plasticity with the planar frieze below and the crudely mannered dentil-cavetto-listel course above. The quatrefoils, with their "pimpled" excrescences, and the awkward cornice of the balustrade are matched above the window by the rudely proportioned details of the gable (Figs. 73, 75): the coarsely scaled bead-and-reel strung along the archivolt like a necklace, the tiny dentils of the cornice, the swirling, but frontal crockets, and the erupting finials have little unity of shape. Even the intarsia begins to mix sharp Cosmatesque geometry with rounded and closed Gothic quatrefoils. However one may judge the qualities of these details, they are at the opposite extreme of taste from Andrea Pisano, or, indeed, Giotto.

---

[3] White feels that Giotto's design is "less fussy" than Talenti's (1966, 172), with which Gioseffi seems to concur (1963, 83 f), in contrast to earlier critics such as Paatz (1937, 133 ff) and Nardini (13), who found Talenti's part architectonically superior.

[4] Becherucci (1965, 244 ff) argues that Andrea survived the Black Death to die in Florence around 1350, when he would have been buried in the Duomo (accounting for the epitaph; see Ch. I n. 27). For reasons that will become clear in this chapter, I cannot accept her conjecture that he was again *capomaestro* of the fabric in those two years, although there is no reason why — if indeed still alive — he might not then have contracted sculpture.

Nevertheless, on its own terms, the style of the Bifora section is both consistent and expressive. Given a decorative, painterly — even picturesque — intent, the Bifora incrustation manifests great resourcefulness and amplitude of imagination. The very incoherency and indigested richness of detail denies structure and intensifies the sense of the decorative. There is movement and life on the surface. The cool, dark lancets of the windows reappear hotly in the flanking, pink-paneled blind tracery. Above the rich gables are suspended sharp, complementary triangles (which in Giotto's design were locked to the cornice). Except for the jamb decoration, the lancet zone is devoid of intarsia or geometric motives. But the balustrade, the tracery, and the gable all embody geometric patterns taken up in the flanking paneling. The treatment of these forms is noteworthy. Except for the bottom panels of the lower Bifora story — adjacent to the planar frieze below — all of the motifs are expressed spatially.[5] There is not only the normal transparency of balustrade and tracery, but the hexafoils in the gables and the quatrefoils in the lateral panels are executed in sharp, deep intaglio.[6] Thus, the emphatic planarity of the panels is relieved by subtle touches of spatial colorism, assimilating their style with the sculptural richness of the window decoration and the rosette friezes. This careful distribution and balance of detail can be seen also in the disposition of color accents. As already noted, pink and white rear paneling insets alternate in a checkerboard pattern, pink appearing at balustrade and gable level on the buttresses, alongside the windows in the blind lancets, and again in the triangles over the gables (balanced by the strips at the foot of the frontispieces). A rather rigid scheme is formed, which is softened, however, by the above-mentioned pink hexafoils and quatrefoils sunk into the white gables and rectangular paneling.

The studied control of color is particularly evident in the distribution of green marble. In the fabric of Giotto and Andrea the *Verde di Prato* is used in a variety of manners; but in the Bifora stories green appears exclusively as the ground for the windows and panels, around which it flows unbroken. It begs to be read as a continuous sea on which, all but literally, the shallow, boatlike panels float. Only the windows cut the surface tension, providing passage to the deep, dark, almost pool-like interior. Such a metaphorical intention would not have been alien to the tradition of the Campanile: one need only recall Giotto's colossal frame image, his tapestry-like curtain wall, and his finials of *abbondanza,* or Andrea's organic analysis of the incrustation and, most specifically, his fibula keystone. Nor would such a conceit be extraneous to the great poetic culture of Florence at this time.[7] Surely the floating, spectral appearance of the Bifora stories, especially at dusk, or moonlit, cannot be without a degree of intent.[8]

[5] Cf. the inverse adjustment of forms at the foot of the Trifora zone (Fig. 70).

[6] Such multifoil intaglio is common in spandrels, gables, etc. in High Gothic architecture (Cf. Branner, 1965, *passim*).

[7] I am informed by Miss Elizabeth Petroff that analogous phenomena are to be found in the self-conscious syntactical manipulations of mid-Trecento Florentine poetry.

[8] In this connection one might note that the modern restoration has given the entire Campanile a somewhat harsh appearance in full sunlight.

At first glance, the Trifora section (Figs. VIII, 70) seems to manifest the same planimetric, decorative richness as the Bifora. One has the impression of similar buttress paneling, window type, and enframing composition. Even the manner, developed in the Bifora zone, of continuation of Giotto's seven-part division — a unifying force evidently considered a determinant *de rigeur* of the elevation of each successive Campanile section — is carried from the Bifora *mutatis mutandi* to the Trifora zone, which lines up subtly with the parts immediately below (Figs. 22, 70). Yet a closer scrutiny reveals basic differences.[9] In the Trifora story the alternating pink-white paneling of the buttresses is left behind. Andrea's consistent use of pink is resumed, and, with the simple revision, the buttresses regain much of their visual strength. Likewise, the architectonically ineffectual rosette friezes are displaced by continuous intarsiate bands functionally akin to those below the Bifora section. A step is even taken beyond Andrea: the tensile effect of the bands is now reinforced by accompanying classicistic stringcourses (Figs. 82-85). In the Bifora section the elements of the elevation assume detached positions, as we have seen, according to the order of an implicit grid and a painterly sense of composition. In the Trifora story, the entire elevation, including the window inside and out, is multiply bound by a girding of stretched bands and stringcourses. The contrast in stylistic logic is particularly clear in the lower supports of the frontispieces. The consoles under the Bifora windows adhere informally to the surface (Fig. 79). In the Trifora elevation the consoles are locked securely in place between two strong moldings, the upper of which, in fact, runs over the corbel structure (Figs. 81, 83).

In the decoration of the Bifora section all of the elements are given full individuality and realization. However sophisticated, the composition is an additive assemblage of static elements on a single, undifferentiated field. In the Trifora section, three distinct forms — the buttresses, the window complex, and the horizontal binding elements — dominate the composition. The scale of the window loses its connection with the flanking paneling, which is wedged into cramped remnant areas between the window and buttresses and sectioned by the stringcourses, whose spacing is not pictorial but systematic. The blind lancets shrink to an abstract likeness of the window shapes; indeed, they seem out of place, primarily referring to the lancets of the stories below. Likewise, the plastic individuality of the Bifora gables becomes a synthetic, planar image formed by intarsia patterns and shaped by the upward flexing of one of the stringcourses (Fig. 70, 84).

This systematic abstraction penetrates even the detail of the Trifora zone. In contrast to the heterogeneity of form in the Bifora section, key elements are now reduced almost to formulas. The Trifora stringcourses are all the same combination of nearly identical dentil and double-leaf moldings (plus a listel), to which the one at capital level adds a bead-and-reel (Fig. 82) and the gable course a narrow band of intarsia. Even the tracery is decorated with a dentil and double-leaf combination (Figs. 82, 87). It is character-

[9] Investigated first by Nardini, 37 ff.

istic of the Trifora story that the loosely angled and disposed jamb frames of the Bifora now take the shape of pink, octagonal prisms that form a continuous, double frame around the entire splaywork (Figs. VII, VIII, 75, 82, 87).

Yet the change in style from Bifora to Trifora sections is not an abrupt one, for the vocabulary is already streamlined in the second Bifora story. The rich leaves of the consoles supporting the frontispiece of the lower Bifora shed their foliage, the outer twisted columns their studs, the balustrade its "pimples"; the horizontal elements of the window lose their dentils, leaves, and relative softness (Figs. 77, 78). The leafwork on the capitals dries up and the impost above forgoes its tondino (Figs. 74, 75).

Accompanying this simplification of window detail is to be noted a classical revival in the cornicework of both Bifora zones. Andrea Pisano had created a vocabulary of incrustation in great part through the development of ingenious forms from Gothic metalwork. His details exerted an influence in the lower Bifora zone. There the first molding, bearing studded quatrelobes (Fig. 77), derives from Andrea's first cornice (Fig. 13), also a source — reaching back to the bronze door — of the manner in which the rosettes above are set in sharp, elongated panels (Figs. 71, 72). Similarly, the disposition of the cornice capping the first Bifora section (Figs. 78, 79) clearly refers to Andrea's last one (Fig. 77). Exactly at this point, where Andrea's follower is so overtly imitative, does the classicism set in. Andrea's exotic vocabulary yields to a simple set of ovoli and leafwork. But something of Andrea's open spacing and fine plasticity is retained here, as well as the basic structure of the cornice. In the next cornice, above the second Bifora (Fig. 80), the scheme is simplified and rationalized by eliminating the dividing tondini. The components as such — bead-and-reel, double-rowed leaf friezes — are more richly classical. But their spacing is so tight and interior relief so low that the individuality of the forms is lost, with the entire cornice assuming the appearance of a richly textured, multiple stringcourse (Fig. 72).

In the simplification of detail at the windows of the second Bifora zone and the accompanying hyperclassicizing of the overlying cornice can be discerned a shift toward the dry classicism and cerebration of the Trifora story, where precisely the style of the cornice of the second Bifora zone is continued in the stringcourses (Fig. 81) and its hardening of detail picked up in the octagonal window frames and razor-sharp edges of the archivolts (Fig. 82).

Do the subtle changes reflect the development of Talenti,[10] who, before he completed the Bifora zones he had designed around 1343, envisioned the different style of the Trifora section, which he would begin in a few years, and took steps to assimilate the second Bifora story to it, as he had already adapted the lowermost forms of the Bifora section to the adjacent fabric of Andrea? Or was the lower Bifora story designed by a mysterious fourth man, who would have immediately followed Andrea, but who disap-

[10] Nardini *(ibid.)* felt so; also Paatz (III, 361 f), who de-emphasizes the differences between Bifora and Trifora sections. Gioseffi also agrees (1963, 90 f).

peared after a few years, to be followed by Talenti, who saw fit to double the Bifora section — as Andrea had Giotto's base — modifying its detail according to his own taste and with an eye toward the Trifora story he planned above?

The latter possibility is intriguing, and would seem at first glance to be substantiated, for example, by a comparison of the tracery: the light, simple Bifora openwork seems irreconcilable with the rich, heavy Trifora version (Figs. 75, 82, 87). Yet this could be explained in part as a shift in source that would be symptomatic of what we shall find to be the increasing weight of Talenti's incrustation style, the former tracery being in a High Gothic mode, and the latter deriving, most noticeably in its intersecting pattern, from the English Decorated. To go a step further, it can be seen that — despite this manner of superficial divergence — the handling of relief, the coloration of the ground, and the vocabulary of outline are identical. The sharp ogives of the Bifora lancets are transferred to the star-arms in the Trifora; and, conversely, the rounded segments of the Bifora oculus are shifted to the lancet decoration of the Trifora. The bead-and-reel in the Bifora archivolt appears in an equally uncanonical manner in the Trifora window, where it leaps from the stringcourse to form part of the fantastic impost structure of the capitals (Fig. 120).[11]

Indeed, the design of the entire Trifora window, with the exception of the disembodied gable, ushers from the Bifora. The crucial difference is that in the Trifora all of the elements are further defined, enriched, articulated, and unified. The rich foliate friezes, capitals, and tracery decoration are set against the pure geometry of the frame, jambs, and archivolts, which now dizzily teem with superabundant intarsia patterns. The comparatively ingenuous Bifora windows seem to have undergone intense reconsideration, emerging in the Trifora systematized, and at the same time more complex.

This very transformation may be said to characterize the whole Trifora elevation. The painterly scheme of the Bifora zone is rationalized, as we have seen, along architectonic, hierarchic lines.[12] But at the same time, the surface of the Trifora zone is enlivened

[11] Which fits very well in a tradition that spans Arnolfo's S. Cecilia Tabernacle capitals (Fig. 237) and those of Brunelleschi's basilicas. Talenti's was not the first example in Tuscany of intersecting tracery, present already in the clerestory of the nave of Siena Duomo (as dated by Klotz in his forthcoming study; cf. the 1969 Wrightsman Lectures of Jean Bony; also below, p. 147), nor was it to be the last Florentine example, for it was embraced by Simone Talenti, in his Or San Michele tracery (1366 ff); cf. Paatz, IV, 487 f, 516 n. 64; Klotz, 1966, 189 ff (with much emphasis on German sources); and my forthcoming study on this question.

[12] The notion to bind the elevation with stringcourses may reflect a tradition. In the Badia tower the upper stories are bound by such ligaments (Fig. 299). At Ognissanti, the parallel is closer: the monofora and bifora are free, but the trifora is connected to the wall by a stringcourse at capital level (Figs. 293, 294; see Ch. VII). The giant size of the Campanile Trifora story may have catalyzed the transfer and development of the motif, the artist wishing to visually stabilize the huge window. The contemporary, derivative campanile of Prato Duomo shares the configuration (G. Marchini, *Il Duomo di Prato* [Milan, 1957], 46 f, and *idem, Il tesoro del Duomo di Prato* [Milan, 1963], 59, cites evidence by which the upper stories can be dated in the late 1350s).

by intarsia motifs, which flower not only in the window frames, to which they were limited in the Bifora section (with but a few exceptions), but over almost the entire story (Figs. VII, VIII). Moreover, they are now highly, almost systematically random — and therefore demonstrative — in their diversity, mixing the Cosmatesque motifs of Giotto, curvilinear Gothic multifoils, and fantastic new patterns. One might say that the painterly order of the Bifora zone has undergone metamorphosis, appearing in the Trifora story not as order but substance. One senses, in the Trifora section, the style of the Bifora in intellectual, architectonic disguise, a posturing which is almost ineffectual because of the weight of the decoration. Indeed, the hierarchic composition itself is conceived in the same terms of intense planarity as the Bifora zone, giving the identical impression of a static, continuous polychrome crust overlying monolithic masonry (Fig. 70).

Seen against the high-tension, crystalline organism of Andrea Pisano's fabric (Fig. I), the fundamental similarity of the Bifora and Trifora stories is sharply manifest. Moreover, the attribution of both to Talenti would fit the trajectory of the further development of his incrustation style, which moves increasingly away from the Giottesque revival with which it began.

In the decoration of the side-aisle exteriors of the first two bays of the Duomo, which dates from Talenti's model of 1355 and design of 1358,[13] is manifest a maturing and consolidation of the current of systematic structuralism that appears in the Trifora section (Figs. 4, 5, 248, 249). The window scheme is identical:[14] an inner screen of heavy tracery over twisted columns; richly intarsiate and double-framed jambs; a frontispiece of twisted columns that rest on bound consoles and carry lean, attenuated pinnacles intersected by a stringcourse, which, flexing upward, forms the upper border of the gable — a pastiche of whirling intarsia work. Other stringcourses divide the surface of the wall, which is decorated with recessed paneling. Two stringcourses hold the frontispiece consoles firmly in place, another the upper window. All run continuously over the buttresses.

Though the scheme is closely derived from the Trifora section (Fig. 70), the style has undergone crucial development. In the Trifora story the treatment of the horizontal ligaments is at the same time compulsive, flimsy, and uncertain. Repeating the same form

[13] The model of May 29, 1355 (Guasti, 81), in addition to providing an acceptable choir design, is also to resolve the defect of the windows ("il difetto delle finestre"), a probable reference to the question of assimilating the low and closely spaced side-aisle windows of the Arnolfian structural fabric into the differently scaled and spaced new design. To accept a project, then raise the issue again after a brief interval has been a characteristic not only of modern planning, particularly in the case of a problematic issue. In any event, the matter is taken up more explicitly on Oct. 17, 1358 when a design for the incrustation of the side-aisle wall is requested ("uno disengniamento chome pare loro chessi volglia lavorare le mura della chiesa dal lato di fuori, chon che finestro e chon che lavorii" [*ibid.*, 119]), which is *de facto* accepted on Nov. 13 (the "ideal" solution offered being out of question; *ibid.*, 120), and broken down into piecework components on Nov. 23 (*ibid.*, 121). See the discussion of Saalman (1964, 475 f, 480 f; see also bibl.).

[14] Noted already by Nardini, 43.

over and over, Talenti did not yet know quite how to accomplish the broad, rich effects he attempted at capital and gable levels. Persevering in the planarity of the Bifora section, he was not able to activate a three-dimensional, articulate interweaving of wall, buttress, window, and horizontal bands in the Trifora incrustation. His endeavor to recast in his new painterly style the interlocking tectonic system of Andrea (and in more sober stones, of the contemporary northern masters)[15] fell short of the stunning level of success Andrea had so effortlessly achieved. Thus, it is not the almost abortive structuralism and intellectuality, but its picturesque richness that is the true strength of the Trifora section. It lies between the unequivocally painterly Bifora zone and the Cathedral side-aisle wall, where what was attempted in the Trifora story is accomplished.

Here the organic dissection of the wall is fully realized (Fig. 248). The binding ligaments are convincingly powerful; indeed, they are so broad, numerous, and plastic that the wall seems almost muscle-bound. To realize this change one need only observe the way the supporting brackets of the frontispiece are held (Fig. 68), or the new solution to the placement of figure sculpture on the gable. In the Trifora section the figure is balanced precariously over a high finial. At the Duomo, it is set on a broad platform riding the muscular, but blunted gable cornice and enveloped by a niche cut deeply into the wall and bound to a powerful stringcourse complex.

Talenti's final statement of the theme is the almost Baroque side portal of the Cathedral near the Campanile — the so-called Porta del Campanile (Fig. 249).[16] Its enormously heavy decoration is carried buoyantly by the powerful, vertically channeled energy of the waves that ride the quiet lintel, the steely segmental arch, and the great leaping gable, finally bursting in frothy tabernacles.

All of this bears directly on the question of the attribution of the Bifora revetment to Talenti. It is clear now that while essential characteristics link his earliest and latest works and set them off from the manner of Andrea Pisano and others, the dynamic character of Talenti's imagination — incontrovertibly manifest in his progressive mastery of structurally expressive incrustation and vertical dynamics from the Trifora of 1351 to the side-aisle walls of 1355-58 and the Porta del Campanile of ca. 1360[17] — all but precludes the possibility that his treatment of the Bifora section, begun eight years before the Trifora, could ever have been other than in a distinctly less evolved manner.

Careful analysis of the interior of the upper Campanile yields the same result: that Talenti was most surely the author of the Bifora as well as the Trifora zone.

The interruption of Andrea Pisano's internal structure seems to have been analogous to that of his incrustation. As already noted,[18] the vaulting of the third chamber is poorer

---

[15] Cf. Ch. III, 61 and n. 62.

[16] Paatz, III, 364 f. I find the lower parts Talenti's as well.

[17] The Porta dei Cornacchini to the north (*ibid.*, 367 f), again completely Talenti's (except for the door frame and the lions, which are Arnolfian and reused), is probably somewhat earlier, and, in any case, more conservative than the portal on the more prominent south flank (Figs. 248, 249).

[18] See Ch. III, 65.

in design than the lower rooms (Figs. 6, 59). Not only does it lack corner responds, but the cornice on which the ribs rest is devoid of Andrea's characteristic deep plasticity. The vaulting is not even finished: the keystone is missing its decorative boss, which, judging from the nude compass, was to have been akin to the fibula keystone of the room below. Moreover, the vaulting seems unnaturally low in comparison with the first two chambers. From the cross section it appears that the height of the third vault was not determined by Andrea, but rather was dictated by the level of the floor above, which, in turn, is integrated with and a function of the post-Andrea incrustation. What seems to have happened is that when Andrea departed, the walls were standing to a height somewhat above his final (exterior) cornice; he had not begun the third vault, though he may have designed and begun work on the keystone, which would particularly have interested him. His successor had no special interest in the chamber, but rather wanted a level platform, as it were, on which to construct the complex fabric above. He calculated at what point in Andrea's wall a vault would have to be sprung in order to provide the platform above at the desired level. He had a simple cornice carved, let it in the wall at the proper height, sprung a simple rib vault from it (including Andrea's unfinished keystone), filled in the space over the webs in the usual manner (with rubble masonry), and ended with the desired elevated substruction.

The fabric above is as complex as the wall structure immediately below is simple.[19] A single, huge chamber rises continuously through both Bifora stories (Figs. 88-90).[20] Its walls are opened following the elevation of the windows, resulting on each side in a massive double arcade at two levels (Fig. 91). Springing from the benches that run at the floor are octagonal corner colonnettes that rise through several tiers to support the rib vault nearly thirty meters above. Halfway up, at the floor level of the second Bifora story, a jutting *ballatoio* on high corbeling divides the space (Fig. 98); in the corners it appears to be supported by the respond system, which blossoms a capital and then seems to continue on through the platform, the coffer-molding bending obligingly around the colonnette (Fig. 100). The wall is further divided and bound by four stringcourses, two per story: the first (Fig. 93) and third (Fig. 97) run at the level of the window capitals with which they are connected, the second (Fig. 92) and fourth (Fig. 99) around the unbroken inner wall, the latter at the base of the vault. The pointed, barrel-vaulted window chambers are given their own system of articulation (Figs. 91, 101). Out of the necessity to have large windows and at the same time broad piers between them, the barrel-vaulted chambers are double-staged. At the first Bifora level, in the setback between the two stages, are placed colonnettes corresponding precisely to the elevation of the window itself; even the bases (Figs. 103, 104) and capitals are similar. The colonnettes are connected by a roll molding (Fig. 101) articulating the setback of the barrel vault. This secondary system of articula-

---

[19] Cf. Paatz's description, III, 362 f.   [20] See Ch. III, 71 f for its function.

tion is linked with that of the main space by the stringcourse at the level of the isocephalic capitals (Figs. 89, 91).

The idea of the double arcade appears to derive from the ground floor chamber. In the Bifora section, the pier is still a muted form — not an independent body but a resultant configuration determined by the window and the shape of its chamber. The impression remains that of a great monolithic wall punctured by lancet openings, rather than a gathering of articulate piers. The fine articulation seems an all but extraneous addition, not conceived integrally with the wall but spun over it like a spider's web.

Thus the Bifora section is composed of three almost independently conceived forms: a massive, nearly monolithic wall; an extremely painterly marble revetment applied to its exterior; and a fine, rational web of structural articulation set on the interior surface. Yet the divergent elements are obviously so well coordinated that only a single mind can have conceived the design. The unprecedented attempt in the Bifora section to create a Gothic version of the total order of the Romanesque Baptistery [21] was not easy to achieve. It was only in the Trifora story that Talenti was able to pull together all three aspects of the fabric into a relatively unified conception.

Of the three modal possibilities given in the Bifora zone — mass, decoration, and cerebration — Talenti chose to strongly emphasize the latter in all aspects of the Trifora section. We have already witnessed the rationalization in the overt style of its incrustation. The modulation of the interior is equally subtle (Figs. 88, 107). Due to the absence of a central pier on each side it was necessary, for structural reasons, to increase the thickness of the corner masses. The window being so broad, this could be accomplished only by extending the inner stage of the pier toward the center axis of each side. This inherently gave the inner pier structure — forming an "L" — a clean shape and distinct detachment from the corner mass. Reworking and extending the manner of interior articulation of the Bifora section, he cut niches in the edges of the "L" and placed in them multistaged colonnettes that continue — as in the Bifora window chambers — as roll moldings on the arch above. For the inner angle of the pier, he appropriated the octagonal colonnette, placing it on the bench and stretching it up to the springing of the rib vault of the Trifora story (Figs. 107, 109, 111-113, 117).

The new formal clarity of the inner, L-shaped pier is thus emphasized by an expanded system of vertical articulation, in which every angle and edge is emphatically delineated, except where the "L" re-enters or runs behind the outer pier mass (Fig. 108). The lack of articulation at this point only sharpens the differentiation of the corner bulk into an inward-oriented "L," connected with the vaulting system, and an outer mass oriented toward the window and octagonal buttresses.

As on the Trifora exterior, not only is the new order intensely cerebral, it is hierarchical, particularly as to the form and placement of the columnar elements and string-

---

[21] Horn, 1943, 123 ff.

courses. The enormous window — the pre-eminent feature of the Trifora zone — has elaborate twisted columns resting proudly on the balustrade (Figs. 83, 108). Inside, the round colonnettes articulating the pier face are set demurely into niches, not projecting into the central space, as does the structurally more telling octagonal colonnette support-ing the vaulting, which sits boldly on the bench.

The new logic is equally clear in the ordering of the stringcourses. In the "loose" elevation of the Bifora zone there are four capitals per respond, with only one juncture left unmarked. But in the Trifora story, the capitals are found at only a single height, the crucial level of the tracery capitals, at which point the richest external stringcourse contin-ues into the chamber and around the entire inner part of the pier (Figs. 109, 113). The two exclusively interior stringcourses below break off at the juncture between the "L" and the outer corner mass (Fig. 109); the two above capital level are contained by the closed upper chamber, where even the vaulting springs without capitals (Figs. 112, 115, 117). The four are roughly paralleled by several purely exterior, marble courses.

The intent is clear: in the Trifora story the L-shaped piers, their connecting arches and strictly overlying wall, and the vault are meant to constitute an inner shell; the remain-der of the corner mass — roughly an outer "L" and the octagonal buttress — together with the incrustation and the window, forms an outer shell. Both layers carry completely independent systems of articulation. At only one point, near the center of the story, are the two shells linked and the marriage celebrated by the singular line of capitals.

One may pursue the workings of this logic yet further. In the Bifora zone, the stringcourses are of two types. The first, which we will designate type A, is a continua-tion of the tracery impost (Figs. 75, 91, 93), and is simplified in the upper Bifora level (Fig. 97). Type B is the dentil plus cyma recta (Figs. 92, 99). In loose correspondence to the elevation of the exterior, both are repeated twice, ABAB. B thus serves for two dis-tinct purposes: in the lower Bifora story it appears merely as a wall-dividing stringcourse (Fig. 91); but in the upper it breaks over the respond system to form the impost of the vaulting (Fig. 97). This denies the close architectonic logic according to which a different form should serve a different function.

In the hierarchic domain of the interior of the Trifora section this rule now takes effect. The two lower stringcourses bind only the inner "L" and must execute numerous intricate bends (Figs. 107, 109). They are therefore given a relatively small and simple profile, cavetto and cyma recta in the lower, the upper cyma recta only (Fig. 107). The third stringcourse continues in *pietraforte* the rich, marble exterior coursing (Figs. 82, 110, 113). Its intersection with the octagonal respond is marked by a weathered capital (Fig. 113) modeled on the marble versions of the frontispiece. The relatively massive classicism of this molding is taken up by the fourth (Figs. 112, 115) and fifth (Fig. 117) above; more than twice the bulk of the lower two stringcourses, they ride the straight walls between the window and the vault, bending clumsily around the corner octagons. The explanation for this seemingly top-heavy disposition of mass and complexity seems to lie essentially in their intended function: to help seat the massive timbers of the bell carriage (Fig. 112).

The internal form of the Trifora story, then, is a decisive rationalization of the possibilities latent in the architectonic aspect of the Bifora zone. As the relatively ambiguous ordering of the Bifora articulation matches its muted pier configuration, the clarity of the Trifora pier is complemented by a rationally hierarchic ordering of all components, vertical and horizontal, of its articulation. The transformation seems to have involved an intensely personal process of self-criticism — similar to what took place in the incrustation — and as such, indicates Talenti as the ideator of both great chambers of the upper Campanile.

But it is not only by the evidence of the Trifora story that the Bifora section falls to Talenti. His other major interior, the Cathedral nave, is in great part a development of ideas stated first in both upper Campanile chambers. The connections are more specific than the quite valid identification of the severe sense of order generated by the nave with the intellectualism of the mature Talenti from the Trifora on. It is obvious that in plan the complex piers of the upper Campanile, conceived as huge bundles of "L's" and octagons, are behind the bundled plan of Talenti's nave shafts (Figs. 194, 252). Indeed, the very scheme of the Cathedral nave bay, a vaulted elevation over double-storied piers cut by a *ballatoio*, arises unmistakably from a shuffling and reconstitution of the double-storied Bifora chamber. The derivation is especially striking in a comparison of the intersection of *ballatoio* and respond (Figs. 100, 253). Although, as we might expect, the vocabulary of shapes is more highly developed in the Duomo, the syntax remains the same, particularly in the singular bending of the coffering course around the octagon.[22] Even the very enrichment of forms at the Duomo derives from the upper Campanile — the cornicework from that in the upper Trifora chamber (Figs. 107, 117), the consoles and balustrade from the exterior *ballatoio* of the Campanile (Fig. 85). Similarly, the complex yet precise shapes of the ribs and wall arches in the Cathedral vaults are prefigured first in the Bifora, then in the rich forms of the Trifora vault (Figs. 99, 117, 255).[23]

The telling base of the Cathedral pier is also to be traced back to the Bifora section. In contrast to the swelling, ponderously spreading base profiles of Arnolfo, Giotto, and particularly Andrea Pisano (Figs. 8, 52, 164, 195), the base structure of the octagonal colonnettes at the foot of the Bifora interior presents a fused, almost monolithic set of

[22] Not only did Talenti provide the Duomo model of 1355, win the pier competition in 1357, and execute the prototype capital thereafter (Grote, 1961, 115 f) but in the controversy over the placement of the *ballatoio* in 1364 (Saalman, 1964, 483 n. 51), it was the anti-Orcagna faction that won, evidently backing Talenti's design (as it had earlier backed his pier model against Orcagna's).

[23] Although Talenti was absent during the construction of the vaults, they follow his style so directly that their form must embody his design, for which there is no record or hint of a modification after the decision concerning the *ballatoio* placement in Oct., 1364, two months prior to his departure (see n. 22 above).

high, dryly turned forms (Fig. 96).[24] The earlier simple, massive plinth is replaced by a slick Gothic socle. The base moldings (torus-scotia-torus) are of identical height and shape. The joint between plinth and base, scotia and torus, does not divide support and load but is merely another edge in a structurally undifferentiated set of succeeding shapes.

The most advanced Gothic base in Florence at its creation around 1343,[25] and a revolution from the tradition of Arnolfo and the Pisani still very much alive in Andrea's Or San Michele and lower Campanile chambers, the new form is continued without much change in the two corresponding bases in the Campanile interior above. In the second Bifora section, the socle is simplified — along with everything else in that story — but the base presents the same equalized, dry form as the initial example (Fig. 95). The Trifora zone version is almost a copy of the prototype below (Fig. 94). The style appears in more complex form at the foot of Talenti's Cathedral piers, designed in 1357 (Fig. 194). The trace of softness and *contrapposto* in his Campanile bases has now completely withered. As noted in Chapter III, the Cathedral piers present high, huge, "cast-iron" profiles combined in such a manner that one can only read them as part of a rising monolithic mass or as leaden rings.

So much of Talenti's Cathedral interior finds its origin in the upper Campanile — and the Trifora story, in turn, in the Bifora — that it seems most unlikely that he could have done the Cathedral nave and the Trifora story without having first stated and tried out his ideas below. Certainly no other known architect can have done the inner parts of the Bifora section.[26] The three interiors form a highly distinctive group in the history of Florentine architecture, though not without an impressive following beginning in the 1370s with the Loggia della Signoria, by Talenti's son (Fig. 258), and Lucca Duomo (see below); earlier (except for the problematic first Campanile chamber) the group finds a single direct antecedent, the ground story of Or San Michele, which, as we have seen, is probably not Talenti's but by Andrea Pisano, who appears to have been, at least by example and together with Giotto, his Florentine master.[27]

The cycle of attribution is complete. Pucci's testimony is borne out. Executed entirely under Francesco Talenti between 1343 and 1364, the upper Campanile was the proving

---

[24] Allowing even for the dry, modern restoration. The absence of the articulation of the Trifora story vaulting system and the lower stringcourses from the Sgrilli section (Fig. 6) I interpret as an omission (Sgrilli also omits the stringcourse cornice from the obviously unrestored third chamber). These forms hardly seem modern inventions. The weathered capitals (Fig. 113) prove the age of corner colonnetes and the replaced blocks (Fig. 107) confirm the originality of the stepped-back elevation.

[25] Cf. the naves of S. Maria Novella, S. Croce, and S. Trinita.

[26] It has nothing to do with the likes of Neri di Fioravanti. Orcagna did not matriculate the mason's guild until 1352, when it evidently became necessary because of his work in Or San Michele (Offner, 1930 ff, IV, I, 3, 8).

[27] In addition to the connections already drawn, the lowest Bifora capitals, carrying two rows of leaves, the lower a wild acanthus, the upper long clasping forms, derive unmistakably from Andrea's second chamber (Figs. 56, 57, 93). Interestingly, thereafter the interior capitals become cool and abstract, as was noted on the exterior.

ground for a development of forms and concepts that achieved full expression in his interior, flanks, and portals of the Cathedral nave in the late 1350s and 1360s.[28] At the same time he may have been linked with the design for the upper floors of Or San Michele, especially the exterior.[29] The sudden disappearance of Talenti's name from the documents in 1369 may signal his death;[30] but in its pier form the remodeling of Lucca Cathedral from 1372 onward[31] so closely follows the Florentine nave, without being a literal or mistaken copy, that one wonders if Talenti did not give the design (Fig. 257). Lucca had no native Gothic and was obliged to search "all Tuscany" for a respectable *capomaestro;*[32] in 1372 Talenti, if alive, would have been the region's major architect.

Lucca was the most direct, but, as already noted, not the only derivative of Florence Cathedral.[33] Talenti's work at the Duomo group forms the major Florentine fabric of the mid Trecento and, as such, is the key source for the development of later Florentine Trecento architecture under his son, and the later *capomaestri,* especially Giovanni d'Ambrogio. Indeed, the last great *capomaestro* of the Duomo, Brunelleschi, even as he initiated a new epoch in architecture, could not but be deeply affected by the work of Talenti and his school.[34]

Thus, the design of the upper Campanile contributes decisively to the evolution of the later Florentine Gothic. We have seen that the ideas it embodies partially derive from the most advanced preceding Florentine architecture. The incrustation revives first Giotto's Campanile design, then Andrea Pisano's theme of interwoven articulation. The complex pier structures depend on the first Campanile chamber and the ground story of Or San Michele. But a great deal of the upper Campanile, including the window forms and much of the rich detail, does not stem from local precedent. Like Giotto and Andrea, Talenti appears to have infused the developing local tradition with extraneous material. And as with his predecessors, the full understanding of Talenti's design can only follow a review of his pre-Campanile years.

---

[28] The post-Talentian incrustation of the last two bays (vividly described by Boito, 1880, 203 f) is a travesty of Talenti's Bifora section, mimicking the window "support" and reducing the planar, decorative principle to the absurd. But Talenti had parodied Giotto. The sequence is thus curiously parallel to the fate of Giotto's style of painting, first in the powerful art of Orcagna, Talenti's exact contemporary, and then in the later work of a Giovanni del Biondo where Orcagna's manner is reduced to decorative mediocrity (cf. Meiss, 1951, 16 ff; Offner [and Steinweg], 1930 ff, Sec. IV, Vol. IV).

[29] Cf. Ch. III n. 118.

[30] In May, June, and July, Talenti is still receiving his monthly stipend as *capomaestro,* 8¹/₃ flor-

ins (Guasti, docs. 220, 222, 224), after which his name disappears. The salary was by then less than Ghini's 13 florins per month (*ibid.,* docs. 220, 223, 225).

[31] E. Ridolfi, *L'arte in Lucca studiata nella sua cattedrale* (Lucca, 1882), 30 ff.

[32] *Ibid.;* see also Braunfels on the common problem of finding *capomaestri* (1953, 220 f).

[33] The later church of S. Lorenzo at the Certosa of the Val di Ema at Galluzzo derives from this architecture (Fig. 256). The configuration of the pier falls between Orsanmichele and the Cathedral. For dating, see G. Bacchi, *La Certosa di Firenze* (Florence, 1930), 65 ff.

[34] As I plan to show in a forthcoming study.

The Talenti were a numerous and not unimportant Florentine family in the Trecento. Already in 1289 a Lapo Talenti is *castellano* of the Florentine outpost of Montecchio, and by 1317 his son Talento is one of the *Dodici Capitani* of the republic.[35] As early as 1284 a Talenti is one of the *priori,* an honor obtained again in 1313 and 1318.[36] Toward the middle of the Trecento the merchant family expands beyond the confines of its native city, to Lucca (1340), Milan (1350s), and perhaps to Pisa.[37]

It is not known when Francesco was born nor into which branch of the family. Presumably it would not have been the Nipozzano branch of his contemporary, Fra Jacopo Talenti, *capomaestro* of Santa Maria Novella from the 1340s to his death in 1372, for it is doubtful that the Opera would have permitted a close relative, however great an authority, to sit in judgment of the important work of another, as Jacopo did three times in connection with Francesco's Cathedral pier model. Certainly they would not have been brothers, as has been suggested.[38]

However, a birth date around 1300 would fit the known facts of Francesco's life. The first notice conceivably referring to him concerns work at Orvieto Cathedral, a payment in 1325 of five *soldi* to a "Maestro Francesco Talenti."[39] Already a master mason, but still in the middling range of the pay scale, Talenti could easily have been about twenty-five. Around 1330-35 he would have married, fathering at least three children: Piero di Franchesco, who dies in Genoa in 1363[40] (survived perhaps by his daughter Antonia who dies in the 1360s[41]); Tessa, mentioned with her husband in 1369;[42] and Simone, who assists his father in the late 1350s carving the prototype Duomo capital,

[35] Passerini, Ms. 192, Biblioteca Nazionale, Florence.

[36] *Notizie istorico-genealogiche appartenenti alla nobiltà e cittadinanza* (Naples, 1953), 398. Prior to 1327, at least two Talenti matriculate in the Arte della Seta (G. Gargiolli, *L'Arte della Seta in Firenze* [Florence, 1868], 282 ff).

[37] In 1340, a branch moved to Lucca, where they soon established themselves and became rather important citizens (Passerini, Ms. 162, Biblioteca Nazionale, Florence). In 1350, an Orlando Talenti (di Firenze) went to Milan and was soon *Gonfaloniere* (Passerini, Ms. 192). In 1358 a Pietro Talenti ("di Fiorenza") is mentioned as merchant in Milan *(ibid.).* A Francesco L. Coli Talenti is mentioned as one of the *Anziani* of Pisa in 1367 (Poligrafo Gargani, No. 1968, Ms. in Biblioteca Nazionale, Florence); in 1370 he is entrusted with the delivery of a tribute from Pisa to the Emperor residing in Lucca (F. Bonaini, ed., "Cronaca Pisana di Ranieri Sardo dall'anno 962 sino al 1400," *Archivio Storico Italiano,* VI

[1845], 173). This would imply that the Pisan branch of the family was not new to the city.

[38] Speculated by many, including S. Orlandi, *Necrologio di S. Maria Novella* (Florence, 1955), 524 f. The location of the documents concerning Francesco's pier model in the archives of S. Maria Novella might also have to do with the fact that Talenti's son, Simone, at least, lived in the S. Maria Novella quarter (H. Siebenhüner, "Simone Talenti," in Thieme-Becker, *Künstlerlexikon,* XXXII [1938], 416).

[39] Fumi, 1891, 49. Appearing far down on a list of 34 *maestri* receiving from 2 soldi, 6 denari up to 8 soldi (for Nicolo Nuti, who is in charge) per day is the entry "M. Francesco Talenti . . . pro V sol. per diem."

[40] Cirri, *Necrologio fiorentino,* XVII (Ms. in Biblioteca Nazionale, Florence).

[41] *Ibid.*

[42] Poligrafo Gargani, No. 1970, Ms. in Biblioteca Nazionale Florence.

matriculates the mason's guild in 1368, and in the late 1370s is briefly *capomaestro* at the Duomo and largely responsible for the piers of the Loggia della Signoria.[43]

When Francesco established himself in Florence is not known. Probably it would have been somewhat in advance of 1343, when he was around — possibly in the workshop of Or San Michele or even the Campanile itself — to take over the best architectural post in Tuscany. At the peak of his powers in the 1350s, Talenti gradually loses control of the workshop. In 1358 Ghini and Arnoldi move in as co-*capomaestri*. In 1364, the Campanile completed and the Cathedral underway following Talenti's model and executed proto-type pier, he is dismissed from the Opera,[44] perhaps partly according to his own wishes. For twenty years he had been *capomaestro* and, in his mid sixties, may have needed a leave of absence. In 1366 he is back as *capomaestro*, with the large, but limited task of executing the *ballatoio* of the nave interior.[45] Talenti's voice is important in judging subse-quent competitions and models for the Cupola and Tribunes;[46] but, no longer the man of the 1350s, when he impelled his pier model through three sittings of the jury until he won, he does not seem to play a vital role in the planning activities of 1366-67.[47] His Bifora and Trifora stories and two bays of the nave stood; it was enough. Besides, his Cathedral model of 1355 was probably the point of departure for the revision of the time.[48] In 1369 he is still receiving the monthly installment of his one-hundred-florin annual salary as *capomaestro*. But after July his name disappears and is not found again.[49]

Born in Florence around 1300, Francesco would have come of age seeing great fabrics rise: the nave of Santa Maria Novella, Santa Croce, the Palazzo Vecchio, the beginnings of the new Cathedral. He aspired to architecture, and to sculpture. But the only master under whom he might have studied seriously, Arnolfo di Cambio, had died in 1302, leav-ing no follower.[50] In the three decades following the passing of the great stonemason there appears scarcely an architectural design of consequence in the city. For the two important projects of sculpture — the Orsini tomb and the Baptistery door — the city has to import Sienese[51] and Pisan masters. Francesco did not witness the birth of the great buildings going up, but only the painstaking execution, no matter how impressive, of late Dugento projects. However competent were the Trecento *capomaestri* of these fabrics, none was the supreme designer Florence needed to realize the Campanile idea in 1334. Turning to the only pre-eminent Florentine master of the arts, the city sought to calm any misgivings

[43] Siebenhüner, 1938, 416, with further data. If not his father's, the Lucca remodeling might well be Simone's.

[44] Doc. 212.

[45] Guasti, doc. 138.

[46] As in *ibid.*, doc. 150.

[47] *Ibid*, docs. 138 ff. Not one of the new designs is his, although some please him more than others.

[48] The nave is Talenti's (cf. n. 22, 23 above), ex-cept for the fourth bay added to the project in

1366-67. His design included a cupola and chap-els, even if on earlier substructures; the measure-ments of June 19, 1357 (Guasti, 95) could refer to a laying out (Saalman, 1964, 477 f) or to a meas-urement of older fabric (Paatz, 1937, 139 ff). The articulation of the choir and cupola clearly derives from the nave.

[49] See n. 30 above.

[50] Guasti, XXXVI ff.

[51] Tino da Camaino (Paatz, III, 369).

about Giotto's qualifications as architect with a public statement confirming his "scientia et doctrina."[52] At his death a few years later, the city must have been embarrassed even further to find itself short of a great native son working in any medium. The sole important designer around was Andrea Pisano, who proceeded to erect a structurally brilliant, eminently modern and beautiful, but disastrously non-Florentine fabric.[53] It was only with the entry of Talenti, who perhaps had been waiting in the wings for the departure of Andrea, that Florence found one of its own, and an extraordinary architect besides.

But if not in Florence, where had Talenti received his rich and sound training? That he first appears working at Orvieto Cathedral is no accident: in the early Trecento the center of vigorous architectural progress closest to Florence was along the Siena-Orvieto axis. Following closely on the heels of the great Dugento fabrics, Orvieto pushed forward with Maitani's grandiose façade (1310 ff), and Siena with the baptistery (1316 ff). Between the 1280s and the 1340s the two cathedral fabrics generate a vital creative heat, fusing ideas from the outside and emanating influence all over the region. The Dugento nave of Orvieto combines ideas from both directions on the road to Rome on which it lies, from Viterbo as well as Siena. In the 1320s Sienese window and pier forms migrate to the cathedral of Grosetto, where they are prepared for the final Sienese fabric, the project and partial execution of the Duomo Nuovo following 1339.[54]

It is impossible to determine at what point in the region, if any, Talenti received decisive training. It very well might have been that he mastered the basic techniques of stoneworking in one of the many Florentine workshops, then expanded his artistic horizons by traveling. But Talenti was acquainted with more than Maitani's façade, on which he was employed in 1325.[55] Indeed, he was intensely aware of every major fabric in the triangle between Siena, Viterbo, and Massa Marittima.

Talenti probably would have made at least one excursion to a site just south of the papal city of Viterbo: the thirteenth century Cistercian monastery, San Martino al Cimino.[56] He would have been impressed by the cast-iron hardness of detail (so different from the fine metallic quality of Andrea Pisano), especially that of the stringcourse

[52] Doc. 1. Cf. Ch. II n. 38, 44.

[53] Villani honors proudly "maestro Giotto nostro cittadino" (Doc. I). But it was just "un maestro Andrea Pisano" that made the Baptistery door — a work "molto bell[a], e di maravigliosa opera, e costo" in which Villani, by his own word, played a proud part as an official of the Calimala (patron guild of the Baptistery), and whose creator, after a decade, would have been more than just another artisan: Yet to the Florence establishment Andrea seems to have remained an outsider (Villani, X, 178).

[54] Cf. A. R. Garzelli, "Problemi di scultura go-

tica Senese," *Critica d'Arte*, XII (1966), n. s. fasc. 78, 17 ff.

[55] Talenti might have accompanied the three Florentine architects called to Siena in 1324 to give a building consultation; there he would have met Nicolo Nuti, summoned (together with Maitani) for the same purpose from Orvieto (G. Milanesi, *Documenti per la storia dell'arte senese* [Siena, 1854], I, 186 ff, docs. 34, 35), and under whom Talenti was working in 1325 (see n. 39 above).

[56] R. Wagner-Rieger, *Die italienische Baukunst zu Beginn der Gotik* (Cologne, 1957), II, 232 ff, dates and discusses the building more precisely

which runs around the entire church interior halfway up the elevation: both the function and the shape of the molding appear at the Campanile in the "impost block" stringcourse of the first Bifora story (Figs. 91, 93, 261, 262, 264). He also might have observed that almost all the archivolts in the church are edged with roll moldings, as in the Campanile, particulary the Trifora arches.[57] In all, Talenti undoubtedly felt a closer affinity to San Martino than to his native Tuscan Cistercian abbey, San Galgano, which shares certain features with San Martino, but whose even more uncompromisingly hard-edged style and more primitive articulation offered little grist for the imagination (Fig. 259).[58] To confirm the influence of San Martino on Talenti we need only turn to the impressive French tracery of the façade window (Fig. 263).[59] Adapting the northern scheme to their own manner of working, the local masters reduced the rounded delicacy of the original to an emphatic planarity and hardness of relief, similar to the style of the Loggia of the Popes down in the city (Fig. 260). In his Bifora tracery Talenti appears to take up not only this relief style, but the very patterns of the hexafoils flanking the San Martino rose.[60]

The connections between San Martino al Cimino and the Campanile are so precise that one wonders if Talenti was not employed there on the façade. One cannot tell. Often we note such very precise derivations; yet Talenti cannot have worked everywhere they are found. And in Orvieto, where his activity is documented, the connections are less than one might expect, as we shall see below.

At the end of another spur of Talenti's travels is the choir of the duomo of Massa Marittima, done in the late thirteenth or early fourteenth century.[61] In it he would have seen a development of systematic Gothic ideas in the scheme of stringcourses (Figs. 265, 267). The disposition of articulation is indeed precisely the system of the Trifora story. Three stringcourses bind choir and side chapels. The lowest is set at the level of the capitals of the side chapels, into which it continues. The second runs, analogously, at the level of the capital bands of the great windows of the choir — set at the roof level of the side aisles. It continues on the interior, linking the windows together and with the side walls of the choir (Fig. 266). This corresponds in scheme to the Trifora section, as does the upward flexing of the third stringcourse to form a pseudo gable. Talenti may even have appropriated the circumscribed hexafoil set in the gable over the main window.[62]

than L. F. di Longhi, *L'architettura delle chiese Cistercensi italiane* (Milan, 1958), 260 ff.

[57] The lantern-like tubular keystone of the S. Martino crossing may be connected with Talenti's Bifora and nave vaults; but the form is already present in Florence in the choir of S. Croce.

[58] Wagner-Rieger, 1957, II, 226 ff. The stylistic distance between the two fabrics is particularly interesting in light of their approximate synchronism.

[59] The twin towers of the façade are not original,

but an example of historicism dating as early as the 17th century (*ibid.*, II, 234 and fig. 74).

[60] Giotto may have had a similar source for his tracery, but his design was infinitely more delicate.

[61] Paatz, 1937, 37 ff (but the connections with "Nicola Pisano's [sic] Sta. Trinita" are invalid, as the present church is mid-Trecento according to Saalman, 1966, 31 ff).

[62] The analogous logic between Massa Marittima and the Trifora is completed by the fact that the

This spare, systematic choir articulation — also found in Massa Marittima at San Agostino and San Francesco — complemented the expressive richness of the façade of the cathedral (Fig. 268), begun towards the middle of the Dugento and completed by Giovanni Pisano.[63] In the middle story it exhibits the latest Tuscan Romanesque capitals, the Baroque forms of which were not only important for Giovanni Pisano, but seem to be reflected in Talenti's singular Trifora capitals (Figs. 82, 87, 120). The principle, at least, of intensely plastic leaf forms and an uninhibited, strongly projecting abacus-impost structure is common — and, within Talenti's ambient at least, exclusive — to the two cases.

As early as 1316, Francesco could have seen the design for the grandiose façade of the Sienese baptistery, built up rapidly thereafter (Figs. 270, 271).[64] If he had been impressed by the systematic logic of the Cistercians and Massa Marittima, how much more the sophisticated power of the Sienese synthesis of northern system and classical detail would have affected him. In this sense the Sienese baptistery façade is a direct antecedent of the Trifora story. Two decades later, Talenti surely would have known the ambitious, exciting Duomo Nuovo project, begun in 1339 (Figs. 272-274).[65] From these two great fabrics he derived forms of critical importance for the Campanile.

Talenti's debt to Siena centers on window configurations. In one respect his fenestration stems from the Florentine tradition: the idea of a balustraded bifora with engaged half columns at the sides and set in a larger framing system is ultimately that of the baptistery gallery (Fig. 160).[66] On this scheme, now in Gothic rendition at the Campanile, are superimposed, rather thoroughly, multiple aspects of the Sienese fabrics.

The disposition of the Bifora frontispiece, for example, seems to have been suggested by the main portal of the Sienese baptistery,[67] where the gable simply rests on the hood

stringcourses not at capital level have no interior-exterior connection; at the interior base of the choir and side-chapel windows, run independent stringcourses, absent on the exterior; likewise, the small-scale, secondary cornice toward the bottom of the choir windows outside does not run over even the entire exterior, but — like the analogous shaft rings of the Trifora buttresses or the interior L-pier moldings — is restricted to a local application. The shapes of the stringcourses vary in Massa Marittima, reflecting diverse functions and building periods; but the most abstract form, cyma recta over a dentil frieze, is precisely that of the Trifora story, where the cyma recta is foliated — as we shall see, in Sienese fashion.

[63] Paatz, 1937, 37 ff. The upper story remains Giovanni Pisano's despite White's objections (1966, 26 f). The connections pointed out by Paatz, and the unique forms and extreme quality of the design — as well as the coloration — seem to allow for no other master.

[64] For the early date of the drawing and execution, see H. Klotz's forthcoming study.

[65] In 1356 he was called to Siena to pronounce judgment on the fatally flawed project (Milanesi, 1854, 251), on which, see White's penetrating discussion (1966, 165 ff).

[66] The intarsia forms below the lower Bifora story derive from S. Giovanni where analogous motifs are found over the galleries; compare also the Trifora section intarsia with the Baptistery exterior and the walls of the gallery.

[67] Derived partially from the latest developments on the Upper Rhine (Klotz, 1966, 185 ff).

molding of the inner portal without any abutment (Figs. 73, 270).[68] On the other hand, the engaged, extremely thin and attenuated posts of the Trifora frontispiece derive from a window type found in the third story of the same Sienese façade (Figs. 70, 270) and later, together with twisted columns, on the exterior side-aisle windows of the Duomo Nuovo, one of which was built just before or contemporary with the Trifora story (Fig. 274). The double, continuous jamb frames of both the Bifora and the Trifora — and particularly the latter — closely reflect the most simplified and systematized Sienese jambs, those of the Duomo Nuovo interior side-aisle windows (Fig. 273). And common to all these Sienese forms and Talenti's Trifora is the binding of the window elevation to the wall by multiple, intarsiate bands and cornices.

The affinities between Siena and the Campanile continue even into highly singular detail. The finials of the baptistery portals were imitated by Talenti above the Trifora gables, where they also were to carry figures, one of which still exists (Figs. 84, 270).[69] The crockets of the Campanile portal, which seem to be by Talenti, are unique in Florence, but represent a Sienese type going back to Giovanni Pisano and found as late as the portals of the baptistery (Figs. 63, 270), which are sources, as well, for the compacted, spiky, classicizing cornicework that characterizes the Trifora (Figs. 222, 271). Talenti's proud tripartite tracery, though common to Florentine towers, is the universal form of the Siena clerestory, which even includes examples of the intersecting pattern in the nave.[70] Finally, the Sienese influence goes beyond the Campanile: Talenti's Cathedral side portal near the tower — the Porta del Campanile — is, in part, clearly a development of the side portal of the Duomo Nuovo (Figs. 249, 274).

In contrast to Talenti's deep and rich connections with San Martino al Cimino, Massa Marittima, and particularly Siena, the influence of the Orvieto façade, where we believe he was employed in 1325, is diffuse and fragmentary. Talenti's name appears but once in the rich Orvieto documents;[71] he may have worked there only a short time, migrating from fabric to fabric. But in any case Maitani's design had perhaps evolved too far; unlike the other fabrics discussed, it presented scarce opportunity for further development (Figs. 275, 276). Its strongest effect on Talenti was undoubtedly a generic influence of its emphatic systematization and its supreme Cosmatesque colorism. But it is also conceivable that certain details, repetitive shapes — some of which he personally may have helped execute as minor stonecarver in the enormous workshop — remained in his imagination to affect his mature work. The twisted columns of the Trifora and the Porta dei Cornacchini

---

[68] Nardini suggests Romanesque sources (40).

[69] See Ch. V n. 58. Talenti's finials are wildly rich, however, in contrast to the earlier Sienese control.

[70] For the early (c. 1300) clerestory dating see Klotz's forthcoming study; cf. n. 11 above. For Florentine fenestration, Ch. VII, 153 ff.

[71] However, the Orvieto documents of 1326-27 are lost and only one survives from 1328, as noted by J. White, "The Reliefs of the Façade at the Duomo of Orvieto," *Journal of the Warburg and Courtauld Institutes*, XXII (1959), 255 ff.

(Figs. 70, 81, 248, 251) bring to mind the deeply and multiply threaded columns of the Orvieto jambs (Fig. 276). Maitani's lubricated, rolling base and cornice moldings (Fig. 277) may have inspired the slick, swelling profiles of Talenti's later work, such as the Cathedral pier and side-wall articulation (Figs. 194, 250), to be sure, affected as well by the sharp angularity of the Siena workshop.[72]

Whatever the effect of the façade, one can be sure that the Dugento interior of Orvieto caught Talenti's eye; not only would he have been fascinated by the dazzling capitals, but the richly consoled *ballatoio* (Fig. 278) so impressed him that three decades later it inspired the version in the Florentine nave. This may in part be due to the fact that before he designed the Cathedral of Florence, Talenti revisited Orvieto: the fine, precise dentilation of the ribs of the choir, rebuilt in the 1330s,[73] is directly antecedent to the Florentine Duomo vaults (Figs. 252, 255, 280).[74]

The ambitious young artisan who left Florence in the early decades of the Trecento to discover and master the great designs of the thriving centers of architecture to the south had succeeded. When he was given the post of *capomaestro* of the Campanile around 1343, he possessed an enormous vocabulary of forms and details wonderfully fresh and new to Florence and that must have astounded the small-time masons who had been finishing the Dugento designs of their fathers and grandfathers.

Indeed, the content of Talenti's imagination was so heterogeneous that he faced a critical issue. The ideas that he brought with him were opposed. There was, on the one hand, what might be called the emphasis of early fourteenth-century Sienese architecture — taking its cue from the North in such works as the façades of the Siena Baptistery and Orvieto Duomo — on system to which individual forms are subordinate.[75] Yet in this very architecture the taste of southern Tuscany and northern Lazio for spiky, vigorously plastic forms continued. In Orvieto, Viterbo, and Massa Marittima the local tradition of stone carving was not in marble, but in tufa, peperino, and travertine. Even classical forms were manipulated to exploit the roughness and texture of the stone, resulting in "uncanonical," free variations and effects quite different from the classicistic cutting of stone in northern Tuscany, especially in Florence. A perfect example is the Romanesque part of the duomo of Massa Marittima, where artists from Lucca and Pisa found creative

[72] Behind the frontal, radial crockets of Talenti's Bifora and Porta dei Cornacchini may lie work on the almost uniquely similar buds in the rinceaux of the second pier from the left at Orvieto, which he could well have fused with rough-edged leaves adorning the elegant stems (Fig. 279); the façade reliefs were executed probably between 1310 and 1330, according to White *(ibid.).*

[73] The tribune was rebuilt following its demolition in 1335 by "Nicola di Nuta" (Fumi 1891,

170), under whom Talenti had done his recorded work at Orvieto (see n. 39 above).

[74] But cf. the less articulate dentilation in the Bargello vaulting of the 1330s and 1340s (Paatz, 1931, figs. 14, 16). G. de Francovich sees Talenti as sculptor possibly as a link between the Sienese tradition of Maitani and Florence ("Lorenzo Maitani scultore e i bassorilievi della facciata del Duomo di Orvieto," *Bolletino d'Arte,* S. II, Vol. VII [1927-28], 366 f). Cf. Venturi, 1901 ff, IV,

[75] See Ch. III, 60 f.   [325, 367.

challenge and freedom in the new material; to appreciate the result one need only compare the lower or mid parts of the façade with the almost contemporary façade of Lucca Duomo (Figs. 268, 305).[76] Giovanni Pisano himself was particularly taken with the expressive, rough style and translated it into polychrome marble at his Sienese façade (Fig. 269), where the fundamental sense of powerful texture binds together Tuscan and French forms, achieving a manner of synthesis notably repeated by a follower at the façade of the baptistery (Fig. 270).

But it would have been difficult for Francesco Talenti to accommodate these two impulses — the expressively systematic and the licentiously individualistic — to each other and to the ancient Florentine tradition of smooth, but plastic classicism of detail, rational decoration, intellectually harmonious order, and a profound sense of structure, an ideal to which Giotto and even Andrea Pisano paid deep homage.[77] Indeed, it was just this that Talenti did not do. We have seen that his revival of Giotto's tower design was superficial, almost fraudulent. The unassimilated richness and roughness of detail that characterize the exterior of the Bifora section — and which continue transformed into the Trifora story — are the outcome of Francesco's long years in the South. Inside, though he develops Andrea Pisano's structural forms from the lower Campanile and Or San Michele, the hyperrational articulation is not only out of touch with the Florentine past, but, in the Bifora zone, even contradicts the painterly style of his own exterior; and at Trifora level, this conflict is, as it were, aired in public, shamelessly parading on the vast faces of polychrome. Then how was it that Talenti was not booted out like Andrea before him?

The fact is that the architecture of Francesco Talenti played a key role in the revolution of the arts that swept Florence in the 1340s and 1350s with Andrea Orcagna as the other leading exponent. His tabernacle in Or San Michele is everything that is Talenti's Campanile: the licentiously extreme, be it in classical detail, Gothic architectonics,[78] or Cosmatesque colorism (Figs. 282, 283). Like the incrustation of the Bifora and Trifora stories, the painting of Orcagna and his school is marked by an abandonment of Giottesque spatiality and tactility, classical weight and contraposto; it turns to hierarchical, Byzantine planarity; it is characterized, Millard Meiss has found, by "aspiring, though tormented, spirituality... emotionally exciting color and light, and a strained, disharmonious unity of plane and space, line and mass, color and shape."[79] If any Orcagnesque image were the painted correlative to Talenti's architecture it would be the chilling

---

[76] Ridolfi, 1882, 16 ff.

[77] Wiernozowski, 1944, 32 ff, notes that in 1313 a Florentine painter was praised because his work (at the Baptistery Tabernacle) "enlightened and delighted the hearts and eyes of the citizens and all who saw it so that they did not perceive anything confused or sinister." Even Andrea Pisano's unorthodox vocabulary and elevation strongly express the Florentine ethos in their harmonious refinement.

[78] Klotz, 1966, 202 f. The Tabernacle dates 1352-59.

[79] Meiss, 1951, 165 and *passim*. For the parallel shifting tides of Florentine politics see Becker, 1967 f, *passim* (with explicit comment on Meiss's thesis, I, 244).

figure of Saint Michael in the Strozzi Altarpiece, 1354-57 (Fig. 284): in the swollen density of his feet and belly are the profiles of the Cathedral piers; in his fearful costume is the wild landscape of the Bifora incrustation; and in the haunted archangel's pose and expression and in the flattening interaction of his outlines with Saint Catherine, the Trifora revetment and Cathedral elevation seem to find their tense, ambiguous rhythms.

Although the great wave of the new style breaks only after 1348, when the disasters accumulating through the mid 1340s — including depression, famine, plague, revolution, and war — climax in the Black Death, a first shock clearly would have been registered in 1343, when the design for the Bifora section was accepted and begun. Francesco's decision as a youth — in the days when the Palazzo Vecchio was just being finished, in the heyday of Giotto — to head south (and perhaps Orcagna along with him) may have had behind it the premonition that what he would find could someday bring him success and fame. That, upon reaching maturity as an architect around the age of forty, Talenti had precisely the background Florence sensed itself wanting along with great abilities as designer and administrator, and that the epochal catastrophe was immanent which precipitated the sweeping cultural revolution that was to give free reign to Talenti's formal bent, occassioned another of those rare confluences of fate that have always marked the genesis of great architecture.

If Florence forgot itself after the Black Death, by 1357 it had recovered a kind of balance, at least for the moment. The magnitude and consequence of the new Cathedral project brought forth in the Florentines their deepest stratum of stylistic sensibilities, which was to re-emerge more permanently only in the Quattrocento. In the heated competition for the nave pier Talenti's first version was rejected because it seemed too rich and fussy. Orcagna, perceiving the underlying desires of his patrons — and perhaps his own — presented a sparer, acceptable design.[80] Talenti was forced to turn back. As he had earlier pretended to revive Giotto's Campanile style, now he appeared to re-establish the piers of Or San Michele and the elevation of Santa Maria Novella. His Bifora stories were all but a parody of Giotto. The Duomo piers, however they may recall the classic models, are characterized, as we have observed, by an irresolutely ambiguous, leaden massiveness and tactilely abhorrent shapes (Fig. 194); in the elevation an effusion of rough foliage punctuates a restless, rising dynamic (Figs. 252, 253). It is not only the queasy tension of the design, but the conflict between old and new that gives Talenti's monumental interior — like his Campanile project and the art of Orcagna[81] — its mid-Trecento tone.

[80] July 17, 1357: Orcagna's design "occhuperà meno all'occhio . . . [è]di meno vilume e di meno ingonbrio della chiesa . . . [and is recommended] per più bello lavorio e per più presto e di meno costo e più legiadro." Talenti's "à troppi lavorii" (Guasti, 100 f).

[81] Meiss, 1951, *passim*.

Chapter VII

Florentine Towers

By 1342, the Campanile of Santa Maria del Fiore already had reached the notable height of about fifty braccia. But in the Bigallo fresco painted that year[1] it appears a nearly inconspicuous shape barely lifting into view (Fig. 285). As the rendition suggests, Florence bristled with structures as high and higher.[2] The painter conveyed well the way the city must have felt, a dense gathering of vertical stone masses contained by the powerful wall. Giotto's Campanile was only one example of its class, even if it was, when complete, by far the largest and most resplendent; and church campanili were but part of a spiky skyline into which rose the towers of the two proud civic palaces and hundreds of private defense structures and tower-like palazzi. In their history lie untold layers of meaning for the Campanile.

Perhaps the oldest in genesis were the church towers. One of the most important traces of pre-Romanesque Florentine architecture was the campanile of Sant' Andrea, a fabric of Carolingian origins that stood until 1889, when it was destroyed with so much of the most venerable part of Florence (to make room for the most vulgar).[3] A finely proportioned shaft roofed by a low pyramid, it was closed at the bottom except for an entrance portal; a third of the way up a simple monofora was set in a characteristically

---

[1] Saalman, 1964, 472 n. 6; 1970, 8 f.
[2] Identifiable from left to right are S. Maria Novella (with transept rose), S. Maria Maggiore (its tower just to the right of the S. Maria Novella transept), S. Lorenzo (its portico just to the right of the S. Maria Maggiore tower), the Badia (with a polychrome tower), the Bargello, the Pal.

Vecchio, the Baptistery, the Duomo — including Arnolfo's façade, the old S. Reparata with its campanile behind it, and the new Campanile to the right (behind which is visible the Arnolfian side-aisle incrustation) — and finally to the extreme right, the unfinished basilica of S. Croce.
[3] Paatz, I, 51.

early medieval recessed plane topped by an arched corbel table; three sets of double monofore divided by cornices followed, possibly as somewhat later additions (Fig. 290). Although there were other early experiments, such as the Ravennate cylindrical campanili of the Badia (Fig. 297, lower part)[4] and perhaps of Santa Elisabetta (Fig. 291),[5] by the twelfth and thirteenth centuries the prototype at Sant' Andrea had assumed canonical form: a quadratic prism divided by simple courses and friezes into roughly cubic stories opened by a sequence of windows larger toward the top, the whole capped by a pyramidal roof. In the definitive rendition of medieval Florence, the Berlin woodcut (ca. 1470) and the related London panel (ca. 1490)[6] can be seen dozens of this type (Figs. 286, 287). The old Duomo tower itself — partially depicted in the Bigallo fresco to the left of the nave — seems to have been a good example.[7]

[4] The stump of the 10th-century cylinder is incorporated in the present tower (Paatz, I, 278).

[5] Preserved as late as the 15th century. Paatz (II, 18 ff) notes the connection of the tower (now incorporated in No. 3 Pza. S. Elisabetta) seen in the Rustichi view with the church, but refrains from calling it the campanile because of the separate bell cote (Fig. 291; the church was also called S. Michele delle Trombe; this mid-Quattrocento Codex of Marco di Bartolomeo Rustichi, now in the archive of the Florentine Archbishop, contains, as we shall partly see, a large number of views of Florentine churches [in great part reproduced in the Italian edition of Davidsohn]). However, the large fenestration and especially the cornices of the cylinder are more typical of campanili than private towers; the extant masonry could fit the period of the original church, which goes back to the 9th century. At some time the tower may have been the campanile of S. Elisabetta; the small church of S. Maria Maggiore also had a very large campanile at one time, and later only a bell cote (see n. 12 below).

[6] My thanks to Mrs. Herbert Bier for supplying the superb photograph of her panel, first published by L. D. Ettlinger ("A Fifteenth-century View of Florence," *Burlington Magazine*, XCIV [1952], 160 ff) according to whom the panel is probably from the workshop of Francesco Roselli, who was closely linked with the invention and propagation of the type of city view involved. The panel is based on the Berlin woodcut and the engraving preceding it (of which a fragment is preserved at the Società Columbaria) of about 1470, but brought up to date (e.g., substituting the crossing cupola of S. Spirito, completed in 1482, for the pyramidal roof that appears in the woodcut) as well as correcting and expanding many aspects. By an analysis of such changes Ettlinger establishes 1489-95 as the date for Mrs. Bier's panel. On the woodcut (and all other Florentine views) see A. Mori and G. Boffito, *Firenze nelle vedute e piante* (Florence, 1926), 12 ff and fig. opp. p. 144.

[7] The tower rising behind the Baptistery in the Biadaiolo view of Florence (Fig. 288), ca. 1340 (Offner, 1930 ff, Sec. II, II, I, 43 ff and pl. XVIII[6]) does not represent the old Duomo tower, as Paatz appears to believe (III, 339 f), but the Bargello (Fig. 330). Conceivably the Cathedral tower could be one of the other two campanili represented (besides the Pal. Vecchio tower); but their late forms seem instead to refer to such recent campanili as S. Maria Novella or S. Pier Maggiore (Figs. 295-300). Around 1340, the new Campanile was still in its early stages, and the old Duomo tower was apparently insufficiently proud to represent the city, particularly if its depiction in the Bigallo fresco (Fig. 285) is at all accurate (its upper parts appearing either incomplete or partly dismantled). It could not have been exceptionally high, for when it was directed on Aug. 16, 1357 (Guasti, 104) to tear down all older structures interfering with the new Cathedral fabric with walls of less than 1½ braccia thickness, the old Campanile is specifically exempted: with such slight walls it cannot have been very high (the new Campanile has walls of more than 5 braccia). And it may have been charred or otherwise damaged from the fire of 1332 (Docs. I, II; see n. 85 below).

It is regrettable that these views are too schematic to determine more detailed characteristics of the almost entirely lost Romanesque Florentine campanili. Nevertheless, two facts allow that many shared the corner pilasters, arched corbel friezes, and progressively opening fenestration of their influential Lombard predecessors (e. g., Fig. 313).[8] In their important campanili, almost all the other Tuscan towns, including Lucca and Siena, made the Lombard type literally their own from the late twelfth through the fourteenth centuries.[9] And the Gothic bell towers of Florence not only themselves depend on the Lombard type but appear to derive from a local tradition long dependent on it.

The adopted Lombard scheme was the point of departure for the definitive wave of Florentine campanile building beginning in the late Dugento, which reflected a phenomenon widespread in Italy and, indeed, Europe.[10] Sometimes the new Florentine bell towers were added to older church fabrics, such as the one opened by three stories of multiple fenestration, including probably trifore at the top, and capped by a spire, begun for San Miniato al Monte in the late Dugento and completed by 1316-18.[11] Early in the Trecento a somewhat simpler, but very high, campanile was erected over the pre-Romanesque stump at the façade of Santa Maria Maggiore; it was finished in time to be included in the Bigallo view (to the left of the portico of San Lorenzo),[12] as was the lower part of the new bell tower of San Lorenzo (destroyed in the Quattrocento). In the latter case, however, the upper story, with its single, huge window and terminal *ballatoio* seen in the Rustichi view (Fig. 292) but obscured in the fresco, probably postdates the Cathedral Campanile version, on which the conformation would depend.[13]

---

[8] See p. 159 below.

[9] M. Salmi, *L'architettura romanica in Toscana* (Milan-Rome, 1927), 26 f, 61 ff n. 73 ff; and p. 157 below.

[10] E.g., Cremona, Modena, the Chiaravalle Milanese (Figs. 317, 319); north of the Alps, Freiburg (Fig. 167), the Strasbourg and Cologne projects, Vienna, Albi, Ely.

[11] Paatz, IV, 213, 217. It collapsed in 1499. From a strict interpretation of the Berlin woodcut (Fig. 287) Paatz reconstructs only bifore; but neither the woodcut nor the more detailed London panel (Figs. 286) distinguish bifore from trifore; and both represent Gothic articulation as Romanesque framing. My reconstruction of the S. Miniato campanile is by analogy to the contemporaneous towers at S. Maria Novella and S. Pier Maggiore (Figs. 295-300), which include a terminal trifora and spire.

[12] Paatz, III, 616, 617 ff. The 14th-century addition was torn down in 1631.

[13] Paatz, II, 465, 472 f. He mistakenly regards it

the same type as the Ognissanti tower: the Ognissanti belfry carries not a monofora, but a trifora, is crowned not by a *ballatoio* but by a corbel table complex, and was meant to carry a spire. Were the upper story or the *ballatoio* at S. Lorenzo early (perhaps contemporary with the Bargello tower, to which it bears obvious similarities) it would have been, of course, an important source for the Campanile. But to me the S. Lorenzo terminal parts seem of a later epoch than the traditionally articulated shaft below, and for several reasons: for one, were it early, the S. Lorenzo tower would be unique in the Bigallo fresco in having its terminal and most consequential parts cut, which the painter with his almost complete freedom of perspective and placement could easily have avoided (he obviously made a careful preparatory drawing for the densely intricate view); besides, the quatrefoiled *ballatoio* would be anomalous among pre-Talentian ecclesiastical campanili but historically understandable as a reflection of Talenti's potent invention,

Other towers accompanied the important church projects of the time, including Ognissanti, Santa Maria Novella, the Badia, and San Pier Maggiore. The first three still stand, and the fourth is depicted with rare clarity in old views, enabling us to establish the stylistic innovations of the movement. Like the towers added to older churches, they did not represent a radical departure from the traditional scheme — with a partial exception at the Badia. Rather the old frame was enlarged; its articulation became more emphatically systematic; the windows took ogival shape; the pyramidal roof was run up to a high, steep spire fronted by gables and richly fringed with Gothic foliage. By well-considered and characteristically subtle Florentine measures the venerable Romanesque archetype was given a Gothic rejuvenation.

The Ognissanti tower seems to be the earliest, rising above the first of the four churches in question (Figs. 293, 294).[14] Framing a beautifully proportioned sequence of pointed monofora, bifora, and trifora, the traditionally heavy, double-layered Lombard wall was adapted to the Gothic by not only elongating the stories, but narrowing the window panels with broader and deeper pilasters, thereby intensifying the vertical impulse. The wall is dissolved as much as is tolerable without negating the fundamentally mural character of the scheme; even the monofora expands almost to the pilaster line of the stories above. Over the trifora is set a continuous arched corbel frieze, its plasticity embellished by the simple corbel frieze that it supports. Derived from the traditional vocabulary — but perhaps inspired by military architecture — the compound corbel structure acts as a justly proportioned, strong but light cornice. However, it was not meant to terminate the campanile; above rises a stump, which judging by its diagonally oriented corner spurs was meant to carry a ribbed quadratic spire.[15]

The campanile of Santa Maria Novella (Figs. 295, 296), the upper parts rebuilt in 1330 following the collapse of the tower of 1305,[16] and the closely related tower of San Pier Maggiore (Fig. 300), built in the first half of the Trecento but destroyed in the eighteenth century,[17] added little to the innovations of Ognissanti. In fact, the boxiness of their stories and the progressively opening total width of their windows seem, in contrast, an almost Romanesque regression. Santa Maria Novella is particularly frigid, especially with the removal of the spire crockets in the eighteenth century. Its virtues are its massing and its subtle proportions and precision of detail rather than the presence of any new ideas. In the cornice there is a precious fussiness indicative of the general stale-

which carried the great crown of the Pal. Vecchio into ecclesiastical architecture, not only at the Campanile but eventually all over the Duomo.
[14] Paatz, IV, 412.   [See 173 f below.]
[15] Curiously, not observed by Paatz (see n. 13 above).
[16] Paatz, III, 666, 674, 683, noting its extremely conservative style. The doubling of columns is

prefigured in the campanile of Siena Duomo (Fig. 307), which seems to be substantially Dugento with late Trecento and early Quattrocento restorations (Lusini, 1911, I, 25 n. 45, 280 ff; Salmi, 1927, 62 n. 75).
[17] Paatz, IV, 633. It does not seem to appear in the Bigallo view (Fig. 285); might this mean it postdates 1342?

ness of Florentine architecture in the post-Arnolfian decades. The sectional proportions of San Pier Maggiore seem to have been somewhat less squat than Santa Maria Novella and the windows larger;[18] its detail as well may have been less conservative, but hardly an advance beyond Ognissanti.

It was at the Badia that the most significant developments in Florentine campanile design prior to Giotto occurred (Figs. 297-299). Over the stump of the round Ottonian campanile it was decided to construct a new, polygonal tower. The transition from the cylinder to a square evidently was judged too abrupt; on the other hand, an octagon, while yielding the smoothest transition, would have resulted in sides too narrow to decently include the necessary structure, windows, and articulation. A hexagon was the natural compromise[19] (as also at the campanile of the Badia a Settimo; Fig. 301). The shape accommodated several stylistic innovations. The reduced breadth of the sides, in combination with the new obtuse angle of the corners, made the traditional Lombard frame of broad pilasters no longer appropriate. This led the architect to consolidate the two broad, flat frontal strips of the earlier corner arrangement into a single, strongly projecting diagonal buttress.[20] This important step, linking the Romanesque tradition to Giotto's Campanile ground plan, was fully exploited by the architect, who ingeniously detached the corbel tables from the wall, running them continuously over the buttresses.[21] Thus, not only is the plan of Giotto's design prefigured, but his armature of corner buttress piers interlocking with independent, overlying cornices and visually supporting a curtain wall as well. If the mysterious polychrome campanile depicted in the Bigallo view is indeed the Badia, which may have been so frescoed,[22] the derivation would have been still more direct. Even without polychrome, the Badia tower was garnished with corner pinnacles and rich crockets[23] and thus helped prepare the way for the acceptance of Giotto's spire.

At Ognissanti a development of both the plain and the arched corbel frieze took place in the cornice. In the Badia the two forms are treated progressively, beginning with the simple corbel table below the lower bifora, followed above by a single arched corbel frieze, which is doubled in the final cornice (a sequence surely reflected in Talenti's three

[18] The impression of the views listed in Paatz, e.g., Fig. 300.

[19] Paatz inexplicably mistook it for an octagon (I, 278). In addition to being the perfect compromise, a hexagon is the easiest geometric figure to construct. Probably for the same reasons it was used in the analogous Badia a Settimo campanile, also a hexagon build over a round stump (see Fig. 301; n. 83 below). In fact Salmi (1927, 61 n. 73) observes that most cylindrical Tuscan campanili are terminated as polygons.

[20] Cf. the exactly contemporary S. Gottardo in Milan (Fig. 318; see 160 f below).

[21] Behind the Badia may lie the crossing towers of Fossanova (Fig. 315) and Cerreto; but the frieze (predating 1325) wrapped around the superstructure of the Pal. Vecchio (Fig. 332) is clearly the direct antecedent for the Badia cornices. See 170 f and n. 77 below.

[22] Paatz I, 274. In old photographs remnants of intonaco are visible.

[23] Clear in the Codex Rustichi view (Fig. 298).

— to be sure, classicizing — cornices of the Bifora zone). The architect employs framing strips to separate the cornices from the wall. The buttresses, cutting through the sequence of horizontals, run to the spire, where they support the originally richly crocketed ribs. The strong tactile quality of the Gothicizing design is particularly sensed in the interpenetration of the rib socles and the gables. The girding of the wall by a simple stringcourse at capital level (following the Ognissanti trifora section) and below the gables is a master's touch, heightening the plasticity of the cornicework, breaking the monotony of surface, and linking the windows with the wall and buttresses.

The upper parts of the Badia campanile, originally constructed together with the church after 1284, had to be rebuilt in 1330 following partial collapse.[24] Its relationship to Ognissanti and its gable decoration — so reminiscent of the apse of Santa Croce — would suggest that the reconstruction closely reflected the version of Arnolfo's time (if not of his hand). But the stylistic break with the original, lower stories of the hexagon, the highly systematic articulation, and the sequential proximity to Giotto's tower seem to indicate a new design. In the balance, the Badia campanile lies midway between Ognissanti and Giotto; in the rebuilding, the architect of 1330 — the master tower builder of Florence who earlier might have put up Arnolfo's Palazzo Vecchio tower[25] — probably combined old and new to everyone's satisfaction.[26]

His cunning modernism is manifest in a final feature: fenestration dynamics. The towers of Santa Maria Novella and San Pier Maggiore emphasize the horizontal spreading of the windows from story to cubic story. Although at Ognissanti the lights grow from one to three, the vertical current generated by the elongated stories is not dissipated by a broadening of the windows; rather the bifora is limited nearly to the width of the monofora, and the trifora to the bifora, with a resultant tension that adds spring to the Gothic lifting. The Badia master, in his more systematic way, eliminated the progression of lights altogether, positing instead the pure verticality of a strong upward expansion of equally broad, or rather equally narrow bifore. The theme of expansion is thereby transformed from the Romanesque dilation into pure Gothic lift.

Although probably disregarded by Andrea Pisano, this rich variety of sequential fenestration was of consequence for Giotto and Talenti. It was perhaps inevitable that Giotto, while carrying forward the structural analysis of the Badia, turned to the most conservative alternative for his pattern of fenestration, preferring to obtain a powerful dynamic by supercharging the spreading configuration with his volatile aesthetic. The virtuoso mason Talenti, on the other hand, fused the advances of the progressive Florentine prototypes, carefully — indeed, intricately — maintaining a common breadth from

[24] Paatz, I, 265, 274, 278.
[25] Cf. n. 21 above and n. 77 below.
[26] It was sufficiently notable to enter the chronicle of Villani (X, 178), who in any event was evidently proud that the rebuilding was sponsored by "M. Giovanni delli Orsini di Roma Cardinale, e Legato in Toscana, e signore della detta Badia."

double Bifora to Trifora, but stretching the shapes dramatically upward. His pattern not only maintains the necessary impression of its Florentine lineage, but presents a common window arrangement of northern Gothic façades: embryonic already at the south tower at Chartres (1142), a single great opening surmounts one or more stories of paired windows at Laon (1190 ff), Reims West (1241 ff), and Cologne (designed ca. 1320).

It was characteristic of Florence to combine tradition and change in transforming the densely planar, inert Romanesque bell tower into the structurally analytic, lifting masonry of Ognissanti, the Badia, and the Campanile masters. This phenomenon of dynamic continuity even at the juncture between Romanesque and Gothic styles, together with the eloquence of the cleanly sectioned, finely articulated shafts (including the less progressive ones) establish the Florentine group as a distinct entity within the Italian scene.

Elsewhere in Tuscany we are presented with a different prospect.[27] There are no Gothicizing campanili in the Florentine sense. Rather one finds either primitive, heterogeneous local specimens[28] or, in the case of most of the monumental towers — with notable exceptions at Pisa, Pistoia, and Arezzo[29] — variants on the Lombard theme, all quite distinct from Florence. This is clearly illustrated by the Dugento bell tower of Siena Duomo, which, despite its ingenious cornices and its thin, airy grace, is but a highly refined, polychrome mutant of the undisguised Lombard scheme (Fig. 307).[30] Lucca maintains the Lombard archetype even more overtly in a long series of magnificent Romanesque examples — San Frediano, San Michele, the Duomo — distinguished by a characteristically Lucchese richness of detail, including crenellated, rather than pyramidal tops (Fig. 305). One might also note that occasionally — unlike Romanesque Florence (with the exception of San Miniato) — the Lucchese tower is set freestanding (the duomo, Santa Maria Forisportam).

A prominent Tuscan exception to the Lombard rule is the campanile of the Pieve at Arezzo. The five tiers of paired bifore that open each side of the massive, sheer shaft can be traced instead to Rome,[31] where a large number of twelfth- and thirteenth-century campanili were added to fabrics dating back to Early Christian times, sometimes within the body of the church itself (e. g., Santa Maria in Cosmedin, S. Francesca Romana, San Giorgio in Velabro) or abutting the flanks or façade (e. g., Santa Croce in Gerusalemme, Santa Cecilia in Trastevere) but on occasion set free (San Lorenzo f.l.m., Santa Maria in

---

[27] The reader will find illustrations — when not included here — of the extra-Florentine campanili in the references cited below and in such publications as the "Attraverso L'Italia" series of the Touring Club Italiano, etc. For Tuscany, Salmi, 1927, is indispensable. The dating (except as noted) is standard. For understandable reasons, Italy south of Rome does not find a place in this discussion (but cf. n. 73 below).

[28] Salmi, 1927, 26 f, 61 f n. 74.

[29] Arezzo Pieve, the cathedrals of Pistoia and Pisa; however, the standard Tuscan type was also at home in these towns, e.g., S. Piero a Grado in Pisa, S. Francesco and S. Domenico in Pistoia, and S. Agostino in Arezzo.

[30] See n. 16 above.

[31] Salmi, 1927, 27, 62 n. 75.

Trastevere).[32] Lacking the corner pilasters, the arched corbel friezes, and progressive fenestration of their Lombard cousins — or predecessors — the Roman bell towers, without exception, are sectioned into nearly cubic stories by classicizing cornicework (largely dentils and rough consoles); each story is opened expansively, but rarely progressively by one to four lights per side; and a stringcourse cuts each story at the springing line of the window arches, swinging up in arcs over the archivolts (Fig. 306). The rich cumulative effect of these details is at the same time characteristically Roman and curiously akin to that of the arch-Lombard Lucchese contemporaries. But both groups contrast with the abstract Florentine style.

North of the Apennines, still different forms are found in Venice and the *terra ferma,* where two distinct types were built. The earliest — indeed, among the first monumental campanili — are the ninth- and tenth-century cylindrical towers freestanding at Sant' Apollinare Nuovo and Sant' Apollinare in Classe at Ravenna (Fig. 308).[33] Their placement and form found the way, not surprisingly, to Pisa in the twelfth century, merging at the cathedral with the local decorative archetype, the marble arcade (Fig. 302).[34] The second group had its *locus classicus* at Venice (Santo Spirito, San Tommaso dei Borgognoni, Santa Croce, San Giorgio, and San Marco; also Torcello, SS. Maria and Donato in Murano) and was marked not only by a frequently freestanding placement but — as we noted in connection with Andrea Pisano — a quadratic shaft articulated by three to five strong lesene closing in arches, broken occasionally and lightly by a frieze, and capped by a broadly fenestrated belfry section and a low pyramid (Figs. 310, 311). The species can be discerned in embryonic separation from the Lombard form at Pomposa (1036) where a multiplicity of lesene is still all but ruled by progressive fenestration (Fig. 309). It attained definitive expression not only in Venice, but with such regional works as the enormous tower set almost freestanding at the façade of San Mercuriale in Forlì, 1173 ff (Fig. 312).[35]

Varied as these central and upper Italian types may be, they shared — in contrast to Florence — a common fate: after their rich Romanesque florescence, stagnation. It was only in Lombardy that a Gothicizing wave comparable to the one in Florence occurred.

[32] See ground plans in R. Krautheimer *et. al., Corpus basilicarum Christianarum Romae* (Vatican City, 1939 ff), *passim.*

[33] On Ravenna and the origin of campanili, see Conant, 1959, 54 f, 301 n. 13 ff, with bibl.; also A. K. Porter, *Lombard Architecture* (New Haven-London), 1917, I, 71.

[34] Salmi, 1927, 61 n. 73; cf. Sanpaolesi, 1956, 51 f.

[35] On the Venetian towers see G. Gattinoi, *Il Campanile di San Marco* (Venice, 1910), Ch. I;

A. Serafini, *Torri campanarie di Roma e del Lazio nel medioevo* (Rome, 1927), I, figs. 103 ff. S. Spirito, S. Tommasso dei Borgognoni (Torcello), and S. Croce are demolished; according to Mothes (1859, 182 and pl. IV) the tower of S. Stefano was a prominent early 14th-century Venetian example of the type. On Pomposa see M. Salmi. *L'Abbazia di Pomposa* (Rome, 1936), 59 ff. Further regional examples include S. Pietro in Bologna, S. Zeno in Verona, Chioggia Duomo.

By the twelfth and thirteenth centuries essentially two Lombard variants were widely established. Both formed quadratic prisms with cubic stories articulated by the corner pilasters and arched corbel and brick friezes that we have noted. Their variance was in the decorative motif, as it were, set within this common tectonic frame. Already presented somewhat misleadingly as characteristic of *the* Lombard campanile was the motif of progressively opening fenestration, beginning as early as the ninth or tenth century at San Satiro in Milan (Fig. 313).[36] The other extreme, seen for example at Sant' Ambrogio (Fig. 314), was to close all but the belfry itself, decorating the stories with light lesene, a delicate ornamental order to be distinguished from the powerfully tectonic Venetian analogue.[37] The thirteenth century found Lombardy filled with innumerable examples not only of both regional antitheses but every intermediate possibility.[38] Senescence clearly threatened the Lombard campanile. Beginning, however, at the end of the century it burst into a new phase of life.

As in Florence, even the old quadratic frame was affected. In Lombardy this did not entail a structuralization but rather a pictorial, dichromatic outlining of the skeleton; a dissolving of the surface with enriched friezes and relief; and even (here, as in Florence) an occasional vertical stretching of the stories (Fig. 316).[39] Noteworthy though these effects may be, the truly signal Lombard innovations and achievements involved a more basic change: the switch to the polygonal tower form.

When the Cistercians brought the octagon — in France not only common in their order but native to the Auvergne, Burgundy, the Midi, and other regions[40] — to Italy as crossing towers, the Italian love of bell towers appears to have encouraged the local chapters to disregard the rule forbidding monumental campanili. The double-staged, octagonal tower of the early thirteenth century at Fossanova (Fig. 315), while in detail purely French, is more elaborate than any comparable French Cistercian example.[41] If so, it was

[36] On the controversial dating of S. Satiro, see E. Arslan, "L'architettura romanica milanese," *Storia di Milano*, III (1954), 503 ff, with further examples.

[37] Cf. *ibid.*, 510 ff.

[38] Cf. *ibid.*, 506 f; Porter, 1917, I, 71 ff; G. T. Rivoira, *Lombardic Architecture: Its Origin, Development and Derivatives* (London, 1910), I, 169 ff, 185 f, 209; II, 251, 286. And every possible mixture of the Lombard with the Venetian types is to be found in the interlying regions and areas influenced by northern Italy (S. Francesco at Assisi, for example).

[39] E.g., at the cathedrals of Parma and Cremona (Figs. 316, 319); cf. A. M. Romanini, *L'Architettura gotica in Lombardia* (Milan, 1964), I, 227 ff, 232.

[40] M. Aubert, *L'Architecture Cistercienne en France* (Paris, 1947), 369 ff; de Lasteyrie, 1926, I, 515 ff. The most remarkable and probably the earliest examples are in Toulouse (St. Sernin and the churches of the Augustinians and the Jacobins).

[41] According to Aubert (1947, 369 ff) the prohibition of stone towers (only low wooden structures for two bells, the largest not more than 500 lbs., were statutorily permitted) was scorned even in France (where, however, at least the scale was relatively restrained), but particularly in Spain and Italy. As a source for Fossanova, Aubert cites the single-storied octagon of the abbey at Obazine (Corrèze) (*ibid.*, 374). Cf. C. Enlart, *Origines Françaises de l'architecture gothique en Italie* ("Bibliothèque des Écoles Fran-

in Lombardy toward the end of the thirteenth century, in a manner consonant with the regional unrestrained appetite for oversize forms more than abundantly decorated, that the builders of the Chiaravalle Milanese not only utterly ignored the prohibition regarding scale in the colossal crossing tower set over their twelfth century church; but, in much the manner by which their forbears had transformed the prismatic stonework of the French Cistercian models into the heavy brickwork of the nave, they recast the detail of the tiered octagons in the local campanile tradition of pilaster strips, arched corbel friezes, and complicated fenestration, all in the latest version of the rich Lombard style (Fig. 317).[42]

At about the same time as the Chiaravalle — it is not yet clear which takes historical precedence — the multi-tiered octagon appears over the enormous Lombard shafts at Cremona (the "Torrazzo"; Fig. 319) and Modena (the "Ghirlandina"). Although unprecedentedly bold for Italy in the superimposed massing of the forms of such divergent character and origin, and highly imaginative in the octagon detail (particularly the "Torrazzo"), neither was the supreme work to give the group more than an impressive novelty. Nor, for that matter, was the Chiaravalle tower. In fact, notwithstanding their variety in detail, all three designs were but preparation for the definitive Lombard Gothic campanile towering over the small church of San Gottardo in Milan (Fig. 318), inscribed in 1336 by its architect Francesco Pegorari da Cremona and built by Azzone Visconti within the Palazzo Ducale presumably as a monument to his clan.[43]

çaises d'Athènes et de Rome," 60) (Paris, 1894), 34.

[42] There is disagreement about the sources of the Chiaravalle tower and its peers. Enlart (*ibid.*, 68 f) predictably suggests French sources, in particular, the Burgundian type of octagonal lantern towers (e.g., Châteauneuf). However he does mention the local tradition of low crossing towers ("tiburi"; e.g., S. Ambrogio in Milan, S. Michele in Pavia). If Enlart equivocates, de Longhi (1958, 72) explicitly denies a role to even the most developed Lombard Romanesque type (e.g., S. Teodoro in Pavia), stressing Enlart's Burgundian examples and also the towers of Toulouse. Finally, reasonably but in an extremely diffuse manner, Romanini (1964, 226 ff) appears to argue for a fusion of the French stepped octagon, both "Burgundian" and Cistercian, first with the Lombard style in the late 12th century to produce the "tiburi" of, e.g., Piacenza Duomo and S. Ambrogio in Milan, then with these very "tiburi" in the 13th century to produce such amplifications as S. Teodoro in Pavia and later, under the force of a "spectacular pictorialism,"

the Chiaravalle, Cremona, etc. That local traditions play a strong role here even in the question of type might be strengthened by including the polygonal towers of the 11th and 12th centuries discussed by Porter (1917, I, 73 ff), which would suggest that the polygonal form, particularly over the crossing, was a substream in Lombardy, overshadowed by the great quadratic "façade" towers until the late 13th century and thereafter, when under a powerful wave of French influence the octagon became the dominant type.

[43] The apparent agreement of most authors on sequence — the Chiaravalle, the "Torrazzo," and finally S. Gottardo — is contradicted by their dating. By inscription, S. Gottardo dates ca. 1336 (Romanini, 1964, 233); but Romanini (*ibid.*, 235) places the "Torrazzo" 1287-1300, and thus the Chiaravalle even earlier, in contrast to P. Toesca (1951, 91) and de Longhi (1958, 760), who believe both latter towers to be early 14th century. On the stylistic relationships between these campanili and for further examples, such as the Crema belfry (1340), see P. Toesca, 1951, 91; de Longhi, 1958, 70 ff; and particularly Romanini,

In it the venerable Lombard shaft is represented as the base: a closed massive block of gray stone less than a quarter the total height. The octagon becomes the primary form, rising initially as an all but closed prism broken by progressively richer, marvelously inventive brick friezes, with uninterrupted marble colonnettes standing free at the angles and lifting the eye to the upper zone. There, at the fourth level, richly formed bifore are set deeply behind the wall plane, which dissolves above in a continuous loggia. Corbeled powerfully forward from this screen is a band of short columns in the plane of the corner colonnettes. Behind, the upper octagon rises and emerges demurely to separate the crown of the lower prism from the transparent belfry with its paired columns. A cornice follows, and the design closes with a justly proportioned cone.

An architectural tour de force fusing into crystalline, yet dynamically pictorial, unity the various native and imported elements embodied in its predecessors, the design — of a quality rare to the Lombard Gothic — is truly worthy of such contemporary Tuscan masterworks as the façades of Orvieto Cathedral and the Sienese baptistery. Indeed, with regard to campanili, the thrust of such a comparison flows in the opposite direction: toward Lombardy. We have observed that elsewhere in Italy only Florence produced a significant series of Gothicizing campanile projects. But prior to Giotto's design, the careful Florentine advances at Ognissanti and the Badia appear hesitant and tentative alongside their bold and numerous Lombard contemporaries. The Florentine campanile builders, in this period, must have felt rather isolated in their region; looking beyond the regional horizon, at least the master of the Badia tower appears not only to have known Fossanova but could hardly have been unaware of the series of colossal Lombard forms. At the Chiaravalle tower, for example, were to be observed continuous angle lesene and overrunning cornice friezes; with San Gottardo the parallelism of direction becomes even clearer in the enrichment and refinement of vocabulary, the Gothicization of articulation, and the upward-flowing impulse.

But, despite the chasm of separation in detail, it is Giotto's project to which the spirit of the Lombard development is closest. In fact, Giotto, at Padua in the first decade of the Trecento, in Milan in 1336, and certainly in the region during the interval,[44] seems not only to have known, but to have been deeply struck by the group, particularly the boldness of Cremona and Modena: whence he evidently derived the impetus, and even the courage, in his Campanile project to place a fiery Gothic octagon on what was to be, after all, an arch-Lombard shaft.

At the same time the North Italian colossi — the second Lombard style to profoundly affect the campanili of Florence — highlight an easily overlooked difference

1964, I, 228 ff, 233 ff (stressing the role of local influences at the Chiaravalle and Cremona, and their fusion at S. Gottardo). The "Ghirlandina" of Modena, while of the type and built by the Milanese Enrico da Campione around 1300 (P.

Toesca, 1951, 91), has been altered beyond stylistic consequence.

[44] See Nardini, 70 ff; on Giotto's maximum possible activity in northern Italy, see Romanini, 1965, 160.

between Giotto's project and its Florentine predecessors: it is much larger, even gigantic. Gigantism was an especially widespread and progressive phenomenon in the High and Late Gothic period. Not only do cathedral naves grow, from Laon to Chartres to Beauvais, but huge towers spring up in Freiburg, Strasbourg, and elsewhere in northern Europe and, as we have seen, in northern Italy. In Tuscany gigantism commences in the last years of the Dugento with the Arnolfian trio in Florence: the Cathedral project, Santa Croce, and the Palazzo Vecchio (ca. eighty-seven meters high, without the fifteenth-century pyramid). The development was, as in the North, progressive. Closely following Giotto's tower design (102 meters with Saint Michael) was the visionary Sienese project of the Duomo Nuovo, which presumably would have been accompanied by a new campanile at least as high as the soaring "Mangia" (Fig. 335) at the Palazzo Pubblico (eighty-eight meters through the upper battlements, 102 meters to the tip); then arose the definitive Florentine nave, which eclipsed Arnolfo's original version; and finally the supreme effort was launched, Brunelleschi's Cupola (107 meters). But had Talenti's spire been built, the Campanile would have risen even higher (111 meters).[45] As if exhausted, the Early Renaissance turned to projects of almost miniature scale by comparison, beginning with the Old Sacristy of San Lorenzo. It is only elsewhere and not until the time of Bramante — and Julius II — that the will to size resurges.

But obviously far more than gigantism is involved in the contrast between the Campanile and its precursors. As in Lombardy, the Florentine tradition, Romanesque in essence, was by the early Trecento rather a stale one; the Badia tower was, despite the advances, in fact its swan song. Giotto and his successors were faced with a hydra-headed task: to conceive a new bell tower of greater scope and splendor than any previous Florentine shaft, not of naked stone but clothed in variegated marble forms consonant with the Baptistery and the Cathedral project; a Campanile that would be original, and modern in style, yet — so prescriptive was the Florentine sense of tradition — to a recognizable degree retaining the outlines of the traditional bell tower type. It was the latter rule that especially set the Florentines apart from their unconstrained Lombard peers, yielding a situation in which little less was demanded of the architects than to pass the Florentine tradition through a metamorphosis in which the larva was still manifest in the butterfly.

Giotto, we have seen, was not an architect by profession. But he was a supreme genius of form. It was this unique combination of the genius and the dilettante by which Giotto's project avoided triteness, on the one hand and, on the other, the too-modern effects that the professional such as Andrea Pisano, intimate with the latest architectural fashion, would have been prone to display. Giotto infused the moribund framework with

---

[45] To an exact par with Cremona, Italy's highest tower! Dimensions of the Campanile projects from Gioseffi, 1963, pl. 76a, 77b (as it stands the Campanile is 81 m to the top of the *ballatoio*).

the power of his arch-Florentine aesthetic, capitalizing on the progressively fenestrated cubes to achieve a volatile upward dynamic, taking the polychrome revetment of the Baptistery and of Arnolfo as the point of departure for a new colorism matched by the pictorial Gothicizing of the — by comparison — stiffly classical Florentine manner of architectural detail. And who else in Florence, even having seen the Lombard extravaganzas, would have envisioned placing on this transfigured relic not the simple pyramid of its predecessors but an approximation of the Freiburgian tower?

It is possible that the historically recorded aspects of Giotto's dilettantism — his structural miscalculation and the omission of overt setback — were in fact but chance historical survivals, reflecting a strain of professional disdain for his work (recall its Dugento content) five decades later in the only points of tangible and therefore preserved criticism. But considering the influence of Giotto's project on later architects; and even more, that it miraculously fused all the unwritten demands of the commission; that, indeed, it was an incontrovertibly spectacular creation, any derision of Giotto's design would probably have been limited to those pertinacious masons whose professional ancestors in Constantinople must have been scandalized at the unprecedented, yes, inconceivable creation of those amateurs Anthemius of Tralles and Isidorus of Miletus,[46] and whose followers resisted the revolutionary architecture of Michelangelo on the Vatican.

It was perhaps in pointed contrast to Giotto's orthodoxy of form that Andrea Pisano scorned the traditional bell tower outline. Giotto, to be sure, employed numerous extra-Florentine motifs in his project; but none quite broke the envelope of tradition, not even the spire, which, after all, retained the common silhouette. Andrea even employed few details of Florentine origin; his project, as we have observed, was in its very essence alien — Venetian in outline, Pisan in articulation, Sienese in dynamics, and of the Gothic goldsmith shop in decor. Not only novel but of great power in conception it was at first welcomed; but Andrea's miscalculated flaunting of the venerable tradition soon lost him his greatest patron.

The reaction swept in Talenti, who, we have seen, turned back to Giotto's project. Indeed, in a manner analogous to Orcagna's revival of archaic imagery and form, the regression went back beyond Giotto, in fact beyond the Gothicizing wall of the Badia and Ognissanti, reaching to the inarticulate, almost monolithic early medieval elevation exemplified at Sant' Andrea (Fig. 290). Unlike Giotto's project, which carried forward the powerful articulation of its immediate predecessors, Talenti's masonry, it has been observed, particularly in the Bifora section, obscures the effective analysis of wall into pier, cornice, and curtain, instead enveloping the tower in a continuous and inert marble crust. Moreover, in place of the spiky spire of the Badia and Giotto's project, Talenti, in his model, seems to have returned to a simple four sided pyramid, an early form, however high.

---

[46] Cf. R. Krautheimer, *Early Christian and Byzantine Architecture* (Harmondsworth, 1965), 156.

Beyond this primitivism, Talenti's conception is linked to Orcagna also by the extremism of effects, noted earlier, together with the attendant tension between old and new.[47] In marked contrast to Giotto's graceful play of decorative and dramatic aspects, Talenti's stories embody a searing conflict between the sheer stasis of the polychrome crust, unchanging window breadth, and the projected unrelieved pyramid on the one hand and, on the other, the explosive expansion of these shapes, with their fiery detail, upward from Andrea Pisano's niches to the Bifora to the colossal Trifora, a staccato jet of disembodied force that was to have climaxed with a spire half again as high as the Trifora story.

Thus each of the Campanile architects expressed a characteristic attitude toward tradition: Giotto, transfiguration; Andrea Pisano, *hubris;* and Talenti, Orcagnesque reaction. As executed, the Campanile bears the marks of a battleground, as it were, of the conflicting aesthetics, temperaments, and attitudes of three very different men of three divergent stylistic epochs. Yet, because each capitalized on the fabric of his predecessors — not only in the disciplined maintenance of Giotto's seven part division, but with subtle and complex stylistic continuities — the totality achieves a tactile coherence, a synthesis of all the Trecento generations of architecture more compelling, or at least fascinating, than any of the three projects in themselves.

As a collective entity the Campanile yields a further consideration. Embodied not only in the iconography of its sculpture, but in the very notion to decorate the tower with statuary, is the humanistic integration of architecture and sculpture that marks the lower Campanile as among the last direct works of a tradition established by Nicola Pisano and in which architecture is conceived both as a frame for sculpture and as sculpture itself; not coincidentally, the major works of the school are mostly pulpits, façades, and fountains. In sharp contrast, the upper Campanile, with the exception of an all but indiscernible set of angels above the Trifora windows (preserved in only a single example),[48] is marked by the complete absence of a sculptural program.

Certainly height was a factor in this differentiation, especially next to the Cathedral façade, where the reconstructed figural program more or less terminates below Bifora level. But equally important was Talenti's background and essential interest. Cut off from the Pisani by choice as much as circumstance, his style was formed, we have seen, in a comparatively pure architectural ambient;[49] rather than a figural artist who also worked

---

[47] That tension is seen in painting between severe hieratic flatness and post-Giottesque mass, fluidity, and pictorialism; between the unrestrained frontal stasis, emotional positivism, and chromatic purity of old and a restless, ambiguous dynamic, repressed emotionality, and shot coloration. Cf. Ch. VI, 149 f; Meiss, 1951, *passim.*

[48] Ch. V, 117 and n. 58.

[49] The reader will observe the decreasing role of sculpture as integral components from Arnolfo and Giovanni's façades to Orvieto (where, at a decent viewing distance, the relief sculpture becomes mere texture) to the Sienese baptistery project, all but sculpturally barren (even the tympana and the rose; Figs. 239, 269, 270, 275.

as architect, Talenti was an architect who executed occasional sculpture; he was an architect's architect. Even his great Cathedral side portal — like all truly medieval architecture — dominates its sculpture, a reversal of the roles played at Arnolfo's façade (Figs. 239, 249).[50] With his Campanile project, Talenti returns the tower to the pure architectonic tradition from which it had sprung and which, in Florence, runs through the Middle Ages from the Baptistery to Brunelleschi, including, in fact, every monumental fabric except the works of the school of Nicola Pisano — the Cathedral façade and the lower parts of the Campanile and Or San Michele.

While relative height and Talenti's architectural universalism were strongly relevant factors here, it is not immaterial that it is the aesthetically repressive, dissonant age of Orcagna — whose pietistic Or San Michele tabernacle can hardly be included in the Pisani canon, achieving instead a manifesto of humanist disintegration — which signals the turning of the Campanile from humanism. So it is a later humanist age that not only returns to complete the sculptural programs of the Campanile and in part the Cathedral façade, but to embark on a new architecture profoundly and humanly sculptural, and on great sculptural programs in architecture. Does it not allusively reflect on the historical position of the Campanile that Talenti's nave was marked in the Cinquecento for a colossal series of apostles[51] and that his son's monumental loggia in the Piazza della Signoria, fringed with but an incidental series of virtues in its original program, became essentially a sculptural framework in the course of the Renaissance.

If the church towers were, in general, the most highly developed in Florence, private towers were the most numerous (in the Dugento well into the hundreds). Even in peaceful times, when the essentially closed, bare, crenelated shafts were garnished with removable balconies (set on corbeling lodged in putlog holes), their gray masses — many as high as one hundred braccia — at best, gave to the city the heavy air of truce (Figs. 323-329). They reflected well a major aspect of the early history of Florence. From the eleventh century well into the thirteenth, the fundamental political and social units were the *consorterie*, packs of families and clans. Their violent struggles for power and tragic defense of honor in great part constituted the local politics of Florence. It is for good reason they are often called the *soci torri* (tower societies), because their strategic bases of power were the towers into which they retreated when fighting the local enemies camped below on the street. Having been forced into the city, the nobility had brought with them their wild ways and violence, building urban castles and keeps.[52]

[50] Cf. Metz, 1938, 154.

[51] C. de Tolnay, *The Youth of Michelangelo* (Princeton, 1943), 168 ff.

[52] On the towers: Lami, 1766, I, 150 ff (structure, associations); Wood-Brown, 1907, 70 ff (theories of formal development); Davidsohn, 1956, I, 819 ff (early history), V, 400 ff (legal status); idem, *Firenze ai tempi di Dante*, tr. E. D. Theseider (Florence, 1929), 452; P. Santani, "Società delle torri in Firenze," *Archivio Storico Italiano*, s. IV, Vol. XX (1887), 25 ff, 178 ff (the *consorterie*, history, destruction); B. Patzak,

Closely related in form to the private towers, which served, especially in the earliest period, also as dwellings, were the military towers and gates of the city walls (Figs. 287, 320-322). Placed at close intervals (200 braccia), the simple, purely functional towers were almost identical to the family keeps, only smaller (forty braccia high) and, though broadly open toward the city, eliminating fenestration altogether on the three outer faces. The gates, with their complex circulation arrangements and *antiportae*, presented the civil architect greater opportunities for design. They were, in effect, the official façade of the city. They carried its arms and emblems (Figs. 285, 288). Some of the more important entries served as watchtowers, and stood to imposing heights. If their fenestration was limited, it was sometimes carefully, even expressively composed, as on the Porta San Niccolò (Figs. 320, 321). Particular attention was given to the disposition of the battlements, especially the form and proportion of their supports and crenelations.[53]

When, in 1250, the commune began its first monumental seat of government, the Bargello[54] (later to include a high campanile), it could not but draw upon the three intertwined traditions of tower building (Fig. 330). The closed bulk of the monument resembled a fortress, complete with removable balconies and stairs as well as powerful battlements.[55] And it was not mere expediency that the few ornate windows the palace has were adapted from church architecture.[56] Far denser and more personal than the modern abstraction, the Florentine state was an almost religious body. The tower, built up around 1290 over the stump of an archetypal, private shaft,[57] included a feature that had always

Palast und Villa in Toscana (Leipzig, 1912), 36 ff (position in development of private architecture, noting, 58 f, an exception to the severe quadratic type, the Torre dei Tosinghi, a round colonnaded tower 130 braccia high, built in 1239, but destroyed shortly later, according to Villani, VI, 33); Schiaparelli, 1908, 63 ff (their role in domestic architecture); I. Hyman, *Fifteenth Century Florentine Studies: The Palazzo Medici and a Ledger for the Church of San Lorenzo* (Doctoral dissertation, New York University, 1968), 1 ff (a masterly history of Florentine domestic architecture from its beginnings through the Trecento); Borgatti, 1900, 20 ff (locations of towers [most were within the precincts of the Roman wall, none outside the confines of the 12th-century wall]); G. Carocci, *Il Mercato Vecchio di Firenze* (Florence, 1884), 83 ff; *idem*, *L'illustratore fiorentino*, Florence, 1880, 47 ff; Gozzadini, 1875, 8 ff (outside Florence); E. Rocchi, *Le fonti storiche dell'architettura militare* (Rome, 1908), 170 ff (on the great medieval Roman private towers of the Conti, the Milizie, *et. al.*); B. Ebhardt, *Die Burgen Italiens* (Berlin, 1917), *passim*

(on Italian fortifications); Braunfels, 1953, 179 ff (their meaning); F. Schevill, 1936, 70 f (eloquent summary).

[53] Cf. Braunfels, 1953, 45 ff, 58 ff (including the suggestion, 49, that by their number the 73 [= 72] towers and 15 [but in 1339 numbered by one writer as 12] gates symbolized the Heavenly Jerusalem depicted in the Apocalypse).

[54] J. Paul, *Die mittelalterlichen Kommunalpaläste in Italien* (Dresden, 1963), 210 ff.

[55] Although the building was heightened in the reconstruction of the great hall in 1340-46 (*ibid.*, 211), one imagines battlements also over the original building (to be sure of a different style in detail).

[56] In Florence, the bifora scheme was limited to religious architecture until the Bargello (Paatz, 1931, 308 ff, gives the source for the Bargello windows), which brought it to civic buildings (as in the Pal. Vecchio and Or San Michele). But no windows other than the monofora were permitted private houses until the Pal. Medici of Michelozzo.

[57] Paul, 1963, 210.

belonged to the ecclesiastical: the belfry. Even if the bells of the Cathedral had been used for civic purposes,[58] they remained the bells of the church. But the bell story of the Bargello tower was executed with long, round-headed openings cut harshly into a massive wall (Fig. 331). The military manner is particularly evident in comparison with the delicacy of even a Dugento church tower such as Ognissanti, not to mention the Badia (Figs. 294, 299). The assimilation of the ecclesiastical image to the military air of the building is flawless, the belfry joining smoothly with the rusticated stump below and the battlements above. The latter, conversely, are supported by an arched corbel table set on consoles, an ecclesiastical form, rather than over the simple, straight corbeling and struts found in military and private architecture. Florence had found fitting expression for the new synthetic tower genre — the civic campanile, a communal defense tower with a belfry.

The proud, mighty new Bargello was but a precursor to the Palazzo Vecchio, where the cornerstone was laid in 1299 and the bells placed in 1323 (Fig. 334).[59] Its monumental simplicity appears to have deceived even the most perceptive modern observers,[60] only one of whom notes the grandiose knot of visual metaphor it embodies. According to Braunfels,[61] the building is a microcosm of the most essential aspect of the city: the crenelated body represents the city wall, the tower at its edge the civic watchtower;[62] the columns on top are symbols of might and pride borrowed from the imperial *rocca* of Frederick II at San Miniato al Tedesco (Fig. 336).[63] But the imagery is even more complex, and the forms that express it are momentous developments of specific architectural traditions.

[58] Braunfels, 1953, 26 ff.

[59] Paul, 1963, 217 ff. After the text below was written (and largely included in the dissertation version of this ms. [1967]), I was fortunate enough to read the proofs, graciously forwarded me by Dr. Jürgen Paul, of his recent *Der Palazzo Vecchio in Florenz: Ursprung und Bedeutung seiner Form* (Florence, 1969), to which I refer the reader for more extensive comment on the building. In the notes below, however, I have taken the opportunity to discuss those parts of Dr. Paul's work particularly relevant to my argument, including some considerations gratifyingly parallel

[60] E.g., White, 1966, 170 f.   [or tangential.

[61] 1953, 201 ff.

[62] The same interpretation might also be applied to the Bargello, except that it does not cross the threshold level of symbolic intensity that largely justifies Braunfels's reading of the Pal. Vecchio (*ibid.*), despite Paul's objection (1969, 67 ff) that the building appears more as a crown in a fortified image — the third wall being completed in the same decades — than as microcosm. It may

have been more than fortuitous that for the base of the tower of the Pal. Vecchio, the Foraboschi tower was chosen which, according to Frey's plan (1885, plans I, II), lay at the end of the former Via del Gardingo that led to the famous Gardingo (or Gardingus), probably the most imposing watchtower of the first city wall (*ibid.*, 90).

[63] A source (destroyed in World War II, but now under reconstruction) first suggested by H. Mackowski, "San Miniato al Tedesco," *Zeitschrift für Bildende Kunst*, n.s. XIV (1903), 168 (noting that Arnolfo was born in nearby Colle Val d'Elsa and would have been deeply impressed). Paul objects that, although the Imperial baldacchino, as an entity, may be an allusion of the Pal. Vecchio, Braunfels's reading of the columns as individual bodies symbolizing might and pride (1953, 201 f) cannot be correct, for how would it be that the Sienese shortly thereafter, at the "Mangia," set up, in place of columns, rectangular piers devoid of such symbolism (Paul, 1969, 67 f); however, it is just such a loss of symbolic meaning that differentiates a derivative form —

Military battlements were normally uncovered. The signal innovation of the crown of the Palazzo Vecchio was the insertion of a covered gallery between the corbeling and the crenelations — suggested, surely, by the projecting upper stories *(sporti)* of private residences (Fig. 285).[64] This step civilized (or should we not say domesticated) the unrelieved militarism of the feature, giving it a sense of play and bringing its tone into harmony with the wall below, where the "ecclesiastical" windows have much the same effect. Probably it was a dilemma that induced this invention. The loosely formed terminating structures of the contemporary private palace would have been out of keeping with the high military bearing of the building. But the ordinary battlement, however perfectly strict, was a relatively slight form which would have been dwarfed by the colossal wall below and tower above, as one readily can see in the simple termination of the mid-Trecento addition to the east of the Palazzo.[65] The galleried battlement has a ballooning plasticity so powerful that the crown becomes a third element along with the huge mass and brilliant surface of the body and the jetting verticality of the tower. Indeed, on the long side (forty-six meters) it seems to have approximately the weight and length of the tower (forty-four meters), which in turn is roughly equal in height to the body (forty-three meters including the crown).

Beneath the enormous tower — the highest in Florence — is the unseen remnant of a private shaft incorporated in the body of the Palazzo (Fig. 333).[66] This massive stump is more than merely hidden by the elevation. Set before it are blind windows (identical to the functional fenestration) which give the illusion of internal spatial continuity behind the great rusticated face. But an even more cunning masking of structural reality occurs above. The exposed trunk of the tower is corbeled slightly forward, so that it aligns with

like the "Mangia" — from the original. But Braunfels does go too far in interpreting the courtyard as the image of the city-within-the-walls.

[64] This is clear in the images of loggiaed private house towers and the Pal. Vecchio in the Bigallo fresco and the Biadaiolo Codex views (Figs. 285, 288). On the *sporti* see Schiaparelli, 1908, 44 ff; and P. Moschella, "Le case a sporti in Firenze," *Palladio*, VI (1942), 167 ff; and Braunfels, 1953, 110 ff. Ebhardt (1917, IV, 116) established the uniqueness of the galleried battlement at the Pal. Vecchio in its time; Rodolico and Marchini's suggested prototype, the fenestration of Roman city gates and walls (1962, 42) is historically as well as formally unconvincing (although one need not rule out the possible influence of fragments of the Roman fortifications in Florence itself). Paul (1969, 74 ff) arrives independently at my interpretation, but seeks out in addition to the Florentine *sporti* hypothetical, now lost galleried battlements in the Hohenstaufen fortifications in southern Italy that would be analogous to forms preserved in influential Arabic and crusader fortresses — a line of argument perhaps even more tenuous than the Rodolico-Marchini thesis, since even the source in question has to be reconstructed.

[65] For the date, Paul, 1963, 222 f.

[66] An often disregarded feature, according to Lensi (1929, 20 ff) the old tower of the Foraboschi, on which the exposed tower rests, is filled up except for a shaft 1.25 x .65 m that runs from the *ballatoio* to subterranean galleries 3 m below the pavement. The upper tower measures 7.96 x 6.35 m, of which more than 5 m of the latter dimension and all of the former rest directly on the old tower (Fig. 333).

the façade of the *ballatoio* on which it would seem to rest by default — a violent extrapolation of the common bell-cote conformation, whether over a church or a civic palace, such as the original belfry at the Palazzo Pretorio of Volterra.[67] But the hollow crown could hardly support the great load. The load is denied; the huge prismatic volume of masonry seems instead to lift — a truly "Gothic" achievement, miraculously reversing in Tuscan stone the natural flow of tectonic forces. Thus dematerialized, the tower is infused with enormous tension, being monstrously massive, yet psychologically weightless.[68]

The imagery of the tower keeps this sense of tension high. The watch box that crowns the shaft is divided into corbeling, fenestration, and crenelation (Fig. 332). The scheme — interpenetrating with the standard watchtower form, such as the nearly con-

---

[67] The commonly held notion expressed by Rodolico and Marchini (1962, 42) that the scheme of the Pal. Vecchio, including the tower, is prefigured in Volterra at the Pal. dei Priori, appears false. Not only is the *ballatoio* missing, but originally the tower was as well, with the bells hung in a small bell cote at the right front corner now cut down to fit with the battlements (Fig. 337). The Volterra tower, which disturbs the rhythm of the battlements, was added later, in part over an internal arch running diagonally between the walls that support the front and right sides of the shaft (Rohault de Fleury, 1870-73, I, Pl. XXXIV, XXXV; the campanile of S. Francesco in Pisa is hung on two walls at a corner in a similar manner, A. del Bufalo, *La Chiesa di San Francesco in Pisa* [Rome n. d.], 15), resulting in a five sided plan visible from the rear (Fig. 337). The present tower is a reconstruction following the earthquake of 1846 (Rohault de Fleury, 1870-73, I, 8); originally the piers were polygonal; but even so the tower was closer in form to the Pal. Pubblico at Siena (1328-48; Paul, 1963, 268) than its source, the Pal. Vecchio. How late the Volterra tower was added is a moot point; its squat proportions are moving in the direction of Michelozzo's 1440 tower at Montepulciano (H. Saalman, "The Palazzo Comunale in Montepulciano," *Zeitschrift für Kunstgeschichte*, XXVIII [1965], 1 ff). Paul arrives independently and on somewhat different terms at similar conclusions (1969, 64 ff), reversing his earlier discussion of Volterra (1963, 276 ff). As a point of incidental information, at least five copies of the "Mangia" tower are to be found in

the United States: the Pilgrim Memorial Monument in Provincetown, Mass.; the Bristol Street Fire Station in Boston; the Broadway Fire Station in Somerville, Mass.; the Armory at 34th Street and Park Ave. in New York; and the best copy of all, the Railway Station in Waterbury, Conn. (cf. the *New York Times*, July 27, 1969, Travel Sec., 3).

[68] Cf. Paul's expressive interpretation of the tensely vibrant "immaterial character" effected by the rich, dense irregularity of the Pal. Vecchio rustication, particularly at a decent viewing distance, and the not uncalculated roughness of the *ballatoio* and tower stonework; even the windows are brought to the surface, maintaining the impression of a skin-like layer at the surface enveloping the whole; Paul relates this emphasis on surface to the ideas of Gross (1948, 240 ff), and attributes to its peculiar tensile power the potency of the visual logic of the tower's relationship to the body (Paul, 1969, 89 ff). Just how revolutionary the Pal. Vecchio tower was in its time is attested by the formally lagging Florentine civic fortress at Scarperia of 1306 ff (M. Richter, "Die 'Terra murata' im florentinischen Gebiet," *Mitteilungen des kunsthistorischen Instituts in Florenz*, V [1940], 373 ff, figs. 8 ff); even the Sienese "Mangia" completely misses the mark, substituting sheer height for the Gothic formal translation. In fact, the closest Italian equivalent to the formal ingenuity of the Pal. Vecchio is the "Torazzo" at Cremona, which achieves a similar floating, disembodied effect by masking true structure, particularly in the upper tier (Fig. 319).

temporary example near the Porta San Niccolo (Fig. 287)[69] — is the same as the main *ballatoio* and yields a similar relationship to the body below, that of voluminous plasticity over pure mass and surface. But every other aspect has been changed. The simple straight corbels and round-headed arches are replaced by elongated, pyramidical spikes, on which rests a pointed arcade with white marble soffits. Below, the wall is partitioned loosely; above, the lower stringcourse is brought down emphatically to the very apex of the arcade. Below, the shapes are simple semicircles, rectangles, and triangles; above, the long pyramids and pointed arcade are set against small, square windows darkly framing white marble columns, and these, in turn, appear against jagged crenelations.[70] Below, the gallery openings align with the crenelations; above, the spacing varies polyrhythmically — seven corbels, three windows, and five merlons. If the shaft of the tower embodies the conflict between the soaring, dematerialized frontal plane and the deep static mass behind, the crown presents an unrelieved tension in the shaping and disposition of every element.[71] A latent violent image, the watchtower seems a monster with omnipresent, narrowed eyes and threatening fangs.[72]

From this grisly shape rises, of all things, a baldacchino. Previously strictly limited to ecclesiastical use, the form carries intimations of the sacred, befitting its new function as carrier of the all-but-sacred bells of the Signoria. Its columns, cast in appropriately massive form, are so powerful that they act, independent of the tabernacle context, as symbols of might and pride, and capture with intended civic *hubris* the meaning of the nearly free-standing columns set at the corners of the boxy terminus of the imperial *rocca* at San Miniato al Tedesco.[73] An arched corbel frieze, adapted from ecclesiastical towers and used

[69] 1325. For the chronology of the third wall, see Villani, VII, 39, VIII, 31, IX, 10 and 256; Braunfels, 1953, 58 ff.

[70] Cf. Paul's comment on the effect of these so-called "Ghibelline" crenelations (1969, 73 f). A symbolic interpretation is out of the question, for how would Siena have come to its square-headed "Guelf" crenelations of the Pal. Pubblico?

[71] Even the stringcourse moldings of the tower have a razor sharpness; the lower forms a highly singular triangular projection with its undersurface horizontal — a shape that cuts light like a knife.

[72] Paul attributes this ferocity to the "Ghibelline" crenelations of the tower ("Die Zinnen waren die Zähne, die die Stadt ihren äußeren Feinden zeigte," 1969, 70 ff). As early as 1331 lions were kept nearby; in 1353 four *marzocchi* of *macigno* were set up at the corners (Lensi, 1929, 24 f).

[73] Cf. 167 and n. 63 above. The density and fluidity of symbolism is astounding. Salmi (1927, 64 n. 83) finds that the "cylindrical pinnacles" of the S. Miniato tower (evidently believing they carried no superstructure) are reminiscent of those that frequently crown Sicilian and southern Italian campanili, in particular the 12th-century tower of the Martorana of Palermo, source for the 13th-century campanili at the cathedrals of Gaeta, Caserta Vecchia, and Amalfi (cf., L. Biagi, *Palermo* [Bergamo, 1929], 42); if Frederick II thus crowned his Tuscan watchtower with an ecclesiastical form taken from his Sicilian empire, now at the Pal. Vecchio the transformed motif is further displaced, and yet because of the baldacchino image and its associations, actually channeled back toward its ecclesiastical origins. Ciboria appear to have been rare in Florence (even the Cathedral appears not to have had one until the mid Quattrocento; see Paatz, III, 409). But there was one great example: the early Dugento apse of the Baptistery, where (whatever the associations with the Pantheon) the profound

here for the first time in Florentine civic architecture, tautly encircles the superstructure of the baldacchino, where it takes on a military air by association with the overlying crenelations and the structural corbeling below.

The expressive compounding of hitherto disassociated forms of ecclesiastical, military, and even private architecture for the new, synthetic genre of communal palace and tower, first attempted in Florence at the Bargello, attained astounding definition in the Palazzo Vecchio. Could its architect — surely one of the immortal — have been Arnolfo di Cambio? What other Tuscan architect had been so thoroughly exposed to Roman rustication?[74] Who else had worked so long and so creatively with ciboria,[75] extending the form even to the façade of the Duomo (Figs. 237-239)?[76] What previous comparable work so closely recalls the manner in which tower rises from body, baldacchino from tower — a manifestation of one of the central phenomena of the Late Gothic — as Arnolfo's Roman tabernacles, particularly the one in Santa Cecilia (Fig. 237), or the side portals of the Cathedral façade (Fig. 239)? Who but a great sculptor would have visualized so profoundly organic an elevation or so anthropomorphic an image as the watchtower? Besides Arnolfo, what sculptor of the time — Giovanni Pisano aside — charged his work with such bold plasticity and monumentality?[77]

integration of baldacchino with the architecture is not without relationship — perhaps even historical — to the synthesis at the Pal. Vecchio.

[74] The rear wall of the Forum of Augustus has been suggested as Arnolfo's source (M. Salmi, "Arnolfo di Cambio," in *Encyclopedia of World Art* [New York, 1959], I, 762); believed in the Quattrocento to be the Palace of Caesar (by Giovanni Rucellai [Hyman, 1968, I, 156 ff]), and its three-storied elevation truly resembling the Pal. Vecchio, the Roman masonry would have been fitting for the medieval Florence that conceived itself not only a daughter of Rome, but rivaling it, as the inscription on the Bargello makes clear (cf. Rubenstein, 1942; Braunfels, 1953, 18 ff; Baron, 1955, I, 50 ff and *passim*). Paul's insistence (1969, 83 ff) instead on the rustication of Hohenstaufen fortresses in southern Italy as the source appears to me nearly as groundless as his derivation of the galleried battlement from the same ambient (n. 64 above), particularly as he does not present convincing evidence that Florence conceived its image in terms of the southern Empire as it did with respect to Rome (although it is certainly not impossible that such Imperial symbolism was operative *along with* the antique — particularly con-

sidering the S. Miniato tower, which, however, in contrast to southern Italy, was in unavoidable proximity to Florence).

[75] White, 1966, 62 ff.

[76] I. e., the side portals.

[77] Several details point directly to Arnolfo: the heads in the corbeling of the *ballatoio* are markedly similar to the capitals from the Badia tower, now in the Bargello (Paatz, I, 274); many of the bifora capitals are extremely close to those of Arnolfo's blind arcade on the inner façade of the Cathedral (Figs. 229, 231); the Sala d'Armi bases and capitals (the bases inverted) are strikingly similar in style to the Arnolfian parts of the Duomo flanks and to the Badia façade. I prefer to think that the whole design is more or less as the original architect — Arnolfo di Cambio — designed it. Even in this period, a plan could be retained after its author's death, e.g., the façade of Orvieto, the Siena Duomo Nuovo, or the Florentine Duomo itself after the definitive project of 1367 — by which even Brunelleschi had to abide. If in conception a unity, it is possible nevertheless that some of the details of the tower represent the inventions of the builder, a man of sharp, hard, systematic tendencies who would have somewhat reworked Arnolfo's design — and

Regardless of its author, the Palazzo Vecchio was not without consequence, on a number of levels, for the genesis and form of the Campanile. The most general considerations are perhaps obvious: the Palazzo Vecchio not only set a level of achievement for the architects of the Campanile, but its multistaged, soaring dynamic gave an impetus for the ardent vertical forces that we have observed in their projects.

There is a more specific connection. Tuscan architecture appears to have engaged, periodically, in a search for novel belfry forms. In the early Dugento, Pistoia[78] set on a massive shaft (the Leaning Tower in quadratic version) an arched and crenelated belfry cube (Fig. 304), a primitive antecedent, perhaps, with the San Miniato *rocca*, for the Palazzo Vecchio terminus. Pisa, itself now something of an architectural backwater, in the mid Trecento crowned its ancient but still incomplete bell tower with a highly inventive, polyrhythmic cylindrical belfry (Fig. 302) that possibly was meant to be domed like cathedral and baptistery.[79] Florence long maintained the traditional belfry in church towers — simply the top story — being at first content, in the Gothicizing period, with enlarging the scale and discretely modernizing articulation. In Florence we have seen that initially it was rather in civic architecture, a new genre free of prescriptive molds, that the most creative belfry developments occurred, tentatively with the Bargello, then definitively at the Palazzo Vecchio in so compelling a form that it was translated into the Sienese idiom within a decade of its completion (Fig. 335) with reflections continuing in Volterra (Fig. 337) and Montepulciano into the fifteenth century.[80] Following the triumph of the Palazzo Vecchio tower, Giotto could hardly have maintained the traditional belfry in his Campanile project, particularly if he realized — as he must have — that the great civic tower is, after all, a relative of the ecclesiastical Lombard colossi, not only in sheer scale but in the radical boldness of the superpositioning of forms. In fact, in the placement of an airy, arched superstructure (the belfry) over a closed, crenelated shaft, and in the multiple rising of form from form a connection with Cremona was almost inescapable (Fig. 319). At the same time, we have seen that Giotto, even if emboldened and inspired by the spectacular massing, turned not, as the Lombards and Arnolfo, to old-fashioned (however potent) prototypes, but instead to the *dernier cri* in Gothic tower forms (Fig. 167.) A particularly happy stroke, Giotto's adaptation of the Freiburgian octagon and spire not only lent a powerful culmination and an airy grace to his composition, it provided as well a novel belfry that was to have been visually expressive of its function: radiation of the bells' compelling sonority (Fig. 134).

perhaps not only at the Pal. Vecchio, but also at the reconstructed Badia tower, the details, particularly the corbeled cornices, being extraordinarily close (cf. n. 21 above).

[78] Salmi, 1927, 48 n. 42.

[79] Sanpaolesi (1956, 33, 62) suggests a cone. However, by analogy with the Baptistery and Cathedral, as well as from what the incomplete fabric itself would appear to demand, a cupola might be a more satisfactory reconstruction — as Peruzzi already imagined in a Uffizi drawing (Arch. 362A, recto).

[80] Cf. note 67 above.

The Palazzo Vecchio and Giotto's project seem to have exhausted the quest for spectacular belfry forms in Florence, for Andrea Pisano's belfry was probably to have been a simple Venetian *cella* (Figs. 310, 311), an opened cube. And Talenti, in his archaizing manner, returned emphatically to the standard pre-Giottesque type in the Trifora, only inflating it to Brobdingnagian scale and spinning a decoration that we have already amply scrutinized.

But if Talenti rejected the Palazzo Vecchio belfry principle there was another key aspect of the great communal palace that was indeed consequential for one of his most successful inventions: the Campanile *ballatoio* (Figs. 70, 85). The corbel frieze system of the earlier Florentine campanili had reached maximum development at the Badia and had been justly rejected by Giotto in favor of classicizing marble profiles ultimately in the tradition of the proto-Renaissance fabrics. While Talenti's intermediate cornices — unlike the idiosyncratic details of Andrea Pisano — were but another variant of the perennial Florentine classicism, for his terminal "cornice" he turned instead to the crown of the Palazzo Vecchio; as it formed a civilized battlement by infusing the purely military frame with urban features, the Campanile *ballatoio* further sublimated the battlement form by casting it in rich marble shapes and surfaces and translating crenelations into a hexafoiled balustrade. In the Palazzo Vecchio the new elements appropriately were taken from Tuscan domestic architecture; the Campanile balustrade, while hardly of local origin, was manifestly of equally just lineage for the marble Cathedral tower. Indeed, not only were such balustrades common on northern Gothic church towers but particularly so in the fourteenth century.[81]

Yet it is essential to realize that whereas in the North the balustrade — much like the planar battlement — commonly draws across the top a narrow, pierced ribbon, which in plan continues the shaft below, at the Campanile the balustrade forms but the transparent upper edge of a high, volumetric shape that is not only, as we have implied, a sublimated battlement, but which carries the sense of being a marble counterpart of the Palazzo Vecchio crown and watchtower.

This relationship involved a dependence beyond that of formal inspiration. The Palace of the Priors was also their fortress;[82] that the civilized battlements crowning the

[81] De Lasteyrie, 1926 f, I, 525 f; the Norman school was particularly active, and its masterpiece, the great "Kreisker" tower of S. Pol-de-Léon (dating from the reign of Jean IV of Brittany, 1345-99) strikingly brings to mind Talenti's *ballatoio*, for topping the quadratic block are: a frieze of circumscribed quatrefoils in relief; a rather strong, double foliate cornice; and a balustrade of circumscribed quatrefoils (and above the balustrade rises a huge quadratic spire and four airy pinnacles; *ibid.*, fig. 565).

[82] One of the Duke of Athen's tyrannical acts was to transform it into more of a real one. Cf. Braunfels, 1953, 192 f and Paul, 1969, 69 ff and *passim*, on the still, to my mind, unresolved controversy over the extent to which the Pal. Vecchio figured as a fortress. Both writers insist that in republican Florence the Pal. Vecchio as *bona fide* fortress would have been out of place — forgetting, it seems to me, that when it was built, the state was not a fully established fact, that uprisings from all sides and civic strife of vio-

edifice inspired the Campanile *ballatoio* in part follows from the, at least implicit, function of the structure as a defense tower, both in practical terms for the clergy and ultimately more tellingly, as we shall see, in a symbolic manner for all Florence. Yet to view the matter in proper perspective, its martial aspect was but part of the full civic meaning of the Palazzo Vecchio. Thereafter any comparable use of the *ballatoio* would entail not only military but civic implications.[83] If Talenti's *ballatoio* sought a transfer of the import of the great civic building to the Campanile, it was not just the military overtones but its broad communal essence.

The thrust of this interpretation is confirmed, if by nothing else, in the fate of the projected Campanile spire: had it been built, the meanings captured and carried by the *ballatoio* would largely have been lost, for in their towers the two great public buildings established, by its conspicuous omission, the spire as a purely ecclesiastical form.[84] This was probably the deepest reason why Talenti's enormous pyramid was never constructed — at least in the Trecento. This is true even though later, in the Renaissance (as Vasari indicates), it was the classical horizontality of the terminus that was gratifying to the new breed of Florentine. Born as a subject rather than as citizen, for him, understandably, aesthetic line counted more than ancient political import; in any case, he had learned to detest all medieval form, churchly or civic — so that, in other words, the spire was ultimately suppressed not because it was ecclesiastical, but simply because it was Gothic.

We have still to confront the most puzzling scene in the history of Florentine towers. Between 1334 and 1357 the Campanile dominated the architectural energies of the commune, at the expense of the Cathedral project, and even Or San Michele during the fiscal

---

lent ferocity were still very much a real threat to its integrity (there was even a special militia of the guilds to protect the priors against local enemies [Schevill, 1936, 154]), that it was prudent to build for the highest communal institution, if not a forbidding fortress then a fortress-like palace. This the Pal. Vecchio clearly was with its minimal ground story fenestration, massive walls, employable battlements (from within the gallery), and keep (Dati [born in 1362] calls the tower "una rocca"; the internal shaft in its substructure leads down to subterranean passages presumably for some dire emergency [Lensi, 1929, 20 f]). And indeed, the creation of the Pza. della Signoria was explicitly "pro decore et *fortificatione* palatii populi Florentini, in quo morantur domini priores..." ([italics mine] Frey, 1885, doc. 81, p. 201, doc. 85).

[83] A phenomenon excluding the merely fashionable imitation of the form at S. Lorenzo and — as it was left incomplete — Ognissanti (cf. 153 f above). At the tower of the Badia a Settimo (Fig. 301), executed together with the fortification of the monastery by Florence in 1371 ff (C. C. Calzolai, *La storia della Badia a Settimo* [Florence, 1958], 74 ff; his discussion of the campanile itself, 111 ff, is misleading; Serafini, 1927, I, 66, dates the tower correctly), a military image is struck by the simple, high corbeling and the belfry reminiscent of the Bargello (and lacking the festive note of the related S. Lorenzo tower).

[84] The pyramidal roof on the Pal. Vecchio tower is a 15th-century addition. Paul (1963, 220) cites the conflicting opinions of its date. But the fresco of the 1340s commemorating the expulsion of the Duke of Athens (Lensi, 1929, 33), as well as the Bigallo view, show no pyramid. The standard was added in the 15th-century (*ibid.*, 21).

privations of the 1340s. Through thick and thin the Campanile went up, the crises and disasters of 1343 and 1348 causing but temporary delays. Why this single-minded devotion to a tower? Why, indeed, was it even begun in 1334?[85]

Surely it was not because Giotto desired a monument to his genius, on which to glorify, in part for questionable motives, the urban arts, as we have noted was suggested by Braunfels.[86] Irrespective of motives, the will of a single man, particularly an artist, however great, would hardly have carried the community to such great expense and effort, especially for more than two decades after his death. Nor was the powerful multiple symbolism of the sculptural program — or even of the bells — more than an incidental factor concerning the building energies: the sculpture was a highly significant resultant of the Campanile as architecture, but not a key determinant in the founding decision and the execution of the tower. And as to the question of the dual architectural meaning of the Campanile — as an extension of the façade and as an independent shaft — in the final analysis it clearly is the latter that is primary: the Florentines never would have built a Campanile principally in connection with a façade when the façade itself was left incomplete.[87]

On the other hand, it may well be that Arnolfo's Cathedral project had been furthered so successfully between 1331 and 1334 on the basis of new leadership and enlarged income that the "altare majus et chorus nove ecclesie" ("main altar and choir of the new church") mentioned in 1334 as completed signaled that a plateau in the Cathedral campaign had been attained.[88] The situation would have been analogous to the late 1350s, when the Campanile reached a point at which it could be "temporarily" abandoned.[89]

---

[85] A new Campanile, strictly speaking, was not needed. As late as 1300 "la campana grossa" had been placed (Doc. II).

Villani (X, 209; Doc. I) notes that the fire which broke out in Jan. of 1333 "contra il campanile vecchio di Santa Reparata" burnt "una casa"; he says nothing about damage to the tower (although it could have been disfigured; cf. Doc. III). Moreover, as Braunfels reasons (1948, 194), were it thereafter an unusable ruin, the *Operai* would not have waited until 1357 to have it dismantled (Doc. 166), but rather would have done so much earlier if only to gain use of its building materials (as the second city wall was destroyed for use in the Cathedral fabric in 1314). See n. 7 above.

[86] Braunfels, 1948, 193 ff.

[87] See Ch. IV.

[88] See Guasti, doc. 36. Villani states explicitly that in 1331 "si ricominciò a lavorare la chiesa maggiore di Santa Reparata" (X, 195; Guasti,

doc. 33). And the funds had to go somewhere! See Grote, 1961, 43 ff; Metz, 1938, 138; Paatz, III, 434 f n. 42. Saalman's attempt (1964, 473 f n. 12) to invalidate the document of 1334 (first published by Davidsohn, 1908, IV, 460) is not successful. His most cogent point is that the choir is mentioned nowhere else, not even its eventual destruction. It could very well be that the measurement of June 19, 1357 is not a laying-out, as Saalman believes (1964, 477 f) but the traditional interpretation that it is a measurement of existing fabric, i.e., including the choir of 1334; the document refering to its destruction might simply be lost, along with so many others.

[89] The timing would have been in accordance with the synchronous advance planning noted in the Campanile construction (Ch. V): the completion of the "chorus nove ecclesie" by Sept. 15, 1334 would have been foreseen early in the year, leading to Giotto's appointment in April and the Campanile's founding already in July, in time to

If so, the new leadership, the Arte della Lana — perhaps together with Giotto — might have seen in the situation the opportunity to achieve a completely new project instead of merely continuing the problematic fabric of their predecessors.[90]

Again, as we have already noted,[91] Florence was bursting with energy and pride in the 1330s and it was only natural that a bold vertical form be built as the Baptistery and the Cupola were in their day. There was indeed a precipitant for the act: anyone who witnessed (as I did during the course of writing this monograph) the misery and incredible filth following the flood of 1966 can well understand why the proud and powerful Florentines of the Trecento projected the gayest, most colorful of all European towers the year following 1333, particularly if in addition to the November flood the fire of January in the vicinity of the old Campanile had indeed damaged it.[92] In those emotionally charged times, the acute Florentine sense of balance may have been activated: against the embodiment of the state in the communal palace towers one would set the bell tower of the Cathedral, against the gray stone mass of the Palazzo Vecchio a gay marble shaft, against the brutal grimness of the Inferno — which at times Florence was — a brilliant fantasy of Paradise.[93]

But such considerations, however valid in themselves, lacking a historical focus and motive power, inevitably fragment. The driving cause for the grand decision and painstaking implementation was something deeper than the possible pause in a building campaign, the ambition of a small (however powerful) group, the positive reaction to disaster, or a diffuse sense of topographic propriety. The extended will of an entire Florentine generation owed itself to something more than the sum of such plausible factors and encouraging, but fleeting situations.

A clue may be found in the unprecedented speed at which the Palazzo Vecchio was constructed. Indeed, it was the Palazzo itself that seems to have first displaced the Cathedral project.[94] The young, vulnerable government of the Priors needed the dignified security of a monumental edifice. No sooner was it complete and the situation otherwise in order[95] — at least momentarily — than the Campanile was proposed and then raised almost as rapidly, and exclusively. The commune evidently felt the monumental new bell tower to be not merely decorous but of compelling necessity.

In the private wars between the *magnati*, the first act of a victor was inevitably the destruction of the opponent's keep, which not only ruined his base of power, but soiled his honor. Adapting, as ever, traditional ways to new ends, the first act of the *primo popolo*, according to Giovanni Villani, was to decree the leveling of all private towers

accomplish a good deal of the foundation work before the rainy season set in.

[90] Cf. Braunfels, 1948, 195.
[91] Ch. IV, 104 ff.
[92] Cf. n. 85 above.

[93] The London panel captures this in the contrast and balance between the shining Cathedral group and the somber civic complex (Fig. 286).
[94] Braunfels, 1953, 166.
[95] Cf. Villani, X, 195 (Guasti, doc. 33).

to fifty braccia.[96] Whether or not the decree — for which no document has been found — was more than Villani casting his party, the Guelphs, in the role of the upholder of impartial justice,[97] one can be sure that following 1250 large numbers of Ghibelline towers, at least, suffered the fate of the fifty-nine Guelph towers recorded to have been destroyed in the counterrevolution of the next decade.[98]

Evidently these and other wholesale demolitions of towers did not suffice. The *consorterie*, with their urban castles and rural economic power, still were strong enough in the early Trecento to pose a threat to the young republic. One of the first deeds of the Priors, upon completion of their own monumental fortress and tower, was to legislate, in the Statutes of 1324, the dismantling of private towers to fifty braccia (the Palazzo Vecchio tower is about 150 braccia high), a revival of the lapsed rule of 1250, had it ever existed. Moreover, it was sternly prohibited that the resulting stumps be armed with any sort of military instruments; such towers would be razed to the foundations, and the artisan responsible for the work would have both hands amputated.[99]

In spite of stiff new regulations supplementing the earlier Ordinances of Justice, the traditional lawlessness and violence of the *magnati* continued, threatening, if not the state itself, the well-being of private citizens. With enormous wealth and power still behind them, it was easy for them to pervert the courts. As late as the 1330s, Marvin Becker informs us, "forty-six *magnati* families were convicted of one hundred forty-six serious breaches of communal laws, including arson, murder, devastation of church property, attacks on communal fortifications, highway robbery, and treason. None of the sentences were ever executed: for relatively small fines, the *Magnati* could have the severest condemnation annulled."[100] One surmises that many towers remained armed, if not illegally high.

It was only under the puritanical government of 1343-48 that the laws were strictly enforced, particularly those against the *magnati*. Moreover, in 1345, at one great stroke the commune allowed fully one half of the *magnati* — those who in years previous had proven their good faith and peaceful intentions — to become citizens, an act that irrevocably broke the power of the nobility and channeled their political energies to the common good.[101] Simultaneously, the systematic reduction — to an unarmed fifty braccia —

[96] Villani, VI, 39.
[97] Santani, 1887, 25 ff.
[98] *Ibid.*, 28. Braunfels takes care to note that under certain conditions — i.e., the complete pacification of the landlords — it was ruled forbidden to *destroy* the towers, valued as city landmarks (1953, 179).
[99] Davidsohn, 1956, V, 400 ff. (Evidently the commune reasoned that while a landlord might still dare to flout the rule, it would be difficult

[though probably not impossible] to find an artisan willing to take on such a perilous commission.)
[100] Becker, "Popular Government," 1962, 373 ff (a penetrating discussion of the political situation of these years, which I have paraphrased in this and the following paragraph).
[101] *Ibid.* Cf. *idem*, 1967, *passim*, for broader (but somewhat diffuse) considerations of the political dynamics of the period.

of all those towers that might have survived the Statute of 1324 and earlier devastations must have occurred.[102]

During the century it had taken to pull down and disarm the towers of the *magnati*, the city had erected not only numerous large-scale ecclesiastical campanili, but the Bargello and the Palazzo Vecchio. One can easily appreciate the political contrast between Florence in 1250, when her streets were but shadowy, violent corridors at the feet of the hundreds of private keeps, and in 1334, when, most — if not all — of these grim shafts trimmed, the populace undertook daily life in view of the high church and civic bell towers they had collectively built. Yet for a community that, after centuries of tower societies, must instinctively have equated, even if now symbolically as much as practically, political potency with the control of a tower, something of deep import was lacking. All the tower building was not enough for the pride of the city, not even the newly finished, colossal tower of the Priors. The governing bodies of the commune were, in a sense, extensions of the logic of the *consorterie;* as is well known, the *podestà*, the captain, the priorate, and their councils remained limited not only in sovereignty, but particularly in representation and access of entry.[103] They remained, as it were, partial corporate entities in a still incompletely formed state. Thus, neither their towers, nor the numerous campanili (especially the old Cathedral hulk) could sate the apparently universal instinct among Florentines if not to have a tower of one's own then to belong, at least, to some tower group[104] — a need now transformed by the magnetic force of the ascendant state into the urgent desire for a definitive, superscaled tower of universal Florentine proprietorship. The obvious way, indeed the only real possibility, was to rebuild the by now politically neutral, yet communally focal and topographically central Cathedral shaft.

The Campanile begun by Giotto was built so energetically only because, during the years of its construction, the will ran so broad and deep. The civic thrust of the relief, of the *ballatoio*, and of the abandonment of the spire is confirmed by the coats of arms at the base, which represent Florence, the commune, and the *popolo* (Figs. II, 7), conspicuously

[102] That towers remained a potential threat is suggested by the fact that the 1324 statute was repeated in 1355 (Schiaparelli, 1908, 64 n. 2).

[103] Cf. Schevill, 1963, I, 153 ff, 208 ff (compare the analogous Sienese situation, W. M. Bowsky, "The 'Buon Governo' of Siena [1287-1355]: A Medieval Italian Oligarchy," *Speculum*, XXXVII, [1962], 368 ff). It was the very mechanism of qualification for office that the Medici were able to turn to their purpose in the Quattrocento (N. Rubenstein, *The Government of Florence under the Medici* [Oxford, 1966], 4 ff, *passim*).

[104] Particularly in the early 14th century, the burghers of Florence were wont to imitate the manners and customs of nobility, and in fact

"pageant, ceremony, and tournament were the hall-mark of *civiltà* in Florentine society until the 1340's" (Becker, 1967 f, I, 14 f). Even the proletariat had a direct and positive relationship to towers, for the Florentine militia, which included every male inhabitant, took definition by gate companies — that is, by the particular gate to which he was assigned to report in case of attack. In this context one might recall that when the Bardi family captured the castle of Vernio in 1337, their name became "Bardi di Vernio" (H. Bodmer, "A School of Florentine Sculptors in the 14th Century: the Baroncelli and Bardi Monuments," *Dedalo*, X [1929 f], 663).

omitting the Church whose name the Campanile carries but from whose Cathedral nave it is — yes, pointedly — isolated.[105] Truly a "universal tower," the Campanile symbolized the triumph of the *popolo* over the *magnati,* yet at the same time lent the noble families a shining new symbol of common honor in compensation for their loss of private pride and power. If so, the Campanile embodied an inversion — and yet a confirmation — of the medieval mentality: the literal image, a Cathedral bell tower replete with a scholastic sculptural cycle and even a direct, private access for the canons, was sacred, but its most trenchant symbolism was profoundly of this world.[106]

Thus, the Campanile, the combined design of three pre-eminent artists of the Florentine Trecento, was the expression of the deepest civic impulse. It was the climax of tower building in Florence as well. After the Campanile not one tower of consequence was lifted over the city.[107] The last great form to rise into the skyline was the Cupola, which brought Florentine architecture full circle, to the Baptistery, where it all began.

---

[105] In Florence the Church's arms are the crossed keys (gules, two keys in saltire, corded of the handles or, the wards in chief; adopted ca. 1260 out of devotion to the chair of St. Peter; included in the arms frescoed between the *ballatoio* corbeling at the Pal. Vecchio). The red cross on a white ground (argent, a cross gules; adopted 1292 for the Gonfalonier of Justice) is the *popolo;* the split shield (per pale, argent and gules) represents the commune (or the alliance of Florence and Fiesole); and the lily (argent, a lily expanded and budded gules; originally gules, a lily argent, inverted after the 1251 triumph over the Ghibellines) and the *marzocco,* of course, symbolize Florence (or the City and Signoria). Cf. H. Wills, *Florentine Heraldry, A Supplement to the Guidebooks* (London, 1900), 123 f, 187. It is telling that, in contrast to the Bargello, the Pal. Vecchio (the battlements), and the Loggia della Signora,

the Campanile omits the ecclesiastical arms — presumably to stress its symbolic independence from the church at which it stands. The Campanile arms exactly parallel those over the secondary portal on the north face of the Pal. Vecchio (Fig. 204).

[106] For H. Bauer *(Kunst und Utopie, Studien über das Kunst- und Staatsdenken in der Renaissance* [Berlin, 1965], Ch. I) even this distinction would be blurred in the Trecento tendency of the Tuscan city — especially Florence — to see itself as a near sacred entity.

[107] And many were torn down, e.g., S. Lorenzo, S. Maria Maggiore. One can hardly term the campanili of S. Spirito and S. Frediano unusually significant forms, although the previous is fascinatingly eclectic, and, in the otherwise unbroken skyline of the Oltrarno, they both figure prominently by default.

Documentation

The Campanile documents have been meticulously published by Guasti (1887) as part of the records of the Cathedral construction. For the convenience of the reader, however, I have extracted from Guasti those entries concerning the fabrication of the Campanile; with a few exceptions, only references to construction — including payments — are included; the usually long-winded, but unequivocal, legal documents concerning the financing of the Cathedral and Campanile projects and also those involving the organization of the Opera, while fully cited in the text and notes, are omitted here.

The documents are renumbered; their original places in Guasti appear in brackets; the date is given according to the common calendar (in contrast to the old-style Florentine year that ran from March 25 to March 24). In a few instances, as noted in the brackets, the reader will find the documents are taken from publications other than Guasti (1887) and in one case (of slight importance) merely a summary is given. For documents other than those of the account books of the *Provveditori* Filippo Marsili (Docs. 13-133, 135-190) and Cambino Signorini (Docs. 191-208) the provenance is indicated in parentheses at the end of the entry; for the full forms of these abbreviations, see Guasti, XXIX ff. To facilitate the analysis in Ch. V, n. 14 of Doc. 12, its items are enumerated.

Following the primary documents are the sources bearing on the history of the Campanile through Vasari, plus one important passage from del Migliore. The numbering here is Roman rather than Arabic.

APRIL 12, 13, 1334 [DOC. 44]

1. In Dei nomine amen. Anno sue salutifere incarnationis millesimo trecentesimo trigesimoquarto indictione secunda die duodecimo mensis aprilis, Consilio domini Capitanei et populi Florentini . . .; et tertiodecimo eiusdem mensis aprilis, Consilio domini Potestatis et comunis Florentie . . .; totaliter approbate acceptate admisse et firmate fuerunt provisiones infrascripte . . .

Domini Priores artium et Vexillifer iustitie una cum offitio Duodecim bonorum virorum, cupientes ut laboreria que fiunt et fieri expedit in civitate Florentie pro comuni Florentie honorifice et decore procedant, quod esse commode perfecte nequit nisi aliquis expertus et famosus vir preficiatur et preponatur in magistrum huiusmodi laboreriorum, et in universo orbe non reperiri dicatur quemquam qui sufficientior sit in hiis et aliis multis magistro Giotto Bondonis de Florentia pittore, et accipiendus sit in patria sua velut magnus magister, et carus reputandus in civitate predicta; et ut materiam habeat in ea moram continuam contrahendi, ex cuius mora quamplures ex sua scientia et doctrina proficient, et decus non modicum resultabit in civitate premissa: habita prius super hiis diligenti deliberatione, et demum inter ipsos Priores et Vexilliferum et dictum offitium Duodecim bonorum virorum, secundum formam Statutorum, premisso facto et obtento partito et secreto scruptinio ad fabas nigras et albas, eorum offitii auctoritate et vigore, et omni modo et iure quibus melius potueruunt, providerunt ordinaverunt et stantiaverunt: Quod ipsi domini Priores artium et Vexillifer iustitite, una cum offitio Duodecim bonorum virorum, possint eisque liceat pro comuni Florentie eligere et deputare dictum magistrum Giottum in magistrum et gubernatorem laborerii et operis ecclesie Sancte Reparate, et constructionis et perfectionis murorum civitatis Florentie, et fortificationis ipsius civitatis, ac aliorum operum dicti Comunis que ad laborerium vel fabricam cuiuscumque magisterii pertinere dicerentur vel possent; pro eo tempore et termino et cum eo salario solvendo eidem de quacumque pecunia deputata vel que deputaretur seu que debeat vel deberet expendi seu converti in quocumque vel pro quocumque laborerio opere vel fabrica quod vel que construeretur vel fieret in civitate Florentie per illum et illos offitiales et personas, et eo

modo et forma et tempore per quem quos vel quas et pro quo et cum quo et quibus et prout et sicut eisdem dominis Prioribus et Vexillifero iustitie et offitio Duodecim bonorum virorum vel duabus partibus ex eis, etiam alio et aliis absentibus et inrequisitis, videbitur et placebit. — (*Provvisioni,* XXVI, 84.)

SEPTEMBER 16, 1334 [DOC. 46]

2. In Dei nomine amen. Domini consules mandaverunt et fecerunt in domo dicte Artis lane, in qua pro dicta Arte iura redduntur, Consilium generale dicte Artis lane . . . more solito congregari. . . . Coram quibus consiliariis et Consilio ego Castellus magistri Raynuccii notarius dicte Artis lane . . . infrascripta proposui . . .

Quinto. Item quod ipsi domini consules presentialiter in officio residentes habeant baliam et possint pro dicta Arte lane, eorum durante officio presentis consulatus, mutuare seu mutuari facere, de pecunia dicte Artis lane, operariis operis ecclesie Sancte Reparate, pro complendo fundamentum campanilis dicte ecclesie Sancte Reparate, usque in summam centum quinquaginta florenorum auri, dum modo procuretur quod dicta danaria redibeantur pro dicta Arte, in casu quo prestentur hinc ad medium mensem decembris proxime venturi . . .

Et super quinta proposita, loquente de prestando danaria operariis opere ecclesie Sancte Reparate, ut in dicta petitione plenius continetur, placuit viginti uno ex dictis consiliariis qui reddiderunt eorum fabas nigras pro sic, quod fiat et observetur in omnibus et per omnia ut in dicta proposita continetur. Volentes vero contrarium ex dictis consiliariis fuerunt octo, qui redidderunt eorum fabas albas pro non. — (*Deliberazioni,* I, 24-26).

JUNE 7, 9, 1339 [DOC. 53]

3. In Dei nomine amen. Anno sue salutifere incarnationis millesimo trecentesimo trigesimonono indictione septima die septimo mensis iunii . . . In Consilio domini Capitanei et populi Florentini . . . infrascripte provisiones pro evidenti comunis Florentie utilitate per dominos Priores artium et Vexilliferum institie . . . edite et facte . . . et que in ipsis provisionibus et qualibet earum continentur et scripta sunt . . . lecta fuerunt . . .

Item, infrascripta petitio, predictis dominis Prioribus artium et Vexillifero institie porrecta et facta, ac etiam infrascripta provisio super ipsa petitione et contentis in ea edita et facta . . ., lecte et lecta fuerunt modo et forma inferius annotatis . . .

— Coram vobis dominis Prioribus artium et Vexillifero iustitie populi et comunis Florentie exponitur pro parte operariorum opere ecclesie Sancti Iohannis Baptiste et operariorum opere ecclesie Sancte Reparate de Florentia, quod cum via sita iuxta plateam dictarum ecclesiarum ex parte versus ecclesiam S. Cristophori, videlicet a domibus filiorum olim domini Biligiardi de la Tosa usque ad domum de Rochis presideat dictam plateam, et sit adeo altior dicta platea quod, propter ipsam altitudinem vie, dicta platea et dicte ecclesie Sancti Iohannis et Sancte Reparate videntur ita basse, precipue in discessu vie del Corso, quod decor ipsarum ecclesiarum multipliciter diminuitur et celatur; et quod si dicta via et via Cursus Adimariorum debassarentur ac etiam debassaretur platea predicta ex latere dictarum viarum decor dictarum ecclesiarum multum augeretur, et ipse ecclesie apparerent satis altiores; quare pro parte dictorum operariorum cum reverentia petitur quatenus, pro honore comunis Florentie et decoratione dictarum ecclesiarum, placeat vobis, una cum offitio Duodecim bonorum virorum, deliberare et per Consilia populi et comunis Florentie stantiari provideri ordinari et reformari facere: quod per offitium dominorum Priorum artium et Vexilliferi iustitie . . . eligantur nominentur et deputentur . . . offitiales pro comuni Florentie quos et quot et quotiens ipsi domini Priores et Vexillifer eligere voluerint ad debassandum et debassari faciendum dictas vias et plateam et alias vias circumstantes, si expedierit vel ipsis offitialibus videbitur, et ad dirigendum et mutandum cursum aquarum viarum circumstantium dictam plateam . . .; dummodo predicte vie et platea debassentur, et predicta omnia fiant omnibus expensis dictarum operarum ecclesiarum Sancti Iohannis et Sancte Reparate, et quod ad predicta vel predictorum occasione nullus alius cogi possit invitus ad solvendum aliquam pecunie quantitatem vel contribuendum in expensis propterea faciendis; et dummodo expense fiende in predictis et circa predicta et eorum occasione fiant et fieri

debeant de consensu et deliberatione operariorum dictarum operarum pro tempore existentium, et aliter non — domini Priores et Vexillifer iustitie . . . providerunt ordinaverunt et stantiaverunt quod ipsa iamdicta petitio et omnia et singula in ea contenta totaliter a populo et per populum et comune Florentie approbentur acceptentur admittantur et firmentur . . .

Placuit et visum fuit centum quadragintanovem ex consiliariis . . . Illi vero ex consiliariis predictis, quibus predicta displicuerunt . . ., fuere solummodo tres numero computati.

Die nono eiusdem mensis iunii. Consilium domini Potestatis et comunis Florentie . . Placuit centum nonagintaseptem ex consiliariis . . . Illi vero ex consiliariis predictis, quibus predicta displicuerunt . . ., fuere solummodo sex numero computati. — (*Provvisioni*, XXIX, 22-25.)

DECEMBER 9, 10, 1339 [DOC. 56]

4. In Dei nomine amen. Anno sue salutifere incarnationis millesimo trecentesimo trigesimonono indictione ottava die nono mensis decembris. Consilium domini Capitanei et populi Florentini . . . Infrascripta petitio dominis Prioribus et Vexillifero iustitie porrecta et facta, ac etiam infrascripta provisio super ipsa petitione et contentis in ea edita et facta . . ., lecte et lecta fuerunt . . . — Coram vobis dominis Prioribus artium et Vexillifero iustitie civitatis Florentie exponitur pro parte consulum Artis lane dicte civitatis et operariorum opere et hedificationis ecclesie Sancte Reparate maioris ecclesie Florentine, quod pro hedificatione et constructione dicte ecclesie et campanilis ipsius, quod noviter construitur omnino expedit et de necessitate opportet quod domus et habitationes dicte ecclesie posite intra claustrum dicte ecclesie et dictam ecclesiam que de novo edificatur, in quibus habitant canonici presbiteri cappellani et clerici qui dicte ecclesie in divinis deserviunt et missas et alia divina offitia celebrant destruantur tollantur et eleventur; quod fieri non poterit sine. Dei offensa et dampno et iniuria dictorum canonicorum presbiterorum cappellanorum et clericorum, et non modica reprensione dictorum consulum et operariorum, nisi primo provideatur eisdem canonicis presbiteris cappelanis et clericis de habitatione domibus loco et terreno in quibus et

super quo, honorifice ut decet tante ecclesie, habitare et stare possint. Et quod etiam dicta ecclesia non habet Cimiterium in quo corpora defunctorum ad dictam ecclesiam devotionem habentium et concurrentium possint commode sepelliri. Et ideo vobis cum instantia supplicatur quatenus placeat vobis, simul cum offitio Duodecim bonorum virorum, deliberare ordinare et firmare et deliberari ordinari et reformari facere per solempnia et opportuna Consilia populi et comunis Florentie: Quod consules et operarii supradicti tam presentes quam futuri vel alie persone de quibus vobis videbitur, vel maior pars ipsorum vel ipsarum, possint eisque liceat semel et pluries et quotiens voluerint, providere et ordinare de loco et locis terreno habitatione et domibus, in quibus et super quo dicti canonici presbiteri cappellani et clerici honorifice habitare et stare possint, et Cimiterio in quo corpora defunctorum ad dictam ecclesiam concurrentium valeant sepelliri; et ipsas domus habitationes seu terrenum extimare et extimari facere, et extimationem quam inde fecerint solvere et solvi facere illis personis quibus seu ad quos ipse domus pertinent seu pertinebunt, de pecunia deputata vel deputanda ad constructionem et pro constructione dicte ecclesie; et etiam ipsas domos habitationes locum et loca et terrenum de quibus eis vel maiori parti ipsorum videbitur, deputare et concedere possint dicte ecclesie pro habitatione et commoditate habitationis dictorum canonicorum presbiterorum cappelanorum et clericorum, et Cimiterio dicte ecclesie; ac etiam pro ipsa habitatione commoditate habitationis et Cimiterio, eidem ecclesie concedere et assignare viam et vias seu eam partem viarum que sunt prope ipsam ecclesiam, in ea longitudine et latitudine et prout et sicut ipsis consulibus et operariis vel illi seu illis quibus commiseritis vel maiori parti eorum, ut predicitur, placuerit et videbitur. Et quod omnes et singuli quorum erant dicte domus hedificia et terrenum seu casolaria que per ipsos consules et operarios fuerint assignate seu extimate dicta de causa, ut dictum est, teneantur et debeant, cum effectu cogi possint per quoscumque rectores seu officiales comunis Florentie, ad instantiam dictorum consulum et operariorum vel illius seu illorum cui vel quibus per ipsos consules et operarios vel maiorem partem eorum commissum fuerit, ad vendendum et concedendum ipsas domos terrenum et casolaria seu hedificia pro

eo pretio et pretiis, et eo modo quo et quibus declaratum fuerit per ipsos consules et operarios vel per maiorem partem eorum — . . . Priores artium et Vexillifer iustitie . . . providerunt ordinaverunt et stantiaverunt: Quod ipsa iam dicta petitio et omnia et singula in ea contenta a populo et comuni Florentie approbentur acceptentur admictantur et firmentur . . . Placuit et visum fuit centum vigintiquinque ex consiliariis . . . Illi vero ex consiliariis predictis, quibus predicta displicuerunt . . ., fuere solummodo triginta numero computati. Die decimo eiusdem mensis decembris. Consilium domini Potestatis et comunis Florentie . . . Placuit centum quinquagintaquinque ex consiliariis . . . Illi vero ex consiliariis predictis, quibus predicta displicuerunt . . ., fuere solummodo quadragintanovem numero computati. — (*Provvisioni*, XXX, [88-94).

APRIL 26, 1340 [DOC. 57]

5. In Dei nomine amen. Anno sue salutifere incarnationis millesimo trecentesimo quadragesimo inditione viij[a] die vigesimosexto mensis aprilis. Actum Florentie apud ecclesiam Sancte Reparate, presentibus testibus Vannuccio ser Cini de Sancto Miniate et Francia Nuccii de Sancto Ieminiano ad hec vocatis et rogatis.

Pateat evidenter quod sapientes et discreti viri dominus Bartholomeus de Castro Florentino, Nardus de Bucellis, Iohannes Guidonis de Antilla, Vannes Donnini, Guido Guaze, Cennes Nardi, Forese Ferrantini, Iohannes Geri del Bello, Fuccius Magistri, Coppus Borghesis, Chele de Aguglone et Vannes Armati, cives honorabiles florentini populares, habito prius colloquio consilio et tractatu super infrascriptis cum reverendo in Christo patre et domino domino Francischo episcopo florentino et calonacis et cappellanis dicte ecclesie, ac etiam cum consulibus Artis lane et operariis dicte ecclesie, ac etiam cum magistro Andrea maiore magistro dicte opere; facto prius et obtento partito inter eos ad fabas nigras et albas; providerunt et deliberaverunt: Quod chalonecha et abitatio chalonechorum dicte ecclesie fiat et construatur iusta dictam ecclesiam versus meridiem et versus plateam de Bonizis. Rogantes me Locterium notarium infrascriptum ut de predictis publicum conficerem instrumentum. — *Capitoli*, XVII, 77.)

JANUARY, 18, 1341 [DOC. 59]

6.   Electo Lunensi et Comiti.

Reverendo patri domino Antonio Dei et apostolice sedis gratia episcopo Lunensi et Comiti, Priores etc. Paternitatem vestram, de qua ex fide confidentiam indubiam retinemus ut in opportunitatibus nostris placabilem se hostendat, presenti amicabiliter deprecamur quatenus de quantitate marmoris pro constructione nostre matricis ecclesie gratiam facientes tractam velitis concedere secundum tenorem cedule intercluse, contemplatione nostra, qui prompti sumus ad omnia per que honor vester suscipiat incrementa. Data Florentie, die xviij ianuarii, none indictionis. — (*Lettere della Signoria*, VI, 29.)

APRIL 2, 1342 [DOC. 60]

7.   [To the Signoria of Siena]

Habemus querimoniam ab operariis nostre matricis ecclesie, quod cum ipsi in fortia et territorio vestro fodi faciant marmorem rubeum, quo eamdem ecclesiam faciunt redimiri, per quosdam maleficos in eo inferuntur enormiter fractiones; quam ob rem opus negligitur, et vestrum Comune in expensis recipit lexionem. Volumus quatenus eidem dapnificationi debeatis viriliter obviare, et inquirere contra dissipatores huiusmodi, et culpabiles acriter condempnare, ne ulterius similem querimoniam sentiamus, et audiamus quod puniti sint tanti facinoris commissores. Data Florentie, die secunda aprilis, x indictionis. — (*Lettere della Signoria*, VII, 15.)

OCTOBER 18, 1343 [DOC. 62]

8.   Pro conductoribus marmoris.

Nos ... Priores artium et ... Vexillifer iustitie populi et comunis Florentie damus et concedimus securitatem et licentiam, usque ad kalendas ianuarii venturi proxime valituram, universis et singulis nautis et conductoribus quibuscumque quarumcumque plactarum barcarum et quorumcumque lignorum navigabilium, de quibuscumque

partibus fuerint ipsi conductores, qui super ipsis plactis et lignis conducerent marmorem per flumen Arni versus civitatem Florentie pro constructione matricis ecclesie civitatis ipsius, quatenus in veniendo conducendo stando et redeundo cum ipsis plactis et lignis navigabilibus sint liberi et securi, nec possint aut debeant molestari per aliquos districtuales nostros aut alios per totam nostram fortiam et districtum. Mandantes universis et singulis districtualibus nostris eorumque regiminibus presentibus et futuris quatenus huiusmodi nostram securitatem et licentiam effectualiter observare debeant et facere observari, sub pena averis et personarum: et eisdem conductoribus prebeant assistentiam et favores, huiusmodi nostram licentiam et mandatum taliter impleturi, quod singulorum obbedientiam gratificare possimus. De quibus presentium latori dabimus plenam fidem, quas post opportunam inspectionem remanere volumus presentanti nicchilominus decetero valituras. Florentie, die xviij octobris, xij indictionis. — (*Lettere della Signoria*, VIII, 34.)

JULY 7, 1344 [DOC. 63]

9.   Domino Iordano electo Lunensi.

Reverende Pater. Dum intelleximus quod dominus noster summus Pontifex prefecit Reverentiam vestram ad episcopalem sedem Lunensem in episcopum et comitem, letati sumus gaudio magno valde; sperantes quod, sicut nostra devotio honores vestros diligit, ita in hiis que statui et honori nostro conferant nostris precibus vestra Benignitas amabiliter condescendat. Cum igitur nostram matricem ecclesiam et eius campanile ad honorem Dei et Sancte Reparate faciamus famosis edificiis construi et honorifice redimiri, et per precessorem vestrum de tracta marmoris ipsius Lunensis ecclesie constitute in partibus Carrarie, eiusdem diocesis, absque solutione pedagii vel gabelle vel alterius oneris usque ad perfectionem eorum fuerit nobis facta concessio specialis, putantes Reverentiam vestram in premissis gratiosam similiter nobis et placabilem invenire, Eandem caritatis affectibus deprecamur quatenus gratiam nobis factam per precessorem vestrum dignemini confirmare et eandem nobis facere de premissis contemplatione nostra, qui honores vestros diligimus tamquam nostros; et pro predictis prudenti viro Iacobo de Albertis dilecto concivi nostro de predictis instructo exhibere fidem credulam et annuere tanquam nobis. Data Florentie, die vij iulii, xij indictionis. — *(Lettere della Signoria*, VIII, 92).

FEBRUARY, 28, 1348 [DOC. 64]

10. Die ultimo mensis februarii. Domini consules [Artis lane] . . . providerunt ordinaverunt et stantiaverunt . . . Item quod ser Antonius de la Fossa, offitialis foresterius dicte Artis, possit teneatur et debeat eius durante offitio circare investigare inquirere et invenire de quocumque lignamine, quomodolibet habito, operato vel laborato, in et pro armaduris voltarum campanilis Sancte Reparate, et in et pro quibuscumque laboreriis dicti campanilis dicte Sancte Reparate . . . Et ipsum lignamen vel eius extimationem dicto laborerio et operariis seu camerario dicti operis pro tempore existentibus reddi restituy consignari dari ac solvy facere ab illis omnibus et singulis quos dictus offitialis viderit vel cognoverit seu deliberaverit ad eius restitutionem consignationem seu solutionem quomodolibet teneri, modis formis terminis et temporibus de quibus videbitur offitiali predicto: et propterea quemcumque vel quoscumque personaliter ac realiter cogere et compellere . . .; et quos culpabiles invenerit punire et condempnare . . . — *(Deliberazioni*, III, 59).

MARCH 20, 1349 [DOC. 65]

11. Convocato Consilio consiliariorum Artis lane civitatis Florentie . . ., domini consules . . . creaverunt eorum et dicte Artis sindicos et procuratores actores factores et nuntios spetiales Nerium Lozi populi Sancti Fridiani et Loysium Iohannis domini Ubertini de Strozis . . .
Item ad emendum et titulo emptionis recipiendum pro comuni Florentie et opere et constructione et hedificatione dicti operis Sancte Reparate cathedralis ecclesie Florentine, ad honorem Dei et beate Reparate et sanctorum Iohannis et Zenobii et aliorum sanctorum et sanctarum omnipotentis Dei, a Iohanne olim Bartoli Firenzis populi Sancti Christofori de Florentia, suo nomine et

hereditario nomine Pieri condam fratis sui et filii olim dicti Firenzis, quoddam terrenum predicti Iohannis et dicti condam Pieri condam fratris sui, positum Florentie in populo Sancti Christofori de Florentia prope campanile dicti operis Sancte Reparate, cui terreno tales dicuntur esse confines: a primo et secundo via, a tertio domine Lette uxoris olim Laurentii ser Niccolay de Ponturmo, a quarto domine Venne uxoris olim Iacobi de Iandonatis, infra predictos confines vel alios, si qui forent plures aut veriores con fines; nec non etiam ad aprehendendum et recipiendum tenutam et corporalem possessionem dicti terreni . . . — *(Deliberazioni*, III, 86).

JANUARY 5, 1351 [DOC. 68]

12. In Dei nomine, et sue dominice incarnationis anno millesimo trecentesimo quinquagesimo indictione quarta die quinto mensis ianuarii.
Discreti viri Manettus Spiglati di Filicaria, Landus Antonii de Albiczis, Alessus Guiglielmi et Filippus Bonsi cives florentini, operarii pro Arte lane construtionis operis sancte Beate Reparate cathedralis ecclesie Florentine, ad dictum opus congregati, volentes intendere ad utilitatem dicti operis et ut ferventius ad laborerium dicti operis intendatur . . ., locaverunt et concesserunt Nerio Fieravantis populi Sancti Petri maioris, Benoczo Niccolay populi Sancti Michaelis Vicedominorum, Niccolao Beltrami populi Sancti Laurentii, et Alberto Arnoldi populi Sancti Michaelis Bertelde, magistris, ad conducendum ad dictum opus, et ibidem consignandum operariis dicti operis sive gubernatoribus eiusdem pro tempore existentibus, laboratas et completas infrascriptas quantitates marmorum; videlicet alborum de Carraria, rubeorum de cava Sancti Iusti ad Montem Rantali, et nigrorum de Monte Ferrato, bona et pastosa et netta pilis vel aliis defectibus, infrascriptarum rationum et bonitatum et mensurarum, ut inferius particulariter continetur, pro infrascriptis preciis et quantitatibus pecunie, videlicet:
(*1*)
Sedecim bracchia stipidorum, ad modinum eis dandum per Francischum Talenti principalem magistrum dicti operis, vel per alium principalem magistrum dicti operis pro tempore existentem; grossitudinis per latum tertie partis unius brac-

chii, videlicet minor petium, et longitudinis unius bracchii et dimidii alterius bracchii, pro pretio et ad rationem librarum otto pro quolibet bracchio: in summa, libr. cxxviij florenorum parvorum.

(2)

Item octo bracchia angulorum ad modum stipidi, ad rationem librarum quactuor f. p. pro quolibet bracchio: in summa, libr. xxxij f. p.

(3)

Duodecim bracchia marmoris rubei, quod poni debet in dictis pilastris, largitudinis duorum tertiorum bracchii, ad rationem librarum duarum f. p. pro quolibet bracchio: libr. xxiiijor. f. p.

(4)

Otto bracchia marmorum rubeorum, quod poni debet inter angulos dictorum pilastrorum, largitudinis quarte partis unius bracchia, ad rationem sol. xx pro quolibet bracchio: libr. viij. f. p.

(5)

Sedecim bracchia marmoris nigri, quod poni debet inter pilastros, largitudinis tertie partis unius bracchii, ad rationem sol. viginti duorum f. p. pro quolibet bracchio: libr. xvij et sol. xij f. p.

(6)

Sedecim bracchia unius cornicis marmoris albi de Carraria, quod poni debet in medio facciarum campanilis inter marmora nigra de Monte Ferrato et rubea de dicta cava Sancti Iusti ad Montem Rantali, largitudinis tertie partis unius bracchii, et grossitudinis quarte partis unius bracchii, ad rationem librarum duarum et soldorum decem f. p. pro quolibet bracchio: in summa, libr. xL f. p.

(7)

Otto bracchia tavolarum marmorum rubeorum de Monte Rantali, largitudinis unius bracchii et octave partis alterius bracchii, ad rationem librarum trium pro quolibet bracchio: libr. viginti quactuor f. p.

(8)

Otto bracchia unius filaris marmorum alborum de Carraria, largitudinis medietatis unius bracchii, et grossitudinis quarte partis unius bracchii, ad modinum convenientem, ad rationem sol. xlv pro quolibet bracchio: libr. xviij f. p.

(9)

Septuaginta quinque bracchia concii pro dicto campanili ex parte intrinseca ponendi cum schala lapidum fortium, ad rationem libr. trium et sol. quinque pro quolibet bracchio: in summa, libras ducentas quadraginta tres et sol. xv f. p.

Dixerunt insuper quod infrascripta marmora et concia sunt que vadunt sive mitti aut poni debent in quactuor fenestris et in isguanciatis et in pectoralibus et davanzalibus et colupnellis rubeis et inpetratis, et il sopra più de seggiolis et omne id quod pertinet ad dictas fenestras, altitudinis decem bracchiorum, quod debet partiri in decem, et totidem dixerunt tangere pro bracchio quolibet.

(10)

Centum nonaginta duo bracchia inter columpnas medii bracchii et columpnas cum duabus branchiis et columpnas tondas que poni debent in medio fenestrarum, laboratas ac tortas secundum modum quo sunt incepte et ad modum dicendum per principalem magistrum dicti operis pro tempore existentem; longitudinis, videlicet ille duorum bracchiorum et ille medii bracchii ad minus, longitudinis quodlibet petium bracchiorum trium cum dimidio alterius bracchii; et ille que poni debent in medio fenestrarum, longitudinis sex bracchiorum et dimidii ad minus pro quolibet petio, ad rationem librarum sedecim f. p. pro quolibet brac-

(11)   [chio.

Centum quinquaginta duo bracchia colonnellorum marmorum rubeorum de cava Sancti Iusti, que cinghiari debent inpetratum isguanciati fenestrarum, ad rationem librarum quinque et sol. decem pro quolibet bracchio.

(12)

Quindecim bracchia colonnellorum marmorum rubeorum, que poni debent ad planum fenestrarum sub pettorali et de supra, ad rationem librarum quinque et soldorum decem f. p. pro quolibet bracchio.

(13)

Septuaginta duo bracchia colonnellorum dictorum marmorum rubeorum, que poni debent ad planum fenestrarum ad pedem isguanciatorum, grossitudinis tertie partis bracchii, et longitudinis duorum tertiorum bracchii, ad modinum eis dandum per dictum principalem magistrum, ad rationem librarum sex f. p. pro quolibet bracchio.

(14)

Septuaginta quinque bracchia inpetrati pro isguancitis fenestrarum, que poni debent in medio colupnellorum rubeorum, largitudinis septem ottavorum bracchii, ad rationem librarum novem et soldorum quindecim f. p. pro quolibet bracchio.

(15)

Quadraginta bracchia tabularum albarum de

marmore de Carraria, largitudinis septem ottavorum, et grossitudinis sexte partis bracchii, que secuntur cum isguanciato fenestrarum ad pedem, quod non est inpetratum, ed in medio colupnellorum rubeorum qui poni debent ad planum, ad rationem librarum quinque f. p. pro quolibet bracchio.

(16)

Septuaginta quactuor bracchia cornicis albe dicti marmoris que cinghiant pilastros et facciuolas usque ad columpnellos, debent esse et redire concii tertia pars unius bracchii per grosseza et largitudinis medii bracchi, laborata ad linguaczas, ad rationem librarum otto sol. duorum et den. sex. f. p. pro quolibet bracchio.

(17)

Viginti octo bracchia dicte cornicis albe pro davanzalibus fenestrarum, tornando di concio tertium unum, et grossitudinis et largitudinis trium quartorum, ad rationem librarum novem soldorum quindecim f. p. pro quolibet bracchio.

(18)

Duodecim tabule pro pectoralibus fenestrarum; de quibus otto tabule debent esse longitudinis, quelibet, bracchiorum duorum et duorum tertiorum; et alie quactuor, quelibet, bracchium unum et duos tertios; et grossitudinis quelibet dictarum duodecim tabularum inter tertium et medium bracchium; compassate et laborate ad modinum eis dandum per principalem magistrum dicti operis pro tempore existentem; et altitudinis omnes duodecim tabule, quelibet earum, unius bracchii, et duorum tertiorum; pro pretio inter omnes flor. centum septuaginta auri, ad rationem librarum trium et soldorum quinque pro quolibet floreno auri.

(19)

Et per lo sopra più de'seggioli, quod debet partiri cum questo medesimo, libras centum septuaginta duas f. p.

(20)

Ottuaginta bracchia lastrichi, quod poni debet sub seggiolis, ad rationem soldorum viginti duorum pro quolibet bracchio, libr. ottuaginta octo f. p. Et voluerunt et in concordia fuerunt dicti operarii quod volebant eisdem magistris dari, de denariis et florenis dicti operis, pro scioperio, florenos viginti quinque auri. De predictis marmoribus et lapidibus conciis debent, ut dixerunt et in concordia fuerunt, fornire decem bracchia dicti cam-

panilis pro altitudine et circum circa. Et debent ipsi magistri suprascripta omnia marmora bene ac sufficienter ac ydonee laborata et completa dare et assignare operariis dicti operis, sive capomagistro sive gubernatori dicti operis pro tempore existenti, ad pedem campanilis ad collam cum qua laborerium ipsum collari debet super dicto campanili, adea bene completa ex facta quod murari possint: et si expediret super ipso campanili dum murabuntur reactare et retochare, omne concium quod expediret omnibus suis sumptibus et expensis faciendo, ac fornimentis pro murando, ita quod proterea dictum opus nichil habeat mictere nisi in murando, et calcinam renam et manuales ac magisterium pro murando. Salvo quod, si aliquid contingeret solvi ad Carrarium pro dogana marmorum alborum; quod tunc et in eo casu solvi debet ipsa dogana de denariis dicti operis. Que omnia marmora, videlicet alba nigra et rubea et concium lapidum fortium facere debent sufficienter ad laborandum dicta decem bracchia campanilis pro altitudine et circum circa. Et voluerunt et pepigerunt dicte partes modis et nominibus quibus supra et cum protestatione predicta, quod si accideret quod dicti magistri conducerent seu conduci facerent ad dictum opus marmora vel de dictis marmoribus ultra quantitatem necessariam ad faciendum et fulciendum dicta decem bracchia dicti campanilis de marmoribus non conciis; quod in dicto casu dictum superfluum marmorum ematur ab eis pro dicto opere pro pretio condecenti. Et si marmora laborata per eos utilia dicto operi superessent, tunc pro dicto opere solvatur eis de laboratis ad rationem predictam et supra scriptam, non excedendo quantitatem marmorum conciorum ultra quantitatem necessariam pro murando uno bracchio pro altitudine et circum circa ipsum campanile. Et quod si aliquod laborerium esset laboratum pro dicto opere et concium ad dictum opus, debent dicti magistri, et pepigerunt, ad voluntatem operariorum pro tempore existentium, sibi illa computare ad et secundum rationes predictas a dicto opere.

Et e converso, predicti Nerius, Benozzus, Niccolaus et Albertus magistri predicti dicta marmora et lapides sive concium lapidum et marmorum conduxerunt a dictis operariis et, obligando se ipsos et quemlibet eorum et ipsorum et cuiusque ipsorum heredes et bona omnia mobilia et immobilia presentia et futura, promiserunt et convene-

runt dictis operariis et michi Bartolo notario tamquam publice persone stipulantibus et recipienti-
bus pro comuni Florentie et dicto opere, et quilibet eorum in solidum et in totum obligando, dicta
suprascripta marmora supradictarum rationum
colorum et bonitatum ac lapides sive concium lapidum conducere seu conduci facere et conducta
et laborata ac concia consignare et dare operariis
sive officiali ac gubernatori dicti operis pro tempore existentibus, omnibus isporum magistrorum
sumptibus et expensis de marmoribus et lapidibus,
naulis, gabellis, magisterio et fornimentis pro con-
ciando et vectura et omnibus aliis quam bene conciis et actis et completis pro murando, videlicet
dicta marmora ad pedem campanilis, et dictas lapides fortes in claustro dicti operis ubi morantur
magistri dicti operis ad laborandum pro dicto
opere, et posita ad pedem campanilis ipsa marmora ad collam ipsius campanilis, in termino
quindecim mensium proxime venturorum, pro
dictis pretiis, sub pena et ad penam quingentorum
florenorum auri, solempni stipulatione premissa:
que pena totiens commictatur et peti ex exigi possit cum effectu quotiens contra factum fuerit sive
ventum; qua pena commissa vel non, exacta vel
non, rata maneant omnia et singula suprascripta
et infrascripta. Et voluerunt et pepigerunt dicti
magistri quod de eorum bono servitio fiendo et
bono laborerio dando ad terminum debitum stare
et stari debeat dicto discretioni vel deliberationi
suprascriptorum locatorum pro tempore viven-
tium vel presentium in civitate Florentie. Et hoc
ideo fecerunt quia dicti operarii, dicto nomine et
cum protestatione premissa, promiserunt eisdem
quod a gubernatore dicti operis pro omnibus predictis dabuntur suprascripta pretia, que adscen-
dere dixerunt summam florenorum quattuor mil-
lium centum auri, videlicet pro quolibet bracchio
florenos quactorcentos decem auri. Et promiserunt dicti magistri et quilibet eorum, pro predictis observandis et executioni mandandis ut supe-
rius continetur, dare quilibet eorum unum suf-
ficientem fideiussorem hinc ad octo dies proxime
venturos, de bonitate et sufficientia quorum fi-
deiussorum stari voluerunt dicto dicti Nerii Fieravantis. Et preceptum guarentigie feci etc.
Acta Florentie in camerecta sita in claustro dicti
operis, ubi morantur notarius et camerarius dicti
operis ad solvendum magistris; presentibus ad hec
testibus Luysio Iohannis de Strozis populi Sancti

Miniatis inter turres, Vinta Tuccii Rigalecti et
Francisco Talenti et Nerio Loczii de Florentia. —
(*Protocollo di ser Bartolo di Neri da Roffiano,*
dal 1348 al 51.)

APRIL 5, 1353 [DOC. 70, p. 72]

13.   Dissermi Giorgio di Benci e Lapo di Vanni
operai, a di v d'aprile 1353, che io faciessi memoria di cierti ristori che furono loro domandati per
Neri di Fioravante e per li compagni, che ànno in
sonmo il campanile, di lavorii che fanno più che i
patti, come a presso dirò.
viij filari di marmo biancho, cioè ij per ciaschuna
faccia, allato alle colonne delle due branche, gros-
so ¹/₄, largho *(lacuna)*, lungho braccia *(lacuna)*.
. . . braccia quadre di concio di pietre forti per la
schala di sotto; che non è ne' patti più d'una ischa-
la, e e' fanno parte dell'altra.
iiij filari, cioè j per faccia, di pietre roze forti dentro a'segiòli; che non lo deono fare per li patti;
lungho braccia vij per filare, che è in tutto braccia xxviij, et è largho ²/₃.

14.   Di vedere se la schala di sopra è più lavorio
faciendola quadra che tonda, o meno; però che la
doveano fare tonda per li patti; e dare il ristoro
a chi il dee avere.

15.   Annoci a rifare, per la cornicie del concio del
macingnio che noi mettiamo del nostro, e per lo
ristrigniere del concio per la cornicie detta, e per
lo ristrigniere anche del concio per lo sguanciato,
che va meno ismusso che non è il disegniamento.

16.   Dissermi i sopradetti Giorgio e Lapo, che io
faciessi alarghare l'uscio della chorte di sopra tanto che v'entrasse il charro charicho, a di 5 d'aprile
1353.

17.   Dissermi che io examinassi i libri di Neri di
Fioravante e de'compagni, che sono nell'opera,
della raxione del sommo; e se non vi fosse su cosa
che fosse prociudicio o neciessità all'opera, che io
gli rendessi loro; detto di. — Vidili: parmi da ren-
derli loro.

[p. 73]
18.   Dissermi che io saldassi raxione co'maestri

che lavorarono a Charrara com Benozo il marmo dell'opera, e fossi in achordo con loro del resto; et eglino con Domenicho Biliotti insieme istanziaro che e'fossono paghati: iscritto per ser Perino notaio. — Fecilo detto di. E truovo che restano ad avere in somma fiorini 59 d'oro, soldi 46, denari 7 di piccioli; cioè Bertino Gherardino Nicholò Doffo Matteo e Taddeo.

19. Dissermi che io faciessi raxione com Benozo, quello che per aviso potrebe venire costo tutto il marmo che il detto Benozo ae fatto a Charrara per l'opera, il quale e' dicie che è in tutto pezi 562. Troviamo questo dì che verrebe, posto in Firenze, con ogni ispesa, intorno a fiorini M; de' quali infino a questo dì ne sono paghati intorno di fiorini iiij^clxxxv, co'carregi che abiamo a paghare noi e quelli che abiamo promessi a'maestri.

MAY 3, 1353 [DOC. 70, p. 74]

20. Anche mi dissero che io dessi a Giachetto Mancini lire 41 e soldi *(lacuna)*, i quali de' avere dal Vinta; e ponessersi a raxione de'maestri da Charrara: é poi sollicitassi che Giachetto rendesse raxione del charmarlinghato.

MAY 3, AUGUST 5, 1353 [DOC. 70, p. 75]

21. E che io faciessi che Neri di Fioravante e Franciescho Talenti si conpromettessero della quistione che ànno insieme in due amici comuni, e fosse il termine xv di, et il terzo albitro si riserbano a loro. — Conpromisersi in Benozo, di volere degli operai, di 5 d'aghosto 1353.

MAY 21, 1353 [DOC. 70, p. 75]

22. Conmisermi, di xxj di magio, che io m'avisassi del modo che Benozo aveva tenuto con que' d'Orto San Michele, nel tempo che istette a Charrara per noi.

JUNE, 1353 [DOC. 70, p. 75]

23. Che io istudiassi sì che per San Giovanni si

vedesse fatto covelle sul champanile. E per ciò fare achattassi da Orto San Michele ij maestri. E levassi per San Giovanni i ponti dell'armadure, a ciò che si vedesse i' lavorio.

JUNE 19, 1353 [DOC. 70, p. 76]

24. Il modo che io òe a tenere delle maserizie che ci sono. — Fanne una ricordanza; e Neri abi a guardare lealmente poi le maserizie, sanza averne nè tu nè egli raxione, però che sarebe impossibile.

25. E del piombo e ispranghe. — Dàllo in guardia sul champanile a pocho a pocho a Giovanni Belchari, sanza averne persona a rendere conto, però che sarebe impossibile.

26. Di fare che que'del sommo lavorino, e rivedere loro raxione. — Rivedila di quest'altra settimana, e non falli, con Franciescho insieme.

27. De'danari si deono dare a'maestri da Charrara. — Da'loro anzi San Giovanni ¹/₁ i dinari; e poi, come n'ài dalla chamera, compili di paghare.

28. Di dare danari a'maestri del sonmo. — Pagha i maestri di quello che lavorano, e oltre a ciò da' a Benozo insino in 4 fiorini.

29. Di fare istare netto a piè del champanile. — Fa' per ora ispazarvi; poi, passata la festa, troverremo modo da spendervi e far aconciare la sepoltura di Francesco Cichalini.

JUNE 25, 1353 [DOC. 70, p. 77]

30. Di dare vino a'maestri. — Dàllo da kalendi innanzi.

31. Di coloro che lusinghano i maestri nostri.

32. Della raxione delle lunette delle finestre fatte per Franciescho Talenti e de'fiorini xv avuti per questa caxione. — Sostieni.

JULY 12, 1353 [DOC. 70, p. 77]

33. Di Francescho Talenti. — Prestali, come più tosto puoi, danari di quatro mesi, e iscontali poi ogne settimana la metà.

AUGUST 14, 1353 [DOC. 70, p. 77]

34. Di fare fare il disegniamento del campanile, e in che modo. — Fàllo fare di legniame.

35. D'ordinare del marmo per lavorare dal sommo in su. — Disse Francesco che ci à lavoro per j anno.

36. Della raxione di Neri Fieravante del sommo. — Dàlli danari per paghare tutti i maestri loro, e tu Filippo sia loro camarlingo, e noi ti faremo provedere.

SEPTEMBER 26, OCTOBER 4, 1353 [DOC. 70, p. 77]

37. Del dare in sommo più che a giornate.

38. Del mandare a Charrara. — Indugia a Ogniesanti.

39. Delle molte carte abisogniano. — Di ragionarne cho'Regolatori.

[p. 78]
40. Del vino per maestri. — Tolsesi via in tutto.

41. Della finestra con Franciescho. — Che e' si paghi per l'opera il maistero che vi fa fare su ad altrui, e per lui nonnulla ponghasi a sua raxione; e quando sarà fatta, si faccia istimare, e il più e il meno vada per lo detto Franciescho.

NOVEMBER 5, 1353 [DOC. 70, p. 78]

42. Di mandare a Pisa. — Manda.

43. Di qual finestrata si compie. — Vedrella.

44. De'sommi. — Date in sommo ogni cosa.

45. De'danari di Franciescho Talenti. — Prestagliele.

NOVEMBER 30, 1353 [DOC. 70, p. 78]

46. Di fare uno prochuratore. — A'nuovi.

47. De'modi di Francescho. — A'nuovi.

48. Delle pietre macignie. — A'nuovi.

JANUARY 7, 1354 [DOC. 70, p. 79]

49. Per avere danari per li maestri e per lo marmo.

50. Delle pietre che ragionòe Franciescho Talenti.

51. Di vedere qual maestro mette meglio all'opera per mandare a Carrara per lo marmo.

MARCH 16, 1354 [DOC. 70, p. 79]

52. Memoria che Neri di Fioravante e Benozo di Niccholò alogharono a Piero Masi a fare il segiolo et il lastricho che e' doveano fare su la volta del campanile; et furono in concordia per questo modo, presente me Filippo Marsili et *(lacuna)*, a di xvj di marzo:
Che e' debono misurare ciò che si vede del detto lavorio ciaschuna parte per sè, e dègli dare del braccio; prima, del braccio del lastricho soldi viij pic. per lungheza; item del braccio della cornicie soldi vj pic. per lungheza; item del braccio delle pietre femmine soldi x pic. per lungheza; item del braccio del lastrone di sopra soldi xiiij pic. per lungheza. Somma in tutto soldi xxxviij per braccio.

DECEMBER 15, 1354 [DOC. 70, p. 79]

53. Della franchigia per la ghabella di marmi da Pisa. — Prochacciala.

54. Del marmo da Vicho Pisano. — Come viene, istudia che sia qui.

55. Del marmo dell'Avenza. — Iscrivi a Pisa e là, e prochaccia che vegnia.

56. Di chambiare Mone, e far fare a Pisa a Domenicho di Noffo. — Fa', e iscrivigli che ci avisi de'modi che vuol tenere con noi.

57. De lo'mpetrato che mancha nel campanile.

FEBRUARY 2, 7, 28, APRIL, 1355
[DOC. 70, p. 80]

58. . . . da Pisa, dì ij di febraio 1354, che aveva ricievuto Domenicho di Noffo:
j barcha di marmi, iv' entro . . . j colonne del sommo; 54 pezi di marmo, 13 del sommo e 41 dell'opera.
A dì 7 di febraio:
. . . barche, iv' entro; iiij colonne del sommo; 39 pezi di marmo dell'opera.
E a di 28 di febraio:
ij barche, iv' entro; v colonne, xx pezi di marmo, dell'opera.
E a di (lacuna) d'aprile:
ij barche, iv' entro; ij colonne, viij pezi del sommo; ij colonne, xij pezi, dell'opera.

FEBRUARY 27, 1355 [DOC. 70, p. 80]

59. La finestra. — Sèguita.

60. Di comperare il marmo di Santa Croce. — Non è tempo.

MARCH 18, 1355 [DOC. 70, p. 80]

61. I fatti da Charrara. — Iscrivi che i maestri se ne vengniano, e rimagnia solo Domenicho, et egli si metta inanzi tutti i marmi, e chonduchanli a Pisa; e poi se ne vengnia, e mandavi Baldino.

[p. 81]
62. De'pregi de'maestri. — Lascia istare.

63. Di comperare i marmi di Santa Croce. — Voglionsi prima conducere i nostri.

64. Della finestra e degli altri lavorii. — Seguita a fare compiere.

65. Del sommo. — Sollicita che ci siano le colonne; e compiuto il sommo, istralcieremo ogne cosa.

66. D'avere il consiglio. — Martedi che viene, e profera salario a que'maestri che richiedi per consiglio.

67. La champana. — Lascia istare.

68. Mandar danari a Pisa. — Mandavi, come più tosto puoi, fiorini 150.

MAY 29, 1355 [DOC. 70, p. 81]

69. Di far lavorare in credenza. — Fàne come ti pare.

70. Del salaro de'maestri. — Isciema a'maestri soldi 2 per uno, e a'manovali soldi 1 per dì.

JUNE 8, 1355 [DOC. 70, p. 81]

71. Del consiglio e salaro de'maestri. — Al chonchiudere si stanzii.

72. La lunetta et altri lavorii di Francescho. — Istimisi quando sia compiuta.

[p. 82]
73. Del consiglio usato del campanile. — Quando avremo il consiglio sopra il disegniamento [for the Cathedral project] di Franciescho.

74. Del sonmo. — Compiasi.

75. De'marmi da Roma. — Commettono a Biagio ne favelli con frate Iacopo m.°

76. Delle maserizie dell'opera. — Fa' ch'elle sieno iscritte e rimangniansi a l'usanza.

JUNE 26, 1355 [DOC. 70, p. 82]

77. Della ruota dalla cholla con don Marcho. —
Faccia la pruova, chi vuole, fuor dell'opera; e se
viene bene, noi l'acietteremo e provederemo.

78. Di stimare la lunetta e gli altri lavorii di
Franciescho. — Ellessero Alberto Arnoldi e Giovanni Fetto, per l'opera; e Franciescho, Ambruogio Lenzi per lui.

79. Di trovare modo d'avere da Pisa quelli
marmi che di neciessità bisognano. — Fa'venire
fino a 50 braccia di tavole di ¹/₁ braccio in some
per lo meglio che puoi.

80. Di fare venire i marmi dall'Avenza a Pisa.
— Che se non seguitano le barche di rechare che
base, che Domenicho tolgha navili in Pisa da ciò,
e vada; e come più tosto puote, il faccia charichare
e conduciere tra luglio et aghosto.

81. Di trarre de'maestri che ci sono non utili. —
Tenete al più maestri che potete, abiendo da for-
nirli; et non abiendo, sì ne traete i meno utili.

82. Di mandare per li marmi rossi a Santo Iusto
a Monte Rantoli. — Cierchate con più maestri
de'pregi; e quando avrete sentito da tutti, sì'l ci
direte, e noi il dilibereremo.

[p. 82 f]
83. Comandarono a Franciescho et a me Filippo,
che qua entro non si inpigliasse cosa niuna di
nuovo, sanza farlo loro sentire. E che ciò che si
compera per l'opera, noi due siamo presenti al-
meno.

JULY 11, 1355 [DOC. 70, p. 83]

84. Marmi rossi. — Ferma il merchato con Andrea, o chon altri, per lo meglio che puoi.

85. D'uno prochuratore. — Non bisognia.

86. De'marmi di Santa Croce. — Andateli a
vedere Francescho e tu, e raportateci.

87. De'marmi da Pisa. — Istudia di far venire

quelle tavolette in some il più tosto che si puote,
e che le tavolette dall'Avenza vegnano a Pisa.

88. De'manovali. — Tòne come puoi.

89. Il salaro de'maestri del consiglio.

AUGUST 31, 1355 [DOC. 70, p. 84]

90. De'maestri meno di sul campanile.

91. De'marmi da Charrara, disse Manno che
v'à inghanno.

JANUARY, 1356 [DOC. 70, p. 85]

92. De'marmi che sono a l'Avenza e a Pisa. —
Mandavi Baldino; e fa'venire una lunetta in ogne
modo, a nostro costo.

93. Del consiglio renduto per li maestri. Del
consiglio si doveva avere in Palagio. — Raxionar-
ne con consoli a tempo.

94. Del consiglio usato del campanile. — Ri-
cordalo.

95. Del sonmo di Neri. — Comandarono a
Francesco e a me, che da sabato di 16 di giennaio
inanzi non fosse dato che fare a Benozo, fuori del
sonmo suo.

96. Di mandare danari a Pisa.

97. Della lunetta. — Aspetta gli altri pezi.

98. Degli Angnioli. — Vedrègli.

99. De'marmi della Misericordia. — Paghali
secondo lo stanziamento fatto.

100. Della lunetta di Francesco. — Aspetta di
darne un'altra in sonmo, e poi il ci ricorda.

FEBRUARY 5, 1356 [DOC. 70, p. 85]

101. Della cholla di Bartolo di San Ghallo. —

Digli, se e' vuole, che ne facci la pruova a sue ispese; e se istarà bene, noi gli renderemo la spesa e provederello.

102.   De' marmi di Santa Croce. — Non ci pare di comperarli, perchè dicie Franciescho non si mureranno di qui a ij anni.

[p. 85 f]
103.   Del consiglio de' maestri sul campanile. — Ellessero Gilio di ser Baldo, Franciescho di *(lacuna)* Rosso, Benedetto Baldini, Sandro Macci. — Fa' che e' ci siano martedì dopo mangiare, dì viiij di febraio. — Furonci i detti maestri, dì viiij di febraio 1355, e providero e consigliarono di concordia, iscritto per carta per mano di ser Palmieri presente notaio di questa opera: Che i' lavorio del campanile seguitava bene; e che ora nel raguagliare delle finestre si dovessero mettere macigni grandi con ispranghe piombate che leghassero ogne cosa. Fucci con loro Bonaguida Simoni proposte.

MARCH 9, 1356 [DOC. 70, p. 86]

104.   Del modo dello stanziare. — Di mese in mese.

105.   De' marmi che sono a Pisa e a l'Avenza. — Istudia che e' vegniano.

106.   Del consiglio usato del campanile. — Farello una volta a nostro tempo.

107.   Del sonmo di Neri. — Vegnia tutto il marmo suo, e poi si facci raxione.

108.   Della lunetta e altri lavorii. — Come ci è un'altra lunetta, di presente la da' in sonmo a chi me' fa.

109.   Degli Angnioli. — Ricoldalci.

110.   Fa' che noi sappiamo ciò che resta a fare Neri e compagni del sonmo.

111.   Fa' che noi sappiamo tutto il marmo che mancha da quello che ci è, e che è tra via, in suso fino a piè dell'andito.

MARCH 18, 1356 [DOC. 70, p. 86]

112.   De legniame per li ponti. — Togliete, e ispendete il meno si puote.

113.   Delle lunette. — Dàlle tosto a chi meglio [ti fa una.
114.   Del pezo del marmo rotto. — Siamo contenti sia paghato sanza ritegnio.

MAY 10, 1356 [DOC. 70, p. 87]

115.   Di marmi neri. — Fatene venire braccia 100 di $^1/_1$ braccio, a soldi 9.

116.   Della quarta lunetta. — Dàlla dopo San Giovanni, per meno si può.

117.   De' chanapi. — Iscrivi a Bologna, e vedi di que' d'Azino, e abine consiglio con più persone, e avisati bene.

118.   Di ripieno. — Fate d'averne o nuovo o vecchio, qual meglio fa per l'opera.

MAY 31, 1356 [DOC. 70, p. 87]

119.   La lunetta di Franciescho. — Istralciaronla.

120.   Gli Angnioli. —

121.   De' chanapi. — Fornitevi al meglio che potete, e con meno spesa, de qui ad aghosto, che avrete migliori chanapi.

122.   Dell'ultima lunetta. — Dàlla per lire 150, o al meglio che puoi.

123.   Il sonmo di Neri, e de'marmi loro. — Metti i marmi avuti dalloro a libro e la stima, e truova modo che e' siano paghati di questi come più tosto puoi.

JUNE 7, 1356 [DOC. 70, p. 87]

124.   Di fare d'avere de' marmi, per inanzi, in sonmo. — Senti. De' marmi neri. — Seguita quello

che è cominciato. De' marmi rossi. — Mandisi per essi dopo la festa.

[p. 87]

125.   Vogliamo che niuno maestro vada a lavorare fuori dell'opera per niuna chagione, sanza diliberagione di tutti e quattro operai, e se niuno va sanza questa diliberagione fatta nell'opera essendo all'uficio, che e' non ci torni poi a lavorare.

[p. 88]

126.   Fa' d'avere questi quattro maestri iscritti qui dallato, per venerdi mattina dì x di giugnio 1356, al consiglio del lavorio, e noi ci sarèno.

JUNE 10, 1356 [DOC. 70, p. 88]

127.   Vogliamo si tolghano macigni dalla Cichala, e parte delle pietre forti da Montisci.

128.   Abi consiglio della ruota.

JUNE 20, 1356 [DOC. 70, p. 88]

129.   Paghate barili j di vino a'maestri per San Giovanni.

130.   Vogliono gli operai e così comandano, che gl' infrascritti pregi si deano a' sonmaioli, e non più: Stipidi, soldi 28 br.; angholi, soldi 14 br.; fondi, soldi 14 br.; cornici di compassi, soldi 9 br.; compassi, soldi 30 l'uno; empetrato in archo di $^7/_8$, soldi 80 br.; empetrati in archo di più raxioni, soldi 35 br.; fregio a rosette, soldi 30 br.; empetrato in volta del $^1/_3$, soldi 30 br.; cornici grosse sfogliate, soldi 35 br.; corniciuze, soldi 5 br.; quadroni a 3 faccie, soldi 35 br.; cornici a 3 mussi in archo, soldi 11 br.; colonnelli rossi, soldi 25 br.; marmi neri di $^1/_1$ br., soldi 6 br.; marmi neri di $^1/_3$ br., soldi 4 br.; pietre forti, br. soldi 13 quadro; coperte macigne, sol. 14 l'una; schaglioni, soldi 13 l'uno; colonnelli di pietra, soldi 10 br.; tavole di $^2/_3$ pianate dalle 5 latora, soldi 10 br.

AUGUST 31, 1356 [DOC. 70, p. 89]

131.   Neri, per lo sonmo. — Istralciaronla e liberarogli della pena di 500 fiorini, salvo 25 fiorini, e istanziarono fossero paghati.

132.   Delle lunette. — Mettile a uscita per compiute, e pon che debino avere lire 30 per una, che riterrai loro tanto che siano compiute.

133.   Ferri. — Chi lavora a sonmo, si facci a suoi ferri.

NOVEMBER 7, 8, 1356 [DOC. 75]

134.   In Dei nomine amen. Anno ab eius incarnatione millesimo trecentesimo quinquagesimo sexto indictione decima die septimo mensis novembris. Actum Florentie, presentibus testibus Francischo Talenti populi Sancte Reparate et Filippo Marsilii populi Sancti *(lacuna)* ad hec vocatis et rogatis.

Iacopus Lippi Nerii, Loctus domini Locti et Filippus Rinaldi de Rondinellis operarii et officiales pro comuni Florentie opere et fabrice Sancte Reparate de Florentia una cum Iohanne Bingerii de Oricellariis corum collega absente, protestantes in principio medio et fine huius contractus quod per infrascripta vel aliquod infrascriptorum non intendunt vel volunt se ipsos vel alterum eorum sen eorum vel alicuius eorum heredes vel bona aliqualiter obligare set solum comune Florentie et dictam operam Sancte Reparate, omni modo via et iure quibus melius potuerunt, pro dicta opera et vice et nomine ipsius opere Sancte Reparate, locaverunt et concesserunt Nascimbeni vocato Sibillino olim Guernieri de Bononia qui moratur Florentie in populo Sancti Laurentii, et Marcho Pieri de Chumo qui moratur Florentie in populo Sancti Michaelis Bertelde, magistris, et cuilibet eorum, ad conducendum et deferendum et apportandum seu deferri et apportari faciendum ad dictam operam Sancte Reparate et in claustro dicte opere, de comitatu Senarum, omnibus dictorum Nascimbenis et Marci et cuiuslibet eorum expensis, marmos in quantitate et usque in quantitatem librarum sexcentum miliariorum ad pondus, cum et sub infrascriptis pactis conditionibus modis pretiis et terminis, videlicet:

Imprimis in illa quantitate petiorum marmi, et in illis mensuris et modinis qui et que eisdem vel alteri eorum assignabuntur per capudmagistrum dicte opere, dum modo non possit vel debeat aliquod petium marmi esse maioris ponderis librarum sexcentarum ad pondus.

Item quod dicti Nascimbene et Marchus et uterque eorum teneantur et debeant dictos marmos apportare seu conducere seu apportari vel conduci facere ad dictam operam hinc ad kalendas mensis ianuarii sub anno Domini millesimo trecentesimo quinquagesimo septimo.

Item quod dicti operarii et eorum successores teneantur et debeant dare et solvere seu dari et solvi facere eisdem Nascimbeni et Marcho pro pretio dicti marmi libras novem et soldos otto f. p. pro quolibet miliario ad pondus dicti marmi apportati et ponderati in claustro dicte opere, in illis terminis et temporibus et pagis quibus et prout videbitur dictis officialibus vel duabus partibus eorum vel eorum successoribus vel duabus partibus eorum ut dictum est.

Que omnia et singula suprascripta et infrascripta promiserunt et solempniter convenerunt dicti officiales dictis modis et nominibus ex una parte, et dicti Nascimbene et Marchus et uterque eorum se in solidum obligando ex altera, inter se et sibi ad invicem et vicissim solempni stipulatione hinc inde interveniente . . .; sub pena florenorum quingentorum auri, quam penam pars non observans alteri parti servanti inter se ad invicem et vicissim modis et nominibus supradictis dare et solvere promisit et convenit . . .

Item eisdem anno et indictione die octavo dicti mensis novembris. Actum Florentie in populo Sancti Laurentii, presentibus testibus Vanne Cennis et Paulo Ugole et Guidone Fey, omnibus populi Sancti Laurentii Florentie, ad hec vocatis et rogatis. Bencius olim Cionis magister populi Sancte Reparate de Florentia, lecto sibi primo et exposito ad intelligentiam per me Benedictum notarium infrascriptum dicto instrumento conductionis dicti marmi . . ., dicens se de eis omnibus plenam habere notitiam, precibus et mandato dicti Nascimbenis in omnem predictam causam extitit fideiussor . . .

Item eodem die. Actum Florentie in ecclesia Sancti Salvatoris, presentibus testibus domino Francischo priore ecclesie Sanctorum Appostolorum et ser Gialdo Giani notario curie domini episcopi Florentini et aliis ad hec vocatis et rogatis, ser Mattheus olim Gherardi de Bononia notarius qui moratur Florentie in populo Sancte

Felicitatis, lecto etiam sibi primo et exposito ad intelligentiam per me Benedictum notarium infrascriptum dicto instrumento conductionis dicti marmi . . ., dicens se de eis omnibus plenam habere notitiam, precibus et mandato dicti Nascimbenis in omnem predictam causam extitit fideiussor . . . Ego Benedictus ser Iohannis Ciay de Pulicciano florentinus civis etc. — (Arch. Diplomatico, provenance *Opera di S. M. del Fiore.*)

NOVEMBER 28, 1356 [DOC. 70, p. 89]

135.   De' consigli usati del campanile. — Farello.

136.   Della nuova condotta de' marmi. — Fermaronsi con Subiellino e con Marcho per charta, iscritto per ser Benedetto di ser Giovanni.

137.   Della fighura. — Senti al meglio si puote.

JANUARY 11, 1357 [DOC. 70, p. 89]

138.   Della fighura con Franciescho. — Faccila; e facciendola bene, n'abi fiorini 25 d'oro, faciendola a chasa.

[p. 90]
139.   Della ruota della cholla. — Fatela fare.

140.   Delle 950 lire. Della petizione della Chamera. — Fa' una petizione, e noi la porgiereno; e contenghavisi dentro, che ove noi abiàno dal Comune danari ij per lira, che e' ci e ne deano 6, e noi il daremo loro compiuto in 4 anni per 40000 fiorini; ove seguitando come si fa, si penerà xx anni, e costerà 70000.

141.   Della nuovo condotta de' marmi. — Istà bene. Iscrivi a Sebellino a Siena, se e' non manda di qui a sabato dì xj di febraio prossimo de'marmi, che tu andrai là a farne fare a sue spese.

142.   Della fighura della M[isericordia]. — Barattate con loro a una lapida delle nostre. — Diliberarono 6 di febraio che la fighura si lasciasse istare, e dessesi loro una lapida con cierti patti iscritti a libro *A* a c . . .

143.   D'allogare i sette Profeti.

FEBRUARY 6, 1357 [DOC. 70, p. 90]

144. Vogliono gli operai, e così comandorono dì vj di febraio 1356, che Neri faccia si, che di concordia Neri di Fioravante e compagni finischano l'opera d'ognie cosa fra qui a xv dì, o e' rimetta lire 150 piccioli che ebe; e se questo non si fa, che tutti i danari che Alberto mosterrà chiaramente essere pervenuti in mano di Neri dal protesto suo in qua, gli faranno tornare all'opera.

MAY 12, 1357 [DOC. 70, p. 90]

145. Della fighura data a fare a Francesco. —

146. De' consigli usati del campanile. — Eborli dì 26 e dì 31 di magio. Consigliarono come è scritto qui di sotto.

147. Della ruota alloghata al Maestruzo. — Rispondi, o vuole la ruota sua e rendere i danari che àe avuti, o aspetti a' nuovi [Operai].

MAY 22, 31, 1357 [DOC. 70, p. 91]

148. Elessero tutti e quattro [Operai], dì 22 di magio 1357, al consiglio: Bartolo, Franciescho di *(lacuna)*; Tommaso, Stefano Metti; Alesso, Bernardo di Piero; Filippo, Neri di Fieravante: per venerdì, di 26 di maggio 1357, a nona; con salario di soldi x per uno.
Renderon per consiglio, dì 31 di magio 1357, iscritto per ser Mino Giani notaio di questa opera:
Che la ruota da piè del champanile cholli fino al finestrato grande, e ivi si faccia uno palcho su i pettorali isportato in fuori e in dentro, ove si cholli e ponghi ciò che si cholla; e da ivi in su, per dentro il champanile, si cholli chon una pichola ruota che sia di sopra.
E che al più tosto che si raguaglia il champanile, che e' si leghi intorno intorno dentro nel muro chon istanghe grosse e suficienti di ferro.

JUNE 10, 1357 [DOC. 70, p. 91]

149. Del modo dello stanziare. — Feciero per

istanziamento che ognie mese si vedessero le spese fatte.

150. Della raxione di Domenicho di Noffo. — Feciero per istanziamento che e' depositi, per di qui tutto luglio prossimo, al camarlingo fiorini 42 d'oro, tanto che la raxione si saldi; e in quanto non faciesse, s'intenda essere debitore in fiorini 42 detti de'marmi da Siena e del modo: e che si mandi il messo dell'opera a notificharlile. Iscrivemmoli una lettera Franciescho e io, che se alla tornata della lettera e' non manda a suficienza, che noi mandereno per esso a sue spese di per nostra parte a' mallevadori, che al tutto truovino modo che de' marmi ci siano di presente e assai; altrimenti prociederemo contro a loro.

151. Della fighura data a Franciescho, e de' danari che sopra ciò dee dare. — Compiala.

[p. 92]
152. Della ruota del Maestruzo. — Aspetta a venerdì. — Furono in achordo con Maestruzo, dì 16 di giugnio, che egli avesse della sua ruota quello che diciesse Franciescho Talenti e io Filippo.

153. Del consiglio renduto per li maestri. — Avremo nuovo consiglio.

154. Degli Angnioli e de l'alie. — Fatele fare subito inorpellate, sì che vi siano per San Giovanni.

JUNE 14, 1357 [DOC. 70, p. 92]

155. Diliberarono che da San Giovanni in là, preso che fosse al tutto il partito della chiesa, che in sul champanile rimanesse a murare [maestri] e manovali.
Giovanni Belchari, Vigi Grilli, Bancho Falchi, maestri su.
Giovannino d'Alberto, Gierino Marchi, Bartolo Vannugi, Biagio Biagi, per manovali su.
Alla ruota giù di sotto: Lapuccio Benucci, Bartolo d' Ellero, Bughante Boncienni.
Giunta Alberti a allacciare.
A seghare marmi: Baldino Nepi, Alesso Naldi.
A portare pietre, ij.

JUNE 15, 1357 [DOC. 70, p. 93]

156. Comandorono a Sibellino, che tra qui a ¹/₁ lulglio prossimo debia mandare de' marmi assai, altrimenti etcetera.

Vuolsi mostrare agli operai una lettera che viene dalla chava a Sibellino.

JUNE 21, 1357 [DOC. 70, p. 96]

157. Vogliamo che la ragione di Domenicho di Noffo si vegia secondo che apare per lo libro suo e per lo libro dell'opera; e veduta, noi la stanzieremo e chalereno del peso del marmo, considerato il ragualglio di tutte le mandate sue chon le ricievute, abattuto 5 per centinaio, come si dee, del peso pisano al fiorentino, che e' cala intorno di libre 5000; e usanza è che sempre chala alchuna chosa. E chonsiderato la dirittura e la buona fede di Domenicho di Noffo, che l'ae avuto a mandare da Pisa, vogliamo che e'si stia a la sua ragione interamente sanza alchuna cosa ritenerli. — Facto.

158. E che del marmo che condusse Ambruogio chapo maestro di San Giovanni e chostò lire 65, e Domenicho detto gli paghò, e gli operai passati voleano che ne riavesse solo quello che è in patto coll'opera, che sarebono lire 60 sol. 9 e den. *(lacuna)* per charichare e ghabella, vogliamo che e' riabia interamente le lire 65 sanza averne danno o pro. — Facto.

159. E che lire 23 sol. 4 pic. paghati per lo camarlingo in viij pezi di marmi ritrovati per Arno, di peso di lib. 5800, e sono posti al quaderno della chassa a debitore in Domenicho detto, si mettano a uscita per l'opera, per paghamento del detto marmo ritrovato: abiendo considerazione che più pezi del segno de l'A vecchio siano venuti mescholati con questo che ae avuto a mandare Domenicho, che è segnato B, e questi ritrovati sono segnati B, possano essere ischambiati per lo chammino per difetto de'piattaiuoli, e i detti pezi tornano più alla ricevuta del detto marmo. — Facto.

JUNE 30, 1357 [DOC. 70, p. 97]

160. Vogliono che io Filippo ragioni con Sibel-

lino del modo di lasciare il mandare tanti marmi da Siena.

161. Che Franciescho et io vegiamo quanto marmo ci bisognia per di qui a un anno, co'maestri che sono ora rimasi sul campanile. — Intorno di clxxx.ᵐ

JULY 5, 1357 [DOC. 70, p. 97]

162. Vogliamo sapere quanto marmo biancho bisognia per j anno. — Troviamo Franciescho e io che bisogniano, per alzare otto braccia nel più alto, in uno anno:

br. 98 di stipidi di due raxioni .	lib.	39200
br. 48 d'angholi	lib.	9600
br. 62 di cornici de' compassi . .	lib.	9300
br. 121 di tavole di ¹/₁ br. . . .	lib.	18150
br. 113 di tavole di ²/₃	lib.	22600
br. 326 di cornice mussa de pilastri	lib.	65200
br. 92 di fondi de' pilastri di ²/₃ .	lib.	23000

Somma libre 187050

JULY 7, 1357 [DOC 70, p. 98]

163. Raunaci mercholedì dì xij, e fa' che ci sia Sibellino e i malevadori suoi.

JULY 28, 1357 [DOC. 70, p. 102]

164. Del non lavorare sul campanile di qui a ¹/₁ settembre. — Dissero d'averne consiglio cho' consoli.

AUGUST 31, 1357 [DOC. p. 107 f]

165. Vogliono che e' si vegia tutti i danari che ae ricevuti Sibellino sopra la condotta de' marmi da Siena, e che e' si mettano a uscita, e ponghansi a libro grande a sua ragione: e che di quello che resta a dare, sia debitore all'opera e non chamarlingo. E feciero la ragione eglino, e trovarono che aveva avuti lire 1746 soldi 17 denari 4 pic. E cosi si misero a uscita in loro presenzia, e istanziaronsi con gli altri danari insieme.

SEPTEMBER 19, 1357 ([p. 109]

166. Alloghanmo a Baldino Nepi e Stefano Vannugi a disfare tutte le mura del campanile vecchio, fino alla risegha della faccia della chiesa; e portare tutte le pietre di filo a'fondamenti sotto le volte, e l'altre abracciare ivi apresso al decto campanile: deono avere in sonmo fiorini *(lacuna).*

OCTOBER 26, 1357 [DOC. 70, p. 110]

167. Della ruota del Maestruzo. — Che e' paghi. Abia fiorini 2 d'oro per sua faticha, e riabiasi la ruota sua.

168. De' maestri bisogniano al campanile. — Comincisi lunedì dì 30 d'ottobre con que' maestri che altrimenti si stanziorno.

169. Di conciare la campana. — Vedete se è per cosa dobiamo far noi; fatela aconciare.

NOVEMBER 15, 1357 [DOC. 70, p. 111]

170. Istanziarono che niuno traesse dell'opera nè maestro nè manovale per niuna chagione, a pena di lire x, sanza parola di tutti gli operai.
Istanziarono per lo notaio, che nè maestro nè manovale nè masserizia nè chalcina nè altro si traesse dell' opera per niuna chagione, a pena di soldi c.

NOVEMBER 17, 1357 [DOC .70, p. 111]

171. Del Maestruzo. — Fate che la sua ruota ne vegnia giù, e paghisi.

NOVEMBER 29, 1357 [DOC. 70, p. 112]

172. Noi soprascritti operai siamo in chonchordia cho Sibilino di Guernieri da Bolognia, il quale de' conducere i marmi da Siena per l'opera, in questo modo cioè: che noi perlunghiamo termine al detto Sibilino da chalendi gennaio 1357, ch'era il suo termine, in fino a chalendi novembre 1358, ch'e' deba avere chondotto al detto termine tuta la quantità del marmo che si chontiene nella char-

ta della sua aloghagione: e questo intendiamo che sia termine perentorio, riserbando a la detta opera ongni ragione che la detta opera avese chontra al detto Sibilino e chontra suoi malevadori e d'ongni pena che fosono inchorsi o achoresono.
Anche siamo in chonchordia chol detto Sibilino, che de' marmi che ci manderà nel detto tenpo de' paghare l'opera la ghabella e la vetura, e soldi cinquanta del migliaio per fattura a la charigha, e pore a sua ragione, e l'avanzo ritenere per danari ch'à sopra presi della detta opera, no rimutando i patti fatti da l'opera a lui.
Io Cetto operaio sopradetto ò fatta quest'iscritta di chomesione de' sopradetti mie' chopagni il detto di.

DECEMBER 7, 1357 [DOC. 70, p. 112]

173. De' sonmi che bisognieranno dare. — Cominciati a'ntendere co' maestri.

174. Del sonmo dato a Francesco Talenti a veghiare. — [p. 113]

175. De'consigli usati del campanile. —

176. De' marmi neri. — Fatene venire.

177. D'alloghare lo 'impetrato murato. — Alloghatelo.

DECEMBER 15, 1357 [DOC. 70, p. 113]

178. Alloghanmo Franciescho Talenti e io Filippo Marsili, questo di, a chompiere cioè chavare e enpetrare tutti i fregi che sono murati e debonsi inpetrare, e non sono altro che pianati, sul campanile, di largheza di ²/₃, a Puccio Bracciuoli, per soldi venticinque piccioli il braccio, di quanto ne farà: e de' cominciare incontanente.

179. Filippo Ghucci legniaiuolo. Per braccia xviiij ¹/₁ di correnti, e j subiello per li aspi, soldi xxj. Per L assi d'abete per lo campanile, a soldi 7 denari 10 l'una, lire xviiij soldi xj denari viij. Per r[ecatura] soldi v denari iiij.

JANUARY 4, 1358 [DOC. 70, p. 114]

180. Della colla nuova per lo campanile. — Togliemmo una colla dal Maestruzo.

181. Del consiglio usato del campanile. —

182. Vogliamo che sul campanile steano ij maestri a' marmi, j a pionbare, j alle pietre, e i manovali che bisogniano; e di subito si faccia la colla nuova, si che e' ve n'abi 2.

183. Della lettera venuta da Sibellino da Siena. — Vogliamo che Sibellino abia lire c, e Nicholò vetturale sia servito di fiorini 40 d'oro, con buono mallevadore.

184. De'danari de' contratti. — Prochacciali.

185. D'alloghare sonmi. — Udirono i maestri, e dissero si prochacciasse con altri maestri di fuori.

186. De' marmi d' Orto San Michele. — Rendeteli loro.

[p. 115]
187. Ebono questo di a consiglio delle 'nfrascritte cose: frate Iacopo Talenti di Santa Maria Novella, Neri di Fieravante, Franciescho Salvetti, M.° Franciescho dal Choro, Giovanni Gherardini, Ambruogio Lenzi, Taddeo Ghaddi dipintore. — Dissero di rispondere d'ogne cosa martedì a dì viiij di giennaio 1357.

JANUARY 30, 1358 [DOC. 70, p. 116]

188. Del mutare le campane. — Mutatele subito.

FEBRUARY 7, 1358 [DOC. 116]

189. Beninchasa di Grazia: ij quercie per le campane, j olmo per ij pali per la colla, fior. xj ^{1}/$_1$; e rechatura, sol. 14 pic.
Piero Giannozi: j chastagnio per le campane, e recatura, fiorini ij ^{1}/$_1$ soldi 15.

FEBRUARY 16, 1358 [DOC. 70, p. 116]

190. A. Leonardo Richobeni, a Nerino Cherichini, Antonio Nerini, in sonmo per aconciare le campane nel luogho loro, lire xiij.

SEPTEMBER 28, 1358 [DOC. 72, p. 118]

191. Franceschi Talenti trovò, dì 28 di setenbre 358, che manchava al champanile: bechadelli grandi e mezani 38, bechadelli picholi 37, archetti interi 30, chornice isfolglate br. xl, cimase che vano sopra i bechadelli br. c6, chornici del ^{1}/$_3$ braccio br. xl, tavole torte br. 138, chornice di due terzi br. c, tavole per lungheza j ^{1}/$_1$ br. e per largheza br. j grosse ^{1}/$_4$ br. c, chornice largha ^{1}/$_3$ grossa ^{1}/$_1$ br. c.

OCTOBER 17, 1358 [DOC. 72, p. 119]

192. Di dire loro de la tornata di Sibellino, e quello che dice, e quello che n'abiamo fatto noi chapi maestri e Chanbino.

193. Franceschi Talenti ae a chasa uno pezzo di marmo del quale, secondo ch'io truovo, de'fare una imagine d'uno Profeta, e dene avere xxv f. d'oro di maestero. Dice che vuole in prestanza sopr'esso x f. d'oro, e io non so s'elgl' à tanto fatto che li si posano prestare. — Dice Anbruogio di si, che si posono prestare.

194. D'una chasa che è a piè del chanpanile dirinpetto a la taverna chessi vuole vendere, se volete si tolgha. — Sappisi il chosto.

OCTOBER 19, 1358 [DOC. 72, p. 120]

195. Chonpari prima, il decto di, Alberto Arnoldi maestro, e dice ch'è aparechiato di torre di questi sonmi.

NOVEMBER 28, 1358 [DOC. 72, p. 121]

196. Di ragionare d'uno dificio che Giovanni di Lapo Ghini vuole fare per chollare, per lo quale l'opera risparmierà ongni di lire iij sol. iij. — Faciala a sue spese, se non viene ben fatto; e se viene fatto, avrà provisione.

197. Di dire loro, chome Puccio Bracciuoli non à fatto il fregio che fa al chanpanile suso, ed è rimaso adietro a l'altro lavorio è ito suso; ch'è cholpa di Francescho Talenti: e cosi anche è rimaso adietro altro lavorio.

[p. 122]
198. Giovanni di Lapo Ghini tolse a fare, di 28 di novembre, uno dificio il quale dee cholare quanto chollano le due ruote, e che vi bisongnerà vij manovali meno che ne le due ruote; e farallo a tutte sue spese: e se viene ben fatto, pagherà l'opera la spesa, e avrà provisione chome piacerà e parrà algl'operai; e se non viene ben fatto, de'-pagare di suo ongni spesa fatta, e non avere provisione. La spesa disse sarebe da fiorini d'oro x o xij.

DECEMBER 18, 1358 [DOC. 72, p. 122]

199. Prestare a Francescho Talenti il salaro di iij mesi, genaio, febraio, marzo. E che Simone suo filglolo ne sia tenuto. — Facciasi.

DECEMBER 20, 1358 [DOC. 72, p. 122 f]

200. Francescho Talenti, Giovanni di Lapo Ghini scrisono e vidono che manchava al chanpanile fino a l'andito: bechadelli minori 39, bechadelli mezani 64, bechadelli grandi 27, cimase 59, archetti 52, tavole torte 142, per lo 'npetrato di ²/₃ br. xlv, cornice grossa ¹/₁ braccio br. lxv.

JANUARY 10, 1359 [DOC. 72, p. 123]

201. Di solecitare Benci Cioni che chonducha i bechadelli del marmo bianco, minori e mezani e magiori, sechondo che promise quando fu tratto di prigione; chè n'avemo grandisimo bisongno.

202. Di ragionare loro chesse si potesse fare chon uno chapomaestro, che sarebe di grande lungha il milglore ch'averne due, per le ragioni che saprai

dire loro. O se potesono fare che Francescho e Giovanni fosono in achordo sarebe buono.

203. Di ragionare loro del nuovo deficio da cholare che facea Giovanni di Lapo Ghini, acciò che sapiano quello ch'ànno a fare chollui.

JANUARY 14, 1359 [DOC. 72, p. 124]

204. Ristoro Cioni vuole tenperare le due ruote, che chollerano due tanti che non fanno con que' medesimi uomini.

JANUARY 15, 1359 [DOC. 72, p. 124]

205. Di dare in somma: archetti, tavolette torte, cimase, chorniciette, bechadelli picholi e mezani e grandi, per lo chanpanile.

JANUARY 16, 1359 [DOC. 72, p. 124]

206. Di dare in somma i bechadelli grandi e mezani e picholi, e archetti e tavole torte e cimase e chorniciette e chapitelli delle cholonne e de' menbri.

JANUARY 29, 1359 [DOC. 72, p. 124]

207. Francescho Talenti, Giovanni di Lapo Ghini, Chanbino Signorini, di choncordia disono a li detti operai, che per ogni via e modo che posono abian de' marmi bianchi per le faccie de la chiesa però che manca, e simile per lo chanpanile; e che ne volevano esere schusati del mormorare che si fa.

JANUARY 30 [DOC. 72, p. 125]

208. Mandarono Giovanni di Lapo Ghini chapo maestro di questa opera a Siena e a la chava del marmo nel chontado di Siena, e chomisolgli le 'nfrascritte chose. [...]
E che vegia se i bechadelli grandi e mezani e picoli checci dee chonducere Sibillino che siano a quelle misure di lungheza e groseza che debono esere; e

chesse trovase che fosono mozi o vero che non fosono a quelle misure che deono esere, che faccia
rechare i grandi i' luogho di mezani e i mezani
i' luogho di picholi, si che l'opera abia i bechadelli
d'ogni ragione a quella misura che dee.

E che prochacci di mandacci del marmo checci de'
chonducere Sibillino di quelle ragioni che posano
rechare le bestie, e spezialmente di bechadelli cimase archetti tavole torte per le n'petrato e chornice grosse di ¹/₁ br. per lo chanpanile.

E checci scriva speso quello che fa e crede fare od
à fatto: e però mandiamo chollui Bartolo di Giovanni, che ne rechi le letere.

MARCH 22, 26, 1359 [DOC. 80]

209. Die vigesimasecunda mensis martii.

Domini Priores et Vexillifer iustitie, una cum
offitiis gonfaloneriorum Sotietatum populi et
Duodecim bonorum virorum Comunis in pala-
tio populi in sufficienti numero congregati, eorum
offitii auctoritate et vigore omnique modo via et
iure quibus melius potuerunt, facto et celebrato
prius inter eos solepni et secreto scruptinio et ot-
tempto partito ad fabas nigras et albas, secundum
formam statutorum, eligerunt nominaverunt et
deputaverunt . . . pro dicto comuni Florentie Scel-
tum Tinghi promotum per ser Franciscum Bruni
priorem, Taddeum Canigiani promotum per Fi-
lippum Machiavelli gonfalonerium, Salvestrum
Manetti Ysacchi promotum per Tellinum Dini de
numero duodecim, Zenobium de Antilla promotum per Franciscum Gosi gonfalonerium, Pinuc-
cium Bonciani promotum per Franciscum Barto-
lini priorem, Taddeum Fini Tosi promotum per
ser Franciscum Bruni predictum, Bonacursum Ac-
zarelli de Filicaria promotum per Laponem Spa-
darium gonfalonerium, Cantinum Angnoli promotum per Amerighum de Sommaria gonfalonerium, in offitiales et pro offitialibus ad reviden-
dum et recircandum rationem et computum
rationis expense facte in et pro laborerio campanilis Sancte Reparate de Florentia, cum illo salario quod concessum est eis per formam reforma-
tionis Consiliorum dicti populi et Comunis nuper
edite, et pro tempore et termino quattuor mensium proxime futurorum.

Die vigesimasexta mensis martii.

Domini Priores artium et Vexillifer iustitie, una
cum offitiis gonfaloneriorum Sotietatum et Duodecim bonorum virorum Comunis . . . eligerunt
et nominaverunt Bernardum Benis Pepe promotum per Bardum Corsi de numero Duodecim in
offitialem, loco suprascripti Silvestri Manecti
Ysacchi devetum habentis, ad revidendam rationem et computum expense facte in laborerio campanilis Sancte Reparate, cum illo salario et pro
illo tempore quo electus fuerat dictus Silvester.
(*L. S.*) Ego Ghibertus fillus olim ser Alexandri domini Chari de Florentia imperiali auctoritate iu-
dex ordinarius et notarius publicus predicta omnia et singula ex actis et libro actorum dictorum
dominorum Priorum et Vexilliferi iustitie et comunis Florentie existentibus penes me sumpsi et
in hanc publicam formam redegi ideoque me sub-
scripsi. — (Arch. Diplomatico, provenance *Arte
della lana.*)

MARCH 29, 1359 [C. Guasti, "Una giunta e una
correzione al mio libro, 'Santa Maria del Fiore,'" *Archivio Storico Italiano*, s. V, Vol. I
(1888), 429 ff]

210. . . . a' maestri, per vino, quando si serò la
volta del chanpanile, dì 29 di marzo, lib. iij. sol.
vij. (Quaderno di prestanze di Stoldo di Lapo
Stoldi chamarlingo de l'Opera, Archivio dell-
l'Opera di S.M.d.F., c. 9).

JULY 12, 1362 [DOC. 91]

211. Operarii operis et fabrice catedralis ecclesie Sancte Reparate de Florentia, simul congregati
in campanile catedralis ecclesie antedicte, pro
eorum offitio exercendo; visa quantitate pecunie
expensa et soluta per Iohannem Salvani olim camerarium dicti operis pro tempore sex mensium
initiatorum in kalendis mensis ianuarii proxime
preteriti mccclxj inditione xv et finitorum die ultima mensis iunii proxime preteriti mccclxij inditione predicta, et causis contentis in dictis solu-
tionibus, et dictam pecunie quantitatem per eum

solutam esse expensam legiptime et in rebus necessariis et utilibus dicti operis; vigore eorum offitii . . ., providerunt ordinaverunt deliberaverunt declaraverunt dictas expensas et quantitatem pecunie per eum expensam, fuisse factas et solutam legiptime et in rebus utilibus et necessariis dicti operis, et dictam quantitatem pecunie potuisse expendi et solvi et prout in exitu dicti camerarii continetur et scriptum est per ser Iohannem ser Marchi notarium pro comuni Florentie dicti operis; videlicet Exitus generalis, libr. sexmiliasexcentum octuoginta otto sol. xviij den. viij; Exitus magistrorum et manualium et illorum qui laborant in sommo, libr. quinqemilia ducentas quinquagintaquatuor sol. unum. In summa, libr. xj^m viiij^c xlij sol. xviiij den. otto. — (*Delib.*, I, 5).

DECEMBER 20, 1364 [DOC. 124]

212. Dicti operarii, considerantes quod ad presens in dicto opere non expedit quod Franciscus Talenti sit in dicto opere, quod a kalendis ianuarii proxime futuri ultra intelligatur remotus etc., et cassus sit et remotus a dicta die in antea. Presentibus testibus Sterio Francischini et Miniato Stefani. — (*Delib.*, II, 7.)

APRIL 6, 1367 [DOC. 166]

213. Operarii . . . deliberaverunt, pro utilitate dicti operis, quod quedam domus dicti operis que est ex opposito campanilis, que dicitur quod empta fuit pro dicto opere pro destruendo eam causa faciendi plateam dicto campanili . . ., destruatur et destrui debeat usque ad fundamentum pro dechore dicti campanilis et causa faciendi plateam dicto campanili; et conmiserunt et mandaverunt Iohanni Lapi Ghini capomagistro quod ipsam faciat destrui ut supra deliberatum est. — (*Delib.*, II, 80.)

AUGUST 19, 1367 [DOC. 183]

214. Operarii . . . elegerunt nominaverunt et deputaverunt Iohannem Andree vocatum Savio in offitialem et guardiam et ad custodiendum campanile e la faccia della chiesa quod non de-

vastetur, et quod custodiat quod non fiat nec proiciatur aliqua bruttura seu cadaver apud campanile, pro tempore et termino unius anni initiati die xviij mensis augusti, cum salario librarum decem quolibet mense, dando et solvendo eidem per camerarium dicti operis de mense in mensem dictum salarium. — (*Delib.*, II, 25).

AUGUST 19, 1367 [DOC. 184]

215. Operarii . . ., considerantes quod frater Benedictus dal Pogiuolo, iam est longhum tempus et usque ad tempus quando campanile dicte ecclesie construebatur, et postea sepe sepius venit et fuit in dicta ecclesia Sancte Reparate ad dandum consilium operariis dicti operis pro tempore existentibus circha constructionem dicte ecclesie et campanilis; et considerantes quod magistris qui venerunt et veniunt ad dandum consilium dicto operi circa dictam ecclesiam solvitur eis, et continuo providetur eisdem, de antiqua consuetudine, pro eorum labore et premio etc.; et ad hoc etiam ut ipse habeat causam veniendi similiter ad consulendum; et considerantes eius necessitatem; stanziaverunt quod camerarius det et solvat dicto fratri Benedicto, pro premio et labore ipsius, florenos quinque auri. — (*Delib.*, II, 25-26).

JULY 11, 1387 [A. Nardini, *Il Campanile di Santa Maria del Fiore* (Florence, 1885), 66 n. 1]

216. Johanni Antonii legnaiuolo, pro mille sexcentis quinquaginta asserellis, pro solidis viginti uno, denaris sex pro centenario, quos dedit et tradidit dicte Opere pro tecto campanilis predicti, et pro manichis pro beccastrinis, ut constat in libris, a cart. XVIII. Libras decem otto, solides decem, den. otto.
Agostino Nicholai Teri fabro, pro libris triginta septem ballectarum pro eo exibitarum dicto Opere pro tecto campanilis, ut constat in libris, a cart. XVII. Libras quatuor, solidos sexdecim, denarios quatuor flor. parvor.

AUGUST 26, 1388 [DOC. 379]

217. Operarii . . ., auditis et intellectis pluribus

et pluribus consiliis redditis per nonnullos sapientes cives et merchatores florentinos ac etiam magistros lapidum . . . super amplitudine et largitudine vie fiende a domo sive porta Falconeriorum usque ad anghulum vie Spadariorum, et cupientes quod dicta ecclesia hornetur viis et aliis ad hornationem dicte ecclesie necessariis; et volentes, ut tenentur et debent ex debito eorum offitii, quod dicta ecclesia habeat de viis ipsi ecclesie circumstantibus vias pulcras et largas et ut decet iustas et honorabiles, ac etiam pro honore et comodo tam civium quam civitatis Florentie . . ., deliberaverunt quod via circumstans ecclesiam Sancte Reparate a domo sive porta Falconeriorum usque ad viam sive angulum Spadariorum mictatur et micti debeat et sit et esse debeat, ab uno muro ab alio, largitudinis vigintiseptem brachiorum et non minus.

Item . . ., cupientes quod dicta via quam citius potest amplietur, et hoc fieri non potest absque destructione domorum Filippi et Luche Pierii Rinerii et aliorum hominum et personarum morantium usque ad viam Spadariorum in aliqua ipsarum domorum parte, et ut dicta destructio sit eis nota et fieri debere ad voluntatem dictorum operariorum . . ., deliberaverunt quod pro parte dictorum operariorum precipiatur et preceptum fiat dicto Filippo et aliis qui manent iusta dictam viam nunc ibi existentem, quatenus hinc ad per totam quintamdecimam diem mensis septembris proxime futuri teneantur et debeant sgombrare et sgomberasse eorum domus, cum ipsi intendant elapso dicto termino procedere ad largitudinem dicte vie et ad destructionem dictarum domorum. — (*Delib.*, XXVI, 8-9.)

SEPTEMBER 2, 1388 [DOC. 380]

218. Operarii . . ., cupientes quod maior ecclesia florentina ornetur ut decet, et maxime de rebus et laboreriis necessariis et opportunis . . ., deliberaverunt quod quando fit seu fiet lastrachum platee Sancti Iohannis, fiat et fieri debeat etiam laborerium de lapidibus marmi ante et prout trait campanile, videlicet ante faciem revolutam usque ecclesiam Sancti Iohannis, et eo modo et forma quo et quibus manet ante dictam maiorem ecclesiam. — (*Delib.*, XXVI, 9.)

MAY 9, 1391 [DOC. 395]

219. Operarii . . . providerunt et deliberaverunt quod ecclesia designi Sancte Liperate, que est apud campanile, destruatur totis muris circumcirca, remanente salvo designo; et quod ubi sunt muri fiant pilastri oportuni in quadrum, et in illo medio fiat graticula de castagniuolis.

Item deliberaverunt quod sepultura magistri Iohannis medici, que est super platea Sancti Iohannis inter ecclesiam Sancte Liperate et Sancti Iohannis, remaneat salva et non devastetur, et quod quando fiet lastricum dicte platee, dictus magister Iohannes possit ponere unum schudicciuolum solum sue armis ad hostium sive sportellum ipsius sepulture. — (*Delib.*, XXXI, 20.)

DECEMBER 26, 1397 [DOC. 408]

220. Deliberaverunt quod ut turpia que odie fiunt sub volta iusta capanile Sancte Reparate inter ecclesiam et dictum capanile tollantur, quod ibi subtus dictum arcum et voltam quantum expedit lastricetur et lastricari debeat cum lastronibus mangnis . . . (*Delib.*, XL, 38.)

SEPTEMBER 13, 1407 [DOC. 441]

221. Operarii . . . deliberaverunt quod sepulture marmi existentes extra ecclesiam Sancte Reparate iusta canpanile debeant et possint reattari per magistros dicti operis, et post dictam reattationem ipsas sepulturas vendere unicuique ipsam vel ipsas emere volentibus, quamlibet ipsarum pro florenis viginti auri. — (*Delib.*, LIV, 2.)

APRIL 12, 1410 [DOC. 455]

222. Deliberaverunt quod Iohannes Ambroxii capudmagister dicte opere . . . possit et valeat vendere cuicunque voluerit de sepulturis sub campanile novis iusta scaleas, pro pretio ad minus florenorum viginti auri, cum hoc quod primo solvatur dictum pretium camerario dicte opere ante quam fiat instrumentum etc. — (*Delib.*, LIX, 3.)

JANUARY 23, 1431 [C. Guasti, *La Cupola di Santa Maria del Fiore* (Florence, 1857), DOC. 68]

223. Prefati domini comsules, una cum operariis dicte Opere, considerantes edifitium Cupole maioris fore prope conclusionem et perfectionem, ac etiam extra omnem mensuram modelli murati penes Campanile; et auditis et intellectis quampluribus personis querelantibus de inhonestate que fit in dicto modello tam vacuationis corporis quam etiam alterius inhonestatis; intendentes predictis obviare pro utilitate prefate Opere et honore pulcritudinis Canpanilis, et ut talia obbrobia removeantur; deliberaverunt quod caputmagister prefate Opere, sine alio partito et deliberatione, illico destrui faciat prefatum modellum; cum hac reservatione, quod armadura Cupole prefati modelli integra elevetur et ponatur in loco tuto, ad hoc ut, si opus esset, de ea possit haberi plena notitia. — (*Libro di Deliberazioni*, Archivio dell'Opera di S. M. d. F.)

FEBRUARY 5, 1431 [G. Poggi, *Il Duomo di Firenze* (Berlin, 1909), DOC. 307]

224. Item deliberaverunt quod capudmagister actari faciat super porta campanilis illud quod ei videtur fore necessarium et honorabile faciendo quemdam capitellum de novo ubi non est et apponi faciat certis locis et apponi faciat certis locis vacuis tres figuras que sunt in opera. — (*Delib.*, 1425-36, c. 136v.)

MARCH 22, 1491 [A. Nardini, *Il Campanile di Santa Maria del Fiore* (Florence 1885), 66]

225. [*Text and provenance not cited; Nardini's resumé*]: Decide 'si termini la porta del campanile come'era stata cominciata, essendo stata sospesa, perchè alcuni avevano proposto rinnuovare la forma degli stipiti.'

SOURCES

[G. Villani, *Cronica* (Florence, 1844), X, 209; XI, 12]

I. A dì 26 di gennaio [1333] di mezzodì s'apprese fuoco contra il campanile vecchio di Santa Reparata dalla via di Balla, e arse una casa.

Nel detto anno [1334], a dì 18 di luglio, si cominciò a fondare il campanile nuovo di Santa Reparata, di costa alla faccia della chiesa, in sulla piazza di Santo Giovanni. E a ciò fare e benedicere la prima pietra fu il Vescovo di Firenze con tutto il chericato, e co'signori Priori e l'altre signorie, con molto popolo a grande processione. E fecesi il fondamento infino all'acqua tutto sodo. E soprastante e provveditore della detta opera di Santa Reparata fu fatto per lo Comune maestro Giotto nostro cittadino; il più sovrano maestro stato in dipintura che si trovasse al suo tempo, e quegli che più trasse ogni figura e atti al naturale. E fugli dato salario dal Comune per remunerazione della sua virtù e bontà.

. . . Il quale maestro Giotto tornato da Milano, che'l nostro Comune ve l'avea mandato al servigio del Signore di Milano, passò di questa vita a dì 8 di gennaio 1336, e fu seppellito per lo Comune a Santa Reparata.

] . . . [

[S. della Tosa, *Annali*, ed. D. Manni (Florence, 1733)]

II. E in quest' anno [1300] si fece la campana grossa in Santa Liparata, che si chiama la Ferrantina, e fecela fare messere Ferrantino de'Ferrantini a onore di messere Santo Zanobio. [Guasti, doc. 23]

E a dì XXVI di gennaio [1333] s'apprese il fuoco nelle case a rimpetto al campanile vecchio di Santa Liperata, e arsono da tre case. [Guasti, p. 34 n. 1]

Del mese di giugno [1334] si cominciò a fondare il bello campanile di Santa Liperata. [Guasti, p. 44 n. 1]

] ... [

[Anonymous ("Incerto"), *Cronaca*]

III. *[Under the year 1333 (sic)]:* Si cominciò a fare il campanile del marmo di Santa Liperata di Firenze. [Guasti, p. 44 n. 1]

] ... [

[A. Pucci, *Il centiloquio, che contiene la cronica di Giovanni Villani in terza rima,* in I. de San Luigi, ed., *Delizie degli eruditi toscani,* VI (1775), 119 f]

IV.   Nell'anno a' dì diciennove di luglio
       Della chiesa maggiore il campanile
       Fondato fu, rompendo ogni cespuglio,
   Per mastro Giotto, dipintor sottile,
       Il qual condusse tanto il lavorio
       Ch' e primi intagli fe' con bello stile.
   Nel trentasei, sì come piacque a Dio,
       Giotto morì d'età di settant'anni,
       E'n quella chiesa poi si soppellio.
   Poscia il condusse un pezzo con affanni
       Quel solenne maestro Andrea Pisano,
       Che fe' la bella porta a San Giovanni;
   Ma per un lavorio che mosse vano,
       Il qual si fè per miglioramento,
       Il maestro gli fu tratto di mano.
   E guidòl poi Francesco di Talento,
       In fin ch'al tutto fu abbandonato,
       Per dar prima alla chiesa compimento.

] ... [

[P. Fantani (ed.), *Commento alla Divina Commedia d'anonimo fiorentino del secolo XIV* (Bologna, 1868), XX, 188]

V.   Compose et ordinò [Giotto] il campanile di marmo di Santa Riparata di Firenze: notabile campanile et di gran costo. Commisevi due errori: l'uno, che non ebbe ceppo da piè; l'altro, che fu stretto: pòsesene tanto dolore al cuore, ch'egli si dice, ch'egli ne 'nfermò et morissene.

] ... [

[L. Bruni, *Historiarum florentini populi* (Florence, 1857), VI, 216]

VI.   Per hoc tempus [1334] marmorea turris quae est ad Reparatae templum fundari coepta est, architectata quidem a Jotto, insigni per eam tempestatem pingendi magistro. Is et fundamentis jaciendis praefuit, et formam, qualem nunc videmus, praestanti magnificentia operis designavit.

] ... [

[L. Ghiberti, *Lorenzo Ghibertis Denkwürdigkeiten (I Commentari),* ed. J. von Schlosser (Berlin, 1912), I, 37, 43]

VII.   [Giotto] Fu dignissimo in tutta l'arte, ancora nella arte statuaria. Le prime storie sono nello edificio il quale da 'llui fu edificato, del campanile di Sancta Reparata furono di sua mano scolpite et disegnate; nella mia età vidi provedimenti di sua mano di dette storie egregiissimamente disegnati.

[Andrea Pisano] fece nel campanile in Firenze sette opere della misericordia, sette virtù, sette scientie, sette pianeti; di maestro Andrea ancora sono intagliate quattro figure di quattro braccia l'una. Ancora vi sono intagliate grandissima parte di quelli i quali furono trovatori dell'arti. Giotto si dice sculpì le due prime storie.

] ... [

[F. Albertini, *Opusculum di mirabilibus novae et veteris urbis Romae* (Rome, 1510) 92r]

VIII.   In Vaticano est porticus S. Petri duplex; in pariete unius est navis fluctuans cum apostolis e musivo depicta ab Iocto Flor. pictore excellentiss. simul cum architectura: ut apparet in praeclara turri marmorea ecclesiae Florentinae.

] ... [

[A. Billi, *Il libro di Antonio Billi,* ed. C. Frey (Berlin, 1892), 6]

IX.   Fece [Giotto] il modello del campanile di Santo Giovannj, il quale doppo la morte sua si seguitó per Taddeo Gaddj, suo discepolo.

] . . . [

[Anonimo Gaddiano, *Il Codice Magliabechiano*, cl. XVII. 17, ed. C. Frey (Berlin, 1892) 53, 55]

X. Fece [Giotto] il modello del campanile di San Giouannj, il quale doppo la morte sua si seguitó per Taddeo di Gaddo suo discepolo. Opero anchora nella scultura et disegno et sculpi di marmo le prime historie, che sono nel campanile, da luj edificato, di Santa Maria del Fiore.

. . . seguito [Taddeo Gaddi] il modello del campanile di San Giouannj, dal suo maestro Giotto incominciato.

] . . . [

[G. B. Gelli, *Venti vite d'artisti*, ed. G. Mancini (Pisa, 1896), 19]

XI. Nè solamente fu [Giotto] valente ne la pittura, ma ancora nella scultura e nella architettura, la quale cosa doppo di lui si è ritrovata solamente in Andrea Cioni [!] e perfettissimamente in Michelagnolo come diremo di sotto, imperò che egli fece il modello del campanile di santa Maria del Fiore et cominciollo, ma non potè finire interponendosi la morte, nel quale sono di suo mano quelle prime storiette di mezzo rilievo.

] . . . [

[G. Vasari, *Le Vite de' più eccellenti architetti, pittori, et scultori italiani*, first edition (Florence, 1550); ed. C. Ricci (Milan-Rome, 1927), 148 f, 184]

XII. Ma quanto e' valesse [Giotto] nella architettura, lo dimostrò nel modello del Campanile di Santa Maria del Fiore, che essendo mancato di vita Arnolfo Todesco capo di quella fabrica, e desiderando gli Operai di quella chiesa e la Signoria di quella città che si facesse il campanile, Giotto ne fece fare col suo disegno un modello di quella maniera todesca che in quel tempo si usava, e, per averlo egli ben considerato, inoltre disegnò tutte le storie che andavano per ornamento in quella opera. E così scompartì di colori bianchi, rossi e neri in sul modello tutti que' luoghi dove avevano [a] andare le pietre et i

fregi con grandissima diligenzia, et ordinò che 'l circuito da basso fussi in giro di larghezza de braccia 100, cioè braccia 25 per ciascuna faccia, e l'altezza braccia 144. Nella quale opera fu messo mano l'anno MCCCXXXIIII e seguitata del continuo: ma non sì che Giotto la potessi veder finita, interponendosi la morte sua. . . . Il campanile di Santa Maria del Fiore fu seguitato e tirato avanti da Taddeo Gaddi suo discepolo in su lo stesso Modello di Giotto: Et è opinione di molti, et non isciocca, che egli desse opera alla scultura ancora, attribuendogli, ch'e' facesse due storiette di marmo, che sono in detto Campanile dove si figurano i modi, e i principii dell'arti; ancora che altri dichino, solamente il disegno di tali storie essere di sua mano.

. . . tanto quanto ancora lo [Taddeo Gaddi] lodarono nella esecuzione buona, ch' e' diede al campanile di Santa Maria del Fiore, del disegno lasciatogli da Giotto suo maestro, il quale avendo fatto la pianta, andò di altezza braccia CXLIIII, et di maniera si murò, che non può più commettersi pietre con tanta diligenza, et è stimato la più bella torre per ornamento et per spesa, del mondo.

] . . . [

[G. Vasari, *Le Vite de' più eccellenti architetti, pittori et scultori italiani*, second edition (Florence, 1568); ed. G. Milanesi (Florence, 1878 ff) I, 398 f, 586, 488 f]

XIII. Dopo queste cose [Giotto] mise mano, l'anno 1334 a dì 9 di luglio, al campanile di S. Maria del Fiore, il fondamento del quale fu, essendo stato cavato venti braccia a dentro, una piatèa di pietre forti in quella parte donde si era cavata acqua e ghiaia; sopra la quale piatèa, fatto poi un buon getto che venne alto dodici braccia dal primo fondamento, fece fare il rimanente, cioè l'altre otto braccia di muro a mano. E a questo principio e fondamento intervenne il vescovo della città, il quale, presente tutto il clero e tutti i magistrati, mise solennemente la prima pietra. Continuandosi poi questa opera col detto modello, che fu di quella maniera tedesca che in quel tempo s'usava, disegnò |I.129| Giotto tutte le storie che andavano nell'ornamento, e scompartì di colori bianchi, neri e rossi il modello in tutti que' luoghi dove avevano a andare le pietre e i fregi, con molta diligenza. Fu il circuito da basso in giro largo braccia cento, cioè braccia venticinque per ciascuna faccia, e l'altezza braccia centoquarantaquattro. E se è vero — che tengo per verissimo — quello che lasciò scritto Lorenzo di Cione Ghiberti, fece Giotto non solo il modello di questo campanile, ma di scultura ancora e di rilievo parte di quelle storie di marmo dove sono i principii di tutte l'arti. E Lorenzo detto afferma aver veduto modelli di rilievo di man di Giotto e particolarmente quelli di queste opere; la qual cosa si può credere agevolmente, essendo il disegno e l'invenzione il padre e la madre di tutte queste arti e non d'una sola. Doveva questo campanile, secondo il modello di Giotto, avere per finimento sopra quello che si vede una punta overo piramide quadra alta braccia cinquanta, ma per essere cosa tedesca e di maniera vecchia, gl'architettori moderni non hanno mai se non consigliato che non si faccia, parendo che stia meglio così. Per le quali tutte cose fu Giotto non pure fatto cittadino fiorentino, ma provisionato di cento fiorini d'oro l'anno dal Comune di Firenze, che era in que' tempi gran cosa, e fatto proveditore sopra questa opera che fu seguitata dopo lui da Taddeo Gaddi, non essendo egli tanto vivuto che la potesse vedere finita.

[Andrea Pisano] fece . . . ancora, secondo il disegno di Giotto, quelle figurette di marmo che sono per finimento della porta del campanile di Santa Maria del Fiore; ed intorno al medesimo Campanile, in certe mandorle, i sette Pianeti, le sette Virtù e le sette opere della Misericordia [sic], di mezzo rilievo in figure piccole, che furono allora molto lodate. Fece anco, nel medesimo tempo, le tre figure di braccia quattro l'una,

che furono collocate nelle nicchie del detto campanile, sotto le finestre che guardano . . . verso mezzogiorno; le quali figure furono tenute in quel tempo più che ragionevoli.

[Taddeo Gaddi] fu molto onorato . . . per avere sollecitamente e con diligenza esseguita la fabrica del campanile di Santa Maria del Fiore col disegno lasciato da Giotto suo maestro: il quale campanile fu di maniera murato, che non possono commettersi pietre con più diligenza, nè farsi più bella torre per ornamento, per spese e per disegno.

] . . . [

[F. L. del Migliore, *Firenze, città nobilissima* (Florence, 1684), 56]

XIV. Nelle Riformagioni leggesi l'istruzione data a Giotto, che ne fù l'Architetto, come lo doveva ordinare, e prescrivere, secondo la volontà, e deliberazion del Consiglio, di cui son'importanti addurne le prime parole, per comprendersi in ciò a che altezza di concetto arrivasse il Popolo di Firenze, dicevanisi adunque, che superata l'intelligenza, etiam, di chi fosse stat'atto a darne giudizio, si costituisse un'edifizio così magnifico, che per altezza, e qualità del lavoro, ne venisse a superare tanti quanti in quel genere, ne fossero stati fatti da'Greci, o da'Romani ne' tempi della lor più florida potenza: perchè se le Piramidi, i Colossi, e gli alti Obelischi fù un de' modi famosi appresso di loro, per il quale, al dir di Plinio, onoravasi chi aveva trionfato, pareva che quì ciò si richiedesse con più ragione magnifico, stante il farsi, non ad onore, o per memoria d'un solo, ma d'un Popolo intero poderoso, d'animo grande, e libero nell'autorità . . .

Bibliography of Works Cited

Ackerman, J. S. "'Ars Sine Scientia Nihil Est,' Gothic Theory of Architecture at the Cathedral of Milan," *Art Bulletin*, XXXI (1949), 84 ff.

Albertini, F. *Opusculum di mirabilibus novae et veteris urbis Romae.* Rome, 1510.

Alpatov, M. "The Parallelism of Giotto's Paduan Frescoes," *Art Bulletin*, XXIX (1947), 149 ff.

Anonimo Gaddiano. *Il Codice Magliabechiano*, ed., C. Frey. Berlin, 1892.

Antal, F. *Florentine Painting and Its Social Background.* London, 1947.

Arslan, E. "L'architettura romanica milanese," *Storia di Milano*, III (1954), 503 ff.

Auber, A. *Histoire et théorie du symbolisme religieux.* Paris-Poitiers, 1871.

Aubert, M. *L'Architecture Cistercienne en France.* Paris, 1947.

Augustodunensis, H. *Gemma anamae*, in J. P. Migne, ed., *Patrologiae cursus completus series Latina*, Paris, 1844 ff, CLXXII.

Bacchi, G. *La Certosa di Firenze.* Florence, 1930.

Bacci, P. *Documenti e commentari per la storia dell'arte.* Florence, 1944.

Baldinucci, F. *Vocabulario toscano dell'arte del disegno.* Florence, 1681.

— — —. *Notizie de' professori del disegno da Cimabue in qua*, ed. G. Piacenza. Turin, 1768.

Baron, H. *The Crisis of the Early Italian Renaissance.* Princeton, 1955.

Bartalini, A. *L'architettura civile del medioevo in Pisa.* Pisa, 1937.

Bauer, H. *Kunst und Utopie, Studien über das Kunst- und Staatsdenken in der Renaissance.* Berlin, 1965.

Becherucci, L. "I rilievi dei Sacramenti nel campanile del Duomo di Firenze," *L'Arte*, XXX (1927), 214-233.

— — —. "La bottega pisana di Andrea da Pontedera," *Mitteilungen des kunsthistorischen Instituts in Florenz*, XI (1965), 244 ff.

Becker, M. "Some Economic Implications of the Conflict Between Church and State in 'Trecento' Florence," *Medieval Studies*, XXIV (1959), 1 ff.

— — —. "Church and State in Florence on the Eve of the Renaissance (1343-1382)," *Speculum*, XXXVII (1962), 509 ff.

— — —. "Florentine Popular Government (1343-1348)," *Proceedings of the American Philosophical Society*, CVI (1962), 361 ff.

— — —. "Economic Change and the Emerging Florentine Territorial State," *Studies in the Renaissance*, XIII (1966), 9 ff.

— — —. *Florence in Transition.* Baltimore, 1967 f.

Biagi, L. *Palermo.* Bergamo, 1929.

Billi, A. *Il libro di Antonio Billi*, ed. C. Frey. Berlin, 1892.

Biondo, F. *Historiarum ab inclinationem Romanorum imperii decades.* Basel, 1531.

Bocchi, F. *Le bellezze della Città di Firenze*, ed. G. Cinelli. Pistoia, 1677.

Bodmer, H. "A School of Florentine Sculptors in the 14th Century: The Baroncelli and Bardi Monuments," *Dedalo*, X (1929 f), 616 ff, 662 ff.

Boito, C. "Il Duomo di Firenze e Francesco Talenti" (1865), in *Architettura del medioevo in Italia.* Milan, 1880, 185 ff.

Bonaini, F. (ed.). "Cronaca Pisana di Ranieri Sardo dall' anno 962 sino al 1400," *Archivio Storico Italiano*, VI (1845), 173 ff.

Bonelli, R. *Il Duomo di Orvieto e l'architettura italiana del duecento trecento.* Città di Castello, 1952.

Bongiorno, L. M. "The Theme of the Old and the New Law in the Arena Chapel," *Art Bulletin*, L (1968), 11 ff.

Borgatti, M. *Le mura e le torri di Firenze.* Rome, 1900.

Bowsky, W. M. "The 'Buon Governo' of Siena (1287-1355): A Medieval Italian Oligarchy," *Speculum*, XXXVII (1962), 368 ff.

Brandt, P. *Schaffende Arbeit und bildende Kunst im Altertum und Mittelalter.* Leipzig, 1927.

Branner, R. *St. Louis and the Court Style in Gothic Architecture.* London, 1965.

Braunfels, W. "Giotto's Campanile," *Das Münster*, I (1948), 193 ff.

— — —. *Mittelalterliche Stadtbaukunst in der Toskana.* Berlin, 1953.

de Brosses, C. *Lettres familières écrites d'Italie, 1739-1740*, ed. R. Colomb. Paris, 1869.

Browning, R. *Men and Women.* Boston, 1863 (orig. ed. 1855).

Brucker, G. *Florentine Politics and Society, 1343-1378.* Princeton, 1962.

Brunetti, G. "I Profeti sulla porta del campanile di Santa Maria del Fiore," in *Festschrift Ulrich Middeldorf*, Berlin, 1968, 106 ff.

Bruni, L. *Historiarum florentini populi.* Florence, 1857.

del Bufalo, A. *La Chiesa di San Francesco in Pisa.* Rome, n. d.

Bunt, C. G. E., and Churchill, S. J. A. *The Goldsmiths of Italy.* London, 1926.

Burckhardt, J. *Der Cicerone.* Basel, 1855.

Calzolai, C. C. *La storia della Badia a Settimo.* Florence, 1958.

Cämmerer-George, M. *Die Rahmung der toskanischen Altarbilder im Trecento.* Strasbourg, 1966.

Carocci, G. *L'illustratore fiorentino.* Florence, 1880, 47 ff.

— — —. *Il Mercato Vecchio di Firenze.* Florence, 1884.

— — —. "Notizie," *Arte e Storia*, XXI (1902), 6.

Cellini, P. "Appunti orvietani per Andrea e Niccolo Pisano," *Rivista d'Arte*, XV (1933), 10 ff.

Chierici, G. "La Basilica di S. Lorenzo in Milano," *Palladio*, n. s. IV (1954), 171 ff.

Cirri. *Necrologio fiorentino*, XVII (Ms. in Biblioteca Nazionale, Florence).

Conant, K. J. *Carolingian and Romanesque Architecture: 800-1200.* Baltimore, 1959.

Curtius, E. R. *European Literature and the Latin Middle Ages*, tr. W. R. Trask. New York, 1953.

Dati, G. *Istoria di Firenze dal 1380 al 1405*, ed. Luigi Pratesi. Norcia, 1904.

Davidsohn, R. *Forschungen zur Geschichte von Florenz.* Berlin, 1908.

— — —. *Firenze ai tempi di Dante*, tr. E. D. Theseider. Florence, 1929.

— — —. *Storia di Firenze.* Florence, 1956.

Dehio, G., and von Bezold, G. *Die kirchliche Baukunst des Abendlandes.* Stuttgart, 1884 ff.

Demus, O. *The Church of San Marco in Venice.* Washington, D. C., 1960.

Divi, A. *Historiarum pars tertia* (Ms. in Biblioteca Nazionale, Florence [Magl. XXXIX. 70]), II, I. 376.

Dorini, U. *Statuti dell'Arte di Por Santa Maria.* Florence, 1934.

Durandus, W. *Rationale divinorum officiorum.* Naples, 1839.

Edhardt, B. *Die Burgen Italiens.* Berlin, 1917.

Egbert, (Mrs.) V. W. *The Mediaeval Artist at Work.* Princeton, 1967.

von Einem, H. "Bemerkungen zur Bildhauerdarstellung des Nanni di Banco," *Festschrift für Hans Sedlmayr.* Munich, 1962, 68 ff.

Enlart, C. *Origines Françaises de l'architecture gothique en Italie* ("Bibliothèque des Écoles Françaises d'Athènes et de Rome," 66). Paris, 1894.

Ettlinger, L. D. "A Fifteenth-century View of Florence," *Burlington Magazine*, XCIV (1952), 160 ff.

Falk, I. *Studien zu Andrea Pisano*. Hamburg, 1940.

———, and Länyi, J. "The Genesis of Andrea Pisano's Bronze Doors," *Art Bulletin*, XXV (1943), 132 ff.

Fantani, P. (ed.). *Commento alla Divina Commedia d'anonimo fiorentino del secolo XIV*. Bologna, 1868.

Fineschi, V. *Memorie sopra il cimitero antico della Chiesa di S. Maria Novella*. Florence, 1787.

Follini, V., and Rastrelli, M. *Firenze antica e moderna illustrata*. Florence, 1789 ff.

Fontana, G. *Cento palazzi fra i più celebri di Venezia*. Venice, 1865.

Franceschini, P. "Per Francesco Talenti," *Arte e storia*, XXII (1903), 131 f.

de Francovich, G. "Lorenzo Maitani scultore e i bassorilievi della facciata del Duomo di Orvieto," *Bolletino d'Arte*, II, Vol. VII (1927-28), 366 f.

———. *Benedetto Antelami*. Milan-Florence, 1952.

Frankl, P. *The Gothic*. Princeton, 1960.

Frey, C. *Loggia dei Lanzi*. Berlin, 1885.

Freyhan, R. "The Evolution of the Caritas Figure in the 13th and 14th Centuries," *Journal of the Warburg and Courtauld Institutes*, XI (1948), 68 ff.

Fumi, L. *Il Duomo di Orvieto*. Rome, 1891.

von der Gabelentz, H. *Die kirchliche Kunst im italienischen Mittelalter, ihre Beziehungen zur Kultur und Glaubenslehre*. Strasbourg, 1907.

Gall, E. *Die gotische Baukunst in Frankreich und Deutschland*. Leipzig, 1925.

Gargiolli, G. *L'Arte della Seta in Firenze*. Florence, 1868.

Garzelli, A. R. "Problemi di scultura gotica Senese," *Critica d'Arte*, XII (1966), n.s. fasc. 78, 17 ff.

Gattinoi, G. *Il Campanile di San Marco*. Venice, 1910.

Gaye, G. *Carteggio inedito*. Florence, 1839.

Gelli, G. B. *Venti vite d'artisti*, ed. G. Mancini. Pisa, 1896.

von Geymüller, H. *Friedrich II von Hohenstaufen und die Anfänge der Architektur der Renaissance in Italien*. Munich, 1908.

Ghiberti, L. *Lorenzo Ghibertis Denkwürdigkeiten (I Commentari)*, ed. J. von Schlosser. Berlin, 1912.

Gilbert, C. "The Earliest Guide to Florentine Architecture, 1423," *Mitteilungen des kunsthistorischen Instituts in Florenz*, XIV (1969), 33 ff.

Gioseffi, D. *Giotto architetto*. Milan, 1963.

Godwin, F. G. "An Illustration to the 'De sacrementis' of St. Thomas Aquinas," *Speculum*, XXVI (1951), 609 ff.

Gosebruch, M. "Giotto's Stefaneschi-Altarwerk aus Alt S. Peter in Rom," *Miscellanea Bibliothecae Hertzianae*, Munich, 1961, 104 ff.

———. *Giotto und die Entwicklung des neuzeitlichen Kunstbewußtseins*. Cologne, 1962.

Gozzadini, G. *Delle torri gentilizie di Bologna*. Bologna, 1875.

Gross, W. *Die abendländische Architektur um 1300*. Stuttgart, 1948.

Grote, A. *Studien zur Geschichte der Opera di Santa Reparata zu Florenz im vierzehnten Jahrhundert*. Munich, 1961.

Guasti, C. *La Cupola di Santa Maria del Fiore*. Florence, 1857.

———. *Santa Maria del Fiore*. Florence, 1887. [Cited as Guasti.]

———. "Una giunta e una correzione al mio libro, 'Santa Maria del Fiore,'" *Archivio Storico Italiano*, S. V, Vol. I (1888), 429 ff.

Haart, F. "Art and Freedom in Quattrocento Florence," *Essays in Memory of Karl Lehmann*. New York, 1964, 114 ff.

Haftmann, W. *Das italienische Säulenmonument*. Leipzig-Berlin, 1939.

Hetzer, T. *Giotto — seine Stellung in der europäischen Kunst*. Frankfurt, 1941.

Horn, W. "Das florentiner Baptisterium," *Mitteilungen des kunsthistorischen Instituts in Florenz*, V (1938), 100 ff.

———. "Romanesque Churches in Florence," *Art Bulletin*, XXV (1943), 123 ff.

Houvet, E. *Cathédrale de Chartres: portail nord*. Chelles, 1919.

Hugo of St. Victor. *Speculum de mysteriis Ecclesiae*, in J. P. Migne, ed., *Patrologiae cursus completus series Latina* (Paris, 1844 ff), CLXXVII.

Hutton, E. *The Cosmati*. London, 1950.

Hyman, I. *Fifteenth Century Florentine Studies:*

The Palazzo Medici and a Ledger for the Church of San Lorenzo. Doctoral dissertation, New York University, 1968.

Isermeyer, C. A. *Rahmengliederung und Bildfolge in der Wandmalerei bei Giotto und den Florentiner Malern des 14. Jahrhunderts.* Würzburg, 1937.

Jahn-Rusconi, A. "Il campanile di Giotto," *Emporium,* XIX (1941), 241 ff.

Janson, H. W. *Apes and Ape Lore in the Middle Ages and the Renaissance* ("Studies of the Warburg Institute," XX). London, 1952.

— — —. *The Sculpture of Donatello.* Princeton, 1957.

— — —. "Donatello and the antique," in *Donatello e il suo tempo: Atti dell'VIII Convegno Internazionale di Studi sul Rinascimento,* Florence, 1968, 77 ff.

Jantzen, H. "Giotto und der gotische Stil," in *Das Werk des Künstlers.* 1939-40, 441 ff.

Jaques, R. "Die Ikonographie der Madonna in Trono in der Malerei des Dugento," *Mitteilungen des kunsthistorischen Instituts in Florenz,* V (1937), 1 ff.

Kallab, W. *Vasaristudien.* Vienna, 1908.

Katzenellenbogen, A. *The Sculptural Programs of Chartres Cathedral.* New York, 1959.

— — —. *Allegories of the Virtues and Vices in Mediaeval Art.* New York, 1964.

Kauffmann, H. *Donatello.* Berlin, 1936.

Keller, H. "Der Bildhauer Arnolfo di Cambio und seine Werkstatt," *Jahrbuch der preußischen Kunstsammlungen,* LV (1934), 204 ff, LVI (1935), 22 ff.

— — —. "Die Bauplastik des Sieneser Doms," *Kunstgeschichtliches Jahrbuch der Biblioteca Hertziana,* I (1937), 141 ff.

Kiesow, G. "Zur Baugeschichte des Florentiner Doms," *Mitteilungen des kunsthistorischen Instituts in Florenz,* X (1961), 1 ff.

— — —. "Die gotische Südfassade von S. Maria Novella in Florenz," *Zeitschrift für Kunstgeschichte,* XXV (1962), 1 ff.

Klotz, H. "Deutsche und italienische Baukunst im Trecento," *Mitteilungen des kunsthistorischen Instituts in Florenz,* XII (1966), 173 ff.

Koch, G. F. "Karl Friedrich Schinkel und die Architektur des Mittelalters," *Zeitschrift für Kunstgeschichte,* XXIX (1966), 208 ff.

Körte, W. "Die früheste Wiederholung nach Giottos Navicella (in Jung-St. Peter in Strassburg)," *Oberrheinische Kunst,* X (1942), 97 ff.

Kosegarten, A. "Einige sienesische Darstellungen der Muttergottes aus dem frühen Trecento," *Jahrbuch der Berliner Museen,* VIII (1966), 103 ff.

Kraus, H. *The Living Theatre of Medieval Art.* Bloomington, 1967.

Krautheimer, R. *Early Christian and Byzantine Architecture.* Harmondsworth, 1965.

— — —, and Krautheimer-Hess, T. *Lorenzo Ghiberti.* Princeton, 1956.

— — —, et. al. *Corpus basilicarum Christianarum Romae.* Vatican City, 1939 ff.

Kugler, F. *Geschichte der Baukunst.* Stuttgart, 1859.

Lami, G. *Lezioni di antichità toscane.* Florence, 1766.

Lányi, J. "Andrea Pisano," in Thieme-Becker, *Künstlerlexikon,* XXVII (1933), 97.

— — —. "L'ultima opera di Andrea Pisano," *L'Arte,* n. s. IV, Vol. XXXVI (1933), 204 ff.

de Lasteyrie, R. *L'Architecture religieuse en France à l'époque gothique,* ed. M. Aubert. Paris, 1926 f.

Lensi, A. *Palazzo Vecchio.* Milan, 1929.

Limburger, W. *Die Gebäude von Florenz.* Leipzig, 1910.

Loessel, S. B. *S. Maria in Vescovio.* Master's thesis, New York University, 1942.

di Longhi, L. F. *L'architettura delle chiese Cistercensi italiane.* Milan, 1958.

Longhurst, M. H. *Notes on Italian Monuments of the 12th to 16th Centuries,* ed. I Lowe. London, 1962.

Longfellow, H. W. *Flower-de-Luce.* London, 1867.

Lupi, C. "La casa pisana e i suoi annessi nel medio evo," *Archivio Storico Italiano,* s. V, Vol. XXVII (1901), 264 ff.

Lusini, V. *Il Duomo di Siena.* Siena, 1911.

Mackowski, H. "San Miniato al Tedesco," *Zeitschrift für Bildende Kunst,* n. s. XIV (1903), 168 ff.

Mâle, E. *L'Art religieux du XIIIe siècle en France.* Paris, 1931.

Manni, D. "Notizie istoriche intorno ad Antonio Pucci," *Delizie degli Eruditi Toscani,* III (1771), iii ff.

Marchini, G. *Il Duomo di Prato*. Milan, 1957.

— — —. *Il tesoro del Duomo di Prato*. Milan, 1963.

van Marle, R. *Iconographie de l'art profane au moyen-age et à la renaissance*. La Haye, 1932.

McCarthy, M. *The Stones of Florence*. New York, 1957.

Meiss, M. Review of F. Antal, *Florentine Painting and Its Social Background* (London, 1947), in *Art Bulletin*, XXXI (1949), 143 ff.

— — —. *Painting in Florence and Siena after the Black Death*. Princeton, 1951.

Metz, P. "Die Florentiner Domfassade des Arnolfo di Cambio," *Jahrbuch der preußischen Kunstsammlungen*, LIX (1938), 121 ff.

Middeldorf, U. Review of H. Kauffmann, *Donatello* (Berlin, 1936), in *Art Bulletin*, XVIII (1936), 570 ff.

del Migliore, F. L. *Firenze, città nobilissima*. Florence, 1684.

Milanesi, G. *Documenti per la storia dell'arte senese*. Siena, 1854.

Molini, G. *La metropolitana fiorentina*. Florence, 1820.

Mommsen, T. E. "Petrarch and the Decoration of the 'Sala virorum illustrium' in Padua," *Art Bulletin*, XXXIV (1952), 95 ff.

Montaigne, M. *Journal du voyage en Italie, 1580-81*, ed. M. Rat. Paris, 1955.

Mori, A., and Boffito, G. *Firenze nelle vedute e piante*. Florence, 1926.

Moschella, P. "Le case a sporti in Firenze," *Palladio*, VI (1942), 167 ff.

Mothes, O. *Geschichte der Baukunst und Bildhauerei Venedigs*. Leipzig, 1859.

Müntz, E. *Les Précurseurs de la renaissance*. Paris, 1882.

— — —. *Florence et la Toscane*. Paris, 1897.

Murray, P. "Notes on Some Early Giotto Sources," *Journal of the Warburg and Courtauld Institutes*, XVI (1953), 58 ff.

Musée des arts décoratifs, *Vitraux de France du XIe au XVIe siècle*, ed. J. Guerin. Paris, 1953.

Nardini, A. *Il Campanile di Santa Maria del Fiore*. Florence, 1885. [Cited as Nardini.]

Nicco Fasola, G. *La Fontana di Perugia*. Rome, 1951.

Notizie istorico-genealogiche appartenenti alla nobilità e cittadinanza. Naples, 1953.

Oertel, R. "Wende der Giotto-Forschung," *Zeitschrift für Kunstgeschichte*, XI (1943-44), 6 ff.

— — —. *Die Frühzeit der italienischen Malerei*. Stuttgart, 1966.

Offner, R. *A Critical and Historical Corpus of Florentine Painting*. New York, 1930 ff (late volumes with K. Steinweg).

Orlandi, S. *Necrologio di S. Maria Novella*. Florence, 1955.

Paatz, W. "Zur Baugeschichte des Palazzo del Podestà (Bargello) in Florenz," *Mitteilungen des kunsthistorischen Instituts in Florenz*, III (1931), 308 ff.

— — —. *Werden und Wesen der Trecento-Architektur in Toskana*. Burg, 1937.

— — —. "Die Gestalt Giottos im Spiegel einer zeitgenössischen Urkunde," *Eine Gabe der Freunde für Carl Georg Heise*, Berlin, 1950, 55 ff.

— — —, and Paatz, E. *Die Kirchen von Florenz*. Frankfurt, 1940 ff. [Cited as Paatz.]

Palmieri, M. *Matthei Palmerii Liber de temporibus*, in L. A. Muratori, ed., *Rerum italicarum scriptores* (n.s. ed. G. Carducci and V. Fiorini). Città di Castello, 1906, XXVI, 113.

Panofsky, E. *Gothic Architecture and Scholasticism*. Latrobe, Pa., 1951.

— — —. *Early Netherlandisch Painting: Its Origins and Character*. Cambridge, Mass., 1953.

— — —. *The First Page of Giorgio Vasari's 'Libro,'"* in *Meaning in the Visual Arts*, New York, 1955, 176 ff.

— — —. *Renaissance and Renascences in Western Art*. Stockholm, 1960.

Passerini. Ms. 162, Biblioteca Nazionale, Florence.

— — —. Ms. 192, Biblioteca Nazionale, Florence.

Patzak, B. *Palast und Villa in Toskana*. Leipzig, 1912.

Paul, J. *Die mittelalterlichen Kommunalpaläste in Italien*. Dresden, 1963.

— — —. *Der Palazzo Vecchio in Florenz: Ursprung und Bedeutung seiner Form*. Florence, 1969.

Pera, L. *Il razionalismo e l'architettura pisana*. Pisa, 1936.

Petrarch, F. "Le 'De viris illustribus' de Pétrarque," ed. P. de Nolhac, in *Notices et extraits des manuscrits de la Bibliothèque Nationale*, XXXIV (Paris, 1891), 134 ff.

Planiscig, L. "Die Bildhauer Venedigs in der ersten Hälfte des Quattrocento," *Jahrbuch der kunsthistorischen Sammlungen in Wien,* n.s. IV (1930), 71 ff.

Poggi, G. *Il Duomo di Firenze.* Berlin, 1909.

Poligrafo Gargani, No. 1968, Ms. in Biblioteca Nazionale, Florence.

———, No. 1970, Ms. in Biblioteca Nazionale, Florence.

Pope-Hennessy, J. *Italian Gothic Sculpture.* London, 1955.

———. *Catalogue of Italian Sculpture in the Victoria and Albert Museum.* London, 1964.

Porter, A. K. *Lombard Architecture.* New Haven-London, 1917.

Pucci, A. *Il centiloquio, che contiene la cronica di Giovanni Villani in terza rima,* in I. di San Luigi, ed., *Delizie degli eruditi toscani,* VI (1775), 119 ff.

Richa, G. *Notizie istoriche delle chiese fiorentine.* Florence, 1754 ff.

Richter, M. "Die 'Terra murata' im florentinischen Gebiet," *Mitteilungen des kunsthistorischen Instiutes in Florenz,* V (1940), 373 ff.

Ridolfi, E. *L'arte in Lucca studiata nella sua cattedrale.* Lucca, 1882.

Rintelen, F. *Giotto und die Giotto-Apokryphen.* Munich-Leipzig, 1912.

Rivoira, G. T. *Lombardic Architecture: Its Origin, Development and Derivitives.* London, 1910.

Robinson, J. H., and Rolfe, H. W. *Petrarch.* New York, 1914.

Rocchi, E. *Le fonti storiche dell'architettura militare.* Rome, 1908.

Rodolico, F. *Le pietre delle città d'Italia.* Florence, 1953.

———, and Marchini, G. *I palazzi del popolo nei comuni toscani del medio evo.* Florence, 1962.

Rohault de Fleury, G. *Les Monuments du Pise au moyen age.* Paris, 1866.

———. *Toscane au moyen age: Architecture civile et militaire.* Paris, 1870-73.

Romanini, A. M. *L'architettura gotica in Lombardia.* Milan, 1964.

———. "Giotto e l'architettura gotica in alta Italia," *Bolletino d'Arte,* III-IV (1965), 160 ff.

Rossi, G., and Salerni, G. *I capitelli del Palazzo Ducale di Venezia.* Venice, 1952.

Rubenstein, N. "The Beginnings of Political Thought in Florence," *Journal of the Warburg and Courtauld Institutes,* V (1942), 198 ff.

———. "Political Ideas in Sienese Art: The Frescoes by Ambrogio Lorenzetti and Taddeo di Bartolo in the Palazzo Pubblico," *Journal of the Warburg and Courtauld Institutes,* XXI (1958), 179 ff.

———. *The Government of Florence under the Medici.* Oxford, 1966.

von Rumohr, C. F. *Italienische Forschungen.* Berlin, 1827.

Runge, L. *Der Glockenturm des Dom zu Florenz.* Berlin, 1853.

Ruskin, J. *Mornings in Florence.* New York, 1903.

Saalman, H. "Santa Maria del Fiore:1294-1418," *Art Bulletin,* XLVI (1964), 478.

———. "The Palazzo Comunale in Montepulciano," *Zeitschrift für Kunstgeschichte,* XXVIII (1965), 1 ff.

———. *The Church of Santa Trinita in Florence.* New York, 1966.

———. *The Bigallo.* New York, 1969.

Salmi, M. *L'architettura romanica in Toscana.* Milan-Rome, 1927.

———. *L'Abbazia di Pomposa.* Rome, 1936.

———. "Arnolfo di Cambio," in *Encyclopedia of World Art,* I. New York, 1959, 762.

Salvini, R. "Arnolfo e la Cupola di S. Maria del Fiore," in *Atti del 1° Congresso Nazionale di Storia dell'Architettura,* Florence, 1936, 31 ff.

———. *Giotto Bibliografia.* Rome, 1938.

Sanpaolesi, P. *Il Campanile di Pisa.* Pisa, 1956.

Ṣantani, P. "Società delle torri in Firenze," *Archivio Storico Italiano,* IV, Vol. XX (1887), 25 ff, 178 ff.

Sauer, J. *Symbolik des Kirchengebäudes und seiner Ausstattung in der Auffassung des Mittelalters.* Freiburg, 1924.

Sauerländer, W. *Von Sens bis Strassburg.* Berlin, 1966.

Schapiro, M. Review of J. C. Webster, *The Labors of the Months in Antique and Mediaeval Art (Princeton, 1938),* in *Speculum,* XVI (1941), 134 ff.

Schevill, F. *History of Florence.* New York, 1936 (new ed. 1963).

Schiaparelli, A. *La casa fiorentina e i suoi arredi nei secoli XIV e XV.* Florence, 1908.

Schlegel, U. "Zum Bildprogramm der Arena-Kapelle," *Zeitschrift für Kunstgeschichte*, XX (1957), 130 ff.

von Schlosser, J. "Giusto's Fresken in Padua und die Vorläufer der Stanza della Segnatura," *Jahrbuch der kunsthistorischen Sammlungen des allerhöchsten Kaiserhauses*, XVII (1896), 13 ff.

———. *Die Kunstliteratur*. Vienna, 1924.

Schnasse, C. *Geschichte der bildenden Künste im Mittelalter*. Düsseldorf, 1876.

Selvatico, P. *Storia estetico-critica delle arti del Disegno*. Venice, 1852-56.

Serafini, A. *Torri campanarie di Roma e del Lazio nel medioevo*. Rome, 1927.

Sercambi, G. *Croniche*, in Istituto Storico per il Medio Evo, *Fonti per la storia d'Italia*, XX, Roma, 1892.

Seznek, J. *The Survival of the Pagan Gods*, tr. B. Sessions. New York, 1961.

Sgrilli, B. S. *Descrizione e studi dell'insigne fabbrica di S. Maria del Fiore*. Florence, 1733.

Siebenhüner, H. "Simone Talenti," in Thieme-Becker, *Künstlerlexikon*, XXXII (1938), 416.

Steger, H. *David Rex et Propheta*. Nürnberg, 1961.

Stubblebine, J. H. "The Development of the Throne in Tuscan Dugento Painting," *Marsyas*, VII (1957), 25 ff.

Swarzenski, G. *Nicolo Pisano*. Frankfurt, 1926.

Tanfani, L. *Della chiesa di S. Maria del Pontenovo, detta della Spina*. Pisa, 1871.

Telpaz, A. M. "Some Antique Motifs in Trecento Art," *Art Bulletin*, XLVI (1964), 372 ff.

Thomas, W. *The History of Italy (1549)*, ed. G. Parks. Ithaca, 1963.

Tintori, L. and Meiss, M. "Additional Observations on Italian Mural Technique," *Art Bulletin*, XLVI (1964), 377 ff.

Toesca, I. *Andrea e Nino Pisano*. Florence, 1950.

Toesca, P. *Il Trecento*. Turin, 1951.

de Tolnay, C. *The Youth of Michelangelo*. Princeton, 1943.

della Tosa, S. *Annali*, ed. D. Manni. Florence, 1733.

Touring Club Italiano. *Umbria*. Milan, 1950.

Toy, S. *A History of Fortification*. London, 1955.

Trachtenberg, M. *The Planning of Florence Cathedral from 1296 to 1366/67*. Master's thesis, New York University, 1963.

Valentiner, A. "Giovanni Balducci a Firenze e una scultura di Maso," *L'Arte*, XXXVIII (1935), 3 ff.

———. "Andrea Pisano as a Marble Sculptor," *Art Quarterly*, X (1947), 163 ff.

Vasari, G. *Le Vite de' più eccellenti architetti, pittori, e scultori italiani*, first edition, Florence, 1550 (ed. C. Ricci, Milan-Rome, 1927).

———. *Le Vite . . .*, second edition, Florence, 1568 (ed. G. Milanesi, Florence, 1878 ff). [Cited as Vasari.]

———. *Le Vite . . .*, ed. K. Frey, I, 1. Munich, 1911. [Cited as Vasari-Frey.]

———. *Die Lebensbeschreibungen*, ed. A. Gottschewski. Strasbourg, 1906.

Venturi, A. *Storia dell'arte italiana*. Milan, 1901 ff.

Villani, G. *Cronica*. Florence, 1844. [Cited as Villani.]

Viollet-le-Duc, M. *Dictionnaire raisonné de l'architecture française du XIᵉ au XVIᵉ siècle*. Paris, 1864.

Vitry, P. *La Cathédrale de Reims*. Paris, 1919.

Wagner-Reiger, R. *Die italienische Baukunst zu Beginn der Gotik*. Cologne, 1957.

Webster, J. C. *The Labors of the Months in Antique and Mediaeval Art*. Princeton, 1938.

Weinberger, M. "The First Façade of the Cathedral of Florence," *Journal of the Warburg and Courtauld Institutes*, IV (1940-41), 67 ff.

———. "Remarks on the Role of French Models within the Evolution of Gothic Tuscan Sculpture," *Acts of the Twentieth International Congress on the History of Art*, Princeton, 1963, I, 198 ff.

Wentzel, H. "Italienische Siegelstempel und Siegel all'antico im 13. und 14. Jahrhundert," *Mitteilungen des kunsthistorischen Instituts in Florenz*, VII (1955), 73 ff.

White, J. *The Birth and Rebirth of Pictorial Space*. London, 1957.

———. "The Reliefs of the Façade at the Duomo of Orvieto," *Journal of the Warburg and Courtauld Institutes*, XXII (1959), 255 ff.

———. *Art and Architecture in Italy, 1250-1400*. Baltimore, 1966.

Wiernozowski, H. "Art and the Commune in the Time of Dante," *Speculum*, XIX (1944), 14 ff.

Wills, H. *Florentine Heraldry: A Supplement to the Guide-books*. London, 1900.

Wood-Brown, J. *The Builders of Florence.* London, 1907.

Wundram, M. "Studien zur künstlerischen Herkunft Andrea Pisanos," *Mitteilungen des kunsthistorischen Instituts* in Florenz, VIII (1957-59), 199 ff.

Zanotto, F. *Il Palazzo Ducale di Venezia.* Venice, 1853.

Photograph Credits

Photographs not listed below are by the author.

Alber Verlag, Freiburg i. Br.: 167

Alinari, Florence: 5, 23, 65, 67, 124, 128, 149, 150, 157, 165, 175, 176, 192, 198, 209, 212, 223, 237, 238, 241, 249, 257, 258, 268, 269, 270, 275, 276, 279, 281, 285, 289, 301, 306, 308, 309, 312, 313, 314, 317, 319, 327, 336, 337, 338.

Anderson, Rome: 126, 133, 136, 137, 140, 141, 142, 143, 144, 145, 146, 153, 156, 168, 240, 304, 310, 316, 318.

Archphoto, Florence: 27, 28, 29.

Barsotti, Florence: 325.

British Museum: 220.

Brogi, Florence: 129, 130, 131, 132, 166, 178, 181, 182, 183, 184, 185, 186, 188, 190, 191, 210, 211, 239, 284, 305, 335.

Fotocielo, Rome: 3

Gabinetto Fotografico Nazionale, Rome: 221.

Heinrich Klotz: 34, 36, 112, 205, 206, 315.

Kunsthistorisches Institut, Florence: 177, 207, 261, 288, 311.

Manelli, Florence: 330, 331, 334.

Museo Civico, Padua: 147, 154, 155.

National Gallery, London: 286.

Pierpont Morgan Library, New York: 1, 4, 300, 320.

Scala, Florence: frontispiece, I, II, VII, VIII, IX.

Sopr. ai Monumenti, Florence: 246.

Sopr. alle Gallerie, Florence: 159, 202, 203, 291, 292, 298.

Sopr., Venice: 152.

Staatliche Museen, Berlin: 287.

Vatican Museum: 169, 170.

Index

Illustrations

I   Giotto and Andrea Pisano: Lower Campanile

II   Giotto: First zone, Campanile

III *Giotto and Andrea Pisano:*
Cornices, first zone, Campanile

V *Giotto: First zone, Campanile. Intarsia*

IV *Andrea Pisano:*
Niche section, Campanile. Detail

VI *Giotto: First zone, Campanile. Florentine Lily*

VII   Francesco Talenti: Bifora zones, Campanile

VIII   *Francesco Talenti: Trifora zone, Campanile*

IX   Giotto's Campanile project,
Museo dell'Opera del Duomo, Siena

X   Giotto, Andrea Pisano,
and Francesco Talenti:
Campanile. Chambers and stairway system
(drawing by P. Waddy)

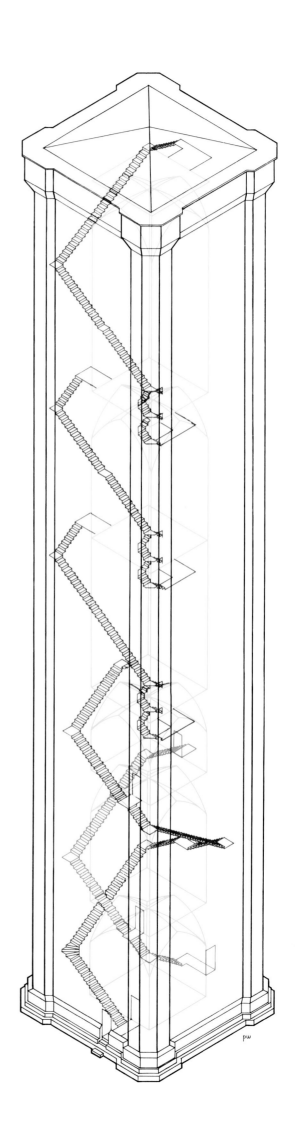

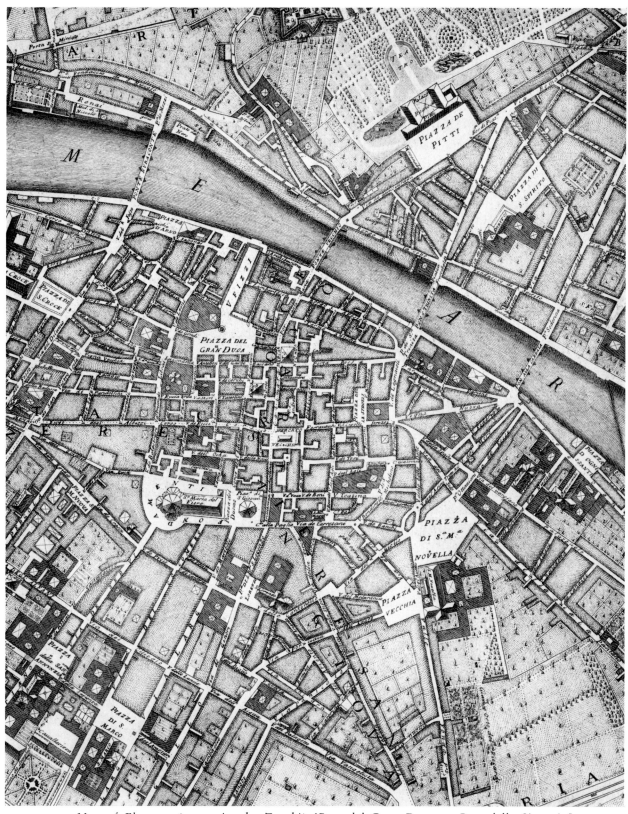

1   Map of Florence (engraving by Zocchi) [Pza. del Gran Duca = Pza. della Signoria]

2   *View of Florence (from the Fortezza del Belvedere)*

3   *Aerial view of Florence (from over the Arno)*

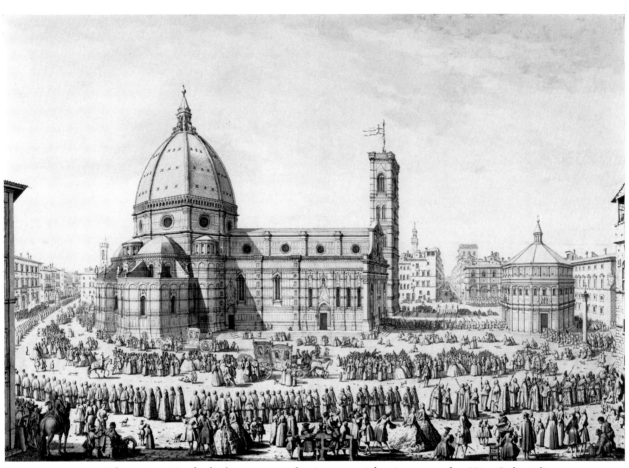

4   *Florentine Cathedral group and piazza, with view up the Via Calzaioli*
(drawing by Zocchi, Pierpont Morgan Library, New York)

5   *Giotto, Andrea Pisano, Francesco Talenti: Campanile (from the southeast)*

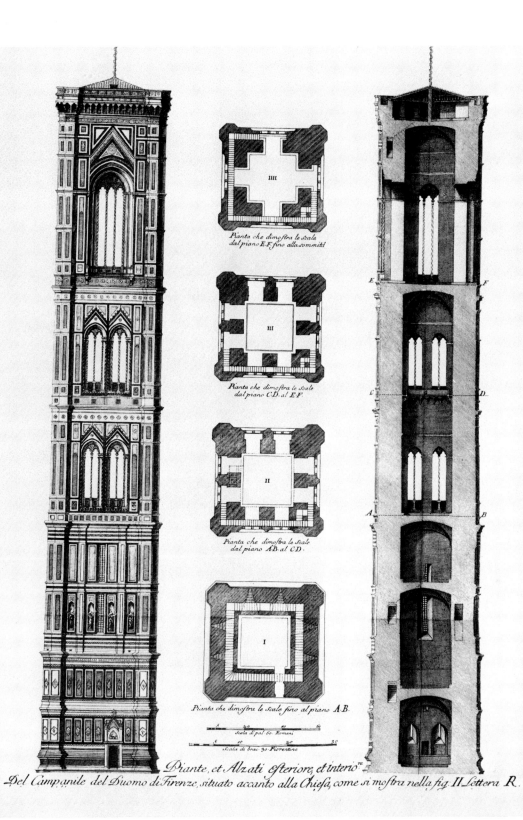

Pianta che dimostra le scale
dal piano E.F. fino alla sommità

Pianta che dimostra le scale
dal piano C.D. al E.F.

Pianta che dimostra le scale
dal piano A.B. al C.D.

Pianta che dimostra le scale fino al piano A.B.

Scala di pal. 60. Romani

Scala di brac. 30. Fiorentine

Piante, et Alzati esteriore, et interiore
Del Campanile del Duomo di Firenze, situato accanto alla Chiesa, come si mostra nella fig. II Lettera R.

6   Giotto, Andrea Pisano, Francesco Talenti: Campanile. Elevation, plans, and cross section
(engraving by Sgrilli)

7   *Giotto and Andrea Pisano: First and second zones, Campanile*

8   *Giotto: First zone, Campanile. Corner detail*

9　Giotto: First zone, Campanile (from above)

10   *Giotto and Andrea Pisano: Cornices, first zone, Campanile*

11   Giotto: First zone, Campanile. First cornice

12   Giotto: First zone, Campanile. First cornice

13 *Andrea Pisano: Second cornice, first zone, Campanile*

14 *Andrea Pisano: Second cornice, first zone, and intarsia, Campanile*

15   *Andrea Pisano: Second zone, Campanile. Relief paneling*

16   *Andrea Pisano: Second zone, Campanile. Cornice*

17   *Andrea Pisano: Second zone, Campanile. Leafwork, detail of cornice*

18   *Andrea Pisano: Second zone, Campanile. Leafwork, detail of cornice*

19   *Andrea Pisano: Niche section, Campanile*

20   *Andrea Pisano: Niche section,*
     Campanile. Cornice

21   *Andrea Pisano: Niche section,*
     Campanile. Detail of upper part

22 *Andrea Pisano and Francesco Talenti: Niche section and upper Campanile*

23   *Andrea Pisano: Niche section, Campanile. West face (sculpture by Donatello
and Nanni di Bartolo)*

24   *Andrea Pisano: Niche section, Campanile. Center detail*

25   *Giotto and Andrea Pisano: First chamber, Campanile. South side*

26   *Giotto and Andrea Pisano: First chamber, Campanile. West side*

27   Giotto and Andrea Pisano: First chamber, Campanile. South side, east niche.
Intonaco removal, April 1969

28   Detail (left) of Fig. 27   29   Detail (right) of Fig. 27

30 *Andrea Pisano: Steep window beneath vaults, west wall,*
first chamber, Campanile

31 *Giotto and Andrea Pisano: First chamber, Campanile. Canted window, north side, east niche*

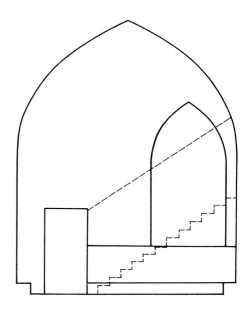

33 *Giotto and Andrea Pisano: First chamber,*
    Campanile. Schematic elevation
    of east side, with position of stair

32 *Giotto and Andrea Pisano: Ground story,*
    Campanile. Cross section, through center,
    looking south (bonding of masonry shells not
    indicated) (drawing by L. Bier)

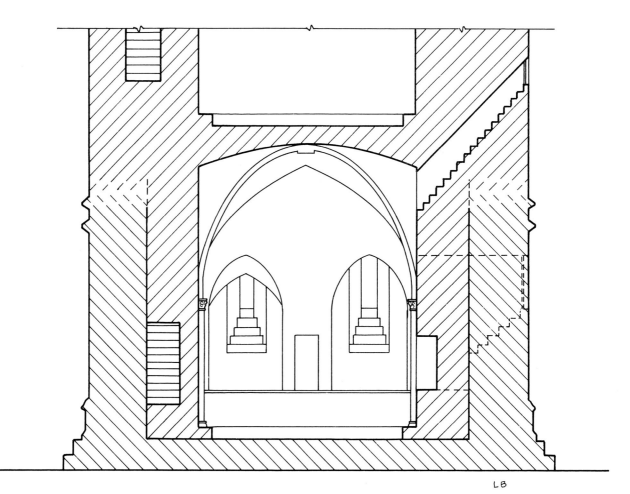

0 1 2 3 4 5 6 7 8 9 10

SCALE IN BRACCIA

GIOTTO

ANDREA PISANO

34 *Andrea Pisano: Main stairway, Campanile.*
First flight (looking south)

35 *Giotto and Andrea Pisano:*
First chamber, Campanile.
Southeast corner

36 *Andrea Pisano: Main stairway, Campanile. Third flight (looking south)*

37   Andrea Pisano: Colonnette base, first chamber, Campanile

38   Andrea Pisano: Colonnette base, first chamber, Campanile

39 *Andrea Pisano: Capital (prototype),*
first chamber, Campanile

40 *Andrea Pisano: Capital,*
first chamber, Campanile

41 *Andrea Pisano: Capital,*
first chamber, Campanile

42 *Andrea Pisano: Capital,*
first chamber, Campanile

43 Andrea Pisano (?): Keystone, first chamber, Campanile

44 Andrea Pisano: Corner detail, first chamber, Campanile

45 Andrea Pisano: Leaf decoration of central pier, first chamber, Campanile

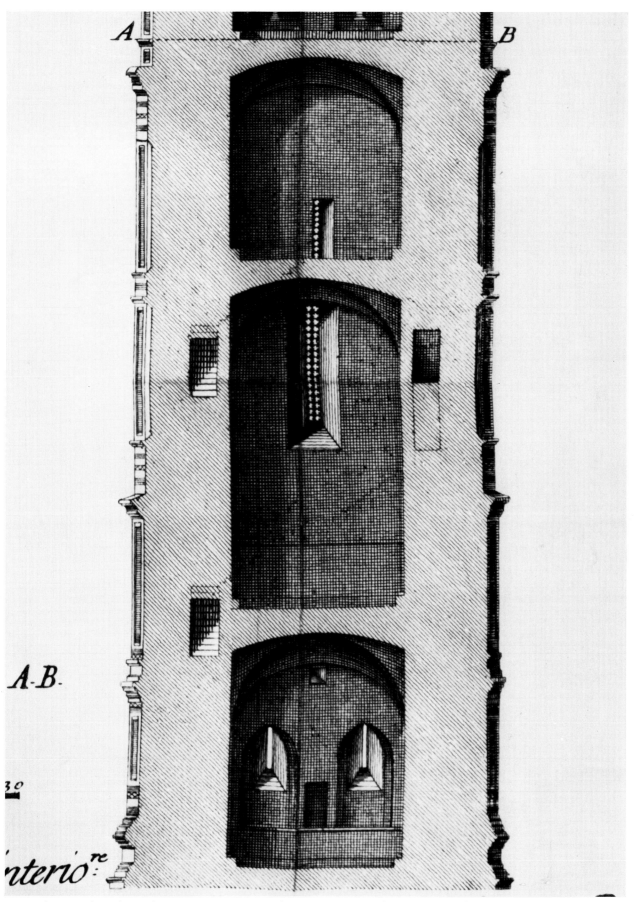

A

B

A·B·

3 0

ˈnteriōᵣₑ

46 *Giotto and Andrea Pisano: Lower Campanile. Cross section, through center, looking west (detail of Fig. 6)*

47 *Andrea Pisano: Second chamber,*
Campanile. East and south sides

48 *Andrea Pisano: Second chamber,*
Campanile. North and east sides

49   *Andrea Pisano: Second chamber, Campanile. Vaulting*

50   *Andrea Pisano: Second chamber, Campanile. "Venetian" window*

51   *Andrea Pisano: Second chamber, Campanile. Colonnette*

52 *Andrea Pisano: Second chamber, Campanile. Colonnette base and ledge*

53   *Andrea Pisano: Second chamber, Campanile. Colonnette base and ledge*

54   *Andrea Pisano: Second chamber,*
     Campanile. Capital

55   *Andrea Pisano: Second chamber, Campanile. Capital*

56   *Andrea Pisano: Second chamber, Campanile.*
     Capital

57   *Andrea Pisano: Second chamber, Campanile.*
     Capital

58   Andrea Pisano: Second chamber,
        Campanile. Keystone

59   Andrea Pisano and Francesco Talenti:
        Third chamber, Campanile. Vaulting

60   *Giotto and Andrea Pisano. First and second zones, Campanile. East face*

61 *Andrea Pisano and Francesco Talenti (?): Street portal, Campanile*

62   *Andrea Pisano and Francesco Talenti (?): Street portal, Campanile. Detail, left*

63 *Francesco Talenti (?): Gable,*
street portal, Campanile

64 *Andrea Pisano and Francesco Talenti (?):*
Street portal, Campanile. Cornice detail, right

65 *Andrea Pisano: Tympanum, street portal, Campanile*

66   *View between Cathedral and Campanile*

67   *Andrea Pisano: Elevated portal, Campanile*

68 Francesco Talenti workshop: Elevated portal, Florence Duomo

69 Andrea da Firenze: The Church Triumphant,
Spanish Chapel, S. Maria Novella, Florence. Detail showing Campanile

70 *Francesco Talenti: Upper Campanile*

71   *Francesco Talenti: Lower Bifora zone, Campanile*

72   *Francesco Talenti: Upper Bifora zone, Campanile*

73   Francesco Talenti: Lower Bifora zone, Campanile. Windows

74 *Francesco Talenti: Upper Bifora zone, Campanile. Tracery and gable*

75 *Francesco Talenti: Lower Bifora zone, Campanile. Tracery and gable*

76   *Francesco Talenti: Lower Bifora zone, Campanile. Capitals*

77   Andrea Pisano and Francesco Talenti:
Niche-section cornice and detail of lower Bifora zone, Campanile

78   *Francesco Talenti: Bifora zones, Campanile. Detail between the two zones (from below)*

79 Francesco Talenti: *Bifora zones, Campanile. Detail between the two zones*

80 *Francesco Talenti: Upper Bifora zone, Campanile. Cornice*

81 *Francesco Talenti: Trifora zone, Campanile. Corner detail*

82 Francesco Talenti: Trifora zone, Campanile. Tracery (south face)

83 Francesco Talenti: Trifora zone, Campanile. Balustrade (south face)

84   Francesco Talenti: Trifora zone, Campanile. Gable, carying angel (south face)

85   *Francesco Talenti: Ballatoio, Campanile. Corner detail*

86   *Francesco Talenti: Ballatoio, Campanile. Platform*

87   *Francesco Talenti: Trifora zone, Campanile. Tracery (east face)*

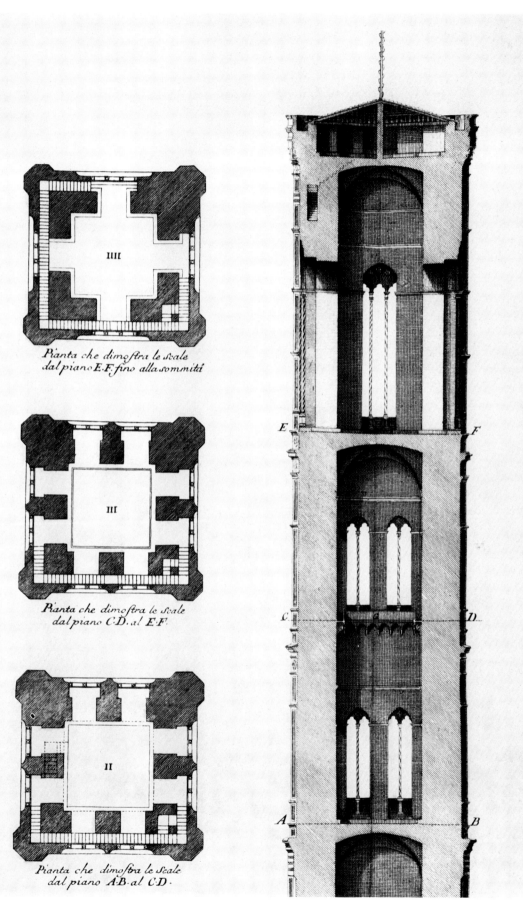

*Pianta che dimostra le scale
dal piano E·F· fino alla sommità*

*Pianta che dimostra le scale
dal piano C·D· al E·F·*

*Pianta che dimostra le scale
dal piano A·B· al C·D·*

88   *Francesco Talenti: Upper Campanile. Cross section and plans (detail of Fig. 6)*

89   *Francesco Talenti: Bifora section, Campanile. Interior (view up)*

90   *Francesco Talenti: Bifora section, Campanile. Interior (view down)*

91   Francesco Talenti: Lower Bifora zone, Campanile. Interior view

92 *Francesco Talenti: Lower Bifora zone, Campanile.
Second stringcourse (without capital)*

93 *Francesco Talenti: Lower Bifora zone, Campanile.
First stringcourse (with capital)*

94 *Francesco Talenti:
Trifora zone, Campanile. Respond base*

95 *Francesco Talenti:
Upper Bifora zone, Campanile. Respond base*

96 *Francesco Talenti:
Lower Bifora zone, Campanile. Respond base*

97   Francesco Talenti:
Upper Bifora zone, Campanile. Interior corner

98   Francesco Talenti: Bifora section, Campanile. Ballatoio

99   *Francesco Talenti:*
Upper Bifora zone, Campanile. Vaulting

100   Francesco Talenti: Bifora section, Campanile. Ballatoio (from below)

102 *Francesco Talenti: Upper Bifora zone, Campanile. Tracery (from inside)*

101 *Francesco Talenti: Lower Bifora zone, Campanile. Window chamber (view up)*

103 *Francesco Talenti: Lower Bifora zone, Campanile. Base, window chamber*

104 *Francesco Talenti: Lower Bifora zone, Campanile. Tracery base*

105 *Francesco Talenti: Lower Bifora zone, Campanile. Twisted column*

106 *Francesco Talenti: Upper Bifora zone, Campanile. Twisted column*

107   Francesco Talenti: Trifora zone, Campanile. Pier

108   *Francesco Talenti: Trifora zone, Campanile. Window and pier*

109   *Francesco Talenti: Trifora zone, Campanile. Window chamber (view up)*

110   *Francesco Talenti: Trifora zone, Campanile. Detail of window stringcourse*

111   Francesco Talenti: Trifora zone, Campanile. Pier (from belfry)

112　Francesco Talenti: Trifora zone, Campanile. Belfry

113　Francesco Talenti: Trifora zone, Campanile. Pier (from belfry)

114 *Francesco Talenti: Stump for spire (southeast), Campanile*

115 *Francesco Talenti: Trifora zone, Campanile. Belfry stringcourse*

116 *Francesco Talenti: Stump for spire (southwest), Campanile*

117 *Francesco Talenti: Trifora zone, Campanile. Vaulting*

118 Francesco Talenti:
Section of frontispiece from lower Bifora
zone, and capital from upper Bifora zone
of Campanile, Museo dell'Opera del
Duomo, Florence (left)

119 Andrea Pisano: Capital from Campanile
niche, Museo dell'Opera del Duomo,
Florence (below)

120   Francesco Talenti: Capital from Trifora zone of Campanile, Museo dell'Opera del Duomo, Florence

*121   Francesco Talenti: Rosette from cornice of lower Bifora zone of Campanile,
Museo dell'Opera del Duomo, Florence*

122   Francesco Talenti: Tracery from Trifora zone of Campanile,
Museo dell'Opera del Duomo, Florence

123   Francesco Talenti: Stringcourse section from Trifora zone of Campanile
(resting on a Renaissance capital), Museo dell'Opera del Duomo, Florence

124   *Andrea Pisano and Francesco Talenti (?): Street portal, Campanile (before restoration)*

125   Giotto and Andrea Pisano: First and second zones, Campanile. Detail (west face)

126 Giotto and Andrea Pisano: Relief and niche zones, Campanile. South face

127 Giotto-Andrea Pisano workshop:
Noah, *first zone (west face), Campanile*

128 Giotto-Andrea Pisano workshop:
Gionitus, *first zone (south face), Campanile*

129 Giotto-Andrea Pisano workshop:
Phoroneus, *first zone (south face), Campanile*

130 Giotto-Andrea Pisano workshop:
Daedalus, *first zone (south face), Campanile*

131   *Giotto-Andrea Pisano workshop:* Weaving, *first zone (south face), Campanile*

132   Giotto-Andrea Pisano workshop: Hercules and Cacus, *first zone (east face), Campanile*

133 *Giotto's Campanile project,*
Museo dell'Opera del Duomo,
Siena. Lower part

134 *Giotto's Campanile project,*
Museo dell'Opera del Duomo,
Siena. Upper part

135 *Giotto's Campanile project, first zone (detail of Fig. 133)*

136 *Giotto's Campanile project, first and second zones (detail of Fig. 133)*

137 Giotto's Campanile project, monofora zone (detail of Fig. 133)

138   Giotto's Campanile project, cornice of triple bifora zone (detail of Fig. 134)

139   Giotto's Campanile project, ballatoio (detail of Fig. 133)

140   *Giotto's Campanile project, double bifora windows (detail of Fig. 133)*

141   *Giotto's Campanile project, single bifora window (detail of Fig. 133)*

142 *Giotto's Campanile project, triple bifora zone (detail of Fig. 134)*

143 *Giotto's Campanile project, octagon (detail of Fig. 134)*

*144   Giotto's Campanile project, St. Michael
(detail of Fig. 134)*

*145   Giotto's Campanile project, angel,
left (detail of Fig. 134)*

*146   Giotto's Campanile project, angel,
right (detail of Fig. 134)*

147   Giotto: Arena Chapel, Padua. Detail (north wall)

148   Giotto: *Arena Chapel, Padua (looking west)*

149　*Giotto: Arena Chapel, Padua.*
Framework detail

150　*Giotto: Arena Chapel, Padua.*
Framework detail

151   *Giotto workshop or following: Chapel vault, Bargello, Florence*

152   *Giotto: Arena Chapel, Padua. Illusionistic cornice of socle*

153   *Giotto, Arena Chapel, Padua. Illusionistic pier (entrance-wall corner)*

154   *Giotto: Arena Chapel, Padua. Illusionistic chapel (east wall, left)*

155   Giotto: Arena Chapel, Padua. Illusionistic chapel (east wall, right)

156   Giotto: Arena Chapel, Padua. Canopy (detail of Last Supper)

*157   Giotto: Arena Chapel, Padua. Canopy
(detail of* Pentacost)

158   Giotto: St. Claire,
*Bardi Chapel, S. Croce,
Florence. Detail*

159   *Giotto: Frescoes, Peruzzi Chapel, S. Croce, Florence*

160 Florence Baptistery. Gallery

161 Florence Baptistery (from the northwest)

162 *Giovanni Pisano: Façade, Siena Duomo.*
Cornicework

163 *Florence Baptistery. Attic*

164   *Arnolfo di Cambio: Socle of Florence Duomo, opposite Campanile*

165　*Cimabue: S. Trinità* Madonna, *Uffizi,*
Florence. Throne detail

166　*Duccio: Rucellai* Madonna, *Uffizi,*
Florence. Throne detail

168   *Ugolino di Vieri: Reliquary of the Holy Corporal, Orvieto Duomo*

167   *Freiburg Münster. West tower*

170   *Model of Stefaneschi Altarpiece (detail of Fig. 169)*

169   *Giotto workshop: St. Peter Enthroned,*
Stefaneschi Altarpiece, Pinacoteca Vaticana

171   Reliquary fragment, Bargello, Florence

172   Reliquary fragment, Bargello, Florence

173   Fra Jacopo Talenti (?): Chiostro Verde,
S. Maria Novella, Florence. Base

174   Arnolfo di Cambio (?): Palazzo Vecchio,
Florence. Window

175 *Mercato Vecchio, Florence (destroyed)*

176 *Giotto:* Caritas, *Arena Chapel, Padua*

177 *Donatello:* Abbondanza (*or* Dovizia), *seen in a late 16th century (?) view of the Mercato Vecchio, Florence*

178   Andrea Pisano: Bronze door, south portal, Florence Baptistery

179   *Andrea Pisano: Bronze door, Florence Baptistery. Framework detail*

180   *Andrea Pisano: Bronze door, Florence Baptistery.*
Framework detail

181 *Andrea Pisano: Bronze door, Florence Baptistery. Canopy*
(*detail of* Namegiving)

182 *Andrea Pisano: Bronze door, Florence Baptistery.*
Canopy (*detail of* Entombment)

183 *Andrea Pisano: Bronze door,*
Florence Baptistery.
Presentation of the Head of St. John

184 *Andrea Pisano: Bronze door,*
Florence Baptistery. Priest's chair
(*detail of* Namegiving)

185 *Andrea Pisano: Bronze door, Florence Baptistery. Portal (detail of* Visitation)

186 *Andrea Pisano: Bronze door, Florence Baptistery. Prison (detail of* St. John Imprisoned)

187 *Andrea Pisano: Bronze door, Florence Baptistery. Platform support (detail of* Entombment)

188   *Andrea Pisano: Bronze door, Florence Baptistery.* Annunciation to Zacharias

189 Andrea Pisano (?): Arms over north portal to courtyard, Bargello, Florence

190 Andrea Pisano workshop: Tomb of Giovanni Cacciano, Cloister of S. Spirito, Florence

191   *Andrea Pisano: Ground story, Or San Michele, Florence. Exterior*

192   Andrea Pisano: Ground story, Or San Michele, Florence. Interior

194　*Francesco Talenti: Pier base, Florence Duomo*

193　*Andrea Pisano: Ground story, Or San Michele, Florence. Pier base*

196   *Andrea Pisano: Ground story, Or San Michele, Florence. Shaft ring*

197   *Andrea Pisano: Ground story, Or San Michele, Florence. Capital*

195   *Andrea Pisano: Ground story, Or San Michele,*
Florence. Base profiles

198 *Or San Michele, Florence.*
Second-story window

199 *Or San Michele, Florence.*
Cornice of ground story

200 *Andrea Pisano: Ground story, Or San Michele,*
Florence. Sheaf of grain, exterior corner

201 *Andrea Pisano: Ground story, Or San Michele,*
Florence. Capital of stairway portal

202   *Andrea Pisano: Ground story, Or San Michele,*
      Florence. Niche of the Arte della Lana

203   *Andrea Pisano: Ground story, Or San Michele,*
      Florence. Niche of the Arte della Seta

204 *Palazzo Vecchio, Florence. Arms over secondary portal on north face*

205 *S. Croce, Florence. Respond base, chapel behind choir*

206 *S. Croce, Florence. Capital, chapel behind choir*

207   S. Maria della Spina, Pisa
      (before restoration)

208   S. Maria della Spina, Pisa.
      Choir, exterior

209   S. Maria della Spina, Pisa. Flank

210   *Andrea Pisano (?): Choir portal, S. Maria della Spina, Pisa*

211   S. Maria della Spina, Pisa. Base profiles
to left of choir portal

212   S. Maria della Spina, Pisa. Side portal of nave

213   *Andrea Pisano (?): Choir, S. Maria della Spina, Pisa. Interior*

214   *Andrea Pisano (?): Choir, S. Maria della Spina, Pisa. Vaulting*

215   *S. Maria della Spina, Pisa. Interior, toward choir*

216   Andrea Pisano (?): Choir, S. Maria della Spina, Pisa. Arcade capital

217   Andrea Pisano (?): Choir, S. Maria della Spina, Pisa. Arcade base

218   Andrea Pisano: Side-aisle cornice, Orvieto Duomo

219   *Andrea Pisano (?): Porta di Canonica, Orvieto Duomo*

220   *Fibula, British Museum*

221   *Paten, Cathedral of Sulmona (Aquila)*

222   *Siena Baptistery. Portal detail*

223   *Palazzo Ariani, Venice. Window*

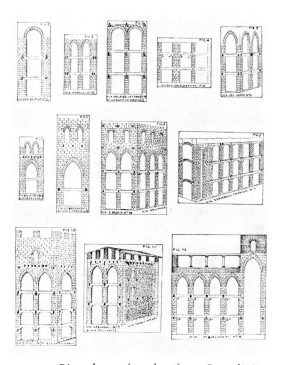

224   *Pisan house façades (from Bartalini)*

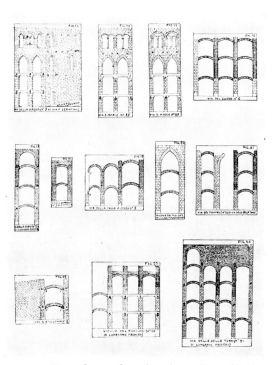

225   *Pisan house façades (from Bartalini)*

226 *Nicola Pisano: Pulpit, Siena Duomo. Capital*

227 *S. Maria Novella, Florence. Capital, left side wall, second pier from transept*

228 *S. Maria Novella, Florence. Capital, right side wall, third pier from transept*

229 *Arnolfo di Cambio: Interior façade arcade, Florence Duomo. Capital*

230 *S. Maria Novella, Florence. Capital, nave, second pier from crossing, right*

231 *Arnolfo di Cambio (?): Palazzo Vecchio, Florence. Window capital*

232 *Nicola Pisano: Pulpit, Pisa Baptistery. Detail*

233 *Giovanni Pisano: Façade, Siena Duomo. Base*

234 *Florence Baptistery. Exterior detail*

235   *S. Maria Novella, Florence. Keystone, side aisle*

236   *S. Maria Novella, Florence. Façade detail*

237 *Arnolfo di Cambio: Tabernacle, S. Cecilia, Rome*

238 *Arnolfo di Cambio: Tabernacle, S. Paolo fuori le mura, Rome*

239　*Florentine school (1587): Drawing of Duomo façade,*
Museo dell'Opera del Duomo, Florence

240   *Lorenzo Maitani: Façade, Orvieto Duomo. Left pier*

241 *Scenes from* Genesis, *cupola, Florence Baptistery*

242 *Nicola and Giovanni Pisano:* Fall *and* Expulsion,
Fontana Maggiore, Perugia

243　Or San Michele, Florence. Second-story vaulting

244 *Florence Duomo. Pier foundation*

245 *Florentine city wall.*
Exposed core at Pza. Torquato Tasso

246 *Florence Duomo. Pier bonding,*
north aisle

247 *Bargello, Florence. Ground-story vaulting of tower*

248   *Francesco Talenti: Porta dei Cornacchini, Florence Duomo*

249   *Francesco Talenti: Porta del Campanile, Florence Duomo*

250 *Francesco Talenti: Side-aisle window, Florence Duomo. Detail*

251 *Francesco Talenti: Porta dei Cornacchini, Florence Duomo. Capital band and cornicework*

252   *Francesco Talenti: Nave, Florence Duomo*

253   *Francesco Talenti: Nave, Florence Duomo. Ballatoio corner*

254 *Francesco Talenti:*
Nave, Florence Duomo.
Keystone, side aisle

255 *Francesco Talenti:*
Nave, Florence Duomo.
Springing of vault

257 *Francesco Talenti or following: Lucca Duomo. View toward choir*

256 *Francesco Talenti or following:*
S. Lorenzo, Certosa di Galluzzo (Florence). View from choir

258 *Simone Talenti et al.: Loggia della Signoria, Florence*

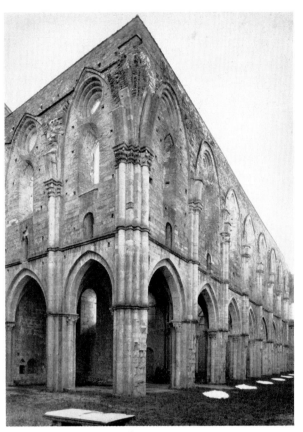

259 S. Galgano. Interior view
of nave wall and transept

260 Loggia of the Popes,
Viterbo. Tracery detail

261 S. Martino al Cimino (Viterbo). Nave

262 S. Martino al Cimino (Viterbo). Crossing

263   S. Martino al Cimino (Viterbo). Façade tracery

264   S. Martino al Cimino (Viterbo). Detail of crossing pier

265 *Duomo, Massa Marittima. Choir exterior*

266 *Duomo, Massa Marittima.*
Detail of choir interior

267 *Duomo, Massa Marittima. Detail of choir exterior*

268   *Duomo, Massa Marittima. Upper façade (tympanum by Giovanni Pisano)*

269   *Giovanni Pisano: Façade, Siena Duomo*

270 *Siena Baptistery. Façade*

271   Siena Baptistery. Façade, center portal

272   Lando di Pietro et al.: Duomo Nuovo, Siena. Detail of main portal,
interior façade

273 *Lando di Pietro* et al.: *Duomo Nuovo, Siena. Interior side-aisle wall*

274 *Side-aisle wall and portal, Duomo Nuovo; corner of transept, Siena Duomo (right)*

275   *Lorenzo Maitani: Façade, Orvieto Duomo*

276   *Lorenzo Maitani: Façade, Orvieto Duomo. Center portal*

277 *Lorenzo Maitani: Façade, Orvieto Duomo. Center portal cornicework*

278 *Orvieto Duomo. Ballatoio, nave*

279 *Lorenzo Maitani: Façade, Orvieto Duomo.*
Leafwork detail (second pier from left)

280 *Nicola di Nuto: Choir vaulting, Orvieto Duomo*

281   Orcagna: Strozzi Altarpiece, S. Maria Novella, Florence

282   Orcagna: Tabernacle, Or San Michele, Florence

283   Orcagna: Tabernacle, Or San Michele, Florence. Capital detail

284 *Orcagna:* St. Michael *and* St. Catherine *(detail of Fig. 281)*

285 *View of Florence, detail of* La Madonna della Misericordia, *Bigallo, Florence*

286　*Francesco Roselli (?): View of Florence. Panel, coll. Mrs. Herbert Bier, London*

287 *(left) Francesco Roselli (?): View of Florence, detail. Woodcut, Kupferstichkabinett, Berlin*

288 *View of Florence (from the* Biadaiolo Fiorentino, *Biblioteca Laurenziana, Florence)*

289 *Domenico di Michelino:* Dante e il suo Poema, *Florence Duomo. Detail, view of Florence*

287 *(right) Francesco Roselli (?): View of Florence, detail. Woodcut, Kupferstichkabinett, Berlin*

290 *S. Andrea, Florence. Campanile (from Coriniti)*

291 *S. Elisabetta (S. Michele delle Trombe), Florence (from the Codex Rustichi)*

292 *S. Lorenzo, Florence (from the Codex Rustichi)*

294   Ognissanti, Florence. Campanile detail

293   Ognissanti, Florence. Campanile

295   S. Maria Novella, Florence. Campanile

296   S. Maria Novella, Florence.
       Campanile detail

297 *Badia, Florence. Campanile*

298 *Badia, Florence*
(from the Codex Rustichi)

299 *Badia, Florence. Campanile detail*

300 *S. Pier Maggiore, Florence. Campanile*
(detail from drawing by Zocchi,
Pierpont Morgan Library, New York)

301 *Badia a Settimo. Campanile*

302 *Pisa Duomo. Transept and campanile (Leaning Tower)*

303   *S. Nicola, Pisa. Campanile*   304   *Pistoia Duomo. Campanile*

305   *Lucca Duomo. Campanile*

306   *S. Maria in Cosmedin, Rome.*
Campanile

307   *Siena Duomo. Campanile*

308 *S. Apollinare in Classe (Ravenna). Campanile*

309 *Pomposa Abbey. Campanile*
(before restoration of windows)

310   Torcello Duomo. Campanile

311   S. Donato,
Murano. Campanile

312   S. Mercuriale,
Forlì. Campanile

313 *S. Satiro, Milan. Campanile*   314 *S. Ambrogio, Milan. Campanile dei Canonici*

315 Fossanova Abbey. Crossing tower

316 Parma Duomo. Campanile

317 Chiaravalle Milanese. Crossing tower

318 S. Gottardo,
Milan. Campanile

319 Cremona Duomo. Campanile ("Torrazzo")

320 *Porta S. Niccolò, Florence (detail from drawing by Zocchi, Pierpont Morgan Library, New York)*

321 *Porta S. Niccolò, Florence*

322 *Porta S. Frediano and adjoining wall, Florence*

323 View north from Palazzo Vecchio (up Via dei Cerchi)

324 Via dei Cerchi, Florence (view toward Palazzo Vecchio)

325 Towers on the Borgo SS. Apostoli, Florence

326 *Tower of the Marsili, Florence*
(Borgo S. Jacopo)

327 *Tower of the Corbizzi, Florence*
(Pza. S. Piero)

328 *Tower and house of the Foresi,*
Florence (Pza. Davanzati)

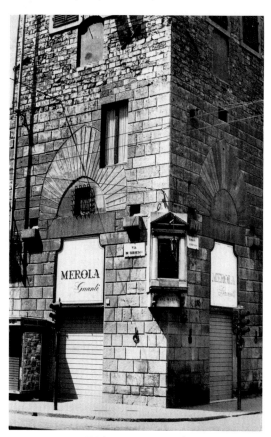

329 *Bishop's tower, Florence*
(Via de'Cerretani/Borgo S. Lorenzo)

330   *Bargello, Florence*

331   Bargello, Florence. Belfry

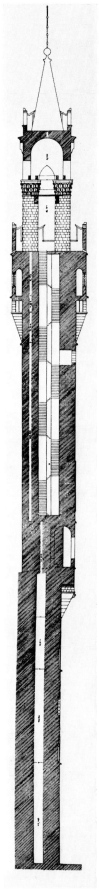

332   *Arnolfo di Cambio (?): Palazzo Vecchio, Florence. Tower detail*

333   *Arnolfo di Cambio (?): Palazzo Vecchio, Florence. Cross section of tower (from Haupt)*

334   *Arnolfo di Cambio (?): Palazzo Vecchio, Florence*

335   *Palazzo Pubblico, Siena*

336 Watchtower of Frederick II,
S. Miniato al Tedesco

337 Palazzo dei Priori, Volterra

Date Due